Sexual Racism and Social Justice

Sexual Racism and Social Justice

Reckoning with White Supremacy and Desire

Edited by

DENTON CALLANDER, PANTEÁ FARVID,
AMIR BARADARAN, AND THOMAS A. VANCE

OXFORD
UNIVERSITY PRESS

Oxford University Press is a department of the University of Oxford. It furthers the University's objective of excellence in research, scholarship, and education by publishing worldwide. Oxford is a registered trade mark of Oxford University Press in the UK and certain other countries.

Published in the United States of America by Oxford University Press
198 Madison Avenue, New York, NY 10016, United States of America.

© Oxford University Press 2024

All rights reserved. No part of this publication may be reproduced, stored in a retrieval system, or transmitted, in any form or by any means, without the prior permission in writing of Oxford University Press, or as expressly permitted by law, by license, or under terms agreed with the appropriate reproduction rights organization. Inquiries concerning reproduction outside the scope of the above should be sent to the Rights Department, Oxford University Press, at the address above.

You must not circulate this work in any other form
and you must impose this same condition on any acquirer.

Library of Congress Cataloging-in-Publication Data
Names: Callander, Denton, editor. | Farvid, Panteá, editor. | Baradaran, Amir, editor.
Title: Sexual racism and social justice : reckoning with white supremacy and desire / edited by Denton Callander, Panteá Farvid, Amir Baradaran and Thomas A. Vance.
Description: New York : Oxford University Press, [2024] |
Includes bibliographical references and index.
Identifiers: LCCN 2023045772 (print) | LCCN 2023045773 (ebook) |
ISBN 9780197605509 (hardback) | ISBN 9780197605523 (epub)
Subjects: LCSH: Sex crimes—Social aspects. | White nationalism. | Social justice.
Classification: LCC HV6556 .S444 2024 (print) | LCC HV6556 (ebook) |
DDC 364.15/3—dc23/eng/20240123
LC record available at https://lccn.loc.gov/2023045772
LC ebook record available at https://lccn.loc.gov/2023045773

DOI: 10.1093/oso/9780197605509.001.0001

Printed by Integrated Books International, United States of America

Contents

Introduction: How Do You Solve a Problem Like Sexual Racism?   1
Denton Callander, Panteá Farvid, Amir Baradaran,
and Thomas A. Vance

SECTION I: HISTORIES AND THEORIES

1. A Queer History of Sexual Racism   31
Denton Callander, Tony Ayres, and Donovan Trott

2. A Look Back at the World's First Online Anti–Sexual
Racism Campaign: Sexual Racism Sux   51
Andy Quan

3. Anti-Black Skin, White Sheets: Challenging Sexual
Color-Blindness Through a Sexual Humility Framework   66
Xiqiao Chen, Jeremy Kelleher, Anthony Boiardo, Dashawn Ealey,
and Daniel Gaztambide

Poetry Interlude

Jezebel   84
Synclaire Warren

SECTION II: REPRESENTATIONS

4. "I Am Dark and Beautiful": Song of Songs, Audre Lorde,
and the Politics of Desire   87
Siam Hatzaw

5. White Desirability and the Violent Radicalization of
Andrew Cunanan   98
Marc Milton Ducusin

vi CONTENTS

6. Undesiring Whiteness and Undoing the White Gaze in HIV
   Prevention Marketing   116
   Ivan Bujan

7. Amitis Motevalli: Exorcising Orientalism   141
   Anuradha Vikram

Poetry Interlude

Shea Butter and Honey   162
   Ilannah Deshazier

SECTION III: LIVED REALITIES

8. "You Just Got to Own It": Māori Girls Un/Doing Settler
   Colonial Sexuality in Aotearoa   167
   Fern Smith and Jade Le Grice

9. Predators and Perpetrators: Cultures of White Settler
   Violence in So-Called Australia   189
   Madi Day and Bronwyn Carlson

10. Consuming Whiteness/Disciplining Desire   206
    Gene Lim

11. Sexual Racism as White Privilege: The Psychic and
    Relational Negotiation of Desire, Power, and Sex   242
    Russell K. Robinson

Poetry Interlude

The Butcher   265
   Synclaire Warren

SECTION IV: SPOTLIGHTING THE STRUCTURAL

12. Curating Desire: The White Supremacist Grammar of
    Tagging on Pornhub   269
    *Chibundo Egwuatu, Zahra Stardust, Mireille Miller-Young,
    and Daisy Ducati*

13. White Supremacy and the Sex Industry: The Racialized
    Stratification of Sex Work in Four Distinct Legal Contexts   296
    *Panteá Farvid, Sarah Epstein, Leigh Lumpkin, Thyme Canton,
    and Michelle King*

CONTENTS vii

14. Sexual Racism and Asian American Egg Donation: Reflections on Experiential Ambivalence 325
Ellen Yom

15. Decentering Whiteness in South Africa: Using Empathic Dialogue to Engage With Race, Identity, Privilege, and Entitlement 336
Matthew Rich-Tolsma and Sizwe Mqalo

Index 359

Introduction

How Do You Solve a Problem Like Sexual Racism?

Denton Callander, Panteá Farvid, Amir Baradaran, and Thomas A. Vance

It is hard to imagine two more provocative topics than racism and sexuality. Each issue on its own can easily ignite a maelstrom of societal anxiety, debate, and discord. Yet, among all this noise there is an undeniable reckoning: racism and sexuality are inextricably and profoundly entwined. For many—scholars and others—the relationship between racism and sexuality is messy and complex, contentious and difficult, important and profound. Indeed, this relationship is so foundational that we should characterize it as not a "relationship" at all, but two mutually defining sides of the same coin. To understand one, you must consider the other and—perhaps most importantly—meaningful and effective antiracism efforts must consider sexuality as central part of antiracism work. "The sex factor," proclaimed American writer and activist James Weldon Johnson in 1939, "is the root and also the route that must be explored in order to uncover the complex functions of polarized racial boundaries and conflict" (Paulin, 2012).

While the inextricability of racism and sexuality is an important and provocative idea, it is by no means a new one (Vidal-Ortiz, Robinson, & Khan, 2018). Johnson was among the first to write and speak publicly on the issue we now call sexual racism, and he was followed by many other great thinkers of the 20th century. In the 1950s, for example, Frantz Fanon used introspection and psychoanalysis to explore racism and sexuality in *Peau Noire, Masques Blancs*, probing his own experiences of marriage to a white woman and writing, "Dans ces seins blancs que mes mains ubiquitaires caressent, c'est la civilisation et la dignité blanches que je fais miennes" (Fanon, 1952).[1] A decade later, the writer and activist Charles Herton coined "sexual racism"

---

[1] Charles Lam Markmann's 1967 translation reads thus: "When my restless hands caress those white breasts, they grasp white civilization and dignity and make them mine."

Denton Callander, Panteá Farvid, Amir Baradaran, and Thomas A. Vance, *Introduction* In: *Sexual Racism and Social Justice*. Edited by: Denton Callander, Panteá Farvid, Amir Baradaran, and Thomas A. Vance, Oxford University Press. © Oxford University Press 2024. DOI: 10.1093/oso/9780197605509.003.0001

2 INTRODUCTION

in his scholarly account *Sex and Racism in America* (Herton, 1965), and shortly after the expression was taken up by the sociologist Charles Stember, who declared it, "the conscious attempt on the part of the [white] majority to prevent interracial cohabitation" (Stember, 1968). In the next decade, June Dobbs Butts—one of the first Black sex therapists in the United States—wrote, "the concepts of sex and race are interwoven in the fabric of American culture to such a degree that it is virtually impossible to separate them" (Butts, 1977). And in the late 1980s, in one of his last public interviews, James Baldwin demurred to a reporter for the *Village Voice* that, "the sexual question and the racial question have always been entwined" (Terkel et al., 2014).

In conceptualizing sexual racism for this collection, we seek to follow these great thinkers in asserting that the *racialization of sexuality* and the *sexualization of racism* are about much more than just intimate relations of dating, sex, love, or marriage. While these worthy subjects have been explored in many studies of racism and sexuality, the bigger picture we seek to bring into focus depicts the construction of desire. Namely, how hegemonic systems of power and oppression determine the ideas, cultures, bodies, and practices that are reified as desirable. As explored throughout this collection, desirability has been, and continues to be, defined exclusively through the coconstituted positioning of white supremacy and anti-Blackness—what prominent sexual racism scholar C. Winter Han calls "the undoubtable desirability of whiteness" (Han, 2021)—realized through violent and ongoing projects of colonialism, imperialism, neoliberalism, capitalism, and globalization. Thus, while it may be tempting to dismiss sexuality as a niche or secondary concern—especially in the face of our world's incredibly painful ongoing struggle with race and racism—the reality is that any meaningful effort to dismantle racism must contend with this foundational component. To return to James Weldon Johnson: sexuality is both the *root* of racism's existence and the *route* for its resolution.

What Is Sexual Racism?

The phrase "sexual racism" has been in circulation since the mid-20th century and defined in multiple ways. In contemporary academic and mainstream discourse, sexual racism has come to be defined largely as racism enacted in the context of sexual or romantic desire. For example, legal and political scholar Sonu Bedi defines sexual racism as "prioritizing an individual as a possible romantic, intimate partner on account of their race in a way that reinforces extant racial hierarchy or stereotypes" (Bedi, 2015), while journalists around the world have mainly defined sexual racism as using racial categories to reject potential sexual or romantic partners (e.g., Brathwaite, 2020; Lopez, 2016; Mahajan, 2017). We share these merely as examples of how research and journalism have tended to conceptualize sexual racism as a specific form of racism defined through intimacies of sex and romance. The definitional component of most contemporary understandings of sexual racism is *context*.

The idea of sexual racism as contextual is deeply problematic, as it supposes that sexuality can be meaningfully disentangled from racism. As we have already argued, however, racism and sexuality are inextricable; just there is no meaningful idea of racism absent of sexuality, so can we not account for sexuality without attending to racism. In our opinion, definitions in popular circulation today undermine this conceptual reality by positioning sexual racism as contextual rather than contending with its ubiquity across all social experience. Contending with these implications, we offer an alternative understanding: "sexual racism" does not qualify or contextualize but instead renders explicit the *sexualized nature of racism* and the *racialized nature of sexuality*. From this perspective, the concept of "sexual racism" can be deployed to create space for scholarship and creative pursuits to more fully unpack the complex dynamics of race, racism, sex, and sexuality.

There are three points we make in support of conceptualizing sexual racism in this broad manner. The first is that sexuality has always been a part of how racism is enacted, and it continues to play an important role in sustaining global white supremacy. Second, the typical framing of sexual racism has produced an overly narrow canon of sexual racism research and discourse that almost exclusively considers interpersonal interactions and individualized desires. While these are relevant and related, they only capture small pieces of a much larger picture. This point does not seek to disparage the wealth of research that in recent years has examined how sexual racism is experienced and enacted in the personal lives of people around the world, but instead invites a renewal of scholarship that can more fully capture and explain the intrapsychic, interpersonal, sociocultural, and structural dynamics in motion. And third, by situating sexuality as central to any understanding of racism, and as racism central to any understanding of sexuality, we hope for meaningful advancement of advocacy and activism. For too long, sexual racism has been relegated to the bottom in terms of "priorities" when

4 INTRODUCTION

it comes to research, journalism, and activism on racism. Yet, it is a core (if not *the* core) of racial oppression in all its multilevel and multifaceted forms. The same argument can be made for the project of sexual plurality, which has struggled to incorporate racism into its foundational ideologies and efforts. Thus, both projects of sexual plurality and antiracism have relegated their respective roles to low status in the world of social justice, not ignored entirely but rarely viewed as pivotal. In our opinion, this has hampered both areas of inquiry. It is our hope that reimagining the relationships signified in sexual racism will excite innovative and effective social change.

To offer transparency, the four of us have played various parts in advancing and articulating the very conceptualizations of sexual racism that we challenge here. In our research, writing, advocacy, art, and clinical practice we have previously relied on and even advocated for a definition of sexual racism as "racism in context." But it was through developing and deploying sexual racism as a concept across our diverse works—including for this collection— that we came to understand the limits of defining it through contextuality. In putting together this collection, we hope to advocate for this understanding of sexual racism—and for bringing together new scholarship on the topic— as part of a larger process toward undesiring whiteness and, simultaneously, undoing sexual racism.

Whiteness, White Supremacy, and the Racialized Global Order

Before delving more deeply into our thinking around sexual racism, it is necessary to outline whiteness as a theoretical framework crucial to this work. While defined in many ways over recent decades, we like Barbara Applebaum's definition of whiteness as:

> Culturally, socially, politically, and institutionally produced and reproduced systems of institutional processes and individual practices that benefit white people while simultaneously marginalizing others. (Applebaum, 2016)

Whiteness derives its foundations from the construction of race as a valuable, "natural" (which is to say biological), and essential category for organizing humans into groups and defining differences between them. Although race is an arbitrary social construction not rooted in any biological reality, it is a useful sociopolitical concept with material realities. Indeed, despite an intellectual understanding of race as socially constructed, it is experienced by people of color as "real, material, and lived" (Ahmed, 2007). Whiteness works, Ahmed argues, to "orientate bodies in specific directions, affecting how they 'take up' space" (2007).

With Ahmed's insights in mind, it might seem confusing that scholars frequently describe whiteness as "invisible" (e.g., McIntosh, 1989). While we do not contest this qualifier outright, it does benefit from further exploration. "Socialized to believe the fantasy that whiteness represents goodness and all that is benign and non-threatening," wrote bell hooks in the early 1990s, "many white people assume this is the way black people conceptualize whiteness" (hooks, 1992). Thus, whiteness is not actually invisible, it is just invisible primarily to white people. The significance of this obfuscation is that it renders the brutality of whiteness invisible, allowing it to co-exist alongside contradictory ideals like freedom and equality.

As Applebaum's definition highlights, whiteness is both rooted in and reinforces white supremacy, which is to say the dominance of white people through overwhelming social, political, economic, and cultural power (Ansley, 1988). Here, it is important to recognize white supremacy as not only about white people but also about the dominance and desirability of certain ideas, values, and ways of being along with social, cultural, and economic practices. Importantly, the desirability of these has been throughout history and to this day predicated on the marginalization and destruction of those associated with nonwhite and non-Christian societies.

Aside from its sociopolitical and cultural ramifications, white supremacy benefits white people—sometimes but not always unwittingly—by affording white privilege. This refers to the "unearned benefits and advantages that accrue to dominant group members solely by virtue of occupying a dominant social position and often regardless of one's attitude, volition, or belief" (Applebaum, 2016). Increasingly, however, we understand that whiteness actually does not benefit anyone, including white people (e.g., Malat et al., 2018), with white privilege a double-edged sword that harms even those who derive from it some kind of benefit. As Baldwin wrote, "the white man is himself in sore need of new standards, which will release him from his confusion and place him once again in fruitful communion with the depths of his own being" (Baldwin, 2021).

6 INTRODUCTION

While relevant to white-majority countries often labeled the "West" or the "Global North," whiteness as a theoretical frame can be meaningfully applied to understand racism around the world. This point is important because it elevates whiteness into an organizing structure for the global order, a way of understanding how race and racism are enacted even in places where white people are the minority. As Michelle Christian articulates:

> Whiteness recognizes the persistence of white domination globally, and in all national racial social systems, even those that are ostensibly without white bodies and white institutions. As a process, always in motion, whiteness embodies a structural position of historical global wealth accumulation and political economic power that reproduces itself through contemporary structural practice. (Christian, 2019)

Beyond a merely theoretical frame, white supremacy has been established as the global reality through the historically linked projects of colonialism, imperialism, and globalization. Put another way, it is not just that we can understand nonwhite contexts through the frame of whiteness but also that the entire world is materially informed by and for the purposes of white supremacy (Allen, 2001; Hale, 2014; Williamson, 2017). Although originally a colonial and then imperial project, globalization has furthered this work, with capitalism playing a central role (Du Bois, 1933; M. Beliso-De Jesús & Pierre, 2020; Spector, 2007). These ideas gave rise to the concept of "racial capitalism," which like our use of sexual racism does not suggest the existence of nonracial capitalism but instead draws attention to the intractable and foundational relationship between racism and the accumulation of capital (Melamed, 2015; Robinson & Kelley, 2000). It is simply not possible and indeed counterproductive to engage one without the other. Taken together, by understanding white supremacy as the global frame it becomes possible to examine the "spectacular and mundane violences that reaffirm empire and the economic, social, cultural, and political power" (Bonds & Inwood, 2016).

The point to be drawn from this brief and by no means comprehensive discussion is that whiteness—and by extension, white supremacy—is the beating heart of societies globally. As we draw deeper into the concept of sexual racism, it is increasingly clear how these projects of domination have used race and sexuality as coconstituting forces to further their violent, nefarious, and egregious work.

Undesiring Colonial and Imperial Sexualities

Race and sexuality have always been integral to the colonial project. While there are many avenues down which one can interrogate the colonization of sexuality and the sexualization of colonialism (Schields & Herzog, 2021), for an understanding of sexual racism there are some that bear close inspection. Of particular note is how the colonial imagination used sexuality to define and subjugate nonwhite, non-Christian others (Meiu, 2015). Under the bloody banner of so-called enlightenment, the supremacy of particular ways of being in relation to whiteness have long been maintained by erotizing, consuming, restricting, destroying, mocking, and otherwise denigrating the sexualities of "barbaric" people of color (Berry & Harris, 2018; Boone, 2015; Massad, 2008; Najmabadi, 2005; Said, 1995). This process derives from and reinforces efforts to label, define, and assign value to certain experiences and practices—often under the auspices of the scientific method and the production of knowledge—effectively producing sex as an object of modernity (Foucault, 1976). In doing so, this work afforded colonial states an important site of power, producing "knowledge" used to justify the eradication, subjugation, and enslavement of Others (Berry & Harris, 2018; Said, 1995; Stoler, 1995).

The same kind of processes that produced sex as an object and established it as a source of power also served the construction of race as a category of human distinction. Although European enlightenment ostensibly espoused ideals of freedom and equality, this ideology stood alongside the enslavement, murder, and genocide of millions of people of color in colonized territories around the world (Mahmud, 1998). Indeed, the very existence of ideologies espousing such ideals demanded an explanation for how freedom and equality could be denied to some segments of humanity (notably people of color but also women and non-Christians, see Fredrickson & Camarillo, 2015). Responding to this demand, systems of modernity—and, to repeat ourselves, the scientific method—worked to validate and propagate the ideas of race, racial difference, and racial superiority; today, we to live with the enduring successes of this yet unfinished campaign (Zuberi & Bonilla-Silva, 2008). To paraphrase such arguments, it is not that race created racism, but that racism created race (Cox, 1959).

Understanding how colonialism established sex and race as sites of power is vital because it directs our attention to a necessary process in the functioning of whiteness: maintaining "racial purity." If whiteness is to remain supreme then it must define a boundary for itself, namely who can and

8 INTRODUCTION

cannot be considered part of the "white race." Without some perception of racial purity, implicit and explicit justifications for white supremacy start to crumble. Sexuality is clearly implicated here because of the threat to racial purity posed by children conceived between white people and people of color. In response to this threat, over time various legal, social, medical, economic, and scientific languages of control have been used to produce and justify brutal tactics to limit interracial partnerships. Examples of this work include forced sterilization, eugenics, antimiscegenation laws, "one drop" rules of racial heritage, among many others (e.g., Berry & Harris, 2018; Kitch, 2016; Lay, 1993; Liz, 2018).

Beyond the implications for procreation, the project of racial purity is also invested in protecting the boundaries and systems of whiteness, including in and through discourses of sexuality. As discussed, colonialism has worked to define "civilized" notions of sexuality by drawing direct contrast with the projected barbarism and savagery of nonwhite Others, establishing important power dynamics, serving the agenda of white supremacy, and justifying colonial subjugation. Thus, the issue is not limited to the desire for certain bodies but also ways of being. Maintaining the racial purity of sexuality has demanded the restriction of so-called deviant expression of sexuality (and gender), including among white people themselves. Sex work is one prominent example of colonial efforts to define and control deviant sexualities, with a growing body of scholarship highlighting the instrumental role of sexual racism in its regulations and oppressions. In the former colonies of South Africa, for example, laws passed in the early 20th century criminalized relationships between white female sex workers and Black men, a reaction to anxieties of Black male sexualities in relation to whiteness (Thusi & Geronimo, 2015). The racialization of sex work and efforts to control it through colonialism can be seen in other parts of Africa and around the world, with implications that continue to endanger sex workers in a multitude of ways (Aantjes et al., 2022; Hunt, 2013; Kaye, 2018).

Same-gender attraction is another prolific example of the colonial racialization of sexuality, which can be found integrated into the imperialism of today. Despite their ubiquity in all parts of the world and through time, same-gender sexualities were punished by law and other forms of social contract in Europe as violent expressions of Christian doctrine were propagated (Monro, 2015). Such legal restrictions derived from and defined a white notion of sexual purity, and through colonialism were imposed around the world including to places where sexuality and gender were expressed with considerable fluidity and freedom. The evidence of this exportation can be seen today. For example, research finds that compared with other states, former British colonies are much more likely to have a history of laws criminalizing same-gender sexualities (Han & O'Mahoney, 2014). While certainly not limited to British colonies, many countries continue to experience the harmful effects of this colonial imposition (Aldrich, 2002; Lennox & Waites, 2013). What is particularly interesting about colonial anxieties around same-gender sexualities is that recent decades have seen whiteness assume a certain flavor of gay politic and seek to impose it on former colonial states through imperialism. In the excellent book, *Desiring Arabs*, Josef Massad describes it thus:

> When the Gay International incites discourse on homosexuality in the non-Western world, it claims that the "liberation" of those it defends lies in the balance. In espousing this liberation project, however, the Gay International is destroying social and sexual configurations of desire in the interest of reproducing a world in its own image. . . . In undertaking [its] universalizing project, the Gay International ultimately makes itself feel better about a world it forces to share its identifications. Its missionary achievement, however, will be the creation of not a queer planet, to use Michael Warner's apt term, but rather a straight one. (Massad, 2008)

It is revealing but not surprising that the project of imperialism would borrow from its long colonial heritage, deploying familiar discursive projections of barbaric nonwhite Others to legitimize control over sexualities perceived as threatening the ideas and practices of white purity. In reality, the most prominent (and well-funded) politic represented in what is often called the "gay rights movement" is defined through systems of whiteness, which reifies white supremacy by marginalizing the interests of Indigenous peoples and people of color while simultaneously claiming notions of diversity and inclusion (Callander et al., 2018; Sykes, 2016). While so-called gay rights represents only one example of racialized sexualities as sites of power, it offers a useful lens through which the bigger picture comes into clearer focus. Indeed, while tempting to think that our social appreciation for race and sexuality have evolved dramatically over the past century, the processes and results are largely consistent: whiteness dictates the terms, and white supremacy is reinforced as a result.

Undesiring Neoliberal Sexualities

Neoliberalism offers another important frame for understanding sexual racism, especially in the current social and political dynamics globally. By promoting cultural values like "privatization, personal responsibility, agentic individualism, autonomy, and personal freedom," neoliberalism is an individualistic and antisocial project, which has infiltrated virtually all aspects of society so that alternative understandings are caste as impractical and naive (Weiss, 2008). Far from eliminating racism or rendering it anachronistic (as some have suggested), Arun Kundnani (2021) deftly argues that neoliberalism uses the desirability of whiteness (which they refer to as the "intellectual legacies of western civilization") to attain its legitimacy. Articulating racism as ancillary to neoliberalism, they go on to say:

> Race is a material feature of the division of labour that neoliberalism produces. Despite its rhetoric of colour-blind market competition, the neoliberal state is a racist state, committed to violently maintaining a racial ordering of labouring and surplus populations. (Kundnani, 2021)

To put this another way, the "free market" can really never be free. This idea, as discussed earlier, is what critiques of "racial capitalism" seek to expound; neoliberalism as a process of individualization necessitates boundaries of difference (especially those defined by race) to give meaning to the organization of labor and capital (Kundnani, 2021).

By seeing neoliberalism as inherently supportive of white supremacy, we can get some sense of the relevance to sexual racism. This relevance is particularly pressing because many neoliberal states have, in recent years, assumed a particular sexual politic rooted in individual "rights" and "freedoms" (Duggan, 2002; Ludwig, 2016). The key here is how neoliberalism establishes sexuality as an individual (and thus, private and antisocial) pursuit, a process that reflexively lends strength to these ideological values. While this individualized sexual politic is often cast as liberatory, like the larger neoliberal project it is actually highly racialized and ultimately very narrow. Indeed, many have discussed how the neoliberal embrace of so-called sexual liberation works to erase racist and colonial histories, and affirms an ideal of "healthy," "normal," or "good" sexuality only as defined by whiteness (Elia & Yep, 2012; El-Tayeb, 2011; Reddy, 2011).

Constructing a narrow ideal of sexual liberation within the neoliberal frame has reinforced the idea that people of color—especially migrants and Muslims—are intolerant when it comes to sexuality, requiring liberation through education, assimilation, and democratic emancipation (El-Tayeb, 2011; Massad, 2008; Shield, 2019). Such tactics continue the long tradition of using sexuality as a tool for white supremacy through a world "built upon neocolonial and racializing logics" (Ludwig, 2016). Further, neoliberalism sets up sexuality as an individual and private pursuit, a matter of individual decision-making, preferences, tastes, and proclivities. Aside from seeming to ignore the reality of sexuality as a predominantly social phenomenon, this setup has the handy effect of removing it from the realm of social and political critique. The result is that explorations of sexual racism become detached from broader social structures and any discussion of the subject are disparaged as infringing on private interests (Bedi, 2015; Smith, 2017).

As we have demonstrated in this section, there is a great deal of important and compelling scholarship that unpacks the enduring complexities and ramifications of racialized sexualities propagated through colonialism, imperialism, and neoliberalism. It is on the shoulders of these giants that we advocate for an understanding of sexual racism that grapples with the sociopolitical and economic underpinnings of lived and structural realities. With any examination of racism, whichever way you turn sexuality is implicitly and explicitly implicated. These ideas cannot and should not be separated. Considering the antisocial and individualistic notions underwriting neoliberalism, however, it is unsurprising that recent examinations of sexual racism have largely lost themselves in focusing on individual experiences of sex, love, and relationships. These are important, no doubt, but only grasp at much larger, ubiquitous, and fundamentally structural issues.

The Lived Realities of Sexual Racism

Our discussion thus far has focused on the systems and structures that give shape to and draw power from sexual racism. Although this landscape provides an important scaffolding for understanding sexual racism, lived and material realities are unquestionably important and warrant deep examination. Put another way, it is important to also consider what sexual racism looks like "on the ground" and in practice. Borrowing from Sara Ahmed, we

12 INTRODUCTION

might call these the "orientations" of sexual racism (Ahmed, 2007), including how sexual racism creates and organizes experiences in different contexts. Given, as we have argued, sexual racism is a ubiquitous force in society, it is possible to see its influence in virtually all aspects of our lives. There are three especially prolific examples that we discuss in the following section, which we feel best illustrate how sexual racism orients the experiences of all people regardless of their race.

Sexual Racism and Interracial Relationships

Interracial relationships offer the first and, perhaps, most obvious lived experience within which to examine sexual racism. In the opening of a special edition for the journal *History of the Family*, editors Julia Moses and Julia Woesthoff highlight how interracial relationships "have been problematized, banned, avoided—and embraced—across the globe and over time for various reasons throughout history," going on to identify that the "core underlying aspect of these dynamics has been concerns about power" (Moses & Woesthoff, 2019). Although globally there remain few legal restrictions on interracial relationships, implicit and explicit social expectations, boundaries, and configurations significantly shape if and how people from different racial backgrounds come together (Gonlin, 2023). And although interracial relationships—especially marriages—have been cast as a solution to sexual racism or at least a sign of its declining influence (Stember, 1968), studies find they can exist as sites of racism even between loving partners (Bat-Shiom & Smith, 2020; Childs, 2005; Craig-Henderson, 2017a, 2017b; Leslie & Young, 2015; Osuji, 2019). It is important to note that while whiteness manifests in relationships of all racial configurations, it is most apparent where one partner is white as the distinction casts into sharp relief the everyday dynamics of white supremacy including in our most intimate spaces. Indeed, research finds that people of color often remain silent when exposed to direct and indirect forms of racism enacted through their relationship and that white partners can become highly defensive and upset when racial topics are broached (Childs, 2005; Craig-Henderson, 2017a, 2017b; Leslie & Young, 2015; Osuji, 2019).

Given the internal and external pressures facing interracial partnerships, it is unsurprising that research from the early 2000s found that interracial marriages between men and women in the United States were more likely to end than same-race marriages (41% vs. 31% ended in divorce at 10 years) (Bramlett & Mosher, 2002). Statistics such as these invite us to wonder about the conditions supporting or undermining interracial couples to resolve the various conflicts imposed by whiteness (Han, 2021; Maffini et al., 2022). The desirability of one's partner should be considered here (e.g., physical, sexual, socioeconomic, cultural, politic) as likely to play a significant role in motivating any interest in seeking a resolution. As we discussed, however, desirability is primarily defined as adjacency to whiteness. This means the likelihood of resolution for conflicts arising from whiteness is derived, at least in part, from the partners' proximity to whiteness itself. This racial component is a complicated loop, especially alongside the other kinds of typical challenges romantic partnerships face in everyday life. While some counseling research and resources exist to support interracial couples (Bat-Shion & Smith, 2020; Dainton, 2015; Greif et al., 2022; Lipscomb & Emeka, 2020), it is important to recognize that common therapeutic models are themselves expressions of whiteness. Based on what is often called "WEIRD" psychology (i.e., research samples, theories, and norms derived almost exclusively from Western, educated, industrialized, rich, and democratic nations; see Henrich et al., 2010), such therapeutic models are tools for maintaining white supremacy. It is reasonable to ask, therefore, what new approaches to therapy and relationship support we might imagine for not only helping couples deal with the daily trauma of whiteness, but also in using their relationship as a vehicle with which to undo sexual racism within themselves.

Sexual Racism Online

Lived experiences of sexual racism are also increasingly centered online, and there is a large amount of recent scholarship that has focused almost exclusively on the enactment of racialized desires in the digital realm. As research on sexual racism has increased significantly in the past two decades, it is no coincidence that this rise has coincided with the proliferation of online sex and dating technologies. Innumerable websites and mobile apps exist to facilitate intimate encounters, and their structures—especially the reliance on textual communication, racial self-categorization, and the ability to search and filter potential matches—have helped make visible individual-level experiences of sexual racism (Curington et al., 2021). These structures, coupled with the private and solitary nature of online dating, offer up a

14 INTRODUCTION

veritable "dating marketplace" that affords a two-dimensional space for sex and relationship shopping while ultimately fostering a highly individualized and antisocial approach to partner seeking (Heino et al., 2010). Significantly, these are hallmarks of the neoliberal (sexual) citizenship, and as discussed this kind of violent individualism is derived from and reinforces systems of whiteness (Nordmarken et al., 2016).

Considering the dimensions of sex and dating online, it is unsurprising that numerous analyses of user profiles—predominantly in white-majority countries—find clear evidence of racial hierarchies rooted in white supremacy (e.g., Feliciano et al., 2009; Lin & Lundquist, 2013; Shield, 2019; Smith, 2017). We cite only a few examples here, noting that the body of research focused on racial rejection and fetishization online is large and growing fast with findings that are pretty consistent about the structural influence of whiteness. Relatedly, research has also started to document the negative effects such experiences can have on the health and well-being of people of color (e.g., Callander et al., 2015; Carlson, 2020; Han et al., 2014; Silvestrini, 2020; Thai, 2020). Beyond academia, the issue of sexual racism online dominates the conversation around race and sexuality, including in news publications, blogs, discussion forums, films, and other mainstream spaces (e.g., Brown, 2018; Holt, 2021; Lopez, 2016; Stokel-Walker, 2018). Typically, this discourse focuses on exclusionary language featured on profiles (e.g., "No spice, no rice") and on the difficult time people of color often have encountering implicit and explicit discrimination while seeking partners online.

Investigations into the negative dimensions of sexual racism as it is experienced online speak to a highly relevant and serious social problem. Yet, in focusing largely on individual experiences the bulk of sexual racism research in recent years loses sight of the bigger picture and reduces the issue to one of private and individualized concern. Rather than offering a deep critique of how white supremacy defines desirability and relationships, the resultant neoliberal takes on sexual racism have led to a myopic discourse of individual "rights." Unsurprisingly, the solutions arising (like removing race/ethnicity filers from online dating platforms) only tinker at the edges of technology while doing nothing to undo their structural dimensions. While such "solutions" may create a small moment of positive public relationships for technology giants, far from undoing sexual racism they often instead further marginalize people of color (Bloodworth, 2020; Gremore, 2020). From this we can conclude that technologies of sex and dating will not and cannot be tools for social justice, but instead—like virtually every other contemporary technology (e.g., O'Neil, 2016)—are only ever capable of reifying white supremacy.

Sexual Racism as Violence

The third and final example we discuss here relates to the ways in which sexual racism transcends the intimate realm to orient everyday experiences often with incredible violence. The most extreme cases are demonstrated through mass murder, such as the 2021 killing by a white cisgender man of six massage parlor workers racialized as Asian in the United States city of Atlanta, Georgia (Fausset, 2021). According to subsequent police proceedings and news reporting, the murderer had a "sex addiction," repeatedly purchased sex from these parlors, and targeted them because they were a "temptation he wanted to eliminate" (Chappell et al., 2021). While some commentators sought to disconnect race from this awful event—itself a discursive tool that helps sustains whiteness (Ichinose, 2021; Korn, 2022)—others highlighted how the hypersexualization of Asian women in policy, popular culture, and other facets of our societies contributes prominently to the violence they experience (Ramiro, 2022). As sociologist Nancy Wany Yuen wrote at the time, "I can't remember ever having experienced racism separate from sexism" (Yuen, 2021). Indeed, the Orientalist fetishization of Asian women is an old and well-documented cultural reality (e.g., Anandavalli, 2022; Azhar et al., 2021), which racializes and sexualizes the Other to diminish their humanity and justify expressions of violence that range from the daily to the deadly (Endo, 2021).

The Atlanta massacre is only one example among many that demonstrate how sexual racism can foster the most explicit forms of violence. In many parts of the world, today's alt-right, neofascist, and white supremacist movements explicitly acknowledge and center sexuality in their ideologies and actions. Notably, the "white replacement conspiracy theory" (which is also known by many similar names) propagates the myth that the "white race" is being purposefully destroyed through strategies including interracial marriage, immigration, birth rates, and abortion. This conspiracy theory centers sexuality by asserting that people of color are having too many children, while also contending that white people are not having enough (Hernandez Aguilar, 2023). The foundations of this myth speak directly to the deeply rooted sexual anxieties permeating whiteness, which have become part of

16 INTRODUCTION

how an audience of (predominantly) cisgender white men are mobilized online (Media, 2022). Tellingly, even the masturbatory behaviors of men in some of these networks are controlled, ostensibly to ensure their virility and the production of white children (DeCook, 2018; Ramirez, 2023). Although this might all sound ridiculous enough as to resemble satire, the lie of white replacement has been a galvanizing force for over a century and its recent distribution online has served as motivation for numerous murders committed by white men around the world (Kestler-D'Amours, 2022; Popli, 2022).

Through these three examples we get some sense of the diverse lived realities—both the contexts and consequences—of sexual racism. These various extremes of sexual racism may seem at odds, but in reality both mundane and murderous expressions find their footing on the same foundation: whiteness. Recognizing this point helps highlight the inherent violence of sexual racism in all settings, including the most intimate, which is especially important given the temptation to cast it as a niche or secondary concern. It also helps elevate the discussion beyond the theoretical and reminds us that there are very real material stakes in play. Far from being secondary, sexual racism is at the forefront of our most pressing social challenges. The question, then, is what needs to be done to undesire whiteness and undo sexual racism in our contemporary world?

This Collection: Undesiring Whiteness Toward Undoing Sexual Racism

It was within this landscape of thinking about sexual racism that we set out to bring together this collection of diverse works. Sexual racism had been activated in our own work and advocacy around the world—Denton as a social and spatial epidemiologist, Pani as an applied and critical feminist psychologist, Amir as an artist and technologist, and Thomas as a clinical psychologist—and we have consistently found need for greater theoretical, conceptual, and practical development. Sexual racism has also been a thread throughout our own social, sexual and romantic lives, shaping how we engage with others and how they engage with us. At times, these struggles have created incredibly difficult and painful experiences of personal reckoning. As mentioned, our reimagining of this concept aims to create space for work that can contend with the complex duality of race and sexuality as it is lived and expressed through social structures. Thus, for the personal as well as for the structural, this multidisciplinary collection aims to make use of that space by bringing together diverse perspectives and encouraging new ideas.

For us, we are invested in undesiring whiteness as an active process of social justice that begins with grasping how ideas, systems, bodies, and ways of being are reified as desirable through ascription to whiteness. From these insights can bloom new methodologies, ontologies, epistemologies, discourses, and interventions toward undesiring. Subsequently, it becomes possible not only to see how sexual racism is done—how it is ascribed onto virtually all aspects of our social experience—but also to work toward undoing its influence. Here, we use explicitly active language because we are most interested in tangible actions. Certainly describing, deconstructing, and destabilizing are essential, but we view their primary purpose of this scholarship to help advance theoretical, conceptual, and practical change. And the purpose of that change? To get closer to the ultimate goals of eliminating racism, in our societies and fostering sexualities unfettered by racism.

Toward these lofty goals, we are overjoyed to have collaborated with a diverse and multidisciplinary cohort of scholars, activists journalists, students, artists, poets, and many others doing work on sexual racism around the world. Each has contributed a unique perspective, representing every continent except South America and with half of the contributors from nonacademic backgrounds or institutions. Three-quarters of contributors are Indigenous and/or people of color, a third are transgender and/or gender diverse, and two-thirds are women or femme. We share these high-level descriptors to give some sense of our various positionalities, as these undoubtedly shape how we see the world and the solutions we propose. Throughout this process, each of us—editors and contributors—have worked to sustain a process of self-reflexivity (Finlay & Gough, 2008), in part to enrich our analyses and interpretations but also to allow this work to evoke changes within ourselves however and wherever possible.

This collection is divided into four sections, with each separated by brief interludes of poetry from Ilannah Deshazier and Synclaire Warren, who plumb the complex interplay of racism and sexuality in ways only poets can. The first section, "Histories and Theories," provides some historical and theoretical accounts of sexual racism among certain populations and in certain contexts. The section opens with an exploration of two films produced two decades apart. In conversation with the films' creators, Tony Ayres and Donovan Trott, this chapter examines the pervasive and stifling influence of neoliberalism on queer sexual politics to propose new ideas that balance the

18 INTRODUCTION

individual with the structural. Next, Andy Quan's autoethnographic account examines the experience of cofounding an online campaign challenging sexual racism, SexualRacismSux.org. This perspective on queer activism in Australia—the highs and lows—uses the gift of hindsight to imagine a way forward, yet again wrestling with the enduring tension between the individual and society. Closing out the section, Xiqiao Chen, Jeremy Kelleher, Anthony Boiardo, Dashawn Ealey, and Daniel Gaztambide use analyses of online data to pose and problematize the notion of "sexual colorblindness." As a counterbalance, they introduce a framework of "sexual humility" to lead the undoing of sexual racism in a space free from shame and morality.

The second section, "Representations," concerns itself with expressions of sexual racism in creative, visual, and other discursive spheres. To those ends, Siam Hatzaw draws on Audre Lorde's politics of desire to unravel the ancient biblical text Song of Songs and its representations of Black female sexuality. Through numerous translations over the centuries, they explore the insertion of sexual racism as it plays out in theological interpretation and their own life. Next, Marc Ducusin offers a compelling examination of convicted murderer Andrew Cunanan, sympathetically positioning him as a radicalized queer figure forged through sexual racism and diversely projected across time via journalism, popular culture, art, and activism. In the following chapter, Ivan Bujan unpacks the constructions of race through erotized HIV prevention marketing in white-majority countries. By critiquing the sexualization of bodies of color, their work proposes new ways for public health to imagine effective and inclusive HIV prevention. This section ends with Anuradha Vikram's powerful recounting of the bold artistic expressions arising from Iranian American provocateur, Amitis Motevalli. They argue that by simultaneously challenging and inviting audiences to unpack the Orientalism of sexual racism, Motevalli lays an evocative foundation from which to undesire whiteness.

The third section "Lived Realities," examines some important and illuminating lived realities of sexual racism. Fern Smith and Jade Le Grice offer a compelling examination of how the sexualities of Māori girls are framed by the unrelenting realities of settler-colonialism in New Zealand/ Aotearoa, including the restriction of sexuality through essentialized notions of public health risk. In their chapter, Madi Day and Bronwyn Carlson also engage with settler-colonialism, applying an anti-colonial framework to examine how the violence of sexual racism is enacted against and experienced by Aboriginal and Torres Strait Islander people in so-called Australia. Taking

INTRODUCTION 19

a deep theoretical dive, Gene Lim wrestles with the promise of undoing sexual racism and the actual reality of trying to decolonize one's own desires. The desire for whiteness, they argue, has material and psychic realities for racialized subjects, which cannot be undone through force of will and may demand a response that is more patient and perhaps more fun. The section ends with an analysis of over 100 qualitative interviews led by Russell Robinson, which reveal the ways in which whiteness gives shape to intimate encounters of intersectionally diverse queer people in the United States.

The fourth and final section, "Spotlighting the Structural," attends to the big-picture dynamics of sexual racism. Chibundo Egwuatu, Zahra Stardust, Mireille Miller Young, and Daisy Ducati begin by examining how digital "tagging" features on prominent pornography websites creates a "grammaire pornographique" that serves the white supremacist agendas of desiring whiteness and sustaining racial capitalism. While proposing some technological interventions that could help address this issue, they ultimately recognize that only through dismantling capitalism can any kind of meaningful change be achieved. Panteá Farvid, Sarah Epstein, Leigh Lumpkin, Thyme Canton, and Michelle King further expand on the racialized organization of sex work, using the dynamics of commercialized sexual encounters to critique the consistent and enduring production of white supremacy in sexualized capitalistic spaces. Next, Ellen Yom offers a reflexive exploration of sexual racism in her scholarship of egg-donation practices among women racialized as Asian in the United States, including how this work has invited new perspectives on her own lived experience. And closing the collection, Sizwe Mqalo and Matthew Rich-Tolsma activate a discursive and self-reflexive practice they call "empathetic dialogue" to delve into the sexualization of their racialized experiences and the racialization of their sexualized experiences growing up in South Africa, including how these foundations have shaped their orientations in the world today.

Overall, this book represents an incredibly exciting and provocative collection of work. As part of the self-reflexive process, however, we must acknowledge that it disproportionately represents perspectives from the Global North, especially the United States and Australia. This gap is major issue for this work, and it highlights that we did not do enough to create safe spaces for and facilitate the inclusion of diverse perspectives, especially from nonwhite countries. We must also problematize the "academic collection" as itself a tool of white supremacy that derives power from exclusionary systems of whiteness and, by extension, the production of knowledge. The very fact the

20 INTRODUCTION

collection is presented almost entirely in English is testament to this point. Contending with the tensions between doing scholarly work and the ultimate desiring of whiteness produced through the systems of that work is a central challenge we set for ourselves at the start of this project. And in many ways, we were only partially successful. While we dreamed of this project as a revolutionary intellectual space, there are many constraints embedded in scholarly book writing that we ultimately did not escape. We might even ask if centering whiteness in our analyses actually contributes to its desirability, if by challenging it we have actually helped reaffirm its significance. While there are no simple resolutions to this problem, one of the ways we have decided to further destabilize the prominence of whiteness in this work is by hosting subsequent events to encourage public engagement—especially from artistic perspectives—in querying the ideas and solutions raised by this collection and its collaborators.

Engaging in this kind of reflexivity is difficult, and there are no easy answers. By no means do we mean to disparage the work of our brilliant collaborators; we are very proud of this collection and believe it makes many important theoretical, conceptual, and practical contributions. Nevertheless, those of us committed to truly undesiring whiteness and undoing sexual racism must contend with a difficult reality: regardless of race, each of us can benefit from these systems in a multitude of ways. These benefits are not always obvious, and their subtlety can lull us into a false sense of having taken meaningful action. This point is central to the whole collection! Whiteness is desirable, and so we are attracted to it even while attempting to articulate and undesire its ugliness. The work of social justice is never done, and we must continue to imagine and experiment with new and previously disparaged ways of undesiring and undoing, especially those freed from traditional modes of knowledge production.

How Do You Solve a Problem Like Sexual Racism?

As we have intimated throughout this chapter, to advance social justice it is necessary that we challenge the desirability of whiteness and confront the ubiquity of sexual racism. This brings us to the central question of this whole collection. What are we actually going to do to undesire whiteness and undo sexual racism? There are many tantalizing potentials proposed by our wonderful contributors, but also some things that we can discount straight away.

As discussed, recent experiences reveal that technology will not undo sexual racism, and education will not undesire whiteness. Indeed, the current forms of such tools ultimately limit their existence only to the service of white supremacy. The challenge with tinkering at the edges with technology and education is that it can feel like the "real" work, but ultimately it only creates the conditions under which systems of oppression endure. That is not to say that technology and education cannot provide some immediate relief to the lived realities of sexual racism, but this relief must always be embedded in larger projects of structural change toward social justice. Across this collection, it seems clear the structural changes most likely to impact sexual racism would be to undesire neoliberalism and capitalism, along with the harms they create through the "benefits" they promote. Last, we urge everyone to actively center sexuality in their antiracism work, and to actively center racism in their sexual plurality work. Continuing to relegate these as lower priorities ensures that truly effective scholarship and praxis will always remain out-of-reach.

One key learning from this collection is the ways in which art and other creative expressions can disrupt the theorization and praxis of sexual racism, particularly in academic spaces. We have been incredibly excited by not only the alternative thoughts but also the alternative ways of thinking introduced by our creative collaborators. Thus, involving creative pursuits directly in the process of undoing sexual racism should be seen as a priority, a complement rather than an alternative to scholarly perspectives. Indeed, active reflexivity between academic and artistic thought may also help undo the siloed dynamics of contemporary research and education, a true multidisciplinarity that challenges rigidly defined scientific expertise (which ultimately only ever maintains the desirability of whiteness). And let us not stop there! Art is one example of potentially disruptive thinking, but we must actively seek out others and create more space for them in the production of knowledge.

This collection came to life during an exciting, dynamic, and difficult time for antiracist work. As we observed and participated in diverse forms of racial activism and advocacy, we repeatedly encountered a distinct inattention to sexuality. The four of us also move in activist circles related to sex and sexuality and we are repeatedly disturbed by how common it is for racism to be entirely excluded from discourse and action. Such a separation is no accident, and there is a long history of antiracism and sexual liberation projects not only kept apart but also pitted in active conflict. As our last and perhaps most important point, we wish to simply yet forcefully

22 INTRODUCTION

demand the meaningful inclusions of sexuality in antiracism activism and the meaningful inclusion of racism in sexual liberation activism. As we have articulated here many times and in many ways, we cannot undesire whiteness without undoing sexual racism, and sexual racism will never be undone without also undesiring whiteness. Ultimately, confronting the inseparable interplay of racism and sexuality is a vital and exciting opportunity for contemporary social justice.

References

Aantjes, C., Crankshaw, T., & Freedman, J. (2022). Impacts of colonial legacies on the rights and security of sex workers in southern Africa. *International Journal of Gender, Sexuality and Law, 2*(1), 273–297.

Ahmed, S. (2007). A phenomenology of whiteness. *Feminist Theory, 8*(2), 149–168.

Aldrich, R. (2002). Homosexuality in the French colonies. *Journal of Homosexuality, 41*(3–4), 201–218.

Allen, R. L. (2001). The globalization of white supremacy: Toward a critical discourse on the racialization of the world. *Educational Theory, 51*(4), 467.

Anandavalli, S. (2022). Not your fetish: Broaching racialized sexual harassment against Asian women. *Journal of Mental Health Counseling, 44*(4), 297–311.

Ansley, F. L. (1988). Stirring the ashes: Race class and the future of civil rights scholarship. *Cornell Law Review, 74*, 993.

Applebaum, B. (2016). Critical whiteness studies. In G. W. Noblit & J. R. Neikirk (Eds.), *Oxford research encyclopedia of education* (pp. 1–23). Oxford University Press.

Azhar, S., Alvarez, A. R., Farina, A. S., & Klumpner, S. (2021). "You're so exotic looking": An intersectional analysis of Asian American and Pacific Islander stereotypes. *Affilia, 36*(3), 282–301.

Baldwin, J. (2021). *The fire next time*. Random House Publishing Group.

Bat-Shion, Y., & Smith, P. (2020). Healing racialized trauma and white fragility in interracial relationships. *Imago Relationship North America* (blog). Retrieved March 20, 2023, from https://blog.imagorelationshipswork.com/racialized-trauma-white-fragility-inte rracial-relationships

Bedi, S. (2015). Sexual racism: Intimacy as a matter of justice. *Journal of Politics, 77*(4), 998–1011.

Berry, D.R. & Harriss, L.M. (2018). *Sexuality & slavery: Reclaiming intimate histories in the Americas*. University of Georgia Press.

Bloodworth, A. (2020, June 3). Why Grindr removing its ethnicity filter is a complex issue. *HuffPost UK*. Retrieved March 20, 2023, from https://www.huffingtonpost.co.uk/entry/ grindr-remove-ethnicity-filter-grindr-dating-app_uk_5ed62d14c5b651b2b317bb4d

Bonds, A., & Inwood, J. (2016). Beyond white privilege: Geographies of white supremacy and settler colonialism. *Progress in Human Geography, 40*(6), 715–733.

Boone, J.A. (2015). The homoerotics of orientalism. Columbia University Press.

Bramlett, M., & Mosher, W. (2002). Cohabitation, marriage, divorce, and remarriage in the United States. *National Center for Health Statistical: Vital and Health Statistics, 23*(22), 1–93.

INTRODUCTION 23

Brathwaite, L. F. (2020). Why dating apps are racist AF—With or without ethnicity filters. *Rolling Stone*. Retrieved March 20, 2023, from https://www.rollingstone.com/culture/culture-features/dating-apps-grindr-ethnicity-filters-1047047/

Brown, A. (2018, January 9). "Least desirable"? How racial discrimination plays out in online dating. *National Public Radio*. Retrieved March 20, 2023, from https://www.npr.org/2018/01/09/575352051/least-desirable-how-racial-discrimination-plays-out-in-online-dating

Butts, J. D. (1977). *Inextricable aspects of sex and race*. Paper presented to the Five College Black Studies Seminar Series, Amherst, Massachusetts. Retrieved March 20, 2023, from https://eric.ed.gov/?id=ED107751

Callander, D., Holt, M., & Newman, C. (2015). "Not everyone's gonna like me": Accounting for race and racism in Australian sex and dating webservices for gay and bisexual men. *Ethnicities, 16*(1), 3–21.

Callander, D., Holt, M., & Newman, C. (2018). Gay racism. In D. Riggs (Ed.), *The psychic life of racism in gay men's communities* (pp. 1–13). Lexington.

Carlson, B. (2020). Love and hate at the cultural interface: Indigenous Australians and dating apps. *Journal of Sociology, 56*(2), 133–150.

Chappell, B., Romo, V., & Diaz, J. (2021). Official who said Atlanta shooting suspect was having a "bad day" faces criticism. *National Public Radio*. Retrieved March 20, 2023, from https://www.npr.org/2021/03/17/978141138/atlanta-shooting-suspect-is-belie ved-to-have-visited-spas-he-targeted

Childs, E. C. (2005). *Navigating interracial borders: Black–white couples and their social worlds*. Rutgers University Press.

Christian, M. (2019). A global critical race and racism framework: Racial entanglements and deep and malleable whiteness. *Sociology of Race and Ethnicity, 5*(2), 169–185.

Cox, O. C. (1959). *Caste, class, and race: A study in social dynamics*. University of California Press.

Craig-Henderson, K. M. (2017a). *Black men in interracial relationships: What's love got to do with it?* Routledge.

Craig-Henderson, K. M. (2017b). *Black women in interracial relationships: In search of love and solace*. Routledge.

Curington, C. V., Lundquist, J. H., & Lin, K. (2021). *The dating divide: Race and desire in the era of online romance*. University of California Press.

Dainton, M. (2015). An interdependence approach to relationship maintenance in interracial marriage. *Journal of Social Issues, 71*(4), 772–787.

DeCook, J. R. (2018). Memes and symbolic violence: #proudboys and the use of memes for propaganda and the construction of collective identity. *Learning, Media and Technology, 43*(4), 485–504.

Du Bois, W. E. B. (1933). *Black reconstruction*. Harcourt, Brace and Company.

Duggan, L. (2002). The new homonormativity: The sexual politics of neoliberalism. *Materializing Democracy: Toward a Revitalized Cultural Politics, 10*, 175–194.

Elia, J. P., & Yep, G. A. (2012). Sexualities and genders in an age of neoterrorism. *Journal of Homosexuality, 59*(7), 879–889.

El-Tayeb, F. (2011). *European others: Queering ethnicity in postnational Europe*. University of Minnesota Press.

Endo, R. (2021). Asian/American women scholars, gendered orientalism, and racialized violence: Before, during, and after the 2021 Atlanta massacre. *Cultural Studies↔Critical Methodologies, 21*(4), 344–350.

Fanon, F. (1952). *Peau noire, masques blancs*. Éditions du Seuil.

24 INTRODUCTION

Fausset, R. (2021, March 16). 8 People killed in Atlanta-area massage parlor shootings. *New York Times*. Retrieved March 20, 2023, from https://www.nytimes.com/2021/03/16/us/atlanta-shootings-massage-parlor.html

Feliciano, C., Robnett, B., & Komaie, G. (2009). Gendered racial exclusion among white internet daters. *Social Science Research*, *38*(1), 39–54.

Finlay, L., & Gough, B. (2008). *Reflexivity: A practical guide for researchers in health and social sciences*. John Wiley & Sons.

Foucault, M. (1976). *Histoire de la sexualité: La volonte de savoir*. Editions Gallimard.

Fredrickson, G. M., & Camarillo, A. (2015). *Racism: A short history*. Princeton University Press.

Gonlin, V. (2023). "Come back home, sista!": Reactions to Black women in interracial relationships with white men. *Ethnic and Racial Studies*, *46*(10), 2020–2042.

Greif, G. L., Stubbs, V. D., & Woolley, M. E. (2022). Clinical suggestions for family therapists based on interviews with white women married to Black men. *Contemporary Family Therapy*, *45*, 333–348.

Gremore, G. (2020, July 2). Grindr ditching the ethnicity filter has created new problems for the very people it aimed to help. *Queerty*. Retrieved March 20, 2023, from https://www.queerty.com/grindr-ditching-ethnicity-filter-created-new-problems-people-aimed-help-20200702

Hale, L. (2014). Globalization: Cultural transmission of racism. *Race, Gender and Class*, *21*(1/2), 112–125.

Han, E., & O'Mahoney, J. (2014). British colonialism and the criminalization of homosexuality. *Cambridge Review of International Affairs*, *27*(2), 268–288.

Han, C.W. (2021). *Racial erotics: Gay men of color, sexual racism, and the politics of desire*. University of Washington Press.

Han, C.W., Ayala, G., Paul, J.P., Boylan, R., Gregorich, S.E., & Choi, K.H. (2014). Stress and coping with racism and their role in sexual risk for HIV among African American, Asian/Pacific Islander, and Latino men who have sex with men. *Archives of Sexual Behavior*, *44*, 411–420.

Heino, R., Ellison, N., & Gibbs, J. (2010). Relationshopping: Investigating the market metaphor in online dating. *Journal of Social and Personal Relationships*, *27*(4), 427–447.

Henrich, J., Heine, S. J., & Norenzayan, A. (2010). The weirdest people in the world? *Behavioral and Brain Sciences*, *33*(2–3), 61–83.

Hernandez Aguilar, L. M. (2023). Memeing a conspiracy theory: On the biopolitical compression of the great replacement conspiracy theories. *Ethnography*, online first. doi: doi.org/10.1177/14661381221146983.

Herton, C. C. (1965). *Sex and racism in America*. University of California Press.

Holt, B. (2021, February 8). Racism thrives in the online dating world: Racial preferences on dating apps "reflect the shameful roots of racism in the United States." *Mashable*. Retrieved March 20, 2023, from https://mashable.com/article/racism-online-dating

hooks, b. (1992). Representing whiteness in the Black imagination. In L. Grossberg, C. Nelson, & P. Treichler (Eds.), *Cultural studies* (pp. 338–346). Routledge.

Hunt, S. (2013). Decolonizing sex work: Developing an intersectional Indigenous approach. In Emily van der Meulen, Elya M. Durisin, and Victoria Love (Eds.), *Selling sex*: Experience, advocacy, and research on sex work in Canada, 82–100. University of British Columbia Press.

Ichinose, H. (2021). *Examining journalistic discourses of Asian Americans in the news: A qualitative critical discourse analysis of news coverage of the Atlanta massage parlor shootings*. [Dissertation]. Malmö University.

Kaye, J. (2018). Settler colonialism, sex work, criminalization, and human trafficking. In Julie Kaye (Ed.), *Responding to human trafficking* (pp. 125–156). University of Toronto Press.

Kestler-D'Amours, J. (2022, May 18). Great replacement: The conspiracy theory stoking racist violence. *Al Jazeera*. Retrieved March 20, 2023, from https://www.aljazeera.com/news/2022/5/18/great-replacement-the-conspiracy-theory-stoking-racist-violence

Kitch, S. L. (2016). Anti-miscegenation laws. In *The Wiley Blackwell encyclopedia of gender and sexuality studies*. Wiley-Blackwell.

Korn, J. U. (2022). Intersectional misogyny and racism against Asian women: Critical race media literacy and the Atlanta massacre. In J. Cubbage (Ed.), *Critical race media literacy* (pp. 73–81). Routledge.

Kundnani, A. (2021). The racial constitution of neoliberalism. *Race and Class, 63*(1), 51–69.

Lay, K. J. (1993). Sexual racism: A legacy of slavery. *National Black Law Journal, 13*, 165–183.

Lennox, C., & Waites, M. (2013). *Human rights, sexual orientation and gender identity in the commonwealth*. University of London Press.

Leslie, L. A., & Young, J. L. (2015). Interracial couples in therapy: Common themes and issues. *Journal of Social Issues, 71*(4), 788–803.

Lin, K. H., & Lundquist, J. (2013). Mate selection in cyberspace: The intersection of race, gender, and education. *American Journal of Sociology, 119*(1), 183–215.

Lipscomb, A. E., & Emeka, M. (2020). You don't get it babe: Intimate partner support coupled with racialized discrimination among intra-racial and inter-racial couples. *Psychology, 11*(12), 1813.

Liz, J. (2018). "The fixity of whiteness": Genetic admixture and the legacy of the one-drop rule. *Critical Philosophy of Race, 6*(2), 239–261.

Lopez, G. (2016, April 13). People have huge prejudices in dating: The Daily Show explains why that's a problem. *Vox*. Retrieved March 20, 2023, from https://www.vox.com/2016/4/13/11420332/daily-show-sexual-racism

Ludwig, G. (2016). Desiring neoliberalism. *Sexuality Research and Social Policy, 13*(4), 417–427.

Maffini, C. S., Paradis, G., & Molthen, F. (2022). Integrating two families: Factors influencing relationship satisfaction among intercultural couples. *Journal of Comparative Family Studies, 53*(2), 237–255.

Mahajan, N. (2017). Are we racist on dating apps? This thread has some questions. *The Quint World*. Retrieved March 20, 2023, from https://www.thequint.com/neon/social-buzz/online-dating-men-speak-how-women-pick-men-racism-online#read-more

Mahmud, T. (1998). Colonialism and modern constructions of race: A preliminary inquiry. *University of Miami Law Review, 53*, 1219.

Malat, J., Mayorga-Gallo, S., & Williams, D. R. (2018). The effects of whiteness on the health of whites in the USA. *Social Science and Medicine, 199*, 148–156.

Massad, J. A. (2008). *Desiring Arabs*. University of Chicago Press.

M. Beliso-De Jesús, A., & Pierre, J. (2020). *Anthropology of white supremacy*. Wiley-Blackwell.

McIntosh, P. (1989). White privilege: Unpacking the invisible knapsack. *Legislative Library of the Northwest Territories, 19*(2), 1–7.

Media, V. (2022). Why the far right are so weird about sex: Decade of hate. *Vice News*. Retrieved March 20, 2023, from https://www.youtube.com/watch?v=jdlXkgUGLv4

26 INTRODUCTION

Meiu, G. P. (2015). Colonialism and sexuality. In E. Blackwood, W. O. Bockting, V. Braun, et al. (Eds.), *The international encyclopedia of human sexuality*. Wiley-Blackwell.

Melamed, J. (2015). Racial capitalism. *Critical Ethnic Studies, 1*(1), 76–85.

Monro, S. (2015). LGBT/queer sexuality, history of, Europe. In E. Blackwood, W. O. Bockting, V. Braun, et al. (Eds.), *The international encyclopedia of human sexuality*. Wiley-Blackwell.

Moses, J., & Woesthoff, J. (2019). Romantic relationships across boundaries: Global and comparative perspectives. *History of the Family, 24*(3), 439–465.

Najmabadi, A. (2005). *Women with mustaches and men without beards: Gender and sexual anxieties of Iranian modernity*. University of California Press.

Nordmarken, S., Heston, L., & Goldstein, A. (2016). Intimate citizenship. In N. A. Naples & J. M. Ryan (Eds.), *The Wiley Blackwell encyclopedia of gender and sexuality studies*. Wiley-Blackwell.

O'Neil, C. (2016). *Weapons of math destruction: How big data increase inequality and threatens democracy*. Penguin Random House.

Osuji, C. K. (2019). *Boundaries of love: Interracial marriage and the meaning of race*. New York University Press.

Paulin, D. R. (2012). *Imperfect unions: Staging miscegenation in U.S. drama and fiction*. University of Minnesota Press.

Popli, N. (2022, May 16). How the "Great Replacement Theory" has fueled racist violence. *Time Magazine*. Retrieved March 20, 2023, from https://time.com/6177282/great-repl acement-theory-buffalo-racist-attacks/

Ramirez, N. C. (2023). The Proud Boys have really strict rules about jerking off. *Rolling Stone*. Retrieved March 20, 2023, from https://www.rollingstone.com/politics/politics-news/proud-boys-trial-rule-book-masturbation-ban-1234666317/

Ramiro, C. (2022). After Atlanta: Revisiting the legal system's deadly stereotypes of Asian American women. *Asian American Law Journal, 29*, 90.

Reddy, C. (2011). *Freedom with violence: Race, sexuality, and the U.S. state*. Duke University Press.

Robinson, C. J., & Kelley, R. D. G. (2000). *Black Marxism: The making of the Black radical tradition*. University of North Carolina Press.

Said, E. W. (1995). *Orientalism*. Penguin Random House.

Schields, C., & Herzog, D. (2021). *The Routledge companion to sexuality and colonialism*. Routledge.

Shield, A.D.J. (2019). *Immigrants on Grindr: Race, sexuality, and belonging online*. Palgrave Macmillan.

Silvestrini, M. (2020). "It's not something I can shake": The effect of racial stereotypes, beauty standards, and sexual racism on interracial attraction. *Sexuality and Culture, 24*(1), 305–325.

Smith, J. G. (2017). Two-faced racism in gay online sex. In P. G. Nixon & I. Düsterhöft (Eds.), *Sex in the digital age* (pp. 134–136). Routledge.

Spector, A. J. (2007). Globalization or imperialism? Neoliberal globalization in the age of capitalist imperialism. *International Review of Modern Sociology, 33*, 7–26.

Stember, C. H. (1968). *Sexual racism: The emotional barrier to an integrated society*. Harper & Row.

Stokel-Walker, C. (2018, September 29). Why is it OK for online daters to block whole ethnic groups? *Guardian UK*. Retrieved March 20, 2023, from https://www.theguard ian.com/technology/2018/sep/29/wltm-colour-blind-dating-app-racial-discriminat ion-grindr-tinder-algorithm-racism

Stoler, A. L. (1995). *Race and the education of desire: Foucault's history of sexuality and the colonial order of things*. Duke University Press.

Sykes, H. (2016). Gay pride on stolen land: Homonationalism and settler colonialism at the Vancouver Winter Olympics. *Sociology of Sport Journal, 33*(1), 54–65.

Terkel, S., Goldstein, R., & Troupe, Q. (2014). *James Baldwin: The last interview and other conversations*. Melville House Publishing.

Thai, M. (2020). Sexual racism is associated with lower self-esteem and life satisfaction in men who have sex with men. *Archives of Sexual Behavior, 49*(1), 347–353.

Thusi, I., & Geronimo, I. (2015). Policing sex: The colonial, apartheid, and new democracy policing of sex work in South Africa. *Fordham International Legal Journal, 38*, 205.

Vidal-Ortiz, S., Robinson, B.A., & Khan, C. (2018). *Race and sexuality*. Polity Press.

Weiss, M. D. (2008). Gay shame and BDSM pride: Neoliberalism, privacy, and sexual politics. *Radical History Review, 100*, 87–101.

Williamson, S. H. (2017). Globalization as a racial project: Implications for human trafficking. *Journal of International Women's Studies, 18*(2), 74–88.

Yuen, N. W. (2021, March 18). Atlanta spa shooting suspect's "bad day" defense, and America's sexualized racism problem. *National Broadcast Corporation*. Retrieved March 20, 2023, from https://www.nbcnews.com/think/opinion/atlanta-spa-shooting-suspect-s-bad-day-defense-america-s-ncna1261362

Zuberi, T., & Bonilla-Silva, E. (2008). *White logic, white methods: Racism and methodology*. Rowman & Littlefield Publishers.

SECTION I
HISTORIES AND THEORIES

1

A Queer History of Sexual Racism

Denton Callander, Tony Ayres, and Donovan Trott

It was the summer of 1989 in New York City's West Village when author and activist, James Baldwin, sat down to be interviewed by Richard Goldstein of the *Village Voice*. Baldwin opined on queer life, identity, and politics, declaring—now famously—that "the sexual question and the racial question have always been entwined" (Terkel et al., 2014). Speaking to one of the themes woven through his literary work, Baldwin went on to say:

> A Black gay person who is a sexual conundrum to society is already, long before the question of sexuality comes into it, menaced and marked because he's Black or she's Black. The sexual question comes after the question of color; it's simply one more aspect of the danger in which all Black people live.

The full transcript of their exchange is certainly worth a read, but this brief excerpt hints at the complex themes Baldwin explored throughout his writing and in his life as a queer Black person in the West. From this intersectional perspective, he asked intersectional questions. In his literary works, notably *Another Country* (Baldwin, 1962), Baldwin used different relationship configurations—particularly multiracial and nonheterosexual—to queer traditional sites of power and imagine new potentialities (Cohen, 1991; Fisher, 2017; Stokes, 2016). Through his writing and especially in his public speaking, Baldwin was explicit that intimacy is only possible when all (including white) people are freed from oppressions wrought in gender, race, and class (Cederstrom, 1984).

Some of Baldwin's contemporaries viewed him as antirevolutionary and an apologist for white supremacy, particularly because he sought to imagine queer relationships among Black men as spaces for undoing racism (Cleaver, 1968; Hove, 2022). More recent analyses have explored how Baldwin sought to *race* and *queer* the individual and interactive natures of pleasure and

Denton Callander, Tony Ayres, and Donovan Trott, *A Queer History of Sexual Racism* In: *Sexual Racism and Social Justice.*
Edited by: Denton Callander, Panteá Farvid, Amir Baradaran, and Thomas A. Vance, Oxford University Press.
© Oxford University Press 2024. DOI: 10.1093/oso/9780197605509.003.0002

32 HISTORIES AND THEORIES

intimacy (Armengol, 2012; Hemming, 2021). "Race and sexuality," it has been argued of Baldwin's novel *Giovanni's Room*, "are not simply interrelated but virtually interchangeable . . . homosexuality becomes, literally and met-aphorically, associated with Blackness at the same time that heterosexuality is . . . indissolubly linked to whiteness" (Armengol, 2012). In this and other works, Baldwin offers a highly provocative and queer study of sexual racism, casting it as the racialization of sexuality and the sexualization of race.

In *The New Black Sociologists*, Antonia Randolph argued for Baldwin's work as offering an important and underused source of social insight and theory pertaining to race and sexuality (Randolph, 2018). This contention reminds us that all literature, film, music, and art "are a form of history and constitute indispensable historical evidence" (Hove, 2022). For a concept as murky and multifaceted, as personal and painful as sexual racism, creative pursuits complement the social sciences for their capacity to unravel and un-pack. In working to undo sexual racism, therefore, there is much to be gained from treating literature, film, music, and art as objects of insight.

This chapter charts a queer history of sexual racism, drawing on two films produced two decades apart. These films—one the creative work of Tony and the other Donovan—use different forms of filmmaking, but both ex-plore the dynamics of race and sexuality from and through the perspectives of queer men of color (Ayres, 1998; Sheridan, 2018). By contrasting these films, examining the public response they generated, and situating their texts within the larger social contexts of the time, we can explore a queer history of *doing* sexual racism while also imagining a queer future in which sexual racism is *undone*.

It is important to note that we chart *a* rather than *the* queer history of sexual racism, bringing to bear our various positionalities as able-bodied queer cisgender men who have lived most of our lives in the white supremacist and unceded colonial territories now referred to as Australia, Canada, and the United States. Alongside these similarities, there are also some differences between us; Tony is Chinese, Donovan is Black, and Denton is white, and while Donovan and Denton are millennials, Tony is a baby boomer. Tony and Donovan are filmmakers and raconteurs, while Denton is a social scien-tist. We highlight this (by no means complete) list of positionalities because they shape not only our lived experiences but also our creative and scholarly interpretations of these issues (Finlay & Gough, 2008). Contending with this reality is part of an ongoing reflexive practice we seek through this chapter and, we hope, our lives more broadly.

Figure 1.1 Film poster for Ayres's 1998 film, *China Dolls*.

A Tale of Two Films

In September of 2021, the three of us sat down to talk about sex, love, film, and sexual racism. In particular, we discussed Tony's 1998 documentary *China Dolls* and Donovan's 2018 comedy feature *No Chocolate No Rice* (Ayres, 1998; Sheridan, 2018) (Figures 1.1 and 1.2). In *China Dolls*, Tony uses his own voice interspersed with the perspectives of other men racialized as Asian to chart the sometimes-painful coming of age as an immigrant and a minority both racially and sexually in 1980s Sydney. In *No Chocolate, No Rice* Donovan portrays a fictional Black gay man struggling, internally and externally, with the complexities of race and sexuality in 2010s Washington, DC, forming part of a larger cast depicting intersectional challenges of race, sexuality, gender and class. Though fictional, *No Chocolate No Rice* draws on Donovan's lived experience, cast through humor to convey these moments in a way that is at once amusing and disturbing (Trott, 2017a, 2017b).

34 HISTORIES AND THEORIES

Figure 1.2 Film poster for Trott's 2018 film, *No Chocolate No Rice*.

While produced in different styles, millennia, and national contexts, both films use autobiographical perspectives to delve into the complex entanglements of racism and sexuality in queer communities.

Denton: Tony, China Dolls explored race and sexuality in a way that wasn't really being talked about, at least in the mainstream discourse at the time. What led you to create this film?

Tony: I think at that time in my career, I was looking at a lot of very personal concerns, things that were troubling me or that I was facing in my life. Often there were issues around the intersection of identities. One of the things that I felt quite profoundly, particularly in my 20s and 30s, was the realization that being Chinese in Australia and being gay wasn't a comfortable or wholly aligned intersection. In fact, quite simply, the places I experience racism most profoundly were male gay place, dominated by white guys. I thought I was alone in that, then I met other people who had from Asian backgrounds who had similar experiences. That's when I realized, "Oh, there's something more at play here," so I then put together *China Dolls*.

Denton: What about you, Donovan? What was the inspiration for your film?

Donovan: For me, I noticed the encounters I had with white men tended to always be clunky and racialized in a way. I began to wonder about why that is, with these experiences culminating in one specific instance, which I depict in the first scene of my movie, where I was called the N-word, hard R, by a sexual partner. That was like, "okay, okay, okay, this is all getting to be a bit much and it's always with white guys!" so I definitely sat back and took a minute. I began talking to my friends of color and we were all coming to a consensus that sexual accounts, or at least the vast majority with white men, seemed to be racialized in some way. That got my brain working. I'm always looking for inspiration and that's why I ended up writing several articles and then making the movie that I made.

One thing our discussions highlighted was just how confusing and isolating it can be to navigate sexuality as a person of color in a white supremacist society, something shown by previous social research with gay men in the United States and Australia (e.g., Callander et al., 2015; Chuang, 1999; Han, 2007).

Donovan: I was curious Tony if there was a time . . . I definitely noticed that when I actually had a conversation with my friends of color about this, it made me feel so much better because I thought I was crazy. I was like: "Is it just me? Maybe I'm presenting in such a way that's encouraging these interactions." Having these conversations with my friends of color definitely made me feel like at least I wasn't crazy.

Tony: Yeah, I thought I was alone in that. I thought it might have just been my personal experience or there was something wrong with me that I was

36   HISTORIES AND THEORIES

somewhat unattractive. I just couldn't fit in the way that the codes worked. As I said, it was when I started sharing these experiences with others that I realized it wasn't really about me personally.

Denton: So would you say these kinds of conversations with your peers were important in prompting the creation of these films?

Tony: Yes, absolutely.

Donovan: For sure. And more than that, big studios lag far behind on delivering nuanced portrayals of queer people of color, which is also why I took matters into my own hands.

As we experienced personal revelations around race and sexuality, so have these films sparked conversations and revelations among others. *China Dolls* in particular attracted interest from scholarly quarters (e.g., Caluya, 2008; Chan, 2006; Donald, 2000), with some contending the film helps "visibilise as well as question the hegemonic forces surrounding [the] constitution, expression and production [of Asian-Australian identity]" (Yue, 2000), while others hold it up as demonstrating the internalized nature of "modern racism" (Leong, 2002). Around the time of its release, Tony himself published a peer-reviewed article exploring the film's themes, which has since been cited hundreds of times (Ayres, 1999). Not all analyses of this work, however, have been affirming. One notable critique decried the "politically correct" lessons of *China Dolls*, especially how it "[failed] to account for desires and identifications that cannot be easily disciplined" (Nguyen, 2012). (As to the latter critique, Tony himself agrees, citing the limited space of a 30-minute film. For more on this often underexamined question, see Gene Lim's chapter "Consuming Whiteness/Disciplining Desire" [Lim, 2024].) Overall, however, the response to *China Dolls* was generally positive.

No Chocolate No Rice also attracted considerable public interest, spurred in part by a companion article Donovan published around the same time in a major media outlet, entitled *An Open Letter to Gay, White Men: No, You're Not Allowed to Have a Racial Preference* (Trott, 2017a). A sign of the times, public response to Donovan's work manifested primarily via social media. "I'm gay and white and guess what? This is bullshit. Everyone has preferences," wrote one presumably white and gay Twitter user who went on to ask the important question: "What's next? We're not allowed to exclude fatties?" (Callander et al., 2023). The hundreds of social media posts responding to the film and article (which we have archived here: Callander et al., 2023) evoked arguments familiar from previous studies of the rhetoric of sexual racism among gay men (Callander et al., 2012; Gregorio Smith, 2017). Others seemed to see these messages as a personal afront, such as one who wrote, "this is way too complicated and comes off as . . . slightly whining . . . i've slept around the rainbow. stop lecturing. love." Along with these public missives, Donovan received many vicious emails. Overall, while there was certainly some positive feedback to his work, the vast majority was negative.

Despite differences in form (i.e., documentary vs. comedy feature), the films deal with similar themes (i.e., sexual racism, intersectionality) and present largely the same conclusions (i.e., desire is socially constructed and, thus, racially mediated). It is, therefore, significant that *No Chocolate No Rice* received a much more negative public reception than *China Dolls*, especially because—as evident in our archive of social media comments (Callander et al., 2023) —public critique of *No Chocolate No Rice* focused almost exclusively on the film's ideas and creators rather than its merits as a creative work. We discussed the different reactions these films received, with social media certainly at the top of our minds.

Tony: I remember when my film came out, it was the days before social media. I think we just had computers.

Denton: It sounds like a blessed time.

Tony: Yeah, and it meant my film was very marginal when it was released. Hardly anyone saw it. It did travel to a lot of queer film festivals, but that was it.

Denton: Donovan, I'm curious about your experiences getting feedback both in the public sphere and maybe in your private life also, as your film did share some very personal moments.

Donovan: Yeah, it's hard to say because I don't have Twitter, which is where a lot of discourse tends to take place. I didn't realize until about a year after things came out that it had gone semiviral. A lot of people who I know of but didn't know had discussed my work and shared it around. I would get a bunch of vicious emails from, I would assume, generally white gays and I would forward them to friends of mine saying, "See, this is what happens when you try to take racism away from white people." It would be this horrible email, some stranger saying: "I'm going to kill you, shut the hell up."

Denton: Yikes, that's terrible.

Donovan: But the thing I thought was really interesting was some Black people within the queer community not pushing back against anything I was saying, but instead fixating on this impression that I was really into white men. With Black people who did not know me, there was this idea that I was really concerned about my relationship with the white gay community, when in actuality I was just calling a spade a spade. I was just saying this thing out loud that I thought we had all experienced. This response just encapsulated for me how people of color can take narratives from the prevailing thread of racism and weaponize it against their own communities. It's one of the ways, I guess, that white supremacy survives. We're aware of the main systems—economic exploitation and the media and all these different things—but then there are other smaller ways in which it keeps itself alive, including by getting communities to turn on one another when they call the thing out.

What is so interesting about the feedback Donovan received—including from other Black queer people—is that it tended to derive from an individualized frame. As we have shown, many people responded to the themes of *No Chocolate No Rice* by casting the issue of sexual racism as a matter of individual preference, their personal sexual liberties, or some failing of Donovan himself. There is no question sexual racism has individual realities, but as articulated by others these always derive from a ubiquitous structural reality (Robinson, 2024). Individualism is at the core of neoliberal capitalist ideologies of the self and society, so it is unsurprising any debate of sexual racism in the West would center individualized perspectives (Callander et al., 2024). Such a center, however, blinds people—with deliberate intent—to the reality of structural inequality, thus sustaining white supremacy and obstructing true democratization (Du Bois & Jones, 2013; Turner, 2008).

In contemplating barriers to undoing sexual racism, our discussion repeatedly returned to the reluctance of many queer people—or at least those groups with whom we are most familiar—to engage openly and honestly with questions of racism and sexuality. On some levels, queerness invites attention to the tension of a nonnormative life—as bell hooks put it, queerness is "being about the self that is at odds with everything around it" (hooks, 2014)—and many creative and scholarly studies of sexual racism have drawn on queer perspectives. Despite the ways in which a queer life can motivate and illuminate new understandings of self and society, many queer (or, perhaps, "gay") people remain incredibly resistant to the very idea of sexual racism.

Donovan: It's been my hypothesis, and I don't think it's a hypothesis at this point, that your queerness does not shield you from having very regressive ideas about the world. If you are a queer man, specifically a queer white man, you can rationalize your queer identity as a reason to hold tighter to more mainstream ideas rooted in racism and misogyny, because you can use your queer identity to say, "I faced something, I some gone through alienation, I have gone through an *ism*." I think that's where the terminology of, "It's just a preference" comes from. It's the pushing away of a larger systemic issue by asserting your agency.

Tony: What's really interesting for me is that sexual racism is such a flash point within the world of gay men, even the idea incites such profound feelings and such defensiveness. Perhaps there's a certain generation of gay men who lived through the sexual outlaw kind of period. So now they feel as though any accusation of racial bias is an infringement on hard fought rights. It makes them feel as though they can't be sexually free and so they end up equating arguments against sexual racism with homophobia.

Donovan: I totally understand what you're saying, because I've had these conversations and they feel like they fought so hard to be themselves and to love who they want to love that challenging the idea of preference is kind of problematic. It's sort of moralistic to their mind. It's kind of, "Well, I fought this hard to love who I want to love and now you're telling me I can't fuck who I want to fuck?!"

Denton: After traveling around and talking to people about sexual racism for over a decade, I can tell you that is an incredibly prevalent idea. What would you like to suggest to people who maintain this belief?

Donovan: What I would suggest is simple. Preferences are not personal.

The Personal and the Structural

The idea that "preferences are not personal" highlights an important truth about our desires: they are created through a complex process of socialization, which more than anything else reflects our environments and contexts. Interestingly, Gilles Lipovetsky called the enactment of preferences the

40 HISTORIES AND THEORIES

"process of personalization," which he viewed as an ultimate act of individualism (Lipovetsky, 1989). Of course, Pierre Bourdieu described preferences as filmy rooted in our social environments (Bourdieu & Nice, 1984), but both he and Lipovetsky were mainly concerned with distinctions between cultural artifacts not people. Bourdieu was right, however, that the distinctions we draw—including about other people—are derived from our sociocultural experience, thus it is vital that we examine those experiences and question how they shape our desires. As study after study find our so-called preferences for sexual and romantic partners are highly patterned and closely mimic broader realities of racism, ableism, cisgenderism, and other forces of oppression (e.g., Albury et al., 2021; Callander et al., 2012; Lin & Lundquist, 2013; Miron et al., 2022), it seems clear that power is the defining feature of desire. Despite this reality, individualism advanced by the neoliberal sexual politic (itself a tool of white supremacy) seems to have convinced many "queer" people the racialization of their sexuality is merely an expression of preference.

Throughout our discussion, we kept returning to the ideas of individualism and the processes of individualization, examining together how they may impact on sexual racism in the West.

Tony: I would find some of these men I found attractive in a social situation, a party situation, when you're a bit tipsy. You would realize there was absolutely no reciprocation. And it wasn't because of anything anyone overtly said, but you would just know you're not in their category. I think that fucks with your head.

Donovan: I absolutely know what you mean. On the flip side, what I encounter most often is these expectations surrounding my Blackness, kind of like: what's your favorite rap song? Basically, many guys I dated wanted a performative type of Blackness that I wasn't giving them and I guess it kind of fucked up their fantasy or whatever. I'm Black and sometimes listen to classical music. Or I'm Black and I like to have discussions about politics. I don't give a fuck about Nicki Minaj, why are you asking me about her? As so, I realized that for them I was just sort like "a Black." It wasn't me who was Black. I was "a Black."

Tony: Yeah. You know what speaks to me about that, is this kind of deep-seated journey to be judged and related to as a total person. As a whole pack, rather than just one aspect of your identity. And I know why it's so operative within the gay male world, dominated as it is by the gaze and what people look like. So, I can understand it, but still just remember yearning to be considered something outside of the cliches of what my race was supposed to represent.

Racial "preferences" as part of the project of individualism rely on stereotypes; it is impossible to say you are attracted to Black men or unattracted to Asian men if you do not maintain some schema about what a Black or Asian man is like. Thus, we can say stereotypes themselves rely on the individualization of personhood, the distilling—as Tony said—of an entire person into racial cliches. To us, this reveals the fraught and ultimately fruitless process of personal individualization. When you separate the unique components of self, these individual parts themselves become meaningless. Put another way, the total of a person is always greater than the sum of their parts. This point is the basis of intersectionality, namely that our experiences of power and oppression arise from many intersecting identities that can only ever be understood in relation to each and can, therefore, never be meaningfully separated (Crenshaw, 1991).

Tracking Anti–Sexual Racism Progress in the Queer West

For nearly two hours, we talked about *China Dolls* and *No Chocolate No Rice*. These films provided us with many opportunities to share our various perspectives on complex questions of desire, and to reflect on the two decades that separate their release. After all our discussion, we were left with an incredibly important question about our recent history of queer sexual racism.

Denton: As you consider each other's films and, perhaps, your lived experiences, I'm curious. Regarding queer sexual racism, do you think things have things changed much in 20 years?

Donovan: I don't think anything has changed. I really don't. I feel like when we talk about the politics of desire, as Tony did 20 years ago with *China Doll* and I carried on doing with *No Chocolate*, the desire part gets all of the attention and the politics part almost always gets lost. People just don't want to engage with it! So we have this question about the nature of desire and the role race plays in that, which is unchanged from the time Tony made his movie to the time I made mine. And from that and from our discussion today, the sort of obvious conclusion is that all roads lead

42 HISTORIES AND THEORIES

to racism and our desires are a product of racism, but people don't want to grapple with that. People don't want to have that conversation, and they don't want to admit what turns them on. They don't want to admit what gets their dick hard is racist.

<u>Denton</u>: I want to push back a little bit and say that I do think that for the first time we are really have a conversation about sexual racism in major public spaces. So, I guess at least our awareness of this issue has grown, although has that actually helped push antiracism forward? Tony, at the end of *China Dolls* you say you've noticed a change in the gay scene, and that the rigid boundaries of the sexual hierarchy are blurring. Do you stand by that statement all these years later?

<u>Tony</u>: I think it's good to talk about this stuff, and I guess I'm a bit more optimistic because back in my day it was so rigid. The only guys who ever approached me in a bar situation, it always felt like they had the right, that somehow I would just desire them because of their whiteness even though they were 25, 30 years older than me. From what I observe when I go out and see the world, I see a lot more Asian men with Asian men, and younger white men with younger Asian men. I don't see that age disparity to the same degree, I don't see the categories as strictly adhered to as before. As Australian society continues to diversify, perhaps more gay men are having their early formative experiences with men of different races. So that might be breaking down things at a level. I try to be optimistic about these things.

<u>Donovan</u>: You're such a good person! I'm not an optimist. I mean, I do believe with every generation comes natural progress. I do believe that. But if we're talking about undesiring whiteness, unlearning racism, I don't know that we're as far along as we think we are. So even with what you're saying Tony, I feel like more work needs to be done to get to the politics part of everything.

<u>Denton</u>: I have to say that I'm leaning more toward Donovan's points on this question of change. Totally agree, Tony, that there is some promise in the fact that we can and do have conversations around sexual racism, but also I wonder if these conversations become a replacement for meaningful action or the nature of the conversations themselves is a limiting factor. Perhaps, as you suggest Donovan, we lack an effective political frame.

Although differing on some of the details, we generally agreed that despite some progress undoing sexual racism among queer people, this work has been slow and not necessarily moving in a liberatory direction. Perhaps 20 years is too short a time to expect observable changes to something as foundational as sexual racism. Even with this point in mind, however, it is still surprising that *No Chocolate No Rice* generated such a negative public reaction, including relative to *China Dolls*; this difference, we believe, simply cannot be explained by context, form, or social media. If the work of undoing sexual racism was really taking place, would not the discursive engagements of queer people in public spaces present at least some evidence of a liberatory shift? Perhaps the film itself is the shift, but the question remains important because discourse can serve as a portend of social change in other ways. Thus, as our recent queer history of sexual racism suggests very limited anti-racist progression, we are bound to ask: why?

Confronting the Sociopolitical Limitations of Individualism

If the purpose of studying history is to avoid its repetition, then to chart a more productive future it is vital we explore why it seems so little progress has been made on the issue of sexual racism among queer communities. Of course, it is necessary to recognize sexual racism as foundational to our societies, which means it will take lifetimes to undo its influence. That not-withstanding, although we believe the nature of a queerness invites attention to the racialization of sexuality, many queer people (especially cisgender gay men) remain resistant to the very idea of sexual racism. Further, although there appears to be growing awareness of sexual racism in some queer quarters, many discussions appear hamstrung by notions of preference and freedom.

Individualism and individualization are perhaps the most compelling explanations we can offer for such limited progress toward undoing sexual racism. We are not alone in advancing this argument. Robin DiAngelo claims, "the Discourse of Individualism is one of the primary barriers preventing well-meaning (and other) white people from understanding racism" (DiAngelo, 2010), while others find arguments of individualism stymies antiracist praxis under a seemingly liberal ideology of equality (Augoustinos et al., 2005). Importantly, social scientists find individualistic values and practices have been increasing globally since the 1960s, especially in white-majority countries (Santos et al., 2017). Certainly, the countries

44 HISTORIES AND THEORIES

in which *China Dolls* and *No Chocolate No Rice* were produced are among the most individualistic in the world, dominated by narratives of individual exceptionalism in the United States and "fair dinkum" egalitarianism in Australia (Clearly Cultural, 2021). Thus, individualism enjoys considerable and growing ideological prominence in our world—especially driven by neoliberalism—which is likely to have impacted upon anti–sexual racism work similar to antiracist work generally.

Individualism and individualization also have implications for the queer sexual racism specifically, which find roots in the Western queer (or perhaps more aptly "gay") political movement developed in the late 20th century. As Steven Seidman and Chet Meeks point out in their compelling analysis, despite prevailing wisdom that gay politics are transformative, in reality they are a politics of normalization and status quo derived from what they call *civil individualism* (Seidman & Meeks 2011). Indeed, many others have highlighted the homogeneity of gay politics as a process of seeking social acceptance rather than instigating social transformation, embracing neoliberal sexual politics by centering on individual "rights" and "freedoms" (Drucker, 2015). Interestingly, in some contexts these politics reject "preferences" of sexuality in favor of bioessentialist arguments (i.e., *born this way*) that seek to naturalize sexual orientation (Wuest, 2019). On the surface it is somewhat confusing such politics can reject the notion of preferences in terms of partner gender yet embrace them in terms of partner race. The foundation for both arguments, however, is a rationale that seeks to fix our desires as stable and "of nature," and far from the fluid and contextual forces of "nurture" through a lifetime of socialization. Thus, this apparent contradiction of semantics is ultimately aligned within a rigid, essentialized, and individualized framing of desire.

Through embracing individualism, contemporary gay politics have also relied on individualization to isolate queerness from the more complex and intersecting dynamics of self. In political and social movements this individualization has centered queerness to the exception of all else, leading to numerous ongoing struggles within Western gay rights organizations, which we have previously called *intersectional crises* (Callander et al., 2018). Failing to contend with the intersectional realities of the people they claim to represent under the increasingly broad umbrella of LGBTQI+, when faced with a challenge such organizations default to the will of the relatively most powerful (i.e., cisgender, able-bodied, and affluent white men and, to a lesser extent, women). Thus, informed by individualism the politics of normalization also come to represent the individualization of a queer identity, casting it as a racially neutral territory that ultimately is oriented to and affirmed through whiteness. Baldwin saw this orientation coming from a mile away:

> I think white gay people feel cheated because they were born, in principle, into a society in which they were supposed to be safe. The anomaly of their sexuality puts them in danger, unexpectedly. Their reaction seems to me in direct proportion to the sense of feeling cheated of the advantages which accrue to white people in a white society. There's an element, it has always seemed to me, of bewilderment and complaint. (Terkel et al., 2014)

There is clearly a lot to unravel in a gay politic developed through and supported by individualism and individualization, which we cannot do full justice here. Instead, we share these thoughts because they relate very directly to any effort to undo sexual racism. As we have already discussed, individualism encourages sexual racism to be framed as a simple matter of *who is fucking whom*. An incredible amount of queer discourse focuses on this issue. While not irrelevant, focusing predominantly on this aspect of sexual racism even within a structural frame affirms an individualistic understanding by (1) suggesting it is primarily about interpersonal interactions, (2) guiding attention to the symptoms rather than the causes, and (3) limiting the responses that people imagine as possible. This last point is perhaps the most important, especially because many queer people seem to hear any discussion of sexual racism as a remonstration of their sexual and romantic lives. As one social media commentator wrote in response to Donovan's *HuffPo* article, "Dating people you know you're not attracted to just to appear non-racist, is a cruel waste of time" (Callander et al., 2023).

The Future of Queer Sexual Racism

By now, it should be clear that mainstream queer politics are not only ill equipped to undo sexual racism but actually work to sustain its place in our societies. Given failings of a gay politics rooted in individualism, we suggest a queer politics rooted in intersectionality offers a far more encompassing, transformative, and productive path toward undoing sexuality racism. While some have claimed intersectionality is a "gateway drug to individualism" (Motaouakkil, 2019), others have cautioned "intersectionality should

46 HISTORIES AND THEORIES

not be constructed as an individualistic project" (Levine-Rasky, 2011). Given intersectionality's capacities to align the experiences and positionalities of an individual within larger systems (always plural) of power and oppression, we find the latter arguments more compelling. From this perspective, we believe intersectionality is uniquely positioned to reconcile multiple levels of social influence, while recognizing, as Tony highlighted, the need each of us has to be "related to as a total person."

Our films were certainly not the first to explore queer sexual racism, and they will not be the last. Indeed, *China Dolls* followed nearly 10 years after Marlon Riggs's documentary *Tongues Untied*, which by the director's own account aimed to "shatter the nations brutalizing silence on matters of sexual and racial difference" (Riggs, 1989). This incredibly important film mixes poetry, music, and personal essays to untangle and retangle queer Blackness in the United States (Levasseur, 1994), ending with the now famous rallying cry, "Black men loving Black men is *the* revolutionary act" (Riggs, 1989). And since *No Chocolate No Rice*, filmmakers have continued to explore sexual racism in queer life including through comedy as in the 2022 film *Fire Island* (Ahn, 2022). This film is significant because it was made by a major studio and received considerable attention for engaging with questions of racism and sexuality among cisgender gay men (Mendoza, 2022; Sander, 2022), but *Fire Island*'s treatment of sexual racism is rather narrow and mainly reaffirms an individualistic frame of this issue. Regardless, there is clearly a growing body of cinematic work from diverse styles engaging with the complexities of queer racism and queer sexuality (for other examples, *Yellow Fever* and other works by Ray Yeung, alongside those of Richard Fung). There is no question that film and other creative works have an important part in transforming the social dynamics of race and sexuality, especially if they can reject individualistic narratives and the politics of normalization.

Naturally, it is easy to write about eschewing individualism by creating a new queer politics of intersectionality and far more difficult to bring this vision to life. DiAngelo was not exaggerating when they described individualism as "such a deeply entrenched discourse that it is virtually immovable" (DiAngelo, 2010). In addition to shaping queer life in the West, Joseph Massad and others have written extensively about how the individualized and bioessentialist queer politics continue to be exported and enforced globally (Massad, 2008). Further, as we have argued individualism is the bedrock of Western ideologies of neoliberal capitalism, an incredible ubiquity that means undoing sexual racism will require nothing less than challenging and transforming the very basis of our societies.

From this perspective, we can safely ignore largely aesthetic interventions like removing racial filters from sex and dating websites (Gremore, 2020) as little more than tinkering at the edges of a wholly corrupt and racist system. While discussions of "corrupt" and "immovable" systems may cast an impossibly daunting light over the future, we must remember that things only remain as they are when we allow the very systems we seek to undo to limit our imaginations. Put another way, individualism may shape our world, but we do not have to let it shape our thinking. In this way, binary conceptualizations—individual/structural, nature/nurture, straight/gay, us/them—become not one-or-the-other, but *both* and everything in between. In these spaces, film and other creative forms can help us break down the rigid structures that sustain and define sexual racism. For if we are truly serious about undoing sexual racism then queer filmmakers, artists, poets, scholars, and everyone else need to dream big, need to dream beyond the individual.

References

Ahn, A. (2022). *Fire island*. Searchlight Pictures.

Albury, K., Dietzel, C., Pym, T., Vivienne, S., & Cook, T. (2021). Not your unicorn: Trans dating app users' negotiations of personal safety and sexual health. *Health Sociology Review, 30*(1), 72–86.

Armengol, J. M. (2012). In the dark room: Homosexuality and/as Blackness in James Baldwin's *Giovanni's Room. Signs: Journal of Women in Culture and Society, 37*(3), 671–693.

Augoustinos, M., Tuffin, K., & Every, D. (2005). New racism, meritocracy and individualism: Constraining affirmative action in education. *Discourse and Society, 16*(3), 315–340. https://doi.org/10.1177/0957926505051168

Ayres, T. (1998). *China dolls*. Film Australia.

Ayres, T. (1999). China doll: The experience of being a gay Chinese Australian. *Journal of Homosexuality, 36*(3), 87–97. http://www.informaworld.com/10.1300/J082v36n03_05

Baldwin, J. (1962). *Another country*. Dial Press.

Bourdieu, P., & Nice, R. (1984). *Distinction: A social critique of the judgement of taste.* Harvard University Press. https://books.google.co.ke/books?id=nVaS6gS9Jz4C

Callander, D., Ayres, T., & Trott, D. (2023). *A brief history of queer sexual racism: Supporting documentation*. figshare. Dataset. https://figshare.com/articles/dataset/A_brief_history_of_queer_sexual_racism_Supporting_documentation/21172003/1

Callander, D., Holt, M., & Newman, C. (2012). Just a preference: Racialised language in the sex-seeking profiles of gay and bisexual men. *Culture, Health and Sexuality, 14*(9), 1049–1063. https://doi.org/10.1080/13691058.2012.714799

48 HISTORIES AND THEORIES

Callander, D., Holt, M., & Newman, C. (2015). "Not everyone's gonna like me": Accounting for race and racism in Australian sex and dating webservices for gay and bisexual men. *Ethnicities, 16*(1), 3–21.

Callander, D., Holt, M., & Newman, C. (2018). Gay racism. In D. Riggs (Ed.), *The psychic life of racism in gay men's communities* (pp. 1–13). Lexington.

Callander, D., Farvid, P., Baradaran, A., & Vance, T. (2024). How do you solve a problem like sexual racism? In D. Callander, P. Farvid, A. Baradaran, & T. Vance (Eds.), *Sexual racism & social justice*. Oxford University Press.

Caluya, G. (2008). "The rice steamer": Race, desire and affect 1 in Sydney's gay scene 2. *Australian Geographer, 39*(3), 283–292.

Cederstrom, L. (1984). Love, race and sex in the novels of James Baldwin. *Mosaic: A Journal for the Interdisciplinary Study of Literature, 17*(2), 175–188.

Chan, K. (2006). Rice sticking together: Cultural nationalist logic and the cinematic representations of gay Asian–Caucasian relationships and desire. *Discourse, 28*(2), 178–196.

Chuang, K. (1999). Using chopsticks to eat steak. *Journal of Homosexuality, 36*(3–4), 29–41. https://doi.org/10.1300/J082v36n03_02

Clearly Cultural. (2021). *Making sense of cross cultural communication: Individualism.* Geert Hofstede. Retrieved February 23, 2023 from https://clearlycultural.com/geert-hofstede-cultural-dimensions/individualism/

Cleaver, E. (1968). *Soul on ice.* Ramparts Press.

Cohen, W. (1991). Liberalism, libido, liberation: Baldwin's *Another country. Genders* (12), 1–21. https://www.utexaspressjournals.org/doi/epdf/10.5555/gen.1991.12.1?role=tab.

Crenshaw, K. (1991). Mapping the margins: Intersectionality, identity politics, and violence against women of color. *Stanford Law Review, 43*(6), 1241–1299.

DiAngelo, R. J. (2010). Why can't we all just be individuals? Countering the discourse of individualism in anti-racist education. *InterActions: UCLA Journal of Education and Information Studies, 6*(1). https://escholarship.org/uc/item/5fm4h8wm#author.

Donald, S. (2000). La Chine in culture/China. *New Formations, 40,* 1–11.

Drucker, P. (2015). 4 The sexual politics of neoliberalism. *Warped: Gay normality and queer anti-capitalism,* 279–304. https://brill.com/display/title/21259.

Du Bois, W. E. B., & Jones, M. H. (2013). *Black reconstruction in America: Toward a history of the part which Black folk played in the attempt to reconstruct democracy in America , 1860–1880.* Transaction Publishers. https://books.google.co.ke/books?id=7IjA4 g0kyNQC

Finlay, L., & Gough, B. (2008). *Reflexivity: A practical guide for researchers in health and social sciences.* John Wiley & Sons.

Fisher, L. R. (2017). Possible futures and grammatical politics in James Baldwin's *Another country. Journal of Modern Literature, 41*(1), 137–155. https://doi.org/10.2979/jmodel ite.41.1.09

Gregorio Smith, J. (2017). It can't possibly be racism: The white racial frame and resistance to sexual racism. In D. Riggs (Ed.), *The psychic life of racism in gay men's communities* (pp. 105–122). Lexington Books.

Gremore, G. (2020). Grindr ditching the ethnicity filter has created new problems for the very people it aimed to help. *Queerty.* Retrieved February 23, 2023, from https://www.queerty.com/grindr-ditching-ethnicity-filter-created-new-problems-people-aimed-help-20200702

Han, C.-S. (2007). They don't want to cruise your type: Gay men of color and the racial politics of exclusion. *Social Identities*, *13*(1), 51–67. https://doi.org/10.1080/135046 30601163379

Hemming, M. (2021). "In the name of love": Black queer feminism and the sexual politics of *Another Country*. *James Baldwin Review*, *7*(1), 138–158.

hooks, b. (2014). *Are you still a slave? Liberating the Black female body*. Presentation to the Eugene Lang College, The New School. The New School. Retrieved February 27, 2023 from https://www.youtube.com/watch?v=rJk0hNROvzs&t=5250s

Hove, M. L. (2022). Intersections of masculinity, sexuality, nationality, and racial identity in James Baldwin. *Cultural Studies↔ Critical Methodologies*, *23*(1), 79–86.

Leong, G. (2002). Internalised racism and the work of Chinese Australian artists: Making visible the invisible world of William Yang. *Journal of Australian Studies*, *26*(72), 79–88.

Levasseur, A. (1994). Marlon Riggs's legacy of simple truth (1957–1994). *Black Camera*, *9*(1), 10–11.

Levine-Rasky, C. (2011). Intersectionality theory applied to whiteness and middle-classness. *Social Identities*, *17*(2), 239–253.

Lim, G. (2024). Consuming whiteness/disciplining desire. In D. Callander, P. Farvid, A. Baradaran, & T. Vance (Eds.), *Sexual racism & social justice*. Oxford University Press.

Lin, K. H., & Lundquist, J. (2013). Mate selection in cyberspace: The intersection of race, gender, and education. *American Journal of Sociology*, *199*, 183–215.

Lipovetsky, G. (1989). *L'ère du vide: Essais sur l'individualisme contemporain*. Gallimard. https://books.google.co.ke/books?id=gj209wiX3bUC

Massad, J. A. (2008). *Desiring Arabs*. University of Chicago Press. https://books.google. com/books?id=TMnMC1vlxVMC

Mendoza, C. (2022). *Fire Island* addresses racism in LGBTQ community. *Newsy*. https:// www.newsy.com/stories/fire-island-addresses-racism-in-lgbtq-community/

Miron, M., Goulet, K., Auger, L., Robillard, C., Dumas, C., Rochon, F., & Kairy, D. (2022). Online dating for people with disabilities: A scoping review. *Sexuality and Disability*, *41*, 31–61.

Motaouakkil, Y. (2019). *Intersectionality: A gateway drug to individualism*. Presentation to TEDxMarrakesh. Retrieved February 23, 2023, from https://www.youtube.com/ watch?v=aEuO3R8ilgI

Nguyen, T. H. I got this way from eating rice: Gay Asian documentary and the reeducation of desire. In M. S. Ma & E. Suderburg (Eds.), *Resolutions 3: Global networks of video* (pp. 241–257). University of Minnesota Press.

Randolph, A. (2018). James Baldwin and the lay race theorist tradition. In *The new Black sociologists* (pp. 30–41). Routledge.

Riggs, M. (1989). *Tongues untied: Giving a voice to Black gay men*. California Newsreel, 1989.

Robinson, R. (2023). Sexual racism as white privilege: The relational and psychic negotiation of desire, power, and sex. In D. Callander, P. Farvid, A. Baradaran, & T. Vance (Eds.), *Sexual racism & social justice*. Oxford University Press.

Sander, S. (2022). Joel Kim Booster reflects on the "pride and prejudice" of *Fire island*'s party scene. *National Public Radio*. https://www.npr.org/2022/06/27/1107839961/joel-kim-booster-reflects-on-the-pride-and-prejudice-of-fire-islands-party-scene

Santos, H. C., Varnum, M. E., & Grossmann, I. (2017). Global increases in individualism. *Psychological Science*, *28*(9), 1228–1239.

50 HISTORIES AND THEORIES

Seidman, S., & Meeks, C. (2011). The politics of authenticity: Civic individualism and the cultural roots of gay normalization. *Cultural Sociology, 5*(4), 519–536. https://doi.org/10.1177/1749975511401272

Sheridan, L. C. (2018). *No chocolate, no rice.* Donovan Trott.

Stokes, M. (2016). " A brutal, indecent spectacle": Heterosexuality, futurity, and go tell it on the mountain. *MFS Modern Fiction Studies, 62*(2), 292–306.

Terkel, S., Goldstein, R., & Troupe, Q. (2014). *James Baldwin: The last interview and other conversations.* Melville House Publishing.

Trott, D. (2017a). An open letter to gay, white men: No, you're not allowed to have a racial preference. *Huffington Post.* https://www.huffpost.com/entry/an-open-letter-to-gay-white-men-no-youre-not-allowed_b_5947f0ffe4b0f7875b83e459

Trott, D. (2017b). Race play 101: My introduction into the world of racist sex play. *Huffington Post.* https://www.huffpost.com/entry/raceplay-101-my-introduction-into-the-world-of-racist_b_595b8fb7e4b0326c0a8d130a

Turner, J. (2008). American individualism and structural injustice: Tocqueville, gender, and race. *Polity, 40*(2), 197–215.

Wuest, J. W. (2019). *Born this way: Scientific authority and citizenship in the American LGBTQ movement* [PhD Dissertation]. University of Pennsylvania. Retrieved February 23, 2023, from https://repository.upenn.edu/edissertations/3404/

Yue, A. (2000). Asian-Australian cinema, Asian-Australian modernity. In H. Gilbert, K. Helen, L. Tseen, & J. Lo (Eds.), *Diaspora: Negotiating Asian-Australia* (pp. 190–199). University of Queensland Press.

2

A Look Back at the World's First Online Anti–Sexual Racism Campaign

Sexual Racism Sux

Andy Quan

Origins

In London one night in 1998, I was flipping through a gay magazine before bed and stumbled on a report of a poll of reader's biggest sexual turn-ons and turn-offs. The former were Americans, athletes, Europeans, I can't remember the others. The number one biggest turn-off chosen was "Orientals." Such a dated and silly category, ranking just above foot fetishes, its place on that page felt like a personal attack. Attacked in my own home, in the comfort of my bed! I was shocked to be reduced to a category to be rated and graded. I'd been turned down in the past because of my race, but this stupid magazine article was different. Instead of being turned down by one person in a bar, I was being rejected by a whole community, *my* community. It hurt.

In 1999, I arrived in Sydney looking for love—or lovers!—and to make a life for myself. Sydney's gay scene was world famous: the Mardi Gras parade and parties, the masculine, athletic men with *that accent*, towering drag queens, beautiful men at Bondi Beach in those tiny lifeguard bathing suits. I knew I'd find community groups, a choir, sports groups: people I could connect and feel safe with. Friends in London and Canada had read about Pauline Hanson and her One Nation party in the news: "Isn't Australia a racist place?," they asked. I hoped not. Born in Vancouver, Canada, of Chinese origins, I had lived in Europe for the preceding four years, in Brussels and London, and had my fill of racism both on the gay scene and in daily life. I was looking for a new home that was culturally diverse and accepting and I hoped Australia would be similar enough to Canada to fit the bill.

Andy Quan, *A Look Back at the World's First Online Anti–Sexual Racism Campaign*. In: *Sexual Racism and Social Justice*. Edited by: Denton Callander, Panteá Farvid, Amir Baradaran, and Thomas A. Vance, Oxford University Press. © Oxford University Press 2024. DOI: 10.1093/oso/9780197605509.003.0003

52   HISTORIES AND THEORIES

It was anger I felt, more than disappointment, when I started using the website Gaydar. Relegated now to the archives of Internet history, Gaydar launched the year I arrived in Sydney, and to my browser delivered many—too many—profiles declaring, for all the world to see: "No Asians." I imagined walking into a store that said "No Blacks" or a company that advertised "No gays need apply." I imagined a young gay Asian teenager in a rural town, isolated, and that his first encounter with the gay world was one that rejected him point blank. It was not that I wanted to date or have sex with men who used racist language, but their attitudes sent such a violent message: You are not desired. You don't belong. You are less.

Rather than stewing in my anger, I decided to take action. I had a personal website at the time to promote my creative writing that explored identity, culture, and racism in the gay community (Quan, 2001, 2005), which was readily repurposed to create what I called the "Gay Asian Male (GAM) pages." My idea, borrowed from letter-writing campaigns by Amnesty International, was that if you made it easy to do something, people might act. I created form letters that could be used to send to posters of offensive ads, be edited quickly and cut and pasted. For example:

Hi

Saw your ad on gaydar when I was surfing the net tonight.

Lots of gay Asian guys like me use this site on a regular basis. We read messages like:

- I am not into GAMs, fems, fats, or pensioners.
- No GAMs
- Not into GAMs, pretentious guys, fakers
- No Asians, sorry.

I'm a pretty confident guy but ads like yours still hurt. I wonder how they affect young guys coming out and surfing the net. Some young 18-year-old in Taiwan or New Jersey who finds out that people consider his race equivalent to something like bad breath.

It IS perfectly acceptable for people to have different tastes but putting a sexual preference based on race in a public space contributes to racism in the gay community, racism which affects all of us—it hurts Asian guys and white guys too.

Maybe consider putting what you're interested in, rather than what you're not interested in, i.e., "looking for masculine guys" rather than "no femmes."

But if someone answers your ad that you're not interested in, just say "sorry, you're not my type" or "sorry, I'm not interested." Or just ignore the message. Treat Asian guys like you would treat white guys that you're not attracted to.

You're not attracted to Asian guys. Fine. Don't remind us everytime we surf the web that people won't even look at us because of our race, or equate us with "fems" or some other supposedly undesirable characteristic just because of our race.

Thanks

The GAM pages displayed four different form letters, with descriptive headings like "short and pointed," "short and polite," and "from a non-Asian supporter." The letter displayed here was labeled "kind of an angry response," but reading it now, I don't think the letter is "kind of angry," it's just direct. It expressed exasperation.

Beyond encouraging others to use these form letters, I also started engaging directly with people online who displayed explicitly racist ideas. For example, in response to an ad from "Two boys in Bondi" that specified "No Asians," I sent a message explaining that their language was hurtful. A few days later, a response:

thanks for your message mate.
It is food for thought and never really thought it like that.
We don't have a racist bone in our bodies, it is purely a matter of sexual preference.
Since you have been so diplomatic and polite, my good deed for the day is to change the ad immediately.

While I considered this interaction a success in helping raise individual awareness, the larger email-writing campaign never really took off. I could see why. Even if others felt the same way as I did, most guys I know don't go online to critique racism or get into arguments with potential partners. Further, confronting racist practices can evoke a hostile response. I get that it's often easier just to say nothing. Indeed, those researching sexual racism among gay men in Australia have repeatedly found that many men of color prefer to say nothing at all lest they increase their exposure to violence and vitriol (Callander et al., 2012, 2016).

54 HISTORIES AND THEORIES

Despite the email campaign's failings, it served as a good entry point to discussions with other activists, including my friend-to-be Tim Mansfield. Tim, a white guy, had many gay Asian friends who shared with him how disturbed they were by racism in online profiles. He thought that getting online racism off the web would make a huge difference to many people. And as he'd noticed that Asian men talking about racism could be discounted and that there was power in a white guy talking about racism, he decided to try to use his white privilege for "good instead of evil." Thus, we joined forces and "Sexual Racism Sux" was born.

Tim and I began meeting, imagining what a campaign against sexual racism could look like. He'd already run a few websites, and his idea was a banner campaign where men could put an electronic banner on their personal profiles or on their websites with a clear message opposing sexual racism online. By May 2000, the campaign was live and hosted via www.sexualracismsux.com. The webpage included an overview of our arguments, some discussion forums, and a section of "frequently asked questions." It also included code that could be copied to display a banner or text on people's sex and dating profiles, which linked back to the site, but was a clear message on its own: Sexual Racism Sux.

Early on, Tim proposed we call the campaign "Sexual Racism Sux." "Really," I remember asking, "don't you think using the word racism will make some men so defensive it shuts down any dialogue?" Tim was adamant, however, that we call a spade a spade and that this particular word would help. As we later wrote on the campaign's website:

> We've consciously chosen to use the word "racism" because 1/ we have noticed racism in the community 2/ we believe that something called "sexual racism" exists 3/ it has evoked strong emotions and reactions.

I predicted, correctly, that the word "racism" would be interpreted by others as "you are racist," but more on that later. I also felt the word "sux" was gimmicky and ugly, but again Tim's arguments won me over: it was recognizable, catchy, a tribute to the Web 2.0 lingo of its time. I confess that all these decades later, the writer in me still cringes to read "sux," but ultimately, I believe the name worked for us. Indeed, a 2011 study of online sex and dating profiles hosted by gay men in Australia—more than a decade after the campaign's launch!—found more than a dozen profiles specifically using the phrase "sexual racism sux" (Callander et al., 2012).

The Campaign

From Day 1, we hoped the campaign could achieve two important aims. In the immediate term, we wanted to reduce racist language in the public (online) sphere and, in the longer term, we wanted to challenge—perhaps even undo—sexual racism. To those ends, we proposed several arguments designed to be understood simply and easily spread:

1. It's not "just a preference" to rule out a sexual partner because of their race. It's prejudice.
2. Saying "no GAMs" or "no Asians" is not "being honest." It's hurtful.
3. Try expressing what you want in your ads, not what you don't want.
4. In the spirit of multicultural Australia, why not try bonking someone from an ethnic group you're not used to?

To the first point, we'd heard the rationale many times that rejecting men of color was "just a preference," like whether you prefer chicken or beef, or classical over country music. So we thought that we'd lead with a rebuttal, and I did honestly (and perhaps naively) believe that naming this as prejudice would help white gay men engage with racism through their own experiences of homophobia. Building on this empathy, we hoped the second point would help men realize that their actions online could hurt real people in the real world. Third, we emphasized the idea of being positive, rather than negative: i.e., say what you want, not what you don't want. The final point was from Tim. I never imagined that we could convince men to broaden their sexual horizons just by proposing it, but I thought the tone was cheeky and fun, so why not?

In promoting positive instead of negative language, our messaging was perhaps not so clear, and the truth is that our thinking at the time may not have been that clear either. By asking men to say what they were looking for, we didn't *really* want men to write in their ads "white man looking for other white men" nor were hoping this would reify men of color as exotic prizes by "white men looking for Asians." Ultimately, we were really focused on reducing the use of phrases like "no Asians," which we viewed as particularly damaging and dangerous. But in our narrow focus on the one phrase, we ended up giving a free pass to those who were expressing sexual racism.

The campaign also involved direct outreach. We were in touch with Gaydar, the major player in online sex and dating at the time. They ignored a lot of

56 HISTORIES AND THEORIES

our suggestions, including one to eliminate "race" as a descriptive part of profiles, and they refused to ban racist language from their website. But they did publish suggestions and produced videos on how to write a profile, which borrowed directly from the campaign's central messages. We were also able to call them out on an advertising campaign during the Sydney Gay Games in 2002. To show how multicultural they were, they'd assembled a large group of young men and randomly draped their bare torsos in flags of many nations. But there was not one Asian model. We met with them along with the gay Asians program manager from the local AIDS council. The Gaydar rep told us that the Asian model hadn't shown up that day. "Try harder," we told him.

The final part of the campaign was responding to the many emails we received. We decided, as a policy, that the cause was better served by unfailing politeness, to not attack critics but try to engage them and explain our points of view. We spent considerable time doing this, though I didn't keep track how much. The campaign's mailing list grew to over 500 individuals, and the website itself received hundreds of hits per month. There was clearly a lot of interest generated by this topic and our advocacy. Eventually, we created a Yahoo group for Sexual Racism Sux, which was active with discussions continuing well into 2009. We learned about trolls, prompting Tim to figure out how to moderate a discussion group, setting up rules and guidelines so we could kick them out. We created a Facebook page, which never took off. Eventually, as Tim and I met long-term partners and drifted away from the world of online partner-seeking, we drifted away from the campaign, although the website still remains active.

Impact

On a broad level, the impact of our campaign was wider than we'd expected. Gay men were active users of the Internet since its earliest days, and this helped spread our message. This dissemination led to attention in the media and journalists offering to write stories about the campaign and radio shows asking for interviews. The local queer community newspaper, the *Sydney Star Observer*, put an article and photo of us on the front page (Figure 2.1; Mills, 2003), which was later republished on Fridae.com, the Singapore-based lesbian and gay portal and news service. Racism in the gay community and sexual racism started to be addressed in community forums and events through Sydney Mardi Gras and ACON.

Figure 2.1 Article on Sexual Racism Sux featured in the Australian queer publication, *Sydney Star Observer* (Mills, 2003).

While both of us had thought of the campaign as a local one, it found purchase internationally as well. The banner was seen on websites globally. I did an interview with a mainstream Vancouver-based community newspaper (Takeuchi, 2006), and for a Melbourne gay community radio show. Years after the campaign started, in May 2014, Australia's multicultural and multilingual broadcaster, SBS, produced a TV episode of a respected program called *Insight* with the topic "Dating Race," on race-based attraction, with mainly straight participants, which was broadcast in the Asia-Pacific region, not just nationally. It surprised me that sexual racism had become part of mainstream discussions. Tim and I were even name-checked in a 2022 editorial about the gay Asian rom-com, *Fire Island* (Tsai, 2022).

Back to when it started, on the community level and individual level, we received positive emails and comments from friends and community members, both men of color and white men. Some commented that they were glad the issue was finally being taken up. Many said they also felt that the language on sites like Gaydar was racist and harmful and it was a good thing to try to address it. But there were many negative responses as well,

58 HISTORIES AND THEORIES

which in some ways helped me realize how naive I was. I had thought the issue was cut and dried. Racist language was harmful and exclusive. Gay online ads were the location of this racism. Getting the language out of public space would be good for Asian men (and all men of color). It would make a friendlier community, hopefully by changing social norms. I believed that the racist language was from ignorance, and that men who used it would change if they knew it was hurting other people. We'd seen our own sexual tastes, and that of our friends, change and shift with time, so we proposed that even if white men had only had sex with other white men so far, this could change. Cut and dried, right?

What I didn't understand at the time was that whiteness and white supremacy reinforce white people and white ideas as the desirable centers of discourse and attention (Ansley, 1989; Applebaum, 2016). These systems work to hide white privilege from those who benefit from it, enabling the purposeful framing of sexual racism as a "preference," in turn denying the foundational role of racism in contemporary sexualities. When we challenged these systems: Well . . . systems don't like to be challenged. It led to denial, pushbacks, and attacks.

While the most common response was that not wanting to have sex with Asian men was "just a preference," some went further, and said it was like being gay or a man, not something they could change. Were we trying to force them to have sex with women too? That language was repeated in responses to the campaign, posted on the website and in direct emails. Suddenly, we were trying to *force* them to have sex with someone they didn't want to. I was surprised at the vehemence with which they defended themselves. They made their sexual "preferences" a defining part of their identity, and something immutable. How their language or actions affected others was not a concern. Someone naming themselves "Freedom For Gays" created their own page that claimed to be "Taking a stand against the sexual Nazis," which was announced to me via an email titled, "I will oppose your left wing campaign every step of the way."

Another common complaint was how could we have any credibility if the campaign didn't combat every prejudice—against overweight men, older men, and more? We defended ourselves by saying we were careful to be inclusive in our language but wanted to be focused. As a gay Asian man and as a person who had many Asian friends, the campaign focused on Asian men, and we were against racism against all groups. We'd have been happy to support other community campaigns. But this really wasn't the objective of our attackers: they just wanted to discredit the campaign.

We also heard from white men, mostly who had lived in or traveled in Asia, who complained that Asian men were racist too, and they had experienced it. But it led them to hostility instead of empathy for the campaign. We explained that we didn't consider the rejection or slights they'd experienced as racism, as they weren't backed by systems of power and oppression. White people may experience discrimination but do not experience racism. Being rejected by an Asian man in a gay bar in Asia was not in a context where one's race was devalued in other ways. We considered it prejudice, not racism. But in the end, it felt like we were wasting time trying to explain this.

If one feels attacked, the simple response is to attack back. Shoot the messenger. The problem was resentful Asian men who couldn't get laid. The problem was Asian men who were racist toward other Asians and chased after white men. The problem, sometimes, was me. A troll emailed regularly, demanding sex, to make up for all the young gay Asian men who had rejected him. A young gay Asian man posted on his website a complaint of a photo of me on my website, which he had found because of the campaign. I was holding a friend's baby in my arms, which made my bicep look big, and I was mocked for my attention-seeking and superficiality. A letter-writer to the editor of the gay community paper writer suggested that the campaign was negative; more positive would be if I went to the once-a-year Mr. Asia event in a local gay bar. Years before today's commonplace online calling out, I was learning that to be a part of a public campaign and put my name to it, I would be expected to be a role model and that my perceived personal behavior needed to match the messages of the campaign.

Other gay Asian men didn't necessarily support the campaign. Some just didn't care. If online racism didn't bother them personally, why make a fuss? One gay Asian man told me he didn't mind seeing "No Asians" on profiles because the racism was upfront, and he didn't have to waste his time. Another critic opposed the campaign, not because of the topic, but because he had the basic belief that people don't change their attitudes.

Lessons

(Sexual) Racism Is Localized and Contextual, but Consistent

A significant lesson for me was that the context for racism is different in every culture and location. We heard from gay men around the world with their own experiences of prejudice, which made me realize I knew little of

60   HISTORIES AND THEORIES

the precise dynamics of sexual racism in different cultures. We heard from a British-born Pakistani and his experiences with blatant racism from white and other South Asian gay "lads." We heard from a Tamil man living in Singapore who reported discrimination from the Chinese majority in the mostly Chinese gay scene, and similar reports of prejudice between ethnic groups in multicultural Malaysia.

For the Sexual Racism Sux campaign, I had unconsciously assumed gay Asian-Australians to be like me: born in the West with parents possibly born in the West as well, and with lived experiences of racism. Perhaps because I had felt racism so personally, I was not able to be objective. Yet gay Asian men in Australia were far more diverse than I'd assumed. Intersectional factors such as language and migration status meant that they could be excluded in more or deeper ways than I. One time at a gay bar, I noticed the white barman serving a white customer before an Asian one, who had arrived first. But the Asian man didn't seem to or chose not to notice. I guessed that he was, perhaps, not used to subtle racism and was not hypervigilant to it like I was.

I guessed that most Asian gay men who lived in Asia didn't connect with the campaign. It made sense in North America, Australia, and western Europe, where Asian men are a minority in the gay scene. In Beijing, Singapore, Tokyo, or Hong Kong, it wouldn't matter if an Asian guy is only looking for white guys, where most Asian guys are going to be dating and having sex and relationships with other Asians. It wouldn't affect the whole gay culture, translate into the same racism as in a white-dominated society, and create a hostile community. Similarly, many gay Asian men in Australia were migrants to Australia from Asia and had grown up and formed their sexual desires in societies where they were the same race as other gay men. Their experiences of sexual racism and racism more broadly were very different from that of a Western-born gay Asian.

Then again, while there were clearly differences, there were similarities. Everyone we spoke to or who reacted to the campaign had some kind of experience with the sexualization of racism and the racism of sexuality. Sure, the dynamics, impacts, and responses tended to differ depending on where, when, and who you were, but they were always there. Are always there. So while sexual racism may be local and is certainly contextual, it doesn't seem to go away.

The Value of an Ally

The emails that came in, the personal, nasty, racist, and aggressive ones, I just couldn't deal with. So we divided the labor: Tim answered emails from (mostly) white critics, being as polite for as long as he was able to, and I focused on answering emails from gay Asian peers. He could talk to people in a way that I couldn't and he could be objective. It was hard to not take those emails personally when they were meant to be personal attacks. Years before Reni Eddo-Lodge's viral blog post, "Why I'm No Longer Talking to White People about Race" which became the basis for a book (Eddo-Lodge, 2020), I felt angry and exhausted trying to explain racism to hostile emailers, but Tim, generally, was able to take a calm and neutral tone:

I discovered that Tim as a white man had access to conversations that I didn't as an Asian man. He overheard white gay men discussing the campaign at the gym, or out and about, who would never talk about it in front of an Asian man. He was an excellent spy. While neither of us had analyzed or discussed the role of allies in antiracist work (such as Kendall, 1998), we knew that a campaign only run by an Asian man would invite criticisms that I was just doing it for personal reasons, that I was angry and resentful, or that I had particular views on gay men of other races, or of my own.

Our approach, of aiming to be polite and respectful to anyone who wrote, would be out of step with today's antiracism campaigners, who I would think would lean toward an Eddo-Lodge-type of response: "I'm not talking to you about racism because I'm not responsible for educating you about racism and it's tiring talking about (and experiencing) racism." But we really did believe, at the time, that changing people's minds was best accomplished through respectful dialogue. I wouldn't take the same approach today, not only because respectful dialogue is more and more rare, but because of what I've come to see as limitations of Sexual Racism Sux.

Could We Have Done Better?

The Sexual Racism Sux campaign was not community-led or -driven. At no time did we ask the men affected by sexual racism what they thought could be done about it, or if they even thought it an important issue. I simply barreled ahead, assuming that my opinions were shared by others. As a result, we

62 HISTORIES AND THEORIES

didn't manage to build a community around the issue, or a substantive one at least, and ended up instead with a disparate group of people who participated in online discussions. While it seemed there were others who supported the campaign, no one else supported it enough to get involved. We didn't connect with other gay men of color, or with the various social or support groups in Sydney at the time.

Even though we aimed for broader changes in the community by spreading ideas and information, too much time was spent engaging with individuals one-on-one. As the main aim of the campaign was practical, to get racist language off the websites, we didn't engage with contemporary understandings of whiteness as described, for example in Applebaum (2016). Naming racist language on gay websites as "sexual racism" seemed radical enough at the time for us, rather than raising awareness of the structures of white supremacy as the core racism within and beyond the realm of sexuality.

The slow, individual, and polite approach we took perhaps reflected the time. We may have thought that communicating through emails, and the comments sections of websites, was a quicker mode than in the past, but none of us could have predicted the speed at which we communicate today, and how we could use apps and the Internet to do it, for good *and* bad. Grindr, which launched in March 2009, is perhaps the best example of this change. Grindr made hunting for sexual partners location-based (as the app told you how far away you were from others) and much more visual: profiles were only allowed to be 250 characters. Men accessed the app more quickly on their smartphones than in front of computers and it seemed to make websites like Gaydar quickly obsolete. I wondered if explicit racism became less frequent, as men's ethnicity was more clearly identifiable and sorting desire was quicker. But that when it did occur, it was more blatant, since using your short word limit to tell potential sexual partners "No Asians" sent a clear message. Grindr also allowed users to be more anonymous than other apps; users may have felt given a free pass to be racist. Still, whether it was implicit or explicit, I came to realize: sexual racism endures.

Gaydar and Grindr both showed me how racism can be facilitated by structures and by technology, in ways that made racism hard to address. The influence of technology was (largely) invisible but incredibly powerful. When I asked why it was necessary for users to say "No Asians" on their profiles, one Gaydar user took the time to explain that for free rather than paid memberships, you were allowed to send and receive a limited number of messages. He received many messages from Asian users and saw writing

"No Asians" as a way of controlling his ability to send and receive messages. This stumped me. I hadn't guessed that the technology, designed to make money, facilitated racist speech. So while individuals could hold racist views that were harmful to other individuals, there was a bigger battle to be waged against the structures of gay communities that benefit some and harm others. I didn't know how I'd begin to do that.

And while technology, and the way it facilitated communication, may have been the basis of the campaign (starting, as you'll recall, in response to gay personal ads on the Internet), communicating ideas through technology should have been the clear focus, rather than the individual conversations that we spent far too much time on. If there was success from the campaign, it was about spreading and communicating ideas, not changing the behavior or beliefs of individuals. Focusing on ideas could have allowed us to be braver and smarter, I think, and could have prodded us to look at our own analyses and beliefs about racism in a much deeper way.

For example, in reviewing the campaign materials for writing this article, I was surprised to see some of the language I used. In the kind-of-angry form email that was a prototype for Sexual Racism Sux, I played into stereotypes and the ways we exclude each other in the gay community, saying men should use positive language like "looking for masculine guys" rather than saying what they didn't want. In that email and in our FAQs section, I said that "it IS perfectly acceptable for people to have different tastes" and that it's not racist to prefer white men.

What was I thinking? Well, I thought that appearing to be agreeable would help a reader accept the next argument, "Don't be racist in public." I'd decided that it would be impossible to stop gay men from being racist, so the best achievement would be for them not to be racist in public spaces, like in their personal ads. I had a very strong belief that we would achieve more social change by not offending people and not getting people offside. I'm a little embarrassed that I considered it sounding angry simply to call out racism and asking someone to change their behavior. If I could go back in time and do the campaign again, I would stop being so damn polite.

Coda

A few years after we'd slowed down in our involvement with the campaign, I attended a meeting called *ConverAsians* at the local AIDS council, known as ACON, which at that time had begun taking a wider remit in LGBTIQ+ health and well-being. There were no more than a dozen of us, and frankly, I can't remember what the topic was, but I do remember at one point the subject turning to sexual racism.

Sitting on the couch were two young men, I'd guess in their early twenties. I found them interesting. They were small and slim and their fashion and haircuts were more like K-pop boy band members than that of the usual Sydney gay boys. One of them shrugged his shoulders and said, "Why bother?" It wasn't a statement of apathy or a critique of activism. What I guessed from the way he carried himself and the expression on his face was that he was from a new generation and different culture of Asian gay men. He hadn't absorbed the ideals of white gay communities to be attracted to white gay men, nor to dress or look like the majority, to fit into an ideal of a white, masculine, athletic man. If someone was racist, why would he care? Why would he waste time on them?

I might have been wrong in my assumptions, but it made me think about the hurt I'd felt, the offense I'd taken and my efforts so that other gay Asians and men of color weren't subjected to blatant racism, stereotypes, and rejection. It would have taken a confidence that I hadn't had, to be able to reject those who were racist or insensitive before they rejected me and block out the noise. Whereas my experience of gay life was in the context of whiteness, affecting my self-esteem, my sex life, and my romantic relationships, it seemed that he was able to step away from whiteness or at least make it not relevant to his life. I was glad for him, though a little jealous.

References

Ansley, F. L. (1989). Stirring the ashes: Race class and the future of civil rights scholarship. *Cornell Law Review, 74*, 993.

Applebaum, B. (2016). Critical whiteness studies. In G. W. Noblit & J. R. Neikirk (Eds.), *Oxford research encyclopedia of education*, 1–23. Oxford University Press.

Callander, D., Holt, M., & Newman, C. E. (2012). Just a preference: Racialised language in the sex-seeking profiles of gay and bisexual men. *Culture, Health & Sexuality, 14*(9), 1049–1063.

Callander, D., Holt, M., & Newman, C. E. (2016). "Not everyone's gonna like me": Accounting for race and racism in sex and dating web services for gay and bisexual men. *Ethnicities. 2016;16*(1): 3–21. https://doi.org/10.1177/1468796815581428

Eddo-Lodge, R. (2020). *Why I'm no longer talking to white people about race*. Bloomsbury Publishing.

Kendall, F. E. (1998). *How to be an ally if you are a person with privilege.* Presentation at the National Conference on Race and Ethnicity.

Mills, D. (2003). When preference reads like prejudice. *Sydney Star Observer.* Retrieved February 26, 2023, from https://sexualracismsux.com/2022/08/12/when-preference-reads-like-prejudice-sydney-star-observer/

Quan, A. (2001). *Calendar Boy.* New Star Books.

Quan, A. (2005). *Six Positions: Sex Writing.* Green Candy Press.

Takeuchi, C. (2006). Personal ad activists won't swallow racism. *Georgia Straight.* Retrieved February 23, 2023, from https://www.straight.com/article/personal-ad-activists-wont-swallow-racism

Tsai, M. (2022). Gay pride and gay prejudice in "Fire island." *INTO.* Retrieved February 23, 2023, from https://www.intomore.com/film/gay-pride-gay-prejudice-fire-island/

3

Anti-Black Skin, White Sheets

Challenging Sexual Color-Blindness Through a Sexual Humility Framework

Xiqiao Chen, Jeremy Kelleher, Anthony Boiardo, Dashawn Ealey, and Daniel Gaztambide

Introduction

This chapter introduces the term "sexual color-blindness" to define discourse, beliefs, and values that ignore the contextual influences of whiteness, white supremacy, and race on sexuality. Building on critical race theorists' analysis of United States constitutional color-blindness, we show how sexual color-blindness—and by extension, sexual racism—is a natural offspring of the liberal and individualistic legality in America. Sexual color-blindness actively constructs a passive desire for whiteness that then expresses itself as benign individualized instincts and desires—leading to sexual racism. Employing an ad hoc qualitative thematic analysis of Internet conversations on Reddit and Quora, we find that sexual color-blind discourse expresses two distinct themes: (1) sexual desire as (benign) preference and (2) sexual desire as essentialized.

Sexual color-blindness is deployed and reinforced in particular schools of thought in the psychological science of attraction, normalizing sexual racism under the rubric of legitimate science. Such information is typically distilled simplistically for public consumption through news media and pop culture, further shaping popular discourse and racist sexual mores/attitudes. In addition, using a psychoanalytic framework, we diagnose sexual color-blindness as a symptom of our neoliberal world and argue that sexual desire is created and sustained socially and systematically. Finally, we propose the framework of sexual humility to encourage discourse and action that confronts sexual racism to undo sexual color-blindness and

---

Xiqiao Chen, Jeremy Kelleher, Anthony Boiardo, Dashawn Ealey, and Daniel Gaztambide, *Anti-Black Skin, White Sheets* In: *Sexual Racism and Social Justice*. Edited by: Denton Callander, Panteá Farvid, Amir Baradaran, and Thomas A. Vance, Oxford University Press. © Oxford University Press 2024. DOI: 10.1093/oso/9780197605509.003.0004

racism and to explore, without shame or moralization, our desires and the structures that produce them.

Positionality Statement

We are a team of individuals with diverse gender, sexual, and racial identities. We are members of the Frantz Fanon Lab for Intersectional Psychology at the New School and are composed of the following members. One first-generation Asian American, straight, cis-woman who was drawn to this work through her own dating experiences, split between marginalization and fetishization and the anti-Asian hate that is not only violently demonstrated "in the streets" but more palpably "between the sheets." Two white gay men who approach this work reflecting on their transgressions and sexual racism—understanding how white gay men are not immune to perpetuating discrimination within an already marginalized community. By applying these experiences, they hope to contribute a lens from within whiteness to understand sexual racism. The last student member is a Black cisgender queer man born and raised in a women-led, multigeneration, community-oriented household in Brooklyn, New York. Although his community devoted itself to the African proverb "It takes a village to raise a child," he quickly understood the messy intersections of his queer, racial, and gender identities as natural byproducts of the inflexible gendered and racialized interactions he experienced as a child. For this reason, he tailors his personal and academic pursuits to dismantle oppressive systems and healing those traumatized by their insidious influences. Lastly, our team includes a faculty mentor and director of the Fanon Lab, a cisgender white Puerto Rican male who has experienced how his phenotype reflects discourses of anti-Black *mestizaje* favoring whiteness in his native Puerto Rico, as well as facilitates "passing" on the U.S. mainland. He has noted how the political economy of sexual desire textured his dating experiences, where context defined how his "race was read" as an object of desire.

We firmly believe that the intersectional nature of our identities shapes our values and the critical lens from which we approach this work. Although we mainly analyze sexually racist phenomena observed in the United States due to our locality, we understand the biases and dangers of falling into an American-centered perspective built on whiteness. As much as possible, we make sure to pinpoint the specific locus of our observations.

Color-Blindness as Legal and Psychic Force

Today, neoliberal discourses of desire stressing individual preference alongside essentialist and biological notions of otherness, devoid of historical and sociopolitical context, are employed in the dating sphere to legitimize personal dating preference based on race (Bedi, 2015; Callander et al., 2015; Curington et al., 2021). Sexual racism represents the last bastion of racial discrimination that is "explained away" (see also the introduction in this volume), even though the existence of racial preference in dating is indisputable and mirrors the bias of a racist, anti-Black society (Collins, 2004; Curington et al., 2021; Rudders, 2014).

We argue that such inability to reflect on biases in intimate spaces is constructed in part by color-blind ideologies in the United States—where skin color or race is not a legitimate factor for de jure legal, political, or public discrimination—skin color or race can be a de facto source of discrimination in the private sphere. To this end, Gotanda (1991) has detailed how color-blind constitutionalism constructs a "private-public distinction"—while racial discrimination in the public sphere is unlawful, privatized discrimination remains sanctioned (or goes unchallenged).

Color-blind constitutionalism intentionally omits a citizen's responsibility for engaging in exclusion or discrimination, as long as it is in the private sphere. For example, a restaurant owner may not exclude an individual from dining based on race, ethnicity, gender, sexual orientation, etc., but they may exercise their right to exclude any individual from their private home simply because they made the decision. The public-private distinction allows for a "protected sphere" within the personal, private domain that legitimates—indeed, renders permissible—stereotyping, bias, and discrimination that fuels inequality (Gotanda, 1991, p. 11). Therefore, private subjects not only can discriminate against others but also are permitted to discriminate against others. Any regulation against private discrimination, therefore, becomes unconstitutional. In this way, color-blind discourses work as a deregulatory force spanning the social, interpsychic, and intrapsychic realms. This dissociation of the public and private is, in turn, mirrored by the psychic dissociation necessary to keep the political separated from the personal.

In *Racial Melancholia and Dissociation*, cultural critic David Eng and psychotherapist Shinhee Han combine Gotanda's critiques of color-blind constitutionalism with psychotherapy case materials to examine the dissociative effects of color-blind ideology:

under the banner of colour-blindness and multiculturalism, discrimination in social life and continuing legacies of whiteness as property are reinvented for everyone as a matter of individual choice and personal preference outside history. From this perspective, everyone in a colourblind and multicultural age is now (racially) dissociated. (2019, pp. 159–160)

Such racial dissociation creates a psychic vacuum where personal choices are disconnected from racialized contexts and motivations, and carved out from larger societal forces. Such disavowal of our personal choices allows for the cloaking of sexual rejection, exclusion, and discrimination as just that—personal choices. In the erotic sphere, such racial dissociation allows us to experience the desire for whiteness, thinness, and wealth in a manner akin to consumer preference—natural, individualistic, private, and pure—masking the underlying white supremacy and market formations that structure both what we find wholesomely attractive and what we perversely fetishize (Curington et al., 2021).

Sexual Color-Blindness as Ideology

We define "sexual color-blindness" as the infiltration of color-blind ideology into the erotic sphere. Sexual color-blindness refers to the discourses, beliefs, and actions that intentionally and unintentionally ignore the impact of whiteness, race, and context on sexual desire, attraction, and intimate partner choices. We argue that sexual color-blindness is a crucial mechanism that prevents reflection on one's desire and reflects tacit racialized scripts—who does and does not have value as a desirous sexual subject?

Sexual color-blindness, defined in these terms, must be understood in relationship to whiteness. To begin to (un)desire whiteness, we must reflect on how our language cloaks and betrays our desire for it. To this end, we wanted to understand how Internet users made sense of sexual racism and how they justified preference, desire, and choice that others may see as sexually racist—in essence, how sexual color-blindness enacts through discourses and practices. We conducted an ad hoc thematic analysis on comments from Reddit and Quora, focusing on conversations related to sexual racism (accessed from May to December 2021). Our search terms included "sex," "sexuality," "sexual," "dating," "partner," "attraction," "discrimination," "racist," "racism," "race," and combinations of each.

70 HISTORIES AND THEORIES

The group then discussed comments that justified sexual racism or rejected the recognition of sexual racism and categorized them into two categories: (1) sexual desire as (benign) preference, and (2) desire as essentialized. We then identified comments that helped illustrate these two categories. To preserve commentators' anonymity, we coded each comment with an abbreviation, which are listed in parentheses following each quotation. In Tables 3.1 and 3.2, each comment's published date and original thread can be found next to the corresponding code.

Sexual Desire as (Benign) Preference

Sexual color-blindness construes preference as a benign, personal, idiosyncratic, and private choice protected under United States legality. A general theme among comments we examined was the distinction between private and public discrimination: "Only dating X race is not racist. People are allowed to have preferences. . . . It is racist to discriminate in hiring, housing, etc., but not when it comes to romance" (R2). The logic of this comment parallels color-blind legality: because private acts are unregulated by law, they cannot be racist. Here, the color-blind law becomes the arbiter of what is racist or not.

Similarly, some comments justify sexual exclusion using the First Amendment: "isn't freedom of association a constitutional right. If so then how is the opposite, the freedom of disassociation, the right to not conjugate

Table 3.1 Comments Scraped From the Online Forum, Quora, Focusing on Conversations Related to Sexual Racism (accessed from May to December 2021)

Code	Published Date	Thread
Q1	2021, Feb 14	"Am I racist if black people aren't my type?"
Q2	2016, May 21	"Is it racist that I prefer to date outside my race?"
Q3	2020, Oct 27	"I recently told a black friend that I do not find black women attractive . . ."
Q4	2018, Feb 8	"Why do people think it is racist to not be attracted to people of a different race?"
Q5	2015, Dec 15	Comment on the post "When will the gay community seriously address racism?"

Table 3.2 Comments Scraped From the Online Forum, Reddit, Focusing on Conversations Related to Sexual Racism (accessed from May to December 2021)

Code	Published Date	Sourced Thread	Post
R2	2021, Dec 16	r/dating	"Why it is racist to prefer to date only someone of your race"
R3	2020, July 6	r/askgaybros	"Related to Sexual Racism (Preferences)"
R4	2021, Feb 8	r/TooAfraidToAsk	"Is it racist?"
R5	2019, Oct 26	r/askgaybros	"Related to Sexual Racism (Preferences)"

with people you do not want to considered racism?" (Q5). Color-blind constitutionalism provides ideological support for exclusion and discrimination in the dating market.

Under neoliberalism, dating is analogous to making a retail choice—"People prefer blondes over black hair, black hair over brunettes. Camaros over mustangs, SUVs over smart cars, purple over green" (Q3). A Quora user articulated this point more explicitly, "black woman who likes to date black men isn't racist. A man who is attracted to women with large breasts. A woman who likes a guy with a big dick. None of those are hateful or '*-ist.' They're just your sexual taste." (Q2).

Sexual preference is portrayed as a personal, aesthetic choice akin to one's inclination towards pizzas or burritos, SUVs or smart cars. Sexual desire as (benign) preference showcases the logic of sexual color-blindness within neoliberal political economies. We discount contextual influences by painting preference as private acts and private choices. Sexual exclusion becomes a benign consumer choice.

Desire as Essentialized

While to some, sexual preference is similar to a consumer choice, to others, sexual desire is instinctual, biological, and naturalized. Much like other biological instincts, the need to breathe, eat, and sleep, sexual desire is understood as natural: "Everyone is attracted to something and most people are attracted to people of their own race/ethnicity. It's nature, and normal" (Q1).

Essentialists argue that desire is unknowable and therefore uncontrollable: "No amount of education, compassion, or understanding can change a sexual preference or attraction. This is not a logical or learned process. It is a biological one" (R3). Many other commenters echoed this sentiment, arguing that one cannot control or force attraction: "you can't decide what turns you on" (R4); "Attraction isn't personal choice—you like who you like" (R5).

Desire as essentialized concludes that desire should not be undermined and questioned, akin to "the permissive discourse of sexuality" developed by Wendy Hollway (1984). The permissive discourse understands sexuality as natural and unrepressed. Analyzing gender differences in heterosexual relationships, Hollway (1984) argues that permissive discourse though seemingly "gender-blind" and "liberating" in reality, ignored social and historical factors, which then reinforced existing power structures and status quo. Extending the permissive discourse to race, *desire as essentialized* articulates the desire for whiteness as also inborn and natural. However, historical realities that constructed such desire are ignored. For example, Internet comments rarely referred to antimiscegenation and Jim Crow laws, which prevented racial mixing and reinforced racial segregation across all institutional levels, marriage, and sexual intimacy. Sexual color-blindness dissociates desire from history, where white supremacist rhetoric categorized nonwhite people and specifically Black people as barbaric, sexually promiscuous, unattractive, and a danger to white women.

These historical realities have contemporary consequences. Analyses of dating trends show that Black women and men are consistently rated lower than all others (Rudder, 2014). Instead, whiteness is the yardstick for universal beauty standards (Collins, 2004), and sexual color-blindness is articulated through the negative, in other words, the absence of anything but whiteness (Mirza, 2003). For example, in the annual *People* magazine's World's Most Beautiful, to date, the number one "spot" has consistently gone to a white person (31/35 women, 31/37 men). Few spots have gone to Black or brown people, and no Asian man or woman has been nominated. Sexual color-blindness manifests as an inability to view attraction and beauty within the larger context of a racist society. Instead, *desire is essentialized*, universal and, of course, universally white.

Evolutionary Psychology/Mainstream Psychology of Attraction

Sexual color-blindness is not only seen in the depths of the Internet but is readily spotted in mainstream academic writings on the science of attraction. Critiques of biological essentialism and determinism in evolutionary psychology have long been taken up by feminist psychologists (Moore & Travis, 2000; Segal, 2000; Tiefer, 1992). In this section, we build on feminist psychologists' critiques of methodological issues, specifically highlighting the lack of diverse samples in evolutionary psychology research.

Evolutionary psychology and sciences of attraction reverse engineer our current standard of beauty and attempt to trace such standards back to prehistoric Darwinian adaptations and sexual selection, framing attraction as a biological process, a natural adaptation, and therefore apolitical (Fisher & Bourgeois, 2020; Gannon, 2002; Moore & Travis, 2000). Through establishing "objective" culture-blind and color-blind measures of attractiveness, and linking such standards to factors crucial to health, survival, and adaptation, evolutionary psychology couches attraction as a universal, biological imperative (Barber, 1995; Cosmides & Tooby 1997). Take, for example, studies on the symmetry of faces that claim symmetric faces and bodies signal developmental stability and health to potential mates (Fink & Penton-Voak, 2002; Jones & Jaeger, 2019; Little & Jones, 2012; Thornhill & Gangestad, 2006). Evolutionary psychologists argue that individuals with symmetric faces are less likely to use antibiotics (Thornhill & Gangestad, 2006). Thus, a symmetric face is aesthetically beautiful and indicates adaptation and survival fitness.

Similarly, it is often argued that sexually dimorphic features (masculine and feminine) signify health, virality, vitality, and physical rigor. Masculine features in men, such as a broader jawline and a deeper brow ridge, signal physical fitness and health, lower susceptibility to respiratory disease, lower antibiotic use, and other disease resistance (Fink & Penton-Voak, 2002; Jones & Jaeger, 2019; Thornhill & Gangestad, 2006). Undoubtedly, these masculine features are influenced by Western Educated Industrialized Rich Developed (WEIRD) standards (Muthukrishna et al., 2020), which also relentlessly enforce heteronormativity (Farvid, 2015).

Strikingly, the studies above have all used samples that are WEIRD, mostly white participants, raising the question of whether findings are more aptly explained by social and cultural factors rather than biological factors.

74 HISTORIES AND THEORIES

A systematic review of studies published in two key evolutionary psychology journals reveals that most samples (81%) were from WEIRD countries, and over 44% were college student samples (Pollet & Saxton, 2019). Universalizing findings based on sampling WEIRD participants is a pervasive problem throughout psychology. Systematic literature reviews of top-tier journals of psychology reveal publications that use a diverse racial makeup are scarce—96% of studies in top APA journals rely on studies drawn from WEIRD samples, and of those studies from the United States, most samples came from white Americans (Arnett, 2008). Furthermore, publications that contextualize their findings or discuss the limitations of their results are rare and underscore the lack of antiracist thinking in psychology (Rad et al., 2018; Roberts et al., 2020).

This lack of reflection on race and diversity constitutes color-blindness and the whitewashing of psychological processes. Such findings raise troubling questions about the integrity of evolutionary psychology, as countless psychological studies demonstrate the importance of race and cultural differences in processes as wide-ranging as cognitive functioning, memory, perception, categorization, parenting, interpersonal relationships, psychopathology, well-being, trauma, identity, and stress (Hughes et al., 2006; Neblett et al., 2012; Sellers et al., 2003).

Despite these scientific biases and methodological issues, the message conveyed by evolutionary psychology is typically taken up in news media and pop culture, communicating to the public that attraction is biological, natural, fixed, and evolutionarily sensical. Such messaging is attractive as it is simple, ostensibly rooted in nature, and, importantly, confirms the status quo (Jackson, 2007; Tavris, 2001).

Psychoanalysis

As detailed in our previous section, some understand our desire as inborn from millions of years of evolution, a host of complex processes that may have nothing to do with individual subjectivity nor anything related to our larger sociocultural environment. However, psychoanalytic thinking shows us otherwise: sexual desire is not a biological instinct but a social construction.

In "Drives and Their Vicissitudes," Freud (1915) distinguishes between drive (*Trieb*) and instinct (*Instinkt*). Confusingly, the English translation has often conflated "drive" with "instinct," "need," or "urges," further muddling the issue (Mills, 2004). Drive can be thought of as libidinal energy that circuits the mind, the body crossing into the outside world via an aim, an object obtainment, and back to the body, creating an endless loop (Freud, 1915). Distinct from animal instinct, one's drive is not prefixed nor biological. Our drive structures our existence beyond the obtainment of objects and stimuli, in other words, "beyond the pleasure principle" (Freud, 2015). Hence, a person can be sexually stimulated by a shoe, a car, or a memory.

The French psychoanalyst Jacques Lacan further elaborates on this point by tying one's drive to the structures of language and society, all via fantasy construction. The production, desire, and the act of sex are caught up in the fantasy of the other we are sexually engaged with, leading Lacan to conclude that "there is no such thing as sexual relation" (1999). Lacan does not deny the existence of sexual relationships here, but that relationship is never biological and always facilitated, lubricated, and supported through fantasy, narrative, and society. That without such fantasy, the sexual act, skin on skin, itself is violent, incoherent, fragmented, and brutal—anything but natural. As Zizek writes, "through fantasy, we learn how to desire" (1992, p. 6).

Contrary to sexual color-blindness, we are not born with inherent sexual preferences. Instead, it is learned through socialization and constructed via narratives of ourselves, others, and the world. It is our ability for language, structure, and social order, that sets up a sexual relationship. The moment a child learns language, they enter an inherited symbolic order where a nexus of laws, conventions, customs, and relationships constructs how the child thinks, relates, fantasizes, and desires. In the case of desire, Lacan proclaims, "man's desire is always the desire of [or for] the other" (Lacan, 1975, p. 17). One never desires alone.

We then must wonder how white supremacy and color-blind constitutionalism infiltrate our sexual preferences, fantasies, and desires and how to undo such influences using radical therapeutic frameworks to change not only one's thoughts or ideologies, but one's desire, drive, and body. As a psychoanalyst and cultural critic, Jamieson Webster writes, "Psychoanalytic work is embedded in a discourse that nonetheless manages to touch this sexual body and change what it is possible to do, no less feel" (2018, p. 15).

Introducing Sexual Humility as a Framework to Combat Sexual Color-Blindness

Tervalon and Murray-Garcia (1998) first coined the term "cultural humility" to describe a way of reflecting a "lifelong commitment to self-evaluation and critique, to redressing the power imbalances" that exist between physicians and their patients. In the context of psychotherapy, Hook et al. (2013) later expanded the term to include the "ability to maintain an interpersonal stance that is other-oriented (or open to the other) in relation to aspects of cultural identity that are most important" to the person on the receiving end of the process (p. 354). Consequently, one must also be aware of historical contexts and address social realities that maintain power imbalances. Grounded in a "not-knowing" stance, we accept and acknowledge that we may not have the answers or solutions; we can only progress and gain understanding (Chun et al., 2010). Sexual humility, we propose, is a commitment to self-reflection and critique of one's sexual preferences and intimate interpersonal actions resulting from historical power imbalances. Through a process of sexual humility, we hold space for ourselves to understand the etiology of our preferences.

We are not arguing for individuals to *diversify* their pool of sexual partners nor *police* their desire, but rather to gain autonomy and understanding over their preferences and deconstruct internalized social attitudes. By intentionally engaging with and examining our sexual experiences, we confront our sexually color-blind thinking and disengage from sexually racist practices.

We introduce a preliminary discussion of what sexual humility might entail as a starting point. Aligned with cultural humility, we believe this process is dynamic, ongoing, and a way of being that is forever changing (Chun et al., 2010; Kyere et al., 2022; Tervalon & Murray-Garcia, 1998). The goal of sexual humility is to gain awareness of our desire and their links to larger societal forces. This process should also be applied to our institutions and societal structures.

Sexual Humility as a Process

Below we outline a suggested process to engage reflexively with our sexual desire and examine biases and blind spots within our "preferences." Each step provides a vignette to demonstrate one possible experience with this work. Although many experiences may not resemble this, we believe this will give a scaffold with which to work. We hope this is a starting point for individuals and institutions to confront color-blind sexual ideology, address power imbalances, and gain autonomy over our sexual desire.

Step 1: Engaging Reflexively With Our Preferences

To begin the sexual humility process, we must engage reflexively by being willing and curious to examine our preferences rather than assume our desire as known. Step one invites participants of all levels to collect data and engage reflexively with the assumed status quo. For example, "Brent," a white, queer man, is confronted on a dating app for listing "No fats, no femmes. White men to the front" in his tagline. Brent's gut reaction is to respond by explaining that his preference is a personal choice, perfectly healthy and natural. Brent engages in the first step by having the willingness to examine his desire reflexively: (1) What physical characteristics do I tend to find attractive? (2) What race do I usually date? Do I gravitate toward certain types of people? (3) How long have these preferences been in place? This first step allows Brent to collect descriptive data on his dating practices. By being willing to take a step back and investigate his desire, he may uncover previously dissociated trends and influences, like race, age, and socioeconomic factors. In our workplaces, departments, and institutions, step one invites us to engage reflexively with existing practices and to process our research protocols, workplace structures, and institutional policies. Engaging with our preferences will set the stage for us to confront embedded sexually racist experiences.

Step 2: Confront and Understand Our Own Sexually Racist Experiences

Step 2 invites us to confront the data we gathered and further interrogate our race-based sexual preferences. The goal of step two is to develop an awareness of the consequences of our existing experiences and practices. Awareness can begin the process of undoing our desire for whiteness. For Black, Indigenous, and people of color, awareness helps us shield ourselves from experiencing sexual racism and help us understand internalized racism and white supremacy that we may perpetuate on other people of color. (1) Have I experienced or committed acts of sexual racism? Did I choose romantic and sexual partners based solely on race, or was I rejected by potential romantic or sexual partners based solely on my race? (2) In what spaces did these acts most occur? (3) If I committed sexually racist acts, what impact did it have

78 HISTORIES AND THEORIES

on the other, and what impact did I have on myself? What did I lose or benefit? (4) How has historical racism morphed our research of relationships, and what is othered (e.g., interracial relationships)? (5) How have we been complicit in assuming whiteness as the standard in our research, practice, and policies?

For example, Brent may realize he prefers to date white men, traversing mainly white spaces and interacting primarily with white people. Brent, however, does not consider that his preferences categorize nonwhite bodies as permanently unattractive and undesirable. Brent begins to disembed his unconscious sexually racist acts and the resulting unintentional harm. This process will give us insight into previously discomforting experiences. Our next step will allow us to hold space for this discomfort for further investigation.

Step 3: Accept and Connect With Our Discomfort

We must constantly and consistently lean into our discomfort to sustain lasting change. First, distressing emotions will rise in this process, and by accepting our distress, we strengthen our emotional capacity to sustain a lifelong effort of self-evaluation, critique, and activism. Second, our emotions have significant meaning. Processing and connecting with our emotions helps us uncover and understand deep-seated biases. Third, by disentangling the meaning behind our emotions, we further gain emotional resilience—the opposite of white fragility—and see how our emotions are personal yet political. To lean into our discomfort, we may ask, (1) How does it feel to know we have racialized preferences or made an intentional ranking judgment? (2) How would it feel to maintain these preferences? (3) How does it feel to have intimate interactions with folks outside of our "type"? (4) How does it feel to support the status quo or confront existing institutions and practices?

For example, Brent may realize he is anxious about race and nonwhite bodies. He feels judgment toward social "others," as he fears being othered. He feels shame and guilt for his practice of sexual exclusivity, making him feel defensive and resentful. Accepting and connecting to his emotions, he realizes he is socialized to desire white bodies and exoticize and fetishize nonwhite bodies. By making the personal political, Brent accepts these emotions, which allows him to dive deeper into the factors that shape them. Combining the other three steps, Brent sees how his desires, beliefs, and emotions are socially contingent and slowly deconstructs how his desires came about. By understanding our discomfort, we can uncover and imagine new ways of relating in these situations in the future.

Step 4: Ignite Our Imagination

Sexual humility fosters and encourages engagement with our relationship to race and holds space for a reformed sexual imagination. As previously detailed, sexual color-blindness dissociates our desires from race and our imagination from radical possibilities. By confronting this dissociation, we can reimagine our sexuality, daily lives, institutions, and the planet beyond racism, oppression, objectification, commodification, and neoliberal capitalism. For Brent, he imagines, (1) How would it be like to not have preferences? How would he navigate dating? (2) What are some ways he can date beyond his comfort zone? (3) How can he center his and others' humanity in the dating process?

Beyond the individual, we ignite our imagination through radical expansion of possibilities, (4) Can we imagine decolonial methodologies in research, including evolutionary psychology? (5) Can we imagine a world without whiteness, anti-Blackness, neoliberalism, and capitalism? What works and what does not work? (6) How can we contribute to change through our particularity? By engaging in step four, we focus on reconstructing our desire through the radical expansion of our imagination. A future image of the self allows for a future image of the collective. We must engage with *each other*'s imagination to heal and rectify our collective sexual desire.

Step 5: (Un)doing Together

We believe (un)doing whiteness is a collective process, (1) How can we remain accountable and practice behaviors that seek to correct power imbalances and (un)center whiteness? (2) How can we inspire others to commit to the sexual humility process? (3) How can we commit to enacting change in our institutions?

Through the previous steps, Brent commits to individual actions that can reverse romantic and intimate power imbalances, such as disengaging with dating app filters, expanding his preferences, and building a more inclusive community. He reinforces his progress by engaging with his friends and community members and hopes to inspire others to commit to the sexual

80 HISTORIES AND THEORIES

humility process. Such community engagement allows him to remain accountable, check his white privilege, process his emotions, and practice behaviors that seek to correct power imbalances.

Concluding Remarks

Sexual color-blindness views human attraction as private, biological, fixed, and apolitical. Sexual color-blindness reflects and reinforces white supremacy under neoliberal sensibilities and perpetuates sexual racism. It is through sexual color-blindness that we repeatedly sustain our desire for whiteness while erasing and disavowing the various cultural, social and political forces that are actively shaping and molding our desires. To uncenter whiteness, we must hijack processes, change libidinal energy, and redirect our drives and desires to encounter the other in its most genuine, most authentic form. To dislodge the desire for whiteness is to dislodge something deeply entrenched in our psyche and bodies.

We propose a process of sexual humility as a beginning of undoing. We argue that true liberation is of the psyche, social, and political, liberating through a proactive engagement with desire on all levels. Individually, we must foster humility, challenge the essentialist notions of desire, and incite critical free choice. Academically, we must confront and reflexively engage with our current theoretical and empirical understandings of desire and attraction. More broadly, we must reflexively understand the consequences of color-blind ideology and its pervasive impact on institutional processes, policies, and structures. By resisting sexual color-blindness and actively practicing sexual humility, ...we advance social justice by undesiring whiteness and undoing sexual racism.

References

Arnett, J. J. (2008). The neglected 95%: Why American psychology needs to become less American. *American Psychologist, 63*, 602–614.

Barber, N. (1995). The evolutionary psychology of physical attractiveness: Sexual selection and human morphology. *Ethology and Sociobiology, 16*(5), 395–424.

Bedi, S. (2015). Sexual racism: Intimacy as a matter of justice. *Journal of Politics, 77*(4), 998–1011.

Callander, D., Newman, C. E., & Holt, M. (2015). Is sexual racism really racism? Distinguishing attitudes toward sexual racism and generic racism among gay and bisexual men. *Archives of Sexual Behavior, 44*(7), 1991–2000.

Chun, M. B. J., Jackson, D. S., Lin, S. Y., & Park, E. R. (2010). A comparison of surgery and family medicine residents' perceptions of cross-cultural care training. *Hawaii Medical Journal, 69*(12), 289–293.

Collins, P. H. (2004). *Black sexual politics: African Americans, gender, and the new racism.* Routledge.

Curington, C. V., Lundquist, J. H., & Lin, K. H. (2021). *The dating divide: Race and desire in the era of online romance.* University of California Press.

Eng, D. L., & Han, S. (2019). *Racial melancholia, racial dissociation.* Duke University Press.

Farvid, P. (2015). Heterosexuality. In C. Richards & M. J. Barker (Eds.), *The Palgrave book of the psychology of sexuality and gender* (pp. 92–108). Palgrave Macmillan.

Fink, B., & Penton-Voak, I. (2002). Evolutionary psychology of facial attractiveness. *Current Directions in Psychological Science, 11*(5), 154–158.

Fisher, M. L., & Bourgeois, C. (2020). Beyond the ingénue: Current evolutionary perspectives of women. *Evolutionary Behavioral Sciences, 14*(1), 1.

Freud, S. (1915). Drives and their vicissitudes. In J. Strachey (Ed. & Trans.), *The standard edition of the complete psychological works of Sigmund Freud* (p. 14). Hogarth.

Freud, S. (2015). Beyond the pleasure principle. *Psychoanalysis and History, 17*(2), 151–204.

Gannon, L. (2002). A critique of evolutionary psychology. *Psychology, Evolution & Gender, 4*(2), 173–218.

Gotanda, N. (1991). A critique of "Our Constitution is colour-blind." *Stanford Law Review, 44*, 1–68.

Greene-Moton, E., & Minkler, M. (2022). Cultural competence or cultural humility? Moving beyond the debate. *Health Promotion Practice, 21*(1), 142–145. https://doi.org/10.1177/1524839919884912

Hook, J. N., Davis, D. E., Owen, J., Worthington Jr, E. L., & Utsey, S. O. (2013). Cultural humility: Measuring openness to culturally diverse clients. *Journal of Counseling Psychology, 60*(3), 353.

Hollway, W. (1984). Gender difference and the production of subjectivity. In J. Henriques, W. Hollway, C. Venn, & V. Walkerdine (Eds.), *Changing the subject.* Methuen.

Hughes, D., Rodriguez, J., Smith, E. P., Johnson, D. J., Stevenson, H. C., & Spicer, P. (2006). Parents' ethnic-racial socialization practices: A review of research and directions for future study. *Developmental Psychology, 42*(5), 747.

Jackson, S., & Rees, A. (2007). The appalling appeal of nature: The popular influence of evolutionary psychology as a sociological problem. *Sociology, 41*(5), 917–930. https://doi.org/10.1177/0038038507080445.

Jones, A. L., & Jaeger, B. (2019). Biological bases of beauty revisited: The effect of symmetry, averageness, and sexual dimorphism on female facial attractiveness. *Symmetry, 11*(2), 279. https://doi.org/10.3390/sym11020279.

Kyere, E., Boddie, S., & Lee, J. E. (2022). Visualizing structural competency: Moving beyond cultural competence/humility toward eliminating racism. *Journal of Ethnic & Cultural Diversity in Social Work, 31*(3–5), 212–224.

Lacan, J. (1999). *The seminar of Jacques Lacan: On feminine sexuality: The limits of love and knowledge: Book XX* (Ed. B. Fink and Trans. J.-A. Miller). W.W. Norton.

82 HISTORIES AND THEORIES

Little, A. C., & Jones, B. C. (2012). Variation in facial masculinity and symmetry preferences across the menstrual cycle is moderated by relationship context. *Psychoneuroendocrinology*, *37*(7), 999–1008. https://doi.org/10.1016/j.psyneuen.2011.11.007

Mills, J. (2004). Clarifications on Trieb: Freud's Theory of Motivation Reinstated. *Psychoanalytic Psychology*, *21*(4), 673–677. https://doi.org/10.1037/0736-9735.21.4.673.

Mirza, H. S. (2003). All the women are white, all the blacks are men—but some of us are brave: Mapping the consequences of invisibility for black and minority ethnic women in Britain. In D. Mason (Ed.), *Explaining ethnic differences: Changing patterns of disadvantage in Britain* (pp. 121–138). Policy Press.

Moore, D. S., & Travis, C. B. (2000). Biological models and sexual politics. In C. B. Travis & J. W. White (Eds.), *Sexuality, society and feminism* (pp. 35–56). American Psychological Association. https://www.apa.org/pubs/books/431628A?tab=2

Muthukrishna, M., Bell, A. V., Henrich, J., Curtin, C. M., Gedranovich, A., McInerney, J., & Thue, B. (2020). Beyond western, educated, industrial, rich, and democratic (WEIRD) psychology: Measuring and mapping scales of cultural and psychological distance. *Psychological Science*, *31*(6), 678–701. https://doi.org/10.1177/0956797620916782

Neblett, E. W., Jr., Rivas-Drake, D., & Umaña-Taylor, A. J. (2012). The promise of racial and ethnic protective factors in promoting ethnic minority youth development. *Child Development Perspectives, 6*(3), 295–303.

Pollet, T. V., & Saxton, T. K. (2019). How diverse are the samples used in the journals "Evolution & Human Behavior" and "Evolutionary Psychology"? *Evolutionary Psychological Science, 5*(3), 357–368.

Rad, M. S., Martingano, A. J., & Ginges, J. (2018). Toward a psychology of *Homo sapiens*: Making psychological science more representative of the human population. *Proceedings of the National Academy of Sciences, 115*(45), 11401–11405.

Roberts, S. O., Bareket-Shavit, C., Dollins, F. A., Goldie, P. D., & Mortenson, E. (2020). Racial inequality in psychological research: Trends of the past and recommendations for the future. *Perspectives on Psychological Science, 15*(6), 1295–1309.

Rudder, C. (2014). *Dataclysm: Love, sex, race, and identity—What our online lives tell us about our offline selves*. Crown.

Segal, L. (2000). Gender, genes and genetics: From Darwin to the human genome. In C. Squire (Ed.), *Culture and psychology* (pp. 31–42). Routledge.

Sellers, R. M., Caldwell, C. H., Schmeelk-Cone, K. H., & Zimmerman, M. A. (2003). Racial identity, racial discrimination, perceived stress, and psychological distress among African American young adults. *Journal of Health and Social Behavior, 44*(3), 302–317.

Tavris, C. (2001). *Psychobabble and Biobunk: Using psychology to think critically about issues in the news* (2nd ed.). Prentice-Hall.

Tervalon, M., & Murray-Garcia, J. (1998). Cultural humility versus cultural competence: A critical distinction in defining physician training outcomes in multicultural education. *Journal of Health Care for the Poor and Underserved, 9*, 117–125.

Thornhill, R., & Gangestad, S. W. (2006). Facial sexual dimorphism, developmental stability, and susceptibility to disease in men and women. *Evolution and Human Behavior, 27*, 131–144.

Tiefer, L. (1992). Commentary on the status of sex research: Feminism, sexuality and sexology. *Journal of Psychology and Human Sexuality, 4*(3), 5–42.

Tooby, J., & Cosmides, L. (1990). On the universality of human nature and the uniqueness of the individual: The role of genetics and adaptation. *Journal of Personality, 58*(1), 17–67. https://doi.org/10.1111/j.1467-6494.1990.tb00907.x

Webster, J. (2018). *Conversion disorder: Listening to the body in psychoanalysis.* Columbia University Press.

Žižek, S. (1992). *Looking awry: An introduction to Jacques Lacan through popular culture.* MIT Press.

Jezebel

Synclaire Warren

Wife of Ahab
Harlot
Meaning wicked one
Jezebel
Jezebel
The color of our skin seems to tell them that we have no honor
Men listening to the so-called language of the body saying "yes" as our
    throats are crying against it
Jezebel
"Nasty Woman" they call as they shame us for taking our womanhood in
    our own hands
They find *her* in us all with every open mouth and head held high
 Seductive surrenders
Bored with their wives
They crawl to the outskirts of the night for women to bring them their
    dreams After they have finished, their belt fastens and again arises the
    sound of "Jezebel"
The blackend whore is more than a story
Broken crossed legs and eyes rolled back, we emerge
To live to be more than their lust

SECTION II
REPRESENTATIONS

4

"I Am Dark and Beautiful"

Song of Songs, Audre Lorde, and the Politics of Desire

Siam Hatzaw

"Desire" is a complicated word. An even more complicated picture emerges when it intersects with race, especially if we conceive of sexuality as an inseparable component of racism. This relationship carries a long history with roots apparent within the ancient texts that continue to shape cultural attitudes. In this chapter, I ground my interpretation of the politics of desire in a theological and literary framework through the Song of Songs, a collection of poetry within the Hebrew Bible, read alongside Audre Lorde's essays *Uses of the Erotic* and *Poetry Is Not a Luxury*, to envision how these texts speak to sexual racism today.

I first read the Song of Songs in my teenage years, when it was presented by a church leader as an allegory portraying the love between God and the Church. Reencountering the text during my research on the theology of the body, I was surprised to discover such explicit expressions of desire for and of a racialized woman within the Bible. Poring over the poems again was an enlightening experience, invoking a re-evaluation of my own understandings of desire. I realized my initial surprise was the result of whiteness infiltrating my perceptions of desirability to plant itself as the norm, to the extent that it had skewed my conceptualization of race within the Bible. This led me to question how and why such a vivid celebration of desire centering a Black woman would be so diluted.

The poet Lucille Clifton wrote, "won't you celebrate with me what i have shaped into a kind of life? [. . .] my one hand holding tight my other hand; come celebrate with me that everyday something has tried to kill me and has failed" (Clifton, 1993). Her words invite us to think about the centrality of whiteness by highlighting the brutality of experience as nonwhite women. Although I recognize "nonwhite" is a term that centers whiteness in itself, I employ it intentionally, borrowing from Clifton's phrasing to emphasize the

Siam Hatzaw, *"I Am Dark and Beautiful"* In: *Sexual Racism and Social Justice*. Edited by: Denton Callander, Panteá Farvid, Amir Baradaran, and Thomas A. Vance, Oxford University Press. © Oxford University Press 2024.
DOI: 10.1093/oso/9780197605509.003.0005

white world we are born into: "both nonwhite and woman, what did i see to be except myself?" (Clifton, 1993). We counter the dominance of whiteness through survival, resilience, yes, but also through celebration. To delight in ourselves, to give in to the act of living so fully, is a method of dismantling.

I learned this through Audre Lorde, whose work plays a pivotal role in my reimagining of desire. *Poetry Is Not a Luxury* begins, "The quality of light by which we scrutinize our lives has direct bearing upon the product which we live" for it's within this light we form ideas "by which we pursue our magic and make it realized" (Lorde, 1985). Clifton's description of what she has "shaped" into a kind of life echoes Lorde's emphasis on beginning with the self, establishing an internal foundation that colors our external experience. Here, poetry provides the language to express mechanisms of transformation. The capacity of poetry to "give name to the nameless" allows each person to access the well of knowledge, creativity, and power we possess—from this reserve we birth ideas for change (Lorde, 1985). Parallels can be drawn between these poetics of unapologetic expression and the poetry of Song of Songs. Both view desire as revolutionary, as Lorde explains, when we connect ourselves with this intimacy, the fears that silence us loosen their grip (Lorde, 1985).

What are these fears? When we are born into this world both nonwhite and woman, we become acutely aware that it is not made for us. Marginalized identities find ourselves navigating a racist, patriarchal, heteronormative, cisnormative, ableist world. Lorde proposes "when we view living as a situation to be experienced and interacted with, we learn to cherish our feelings and respect them as a source of power. *I feel therefore I can be free*" (Lorde, 1985). When confronting white supremacy, Lorde's message invites me to interrogate my notion of resistance as *solely* a practical struggle realized in protest, justice, reparation—instead also turning inward and evaluating how this friction resides in myself, moving through a world constructed by and for whiteness. As nonwhite women, the insidious nature of both white supremacy and patriarchy encourages us to separate ourselves from our feelings. By assessing how whiteness warps our politics of desire, we can begin to allow our feelings the power inherent within them.

In *Uses of the Erotic*, Lorde describes how of the many kinds of power, the erotic is a resource that functions by opening a "fearless underlining of our capacity for joy" (Lorde, 1978). Defined as "an internal sense of satisfaction to which, once we have experienced it, we know we can aspire," the erotic expands our definitions of desire to include both the sexual and the sensual, connections with others and ourselves (Lorde, 1978). To desire is an intimate, instinctual act whether in the form of desiring another, desiring ourselves, or desiring more from life. Its definition has been corrupted, morphing "erotic" into a word whispered only behind closed doors. For oppression to work, it must corrupt the sources that provide energy for change, therefore we've been taught to "vilify, abuse and devalue" (Lorde, 1978) the erotic, evidenced by the age-old connection between women and temptation that stems from the concept of original sin. She encourages a reimagination which moves away from vilification, instead thinking of the ways our bodies open to rhythms, recognizing "satisfaction is possible, and does not have to be called marriage, nor god, nor an afterlife" (Lorde, 1978). Here lies the root of the fear. When we come to recognize the depth of satisfaction we can feel, we demand more from our lives. When we are in tune with the erotic, recognizing our responsibility to ourselves to pursue desire, it becomes a prism through which power is refracted. In turn, the poetic "coins the language" to "express this revolutionary awareness" (Lorde, 1985). Through these functions of the erotic and the poetic, I approach the Song of Songs.

Song of Songs is a collection of poems dating from 10th century BCE. It forms part of the Megillot, five scrolls read on religious festivals of the Jewish calendar. Tod Linafelt describes how, "in alternating voices, two young and obviously unmarried lovers take great delight in describing each other's bodies and their desire for one another. In these descriptions, all borders become fluid and begin to dissolve" (Linafelt, 2002). Here we have a couple sharing odes to each other's bodies found in the middle of the Bible. To find such an explicit account alongside scripture that has long been used to advance purity culture raises questions, which allegorical interpretations attempt to answer. Some readings position Song of Songs as a metaphor for the relationship between God and the Israelites, or Christ and the Church or the soul itself. Alice Connor writes that some view this as a celebration of love and sex as gifts from God, while others see it as performance art reenacting a fertility rite for good harvest, but ultimately, it is about "seeing the truth of ourselves, unvarnished and vulnerable in our nakedness" (Connor, 2017). One function of the erotic is the power that lies in sharing pursuits with another, as the sharing of joy lessens the threat of difference (Lorde, 1978). Through this dynamic, Song of Songs becomes—to borrow Lorde's language—an assertion of the life force of this woman and her capacity for joy.

90 REPRESENTATIONS

In spite of this, when we look closer, the embedded presence of sexual racism becomes apparent. The opening chapter reads, "I am dark but beautiful, O women of Jerusalem—dark as the tents of Kedar, dark as the curtains of Solomon's tents" (Song of Songs 1:5 NLT). The majority of translations are a variation of "I am dark but beautiful," however, a handful render the verse, "I am black and beautiful" (NRSV)—two similar sentences with vastly different meanings. Many translations choose "but" or "yet" as the conjunction, while few choose "and." The issue of racism in (mis)translation is evident. The Hebrew word in question is *vav*: "to add or secure, frequently used as a prefix to mean 'and' in the sense of adding things together" (Brenner, 1999). This *can* sometimes be translated as "but" depending on context, which raises difficulties. The act of translation is riddled with complications, including how the text can inherit the biases of its translator. Kate Lowe examines the consequences of this mistranslation through "the adoption of the 'Black, but . . .' formulation" (Lowe, 2012). The female character is "made to justify or explain her beauty, as though black skin were in itself a barrier," and the "newly adversarial nature of the phrase was adopted as a linguistic and cultural formulation" (Lowe, 2012). In other words, racist biases were inserted *into* the text, not extracted. Translation of the Septuagint aimed to be as literal as possible, prioritizing sacrality of the original over fluency, therefore Lowe stresses that although *vav* has a varied semantic range in other contexts, in this case, it could not mean "but": "So the meaning of this verse is clear: 'I am black and beautiful'" (Lowe, 2012). How, then, did this change come about?

Lowe traces this back to a late 4th-century CE Latin translation of the Bible known as the Vulgate, in which the Christian theologian Jerome of Stridon instituted the Latin word *sed* ("but"). "Assuming that his knowledge of Hebrew was sufficiently good for him not to have mistaken the range of the word *vav*, for him, he must have felt an opposition between 'black' and 'beautiful,' thus the 'black but . . .' formulation entered the Western repertoire" (Lowe, 2012). Crucially, Jerome revised a translation that survives in only one manuscript in which he *did* render the verse "I am dark and beautiful"—revealing a conscious decision took place. Lowe emphasizes that this analysis is an oversimplification of the complicated process of translation, however, it is clear Jerome inserted an oppositional contrast between blackness and beauty and the reasons for its existence should be sought in his surrounding culture.

These complications stem from the multiple possibilities the words "black" and "and/but" represent, especially in poetic contexts. Rabbinical tradition includes four levels of coexisting interpretations, of which Alice Bellis focuses on two in her analysis: the peshat פשט which is the literal meaning, and the derash דרש, the comparative meaning (Bellis, 2021). She argues that the word "black" in 1:5 actually refers to the Shulamite woman being sunburned from working in the vineyards, describing how Ancient Mediterranean upper-class culture shunned the harmful effects of the sun such that any preference for lighter skin in the ancient world was "as much a fact of life as the desire on the part of white, affluent Westerners in the second half of the twentieth century to get tans" (Bellis, 2021). By rendering the verse "I am burnt but beautiful," Bellis proposes the text is not a reflection of colorism but classism, darker skin being indicative of lower classes who faced prolonged exposure through agricultural labor. The Shulamite woman was assigned this as a punishment: "My mother's sons were angry with me and made me take care of the vineyards; my own vineyard I had to neglect" (1:6 NIV). This imagery invites several symbolic possibilities. Some scholarship argues that her vineyard symbolizes her body, therefore neglecting her vineyard likely represents a violation of sexual norms by not "preserving" her virginity (Bellis, 2021). Bellis suggests that the idea of the Shulamite being proud of her sunburned skin "imposes mid-twentieth century thinking on an ancient text. It is more likely that the Shulamite is an upper-class woman whose brothers have forced her to labor in the vineyards" (Bellis, 2021). This interpretation opens avenues for crucial reflections on class consciousness within the Bible, specifically how race and class interact with gender and sexuality within structures of oppression. This is crucial to biblical contexts in which readers encounter female characters whose bodily and sexual autonomy are violated—characters often identified as foreigners to the dominant group within their story or of a lower class. Therefore this fresh perspective on the Shulamite woman's class, as well as the symbolism her vineyard alludes to, makes her proclamation in 1:5 all the more powerful.

If we accept Bellis's literal translation of "black" as "burnt," the intention of the verse arguably remains the same. Given the historical and geographical context of the text's origin, we can assume none of the characters would be racialized as white by modern definitions—racial identities are socially constructed meaning definitions are constantly in flux—therefore the Songs are still in praise of a dark-skinned woman's beauty. I apply a hermeneutics of appropriation, defined by Paul Ricoeur and John B. Thompson: "writings are written for anybody to read and any reader can be a potential audience. This is the unknown reader whom the text procures, different from the intended audience of the writer" (Wabyanga, 2021). Applying my own hermeneutics of appropriation, I draw back to *Poetry Is Not a Luxury* to emphasize the function of poetry as giving name to the nameless. When we consider language as a living form, signs whose meanings are completed by the reader through interpretation of the signifier, the focus of exegesis shifts from establishing literal translations onto what the passage represents. Although Bellis's reading may be a more accurate translation that amplifies the intersectionality of race, class, and sexuality, I approach the text through a different light: at the center is a woman's declaration of her beauty. The speaker confidently presents her self-worth against a wider backdrop of biblical stories in which women (and their bodies) are often regarded as possessions for trade. In light of the multitude of biblical women whose sexuality becomes intrinsically linked with trauma, possession or survival, here we find a woman whose sexuality is unapologetically a channel for joy. By embracing the Songs' eroticism, not only do we find representation of dark skin as desirable, we also encounter bodily autonomy and consent, a vital narrative within an ancient text rife with gender-based violence. In this way, the verse becomes a lyric of protest.

Robert Kuloba Wabyanga offers a Black African reading of the text as a protest song "against historical and contemporary injustices and stigma suffered by the race for 'being' while 'black'" (Wabyanga, 2021). His reading considers the text in light of historic cultural conditioning that has associated "black" and its synonyms with evil, oppositional to "light" associated with grace and purity. Exegesis of the verse by theologians Origen and Gregory of Nyssa interpreted 1:5 allegorically as a reference to sinfulness, rather than ethnicity (Scott, 2006). Wabyanga discusses a "gas-lighting approach on Africans" that "served missionary and colonial racist interests, as indeed so many black people came to believe that their own story, names, images, culture and religion were evil and that they themselves were hell bound if they maintained their pride and identity" (Wabyanga, 2021). Whiteness creates a world in which racialized people internalize racism so that even on the most personal level, "ideals" of desirability are enforced and reproduced. Counter to this, Wabyanga states that the oppressed in the Song of Songs is not contained, rather, "She is assertive! She uses the music podium to sing of her worth with pride. . . . That statement, 'I am black and beautiful,' is important in protests in contexts where beauty is understood from a white perspective that regards the black colour, hair and face or figure as ugly" (Wabyanga, 2021). He gives tribute to figures such as Stephen Biko during the antiapartheid protests in South Africa and his "Black is beautiful" campaign, and Martin Luther

King Jr., who cried out, "I am Black and Beautiful!" By weaving threads between this ancient proclamation of Black beauty and more recent collective movements, Wabyanga's interpretation creates a tapestry of protest against white supremacy. He concludes that, read in this way, this verse serves to "reaffirm our humanity, dignity, value and pride as black people" (Wabyanga, 2021). While my analysis draws from Wabyanga's reading of Song of Songs as an act against injustice, it diverges from its deromanticization, instead amplifying the romanticism to build on eroticism as a site for protest.

To cement eroticism as a form of protest, I turn to Stephen D. Moore's scholarship queering Song of Songs. It is difficult to ignore the heteronormativity of the text with its explicitly gendered expressions of love. Moore argues allegorical interpretations "sprang from disinclination, discomfort, or downright disgust on the part of pious male exegetes" at the prospect of imagining a woman's sexuality (Moore, 2000). Such readings can become discourses of sexual repression, proposing that for medieval Christian commentators, interpreting the Songs as literal expressions of sex was unthinkable, however (ironically) allegorizing the text had the effect of turning it into something even more unthinkable: "not just the expression of an erotically charged relationship between a nubile young woman and her virile young man . . . but the expression of an erotically charged relationship between two male parties instead" (Moore, 2000). Allegorical readings refuse to acknowledge how the text "is suffused with erotic desire" (Moore, 2000). Can we separate the language from the eroticism it is steeped in? Moore asks, "Is it even possible any longer to read with a straight face the staggering profusion of delicious nonsense occasioned by this discomfort and disgust? 'The meeting of your thighs' . . . This refers to the coming together of Jews and Gentiles in the one Church of Christ. . . . 'Your two breasts are the two Testaments, from which the children begotten in Christ draw milk for their growth,' and so on ad infinitum" (Moore, 2000). Ancient commentators refused to entertain the prospect that this could be an ode to sexuality, instead invoking metaphors for religious bonds.

For Moore, this erasure that stemmed from discomfort toward the fantasy of female sexuality inadvertently opened opportunities for queering the text. I lean on Moore's scholarship by challenging this discomfort. Given its context, how could the erotic be ignored? Ilana Pardes writes, "There is something utterly refreshing in the frank celebration of love that is found in the passionate exchanges of the two. Nowhere else in the Bible are bodily parts—hair, nose, eyes, lips, tongue, breasts, thighs—set on a pedestal; nowhere else

94 REPRESENTATIONS

are the sensual pleasures of love—tastes, colors, sounds, and perfumes—relished with such joy; nowhere else is sexual desire spelled out with so much verve" (Pardes, 2019). Her commentary draws me back to Lorde's reminder to connect with the sensual, that poetry is not a luxury, instead it functions as a way of meaning-making in a world that feels disconnected and senseless. This is particularly crucial for racialized people, even more so for those of marginalized genders, whose bodies are rarely relished with such joy. Our relationships to our bodies, and to other bodies, are conditioned by whiteness, therefore inseparable from our racialization.

Growing up in a world where whiteness is the baseline from which all that deviates is Othered, we internalize the message that we are not welcome in these spaces. When it comes to the Bible, this is all the more infuriating as these were never white spaces to begin with; to see ourselves reflected in these characters invites us to envision how divinity resides in us all despite biblical whitewashing. In verse 1:5, we witness a clear statement in praise of a Black woman's beauty, corrupted through a single word. This illuminates two crucial points for the politics of desire: first, how far into ancient history sexual racism extends, and second, how alarming it is that, centuries later, so little has changed. Sexual racism must be dismantled on both an individual *and* a structural level. We can practice self-love with all of our being, but we will still struggle when the world is set up to be against us at every turn. Thus, "the labour of decolonising these representative paradigms is structural. To believe in the *possibility* of love, we must comprehend the fact that we do not obliviously fall into it, but are coded in and out of it" (Gebrial, 2017). In light of these darker sides of desire, Gebrial's statement leads us back to Song of Songs by highlighting how desire is racially coded, and the labor we must practice to decode ourselves. There are obvious parallels between "I am black and beautiful" and the Black Is Beautiful cultural movement of the 1960s. Such campaigns reject that which seeks to suppress us via projected codes of social value, instead embracing a kind of self-acceptance in the face of suppression that I do believe is radical.

I find in Song of Songs a source of empowerment for racialized women, reminding us we have *always* been deserving of love. However, the issue of translation in verse 1:5 echoes contemporary discourse on how desire is coded to discern which bodies are deserving of love, a (mis)translation that reflects how sexual racism is deeply entrenched in our cultural histories. This is particularly vital when situated in the wider context of the historic whiteness of theology as a field. Erasure of the Shulamite woman's assertive proclamation of her own beauty contributes to the underlying thread of whiteness that has come to dominate exegesis. Bellis argues that in the history of biblical interpretation, "What have masqueraded as neutral readings were actually biased in the dominant group's direction, that is, white men of a particular class, nationality, and age. . . . When underrepresented groups join the interpretive community, such misinterpretations often come to light" (Bellis, 2021). My analysis contributes to the interpretive community, in which we are witnessing a reorientation away from the whiteness of biblical hermeneutics through exciting developments within postcolonial, feminist, and liberationist theologies. Drawing inspiration from theopoetics, Audre Lorde's essays offer a compelling lens through which to view the erotic as a moment of true connection to emotions. This means taking time to reflect on the things that bring us satisfaction, and building more of these into our lives. Lorde argues we have been "raised to fear the yes within ourselves," but when we embrace this yes through the poetic and the erotic, it gives us "the energy to pursue genuine change within our world" (Bellis, 2021). Of course, poetry will not fix all of our problems, and practicing self-love will never dismantle systemic oppression. Far from it. Language may well be power, but it must be combined with action to create constructive change. Yet, all of this begins with reflection. How are we coded in and out of love? How does whiteness reside within us, in who and how we desire?

Despite being centuries old, Song of Songs is a rich resource for reimagining our understanding of love. Even within its narrative structure:

> the rapid, unexpected shifts between voices and moods . . . are not the result of sloppy editing but rather part of an underlying notion that the ultimate song of love must convey in its form something of the baffling, dreamlike qualities of amorous pursuits. Love in the Song is too powerful, even explosive, an emotion to be contained within clear boundaries. Words, like kisses, are drenched in wine. If there is any logic, it is an associative dream logic. (Pardes, 2019)

The Song conveys love as too powerful an emotion to be contained by boundaries of language and logic. Lorde, too, views love as a force powerful enough to transform the ways in which we move through the world. Pardes suggests that the Shulamite woman knows that "what makes love the emotion that looms so large in our lives is the very fact that it is uncontrollable, that it continues to surprise us daily as we wander in the bewildering landscapes of our amorous pursuits" (Pardes, 2019). This reminds me of Lorde's pursuit of eroticism in her day-to-day life, describing it as a kernel that, "when released from its intense and constrained pellet, it flows through and colors my life with a kind of energy that heightens and sensitizes and strengthens all my experience" (Lorde, 1978). My reading envisions the Song of Songs as a creative proclamation that resonates with racialized women, an assertion of love (and self-love) that decenters whiteness, and a poetic form that explicitly gives name to—and delights in—our desires. I return to the words of Clifton, a mirror to the pure and unapologetic poeticism of Song of Songs. All of these works, in conversation through the centuries, revel in self-expression, demonstrating an innate capacity not just for survival but for joy. The poetic aligned with the erotic invites us to embrace what we have each shaped into a kind of life: one hand holding our other, in celebration of ourselves.

References

Bellis, A. (2021). I am burnt but beautiful: Translating song 1:5a. *Journal of Biblical Literature*, *140*(1), 91–111.

Brenner, J. (1999–2021). Vav. *The ancient Hebrew alphabet*.

Clifton, L. (1993). won't you celebrate with me. In *The Book of light*. Copper Canyon Press. https://www.poetryfoundation.org/poems/50974/wont-you-celebrate-with-me

Connor, Alice. (2017). Song of Songs: The sexy, sexy bible. In *Fierce: Women of the bible and their stories of violence, mercy, bravery, wisdom, sex, and salvation* (pp. 89–95). 1517 Media.

Gebrial, D. (2017). *Decolonising desire: The politics of love*. Verso.

Keats, J. (2016) [1820]. Ode to a nightingale. *Keats: "Ode to a nightingale" and other poems*. Pocket Poets. Michael O'Mara Books.

Linafelt, T. (2002). Biblical love poetry (. . . and God). *Journal of the American Academy of Religion*, *70*(2), 323–345.

Lorde, A. (1978). Uses of the erotic. *The master's tools will never dismantle the master's house*. Penguin Random House.

Lorde, A. (1985). Poetry is not a luxury. *The master's tools will never dismantle the master's house*. Penguin Random House.

Lowe, K. (2012). The global consequences of mistranslation: The adoption of the "Black but . . ." formulation in Europe, 1440–1650. *Religions 3*(4), 544–555.

Moore, S. (2000). The Song of Songs in the history of sexuality. *American Society of Church History, 69*(2), 328–349.

Pardes, I. (2019). *The Song of Songs: A biography*. Princeton University Press.

Rao, P. (2019). Paying a high price for skin bleaching. *Africa Renewal*. UN.

Scott, M. (2006). Shades of grace: Origen and Gregory of Nyssa's soteriological exegesis of the "Black and beautiful" bride in Song of Songs 1:5. *Harvard Theological Review, 99*(1), 65–83.

Wabyanga, R. (2021). "I am Black and beautiful": A Black African reading of Song of Songs 1:5–7 as a protest song. *Old Testament Essays, 34*(2), 588–609.

Woan, S. (2008). White sexual imperialism: A theory of Asian feminist jurisprudence. *Washington and Lee Journal of Civil Rights and Social Justice 275*, 275–301.

5

White Desirability and the Violent Radicalization of Andrew Cunanan

Marc Milton Ducusin

Introduction

Since Gianni Versace's 1997 murder, the gay, biracial, Filipino-American killer Andrew Cunanan has exerted a morbid fascination. Characterized as a kept man who thrived on the favors of older, affluent, white lovers until desperate circumstances sent him on a bloody spree, Cunanan performed a sordid cautionary tale for a tabloid-hungry public. Yet, as Filipino scholars have noted, the American media largely ignored or misapprehended Cunanan's racial and ethnic identity, with initial news reports and wanted posters profiling him as white (Clarkson, 1997, p. 175) or "racially unidentifiable" (Bacareza Balance, 2008, p. 87). His racial illegibility stemmed from a mestizo physicality not only recognized by Filipino culture but also idealized for its proximity to whiteness (Punzalan Isaac, 2006, p. xxi). As a gay sex worker who relied on his attractiveness to white American men, Cunanan navigated a culture that marginalizes Asians often by sexually fetishizing or rejecting them. The racist specter of white desirability thus haunts his story in ways little examined by popular depictions and news coverage.

Cunanan's killing spree occurred when I was 16, in a rare adolescent recollection of mainstream Filipino visibility. Decades later, when Ryan Murphy's television anthology series *American Crime Story* presented *The Assassination of Gianni Versace* (2018), I admired its compassionate portrayal of both the murderer and his victims as gay men failed by a homophobic society, but Asian reviewers rightly decried its comparative underplaying of race (Duan, 2018; Kang, 2018). An understanding of Cunanan's cultural impact can thus benefit from a deeper exploration of how racism and sexuality intersect in the idealization of whiteness and the marginalization of queer

---

Marc Milton Ducusin, *White Desirability and the Violent Radicalization of Andrew Cunanan* In: *Sexual Racism and Social Justice*. Edited by: Denton Callander, Panteá Farvid, Amir Baradaran, and Thomas A. Vance, Oxford University Press.
© Oxford University Press 2024. DOI: 10.1093/oso/9780197605509.003.0006

Asian bodies. This intersectional perspective enables us to interrogate whiteness and sexual racism in the much-scrutinized media narrative of one of pop culture's most notorious Asian-American figures. By offering a mix of cultural analysis and personal reflections on this narrative and the dialogue surrounding it, I illuminate how Cunanan's victimization of white men violently overturned the power dynamics by which Western culture and gay communities have marginalized people like him.

Representation, Identification, and Assimilation in a Culture of White Desirability

In Sara Ahmed's (2017) phenomenological reading, whiteness is "an effect of racialization, which in turn shapes what it is that bodies 'can do'" (p. 150). The complexities of Cunanan's racialization as a half-Filipino man who occasionally passed as the "scion of a Jewish family" (Clarkson, 1997, p. 48) or a Mexican plantation owner's son (Punzalan Isaac, 2006, p. xxii) exemplify how contiguity to whiteness has historically represented a means for some bodies of color to overcome social restrictions. In Cunanan's case, the bloody culmination of his exploits made him "a notorious symbol of the deadly consequences of crossing the lines of racial, sexual, and class boundaries" (Bacareza Balance, 2008, p. 88). Although condemnation of Cunanan's crimes understandably dominates the discourse around him, his social transgressions also raised public ire. News coverage judged him as a sexual deviant, gold digger, and social impostor—an "adroit and tireless liar" (Lacayo, 1997, p. 29) and "gaudy pretender" (Thomas & Larmer, 1997, p. 20)—as much as a murderer. Yet, his marginalization and efforts to overcome it have elicited empathy from academics and artists of color, particularly those of Filipino descent. Scholars Allan Punzalan Isaac (2006) and Christine Bacareza Balance (2008) have dissected Cunanan's fraught cultural significations, while the playwright, novelist, and poet Jessica Hagedorn presented a fictionalized account of his story in her book and lyrics for a musical theater piece titled *Most Wanted* (2007). Subsequently, the half-Filipino actor Darren Criss earned critical acclaim and multiple awards for his chilling yet sensitive portrayal of Cunanan as an embittered outsider in *The Assassination of Gianni Versace* (2018). These voices and representations counterbalance other accounts' lack of racial awareness, while addressing why a vilified killer resonates with marginalized communities. Consistent

100 REPRESENTATIONS

across these various interpretations of Cunanan is the tension of his liminal relationships to American culture and whiteness.

Filipino identification with Cunanan reveals an anxious desire for social inclusion, representation, and acceptance. In *American Tropics: Articulating Filipino America*, Punzalan Isaac (2006) noted a collective Filipino "longing to be reflected in [. . .] [a]ny American drama, even for the wrong reasons" (p. xviii). Bacareza Balance (2008) likewise commented on Cunanan's instant recognizability to Filipinos as "one of us" (p. 87), a fellow outsider negotiating white society:

> On a smaller and less violent scale, we could relate to [. . .] his experience of being outside a group yet wanting to belong. We honed in on Cunanan's earlier actions as part of the processes of adaptation necessary for survival, although the news rendered his behavior as erratic and strange. His violent actions were excessive forms of the intricate and improvised steps we who are outside the norm perform daily in this cultural cha-cha with America— maintaining our own rhythm while adjusting to others, making sure not to step on too many toes, and feeling the need to add an extra swing in the hips for accent and flair. (p. 88)

Similar themes of cultural integration underlie Jessica Hagedorn's reflections on adapting Cunanan's story as the musical *Most Wanted*, which ran briefly in La Jolla, California, in 2007: "it's about the outsider [. . .] and it's about race and class and sex, and living in America and a sort of twisted immigrant's dream" (Boehm, 2007). While promoting *The Assassination of Gianni Versace* over a decade later, Darren Criss expressed his own sense of connection to Cunanan in more universal terms of human yearning: "Who doesn't know what it's like to feel unloved, or want to rise above your station, or just on a very simple level be liked?" (Dibdin, 2018).

All these observations harmonize with my own memories as a then-teenaged Filipino Canadian reading about Cunanan in the news, but my troubling sense of affinity also hinged on a nascent queer consciousness I was not ready to confront. At an age when I had not yet begun to identify as gay, I saw myself mirrored in the dark-haired, olive-skinned young man remembered by classmates as a good student and by relatives as a sensitive, bookish youngster who "locked himself up with encyclopedias"— later growing up to flaunt his fabulousness in a red leather jumpsuit at a high-school dance (Chua-Eoan, 1997; Thomas & Larmer, 1997). Queer theorist Eve Sedgwick's (1990) concept of "camp-recognition" supplies a useful lens for this jarring realization of kinship with a figure of flamboyant menace. For me at 16, the transgressive jolt of recognition upon viewing camp artifacts—"What if the right audience for this were exactly *me*?" (Sedgwick, 1990, p. 156)—was akin to the extreme mix of "pleasure [and] horror" that Punzalan Isaac (2006, p. xviii) described in seeing oneself reflected through the avatar of a wanted murderer, exoticized in the dominant media narrative.

This profound unease of self-recognition in a figure of criminal monstrosity is compounded by Filipino culture's desire for whiteness and its privileges in Western society. As Punzalan Isaac (2006) showed, this desire informed how Filipino community newspapers responded to Cunanan's story:

> Identification with and simultaneous disavowal of Andrew indicates the conflicted position of Filipinos as postcolonial and ethnic Americans concerned with proper public presentation to an imagined (white) American audience. The Filipino American press depicted the mestizo Andrew as having embodied the promise of assimilation, by passing socially, economically, and even phenotypically into the white American world, but something went awry. [. . .] At what point did that Filipino American face evincing visible whiteness as a sign of assimilation into a national body stray from that promise? (pp. xix–xxii)

Whereas the mainstream national media protested the crimes of a "gay prostitute" (Punzalan Isaac, p. xviii), Filipino Americans bristled at the distortion of their aspirations to American ideals of success and beauty—ideals that the Filipino cultural imagination equates with whiteness.

Scholars of Filipino culture have noted the dominance of white beauty standards and their association with affluence and power (Illo, 1996; Natividad, 2006; Root, 1997). In a thesis on cosmetic skin-lightening in the Philippines, Beverly Romero Natividad (2006) contended that an identity crisis has plagued ethnic Filipinos since colonization, whereby "their idealization of whiteness contradicted their perception of themselves" as belonging to a nonwhite race (p. 2). This double bind of approximating whiteness while still being "othered" extends to the collective experience of Asian Americans: a group sometimes perceived as "nearly white" through the model minority myth, yet inexorably racialized (Chou, 2012; Tuan, 2003). Another cultural phenomenon familiar to Filipino experience is the colorist

102   REPRESENTATIONS

privileging of mixed-race, specifically part-Caucasian facial features. Within a "racial schema that recognizes a long history of cultural and national mixing," Cunanan possessed the "mestizo Filipino good looks often depicted, even celebrated, in Filipino and Filipino American magazines, newspapers, and movies" (Punzalan Isaac, 2006, p. xxi). This perception of his attractiveness further distinguished Filipino sentiments from those expressed in the national media. Whereas a letter to the editor of *Time* (Wojtalewicz, 1997, August 18, p. 7) praised the magazine for not putting "Cunanan's terrifying face on their cover," a *Filipino Express* interviewee lamented the wasted life of the "handsome, intelligent" former altar boy (as cited in Punzalan Isaac, 2006, p. xxi).

Biographical details of Cunanan's young adulthood affirm his own desired conformity to white beauty ideals and discomfort with being half-Filipino. Maureen Orth's *Vulgar Favors* (1999) maintained that Cunanan downplayed his ethnic background at Berkeley in 1989. Although "Filipino was the hot race on campus that year"—suggesting temporary racial fetishes as another kind of marginalization rather than any meaningful acceptance—"Andrew wanted to be blond and blue-eyed" (Orth, 1999, p. 71). As Wensley Clarkson (1997) recounted in *Death at Every Stop*, Cunanan also disliked his surname "because he felt it made him sound Filipino," preferring instead "to reinvent himself as a Latino" under aliases such as "Andrew DeSilva" and "David Morales," which "seemed much more glamorous and impressive to any would-be suitors" (p. 26). This adoption of pseudonyms evoking Hispanic European heritage is again consistent with the value that Filipino culture places on whiteness (Natividad, 2006, p. 2).

White standards of desirability likewise proliferate among gay Asians of various cultures, influencing their perceived attractiveness. Chong-suk Han and Kyung-Hee Choi's (2018) empirical case study demonstrated how "racialized hierarchies of desire" affect gay men of color in Los Angeles (p. 145). An earlier Australian study on racialized language in gay and bisexual men's online profiles (Callander et al., 2012) evinced white male privilege "in dictating the norms of sexual desire in relation to race" (p. 1061). Han (2021) further observed that the overwhelmingly white gay media still excludes men of color, save for exoticized depictions fulfilling gay white male sexual fantasies (p. 2). Gay community organizations further privilege whiteness, prioritizing visible assimilation as a means of cultural acceptance, with the outcome that "to be gay in America today is to be white [. . .] and well to-do" (Han, 2021, p. 22).

These cultural hierarchies enmesh racial desirability with socioeconomic capital, providing an intersectional context through which to read Cunanan's circulation among American gay communities in the 1990s. His relationships of convenience with older, wealthier white male benefactors fit into a familiar pattern among gays that bolsters white privilege while denigrating Asian men. In Tony Ayres's (1998) documentary *China Dolls,* gay Filipino-Australian interviewees candidly attested to the accepted desirability of white romantic partners and the negative perceptions of Asians dating older white men. In one interviewee's words, "Asians who have relationships with older men, they're seen with malice by other gay men as being, you know, a leech." This racialized stigma would thus have consigned Cunanan to a predatory role even if he had had no mercenary designs on his older paramours. Within such a scheme, permanent social advancement remains largely inaccessible for those on the margins, undermining the assimilationist possibilities that lighter-skinned mestizos embody for Filipinos. Cunanan's exploitation of "social skills and symbolic capital—charm, manners, conversation skills, connections, money, and looks" as well as sexual companionship earned him only temporary "class mobility, as long as his looks and credit cards held out—both short-lived currencies" (Punzalan Isaac, 2006, p. xxii). As a mixed-race gay man of color whose attractiveness to benefactors was delimited by white desires and desirability, Cunanan occupied a precarious position of intersecting disadvantages—in many ways, a perfect storm for radicalization.

Racialization and Radicalization

To view Cunanan as radicalized, pushed to extreme actions subverting the dominant order, is to resist reading his crimes as an individualistic aberration, instead exposing their broader systemic implications. This structural reading casts his deeds in a revisionist light that I wish to entertain by drawing on other responses to his story. Not all empathetic commentators on Cunanan have tempered their remarks with ambiguity or disavowal. The late AIDS activist and Indigenous Mexican American surrealist poet Ronnie Burk (1997) created a one-page flier in which he hailed Cunanan as a radical underclass folk hero retaliating against privileged oppressors. A controversial figure himself as a member of ACT UP's recusant San Francisco faction, Burk gained notoriety for condemning the pharmaceutical industry and, more troublingly, questioning the link between HIV and AIDS (Nelson, 2001, p. 325). No less extreme were his views of Cunanan's killing spree. Titled "SHOOT THE RICH! Homage to Andrew Philip Cunanan," Burk's (1997) text is a concise manifesto that challenges and sneers at "a society where police shoot black and [Latino] teenagers daily . . . a society fueled by racism, homophobia, misogyny, and class [privilege]" (Figure 5.1).

Fellow activist and artist Todd Swindell recalled accompanying Burk to wheat-paste this flier around San Francisco's Castro district, only to find copies later torn down or defaced by incensed members of the public (T. Swindell, personal communication, January 9, 2022). If Burk's screed, fueled by decades of intersecting racial, sexual, and economic injustice, seemed extreme in 1997 for comparing American society with decadent European aristocracies, it now reads as prescient of 21st-century movements protesting economic inequity, systemic oppression, whorephobia, and police brutality. But unlike the unifying cry of ACT UP's "Queer Nation Manifesto" (1990), which envisioned an "army of lovers" facing "the rejection of society [. . .] just to love each other" (p. 66), Burk's diatribe condemned the economic and racial privileges dividing men who have sex with men. Recalling Burk's work, Swindell described "a deeper wound that's ignored in the legacy of Versace's murder, of exploitation and commodification of the marginalized, and the way assimilation within the gay status quo perpetuates this divide" (T. Swindell, personal communication, January 13, 2022). Addressing these schisms in his flier, Burk may not have directly interrogated white privilege as he did in other expressions of his activism, but he unequivocally denounced the system for harming people of color.

So great was Burk's empathy for Cunanan that he penned another short piece, a handwritten note accompanying a photo (clipped from *Newsweek*) of a young Cunanan with his father (Figure 5.2):

> People forget Andrew Philip Cunanan was a human being who loved and felt pain and rejection. A little boy who wanted to be loved. We pay the price for every suffering child. I know his rage and I love him for lashing out and I don't care what even my dearest friends think of my opinion. He was a hero of the gay community to be canonized!

More personal than the "Shoot the Rich" flier, this piece hints at the pain flowing from intersectional oppression. Emphasizing the individual consequences of social injustice, it humanizes Burk's portrayal of Cunanan

WHITE DESIRABILITY AND VIOLENT RADICALIZATION 105

Figure 5.1 "SHOOT THE RICH! Homage to Andrew Philip Cunanan" (Burk, 1997).

as a radical. The sentiments resemble Darren Criss's affinity with Cunanan's desire "on a very simple level [to] be liked" (Dibdin, 2018). In my email correspondences with Swindell, he partly attributed Burk's identification with the hunted spree killer to how "the extreme nature of Cunanan's actions appealed to Ronnie's attraction to heightened theatrics," while noting that

Figure 5.2 Personal missive from Burk on Cunanan in *Newsweek* (ACT UP Archive).

the connection seemed to run deeper, as shown when Burk responded to Cunanan's death by morbidly joking to friends that his son had died (T. Swindell, personal communication, January 13, 2022). Although we will never know whether the political agenda that he ascribed to Cunanan reflects the killer's motives to any degree, Burk's perspective underlines how Cunanan's crimes operated within interlocking power structures that marginalized queer sex workers of color while protecting elite, white, and often closeted clientele.

If Cunanan's actual victims—a war veteran, architect, real-estate developer, working-class caretaker, and celebrity fashion designer—do not deserve to be viewed as oppressors or targets of assassination, the societal forces that intersected to disenfranchise him are readily embodied in other real-life figures whose harmful political actions have drawn radical ire. The ACT UP manifesto (1990, p. 72) raged against Jesse Helms and Ronald Reagan. In Tony Kushner's *Angels in America* (1992), one of the most celebrated works of queer art from the era of the AIDS crisis, the attorney and political fixer Roy Cohn emblematizes the hypocrisy of powerful, closeted white men who persecute homosexuals while enjoying same-sex encounters. In the decades since Kushner's play premiered, Cohn's political legacy has extended to the administration of Donald Trump, whom he mentored (Brenner, 2017), while the figure of the conservative Republican privately soliciting gay sex yet publicly supporting homophobic policies has become a tabloid cliché. Burk's damning vision of a "ruling class we know to be hypocritical to the core" is all too familiar in the contemporary landscape.

Burk's appraisal of Cunanan as an "assassin"—a killer of prominent, powerful figures—resonates with Ryan Murphy's better-known *American Crime Story: The Assassination of Gianni Versace* (2018). The "assassination" label imbues Cunanan's killings with a larger social meaning, even if the series does not directly purport that his actions were, as Burk believed, politically motivated. As a popular entertainment beholden to mainstream viewers' sensibilities, the series could hardly have championed Cunanan as did Burk, but its script and Criss's performance likewise render him sympathetic by contextualizing his violence within the homophobia of American culture and its disempowering of queer bodies. In interviews with *Harper's Bazaar* and *Vanity Fair*, screenwriter Tom Rob Smith went so far as to liken Cunanan's character arc to "a story of radicalization" (Dibdin, 2017, para. 4):

> If you can't communicate to the world through creation, you communicate [. . .] through destruction. And that's how a very clever, genuinely clever young man who had never hurt anyone ended up doing this horrific, horrific thing. The process seems much closer to radicalization and terrorism than it is to the pathology of a serial killer. (Miller, 2018, para. 11)

108 REPRESENTATIONS

As with Burk's manifesto, Smith's labeling of Cunanan as a radicalized assassin emphasizes his victimization of powerful people, with Versace representing a pinnacle of material success and societal adoration from which Cunanan was alienated. The first episode visually establishes the social divide in an opening montage that juxtaposes the fashion designer waking in his palatial home and his soon-to-be assailant desperately roaming the shores and streets of Miami Beach. Rather than also exploring the racialized gap between the Italian Versace and the half-Italian, half-Filipino Cunanan, however, the script mirrors them as two gay men of humble origins who both craved success and glamour only to be irrevocably cast, through their own choices, in oppositional roles—a dichotomy made overt in the episode titled "Creator/Destroyer."

At the expense of a fully intersectional rendering of the story, this narrative choice foregrounds class and sexuality while eliding the racial dynamics that separated Cunanan from the other gay men in his life. The elision reflects what Kimberlé Crenshaw (1991) pinpointed as "the failure of identity politics," namely that it often "conflates or ignores intragroup differences" that shape marginalized people's experiences (p. 1242). Emphasizing the gayness that Cunanan had in common with most of his victims, Ryan Murphy's (2018) series downplays the racial distinctions that indelibly mark their experiences of same-sex companionship and desire. Inadequate or flawed treatments of race have elicited extensive criticism of Murphy's works overall (e.g., Braxton, 2016; Bruney, 2020; Cadenas, 2015; Zoller Seitz, 2016), but *The Assassination of Gianni Versace* especially demonstrates the consequences of this oversight (Duan, 2018). The effects of race are perceptible yet underarticulated throughout the series, often subsumed within class asymmetries and themes of romantic disappointment, whether deliberately to render Cunanan's plight more relatable to white viewers or reflecting a lack of racial consciousness among the predominantly white creative team.

As the episodes proceed in reverse-chronological order, Cunanan's slayings of earlier victims—all white men—channel his outrage at economic disenfranchisement and failed relationships. The killing of Chicago real-estate tycoon Lee Miglin, whom the series portrays as sexually involved with Cunanan, is depicted as the symbolic torture and assassination of a rich older man who stood in for his other affluent lovers. A scene in episode two foreshadows the Miglin murder, as Cunanan physically binds and subdues another older white man whom he picks up while turning tricks on the beach. Wrapping his client's face in duct tape and pinning him down on

WHITE DESIRABILITY AND VIOLENT RADICALIZATION   109

the bed, Cunanan enacts a sadistic power play, taunting the man with a pair of scissors while exhorting him to "Accept it." The overturning of privilege becomes even more pronounced when Cunanan similarly taunts Miglin in the next episode, belittling his professional ambitions before physically and verbally dominating him to lay bare the reversal of power: "So dominant out there, so submissive in here. So powerful out there, so pathetic in here." The imagery and language are shocking partly because Cunanan's real-life crimes occurred in a world where queer sex workers of color are statistically more likely to be victims of violent attacks than perpetrators, and stigmas around sex work still impede the reporting of antigay violence (Scheer et al., 2021, p. 144). In this unequal playing field, Cunanan's sadistic power games suggest a twisted revenge fantasy not far from the reckoning that Burk (1997) imagined.

Throughout these unnerving scenes, the subversion of socioeconomic power by a racially ambiguous subject invites consideration in terms of white privilege, even if the script never comments on the victims' whiteness. Whether this silence stems from the lack of writers of color behind the scenes or from a choice to prioritize gay themes over racial ones, it reinforces mainstream media's centralization of white experience as an unquestioned norm, as if to assume that the antihomophobic messages of Murphy's series exist in a racially neutral space. In contrast, Jessica Hagedorn's text for *Most Wanted* (2007) directly confronted racial themes by having its Cunanan character—renamed Danny Reyes—connect with a mixed-race journalist, and by centralizing a queer, racialized voice through the figure of a Black drag queen who acts as narrator (Bacareza Balance, 2008, pp. 92–93). Bacareza Balance (2008) praised the musical precisely for capturing "the intricacies of desire to be another race" alongside the desire for fame and acceptance (p. 95). Hagedorn or other writers of color might have brought similar sensibilities to Murphy's series, in which white desirability becomes at most an unspoken tension, discernible only through the racially conscious casting of Criss and a few tantalizing moments of acknowledgment in the script, which I examine later. While the series has achieved far greater visibility than Hagedorn's musical, which has not been staged since its initial workshop production, Murphy and his collaborators could have enriched their queer-focused approach by exploring racialization and racism in Cunanan's spree and his relationships with other gay men.

The documented details of Cunanan's first two murders warrant especial commentary on racial dynamics that the series largely avoids. News coverage

110 REPRESENTATIONS

highlighted the early victims' normative Midwestern American whiteness, with Orth (1997) describing clean-cut former naval officer Jeffrey Trail and architect David Madson as having "walked off a Kellogg's Corn Flakes box" (p. 270). The series depicts Cunanan's romantic rejection by Madson as the loss of his "last chance" at conventional domestic bliss and white middle-class respectability, but his friendship with Trail may better illuminate white desirability's significance. Orth and other sources repeated Steven Zeeland's anecdote that Cunanan playfully called Trail an "alpha male" in the parlance of Jane Goodall's studies on chimpanzee hierarchies (Chua-Eoan, 1997; Orth, 1999; Zeeland, 1997). As Zeeland (1997) recounted, Cunanan once jokingly spread his legs in front of Trail to mimic a subordinate chimp presenting its genitals in obeisance to an alpha. Even in jest, Cunanan's deference to Trail conjures up Orientalist stereotypes of Asian submissiveness to white superiority that have long inflected Western perceptions of Asians (Chou, 2012), but the teleplay omits this racially charged incident.

The closest the series comes to exploring race in Cunanan and Trail's relationship is a scene at a gay bar in episode seven, when Cunanan attributes his lack of sexual success to not having the right physical appearance. He indicates a pair of clean-cut white bar patrons, one blond and one brunet, as conversely having "a look that people want." Nothing in the dialogue specifically racializes this desirable "look," but a racial meaning is hard not to infer in context, given that hair color and complexion are the two bar-goers' only visible markers of difference from Cunanan apart from their preppy attire, which itself connotes upper-middle-class white privilege. With no other textual clues, Criss's performance and mixed-race identity thus bear the full burden of representing racialized experience in the scene.

Later in the same episode, the series' one direct depiction of sexual racism occurs in a fictionalized scene of Cunanan seeking work at an escort agency, only to be humiliatingly rejected for not fitting the racialized categories that cater to gay white male clientele. The writers navigate the thorny intersections of sexuality, gender, and race in the economically inflected domain of sex work, where desirable bodies are explicit commodities, and the channeling of desire through identity determines a worker's commercial viability. "Straight men like Asian women," the agency director tells him, "but gay clients don't ask for Asian men [...] and they never ask for Asians with attitude." As an Asian viewer already familiar with Cunanan's story, I found this scene incisive, and I wish the series had included more moments like it—moments capturing Asian male anxieties in the racially charged world of gay sex, heightened by the stakes of economic survival. The frank dialogue exposes the treatment of Asian bodies as less desirable than other bodies of color in a context where stereotyping determines their sexual currency. Cunanan quickly learns that the escorting profession accommodates gay desires but not Asian men. In a deeply degrading moment, the director asks him to show her his penis, implicitly to disprove the stereotypes about Asian genital size. The script also nods to the complexity of mixed-race identities when Cunanan suggests that he might pass for Portuguese or Latino if his Asian-ness is unmarketable, but the director dismisses him for not belonging to the expected physical type ("My Latinos are studs").

For all that the scene illustrates the oppressive racialization of sex workers, however, it falls short of connecting anti-Asian discrimination to the idealization of whiteness. Fixating on racial fetishes, the agency director never admits that white escorts are the assumed norm. The writers may have intended a critique of white desirability as a subtext, but when taken in tandem with the series' other silences and partial gestures, the narrative gap feels like yet another missed opportunity, a crucial omission underlining the need—and frequent failure—to interrogate whiteness in antiracist projects.

Conclusion

I highlight the above scenes because, for all their shortcomings, they reiterate the identifiability of Cunanan's narrative within cultural patterns of Asian and Filipino experience, suggesting that his individual circumstances, while borne out to tragic ends, were not exceptional but representative. This broader meaning deepens the personal resonance that his story has long held for me and others. Revisiting this maligned figure who haunted my late adolescence, I find myself no longer disturbed by his ambiguity but grateful for the multipronged perspective—Asian, Filipino, and gay—that enables me to view him as well as his victims with compassion. Even if Murphy and his writers erased the narrative's complex racial dimensions, the on-screen Cunanan, like the one first glimpsed in newspapers and magazines 24 years ago, bears an undeniable familiarity for Filipino viewers, especially those of us who are queer. The radical "audacity and rage" that Burk (1997) saw in Cunanan are akin to frustrations common among the lived experiences of Asians facing sexual racism and other quotidian oppressions in white America. The late Filipino American writer Alex Tizon (2014) sensitively articulated the "feelings of bitterness or exclusion from the main vein of life, among Asian American men" (p. 104), while recalling his own Filipino immigrant family's "adulation of all things white and Western" and how their "open derision of all things brown or native or Asian was the engine of their self-annihilation" (p. 34).

Channeling these destructive energies into physical violence, Andrew Cunanan was an extreme case of a queer racialized subject reacting against the limits of a culture that empowers white men as desiring subjects and constructs whiteness as desirable. Whether or not he was the radicalized figure that Burk (1997) or the creators of *American Crime Story* (2018) depicted him to be, the cultural norms and systemic conditions that overdetermined his fate and that of his white victims are as instructive as any clues we have about his individual motives. The impetus behind my reading, however, is not to justify his killings of innocent people or to overstate the impact of racially motivated sexual rejection, but rather to question how the inextricable realities of economic inequality, sexual injustice, and racism marginalize people and engender violence. All these intersections have a transformative effect; a change to one would alter the narrative. Cunanan's case thus contrasts with that of another radicalized half-Asian spree killer: 22-year-old Elliot Rodger, who murdered six people in Isla Vista, California, in 2014, leaving behind a manifesto that directly attributed his deeds to a misogynistic rage borne of sexual rejection by white women. Differing from Cunanan in sexuality and socioeconomic privilege, Rodger was a young straight man from a wealthy family, killing with a sense of heterosexist masculine entitlement aligned with male supremacist ideology. These leanings prompted the International Centre for Counter-Terrorism to classify him as a misogynist terrorist (DiBranco, 2020), politically far-removed from the antiracist, anticapitalist radicalism that Burk (1997) associated with Cunanan's violence.

At the start of this chapter, I referred to Cunanan's "cautionary tale," but I would offer this label while resisting the urge to reduce a complex story to facile, one-sided moralizing. Rather, I believe that the narrative not only highlights the dangers of violent extremism but also reminds the privileged that the oppressions from which they benefit demand reprisal. This double warning bears radical potential in many positive ways. It provokes us to imagine a culture that fully values the lives of queer people, sex workers, and people of color while rejecting the oppressions wrought by colonial and capitalist values. Such a culture would not desire whiteness as a physical or social ideal; nor would it raise Filipinos to perceive their value through the lightness of their skin or teach gay Asians to prize their bodies only in relation to white desires. In such a culture, consensual commodified sex would not reinforce noxious racial hierarchies, and the racist gatekeeping of opportunities would not widen the economic asymmetries that keep entire classes of society from flourishing. In such a culture, perhaps, the stories of people like Andrew Cunanan would be radically different.

References

ACT UP. (1990). Queer nation manifesto: Queers read this. In B. Fahs (Ed.), *Burn it down! Feminist manifestoes for the revolution* (pp. 63–84). Verso.

Ahmed, S. (2007). A phenomenology of whiteness. *Feminist Theory, 8*(2), 149–168.

Ayres, T. (1998). *China dolls*. National Film and Sound Archive of Australia.

Bacareza Balance, C. (2008). Notorious kin: Filipino America re-imagines Andrew Cunanan. *Journal of Asian American Studies, 11*(1), 87–106.

Boehm, M. (2007, October 2). A musical on trial. *Los Angeles Times*. https://www.latimes.com/archives/la-xpm-2007-oct-02-et-mostwanted2-story.html

Braxton, G. (2016, January 17). With *People v. O.J. Simpson*, Ryan Murphy's track record on race goes on trial. *Los Angeles Times*. https://www.latimes.com/entertainment/tv/showtracker/la-et-st-people-v-oj-simpson-ryan-murphy-race-20160114-story.html

Brenner, M. (2017, June 28). How Donald Trump and Roy Cohn's ruthless symbiosis changed America. *Vanity Fair,* (684), 84–89, 120–123. https://www.vanityfair.com/news/2017/06/donald-trump-roy-cohn-relationship

Bruney, G. (2020, May 1). *Ryan Murphy's Hollywood dislocates its shoulder patting itself on the back*. Esquire. https://www.esquire.com/entertainment/tv/a32335599/hollywood-ryan-murphy-netflix-racism-representation/

Burk, R. (1997, July). *Shoot the rich! Homage to Andrew Philip [sic] Cunanan*. ACT UP Archives. https://actuparchives.com/shoot-the-rich-ronnie-burks-homage-to-andrew-cunanan/

Cadenas, K. (2015, September 22). *Ryan Murphy, racist?* Complex. https://www.complex.com/pop-culture/2015/09/ryan-murphy-are-you-racist

Callander, D., Holt, M., & Newman, C. (2012). Just a preference: Racialised language in the sex-seeking profiles of gay and bisexual men. *Culture, Health & Sexuality, 14*(9), 1049–1063. https://doi.org/10.1080/13691058.2012.714799

Chou, R. S. (2012). *Asian American sexual politics: The construction of race, gender, and sexuality*. Rowman & Littlefield.

Chua-Eoan, H. (1997, August 4). Dead men tell no tales. *Time Magazine, 150*(5), 30–32. http://content.time.com/time/magazine/article/0,9171,986785,00.html

Clarkson, W. (1997). *Death at every stop: The true story of serial killer Andrew Cunanan, the man who murdered designer Gianni Versace*. St. Martin's Press.

Crenshaw, K. (1991). Mapping the margins. *Stanford Law Review, 43*(6), 1241–1299.

Dibdin, E. (2017, August 10). *Darren Criss talks getting inside the mind of Gianni Versace's killer*. Harper's Bazaar. https://www.harpersbazaar.com/culture/film-tv/a11664541/american-crime-story-season-2-versace-darren-criss/

114 REPRESENTATIONS

Dibdin, E. (2018, February 8). *Darren Criss has never wanted to be ordinary: The star of The assassination of Gianni Versace: American crime story explains how he found humanity in the sociopathic killer he plays on TV*. Esquire. https://www.esquire.com/entertainm ent/tv/a16674052/darren-criss-interview-assassination-of-gianni-versace/

DiBranco, A. (2020, February 10). *Male supremacist terrorism as a rising threat*. International Centre for Counter-Terrorism. https://www.icct.nl/index.php/publicat ion/male-supremacist-terrorism-rising-threat.

Duan, N. (2018, March 7). *In The assassination of Gianni Versace, Ryan Murphy proves— again!—he can never get race right*. Quartz. https://qz.com/quartzy/1222574/ryan-mur phy-proves-again-he-can-never-get-race-right/

Hagedorn, J., & Bennett, M. (Writers), Greif, M. (Director). (2007, October). *Most wanted*. A Page-to-Stage production performed at La Jolla Playhouse Theatre.

Han, C., (2021). *Racial erotics: Gay men of color, sexual racism, and the politics of desire*. University of Washington Press.

Han, C., & Choi, K. (2018). Very few people say "no whites": Gay men of color and the racial politics of desire. *Sociological Spectrum, 38*(3), 145–161.

Illo, J. F. I. (1996). Fair skin and sexy body: Imprints of colonialism and capitalism on the Filipina. *Australian Feminist Studies, 11*(24), 219–225.

Kang, I. (2018, January 19). *The deracination of Andrew Cunanan: Why is The assassination of Gianni Versace interested in its protagonist's sexuality but not his race?* Slate. https://slate.com/culture/ 2018/01/the-assassination-of-gianni-versace-erases-its-main-characters-racial-identity.html

Kosofsky Sedgwick, E. (1990). *Epistemology of the closet*. University of California Press.

Kushner, T. (1992). *Angels in America: A gay fantasia on national themes*. Theatre Communications Group.

Lacayo, R. (1997, July 28). Tagged for murder. *Time Magazine, 150*(4), 32–35. http://cont ent.time.com/time/magazine/article/0,9171,138062,00.html

Miller, J. (2018, January 31). The assassination of Gianni Versace: The mysterious murder of Lee Miglin. *Vanity Fair*. https://www.vanityfair.com/hollywood/2018/01/versace-murder-lee-miglin-andrew-cunanan

Murphy, R., Jacobson, N., Simpson, B., Woodall, A., Smith, T. R., Minahan, D., Falchuk, B., Alexander, S., Karaszewski, L., Vucelich, C., Cohn, M., Kovtun, E., Eyrich, L. & Krueger Mekash, E. (Producers). (2018). *The assassination of Gianni Versace: American crime story* [Television series]. FX.

Natividad, B. R. (2006). *Rendering whiteness visible in the Filipino culture through skin-whitening cosmetic advertisements* (2974) [Master's thesis, California State University, San Bernardino]. Theses Digitization Project. https://scholarworks.lib.csusb.edu/etd-project/2974

Nelson, J. (2001, September 1). The AIDS deniers. *GQ, 71*(9), 322–329, 372. https://www. gq.com/story/the-aids-deniers

Orth, M. (1997, September). The killer's trail: Andrew Cunanan and Gianni Versace. *Vanity Fair*, (445), 268–275, 329–336. https://www.vanityfair.com/magazine/1997/09/cunanan199709

Orth, M. (1999). *Vulgar favors: The hunt for Andrew Cunanan, the man who killed Gianni Versace*. Bantam Books.

Punzalan Isaac, A. (2006). *American tropics: Articulating Filipino America*. University of Minnesota Press.

Root, M. P. P. (1997). Contemporary mixed-heritage Filipino Americans: Fighting colonized identities. In M. P. P. Root (Ed.), *Filipino Americans: Transformation and identity* (pp. 80–94). Sage.

Scheer, J. R., Breslow, A. S., Esposito, J., Price, M. A., & Katz, J. (2021). Violence against gay men. In E. M. Lund, C. Burgess, & A. J. Johnson (Eds.), *Violence against LGBTQ+ persons: Research, practice, and advocacy* (pp. 135–148). Springer.

Thomas, E. & Larmer, B. (1997, July 28). Facing death. *Newsweek*, 130(4), 20–30. https://www.newsweek.com/facing-death-174404

Tizon, A. (2014). *Big little man: In search of my Asian self*. Houghton Mifflin Harcourt.

Tuan, M. (2003). *Forever foreigners or honorary whites? The Asian ethnic experience*. Rutgers University Press.

Wojtalewicz, B. (1997, August 18). [Letter to the editor]. *Time Magazine, 150*(7), 7.

Zeeland, S. (1997, July 23). Killer queen: Andrew Cunanan, my love rival. *The Stranger*, 6(44), 10–17. https://www.marksimpson.com/2018/02/05/killer-queen-andrew-cunanan-love-rival/

Zoller Seitz, M. (2016, January 25). *Ryan Murphy's* The People v. O.J. Simpson *puts more than just Simpson on trial*. Vulture. https://www.vulture.com/2016/01/tv-review-the-people-v-oj-simpson.html

6

Undesiring Whiteness and Undoing the White Gaze in HIV Prevention Marketing

Ivan Bujan

In 1984, one of the world's first AIDS organizations, the San Francisco AIDS Foundation (SFAF) introduced erotically explicit HIV prevention marketing for men who have sex with men. Created early in the AIDS crisis, SFAF's campaign featured a headless, naked Black male body with his back turned to the camera, showing off a well-rounded butt (see Figure 6.1). Behind the Black man's silhouette is a second male figure, this one white and with his hand crossing the muscular back of the other body. The poster reads "YOU CAN HAVE FUN (and be safe, too)" followed by safer sex and other harm reduction instructions. Because of its visual framing, SFAF's poster invites spectators to "consume" a hypervisible naked Black body. What, then, might differences in the visual positions of the poster's two models suggest about the assumed spectator, and—building on this—what might it signal about the larger story of race and sexuality in HIV prevention marketing?

As writer Daniel Demens recollects, the poster stirred controversy when published in a newspaper the *San Francisco Chronicle* (2014). According to Demens, many gay bars in San Francisco refused to display the poster because they found its racial overtones unacceptable, but it was still very popular and displayed in bathhouses and bars around the United States. As with other prevention ads geared toward gay, bisexual men, and other men who have sex with men (MSM) at the time, SFAF's poster seems to promote "a beautiful body" to "sex-up" life (Gilman, 1995, pp. 115–172). It sexualizes the male form and depicts (or at least hints at) moments of pleasure. Mostly, this type of advertising replicated the aesthetics of ads for gay saunas and sex clubs found in publications targeted to MSM prior to the 1980s (Brier 2009; Fiahlo & Katz, 2013).

Ivan Bujan, *Undesiring Whiteness and Undoing the White Gaze in HIV Prevention Marketing* In: *Sexual Racism and Social Justice.* Edited by: Denton Callander, Panteá Farvid, Amir Baradaran, and Thomas A. Vance, Oxford University Press.
© Oxford University Press 2024. DOI: 10.1093/oso/9780197605509.003.0007

Figure 6.1 "YOU CAN HAVE FUN (and be safe, too)." San Francisco AIDS Foundation (1984).

While not immune to government censorship and other forms of structural homophobia, the production of eroticized materials has long been rationalized by HIV activists through discourses of education and behavior change (Crimp, 1987; Escoffier, 1998; Leonard & Michell, 2000). Similar

118 REPRESENTATIONS

trends in HIV prevention that foreground racialized desire in marketing have persisted since these earlier days, including today, when condoms are now complemented with highly effective biomedical prevention strategies like treatment-as-prevention and HIV pre-exposure prophylaxis (PrEP). Although venues of advertisement now favor digital spaces, in many ways their aesthetics remain the same: erotically explicit imagery of muscular, lean, young, cisgender, and abled male bodies (see Figure 6.2). As with decades past, this imagery—advertently or otherwise—engages in and represents the complex politics of sexuality and racism, and in doing so, offers a compelling opportunity for analysis.

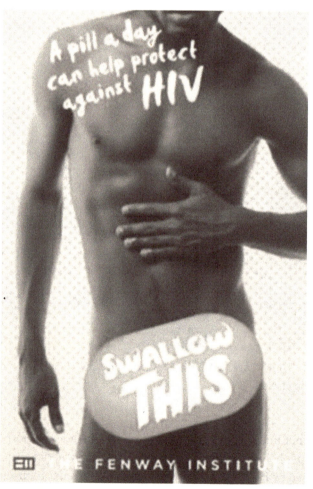

Figure 6.2 "Swallow This." The Fenway Institute (2018).

Guided by more than four decades of HIV campaigns—from condom promotion in the 1980s to more recently PrEP in the 2010s—this chapter asks questions about how race is depicted in HIV prevention marketing (i.e., are men of color positioned as objects or agents of desire?) and the purpose race serves in such depictions (i.e., to engage gay men of color or offer them up for white consumption?). When posing these questions, I am curious about what depictions of racialized sexuality and sexualized race in HIV prevention marketing can reveal about larger and reflexive systems of white supremacy and, by extension, biomedical consumerism. The chapter scrutinizes how interplay between the "white gaze," masculinity, and racism have dictated visual cultures of HIV prevention.

Recognizing and destabilizing the interplay of the white gaze, masculinity, and racism is a useful critical lens through which to view HIV prevention toward imagining new possibilities. Although I predominantly focus on prevention marketing, this critical lens is applicable to HIV public health writ large: from the creation of "at-risk" categories and "key populations," to visual representations (and exclusions) of race in prevention ads, and beyond. As I explore, HIV prevention essentializes race, sexuality, and desire as coconstructed "risk" categories, enacting and reinforcing various stereotypes and ignoring intersectional complexities through an often uncritical process of so-called *population health*. Since marketing campaigns are a result of multiple parties working toward an end goal of selling some kind of product (i.e., condoms, PrEP, behavior change), we can assume the same forces that narrowly essentialize marginalized social identities in other forms of media would inform the mass media of public health. From this perspective, I ask one more question: who and what shapes the commodification of race and sexuality in HIV prevention?

Undesiring the "White Gaze" in HIV Prevention

Many people regard erotically explicit advertising as a major turning point in public health messaging, which awakened new possibilities of engaging with a more "real" projection of lived experience (Brier, 2009; Escoffier, 1998; Gilman, 1995). In this erotic advertising, racialized—including interracial—imagery invites attention to racialization of sexuality and the sexualization of racism. One way of interrogating the sexual racism of HIV prevention is through critical whiteness studies, including the "white gaze" concept.

Whiteness is central to the organizations of global cultural, economic, political, and sexual hierarchies, but it often remains unexamined and invisible (Applebaum, 2016). When writing about relations between Blackness and whiteness in a national framework, scholar E. Patrick Johnson (2003) argues, "[w]hen white Americans essentialize blackness [...] they do so in a way that maintains 'whiteness' as the master trope of purity supremacy, and entitlement, as a ubiquitous, fixed, unifying signifier that seems invisible" (p. 4). Further, scholar Richard Dyer (2003) suggests that "racing whites is to dislodge them/us from the position of power, with all the inequities oppression, privileges, and sufferings in its train, dislodging them/us by undercutting the authority with which they/we speak and act in and on the world" (p. 301). The supposition from this previous work is that recognizing and interrogating whiteness is one way to help destabilize the power dynamics it represents and reinforces.

One of the ways whiteness expresses itself while also sustaining its authority and primacy is through the "white gaze." Scholars define the white gaze as a set of various mechanisms that depict and produce racial difference from a place of white experience (and privilege), which defines and propagates what appear as universal truths but, in reality, are stereotypes that rarely correspond with the experiences of people being gazed (Fusco, 1994; Mercer, 1994; Wilkins, 2021; Yancy, 2017). In this way, the white gaze is an expression of power, "an interpretive framework through which white people define, distort, and ultimately seek to destroy Blackness [and other forms of racialization] to reinforce the racial order and for political gains (Wilkins, 2021, p. 81). While some mechanisms of the white gaze are rooted in desire to destroy, as seen in, for instance, historical lynching images or more recently, recorded police brutality, others solicit pleasure in stereotypes that hypersexualize, patronize, objectify, and commodify racial alterity (Wilkins, 2021; Yancy, 2017, p. xxxii). The white gaze has also been studiously used as a tool to prevent racing white people by placing them in the position of lookers who create meaning and use their gaze as a surveillance technology for others. In these ways, the white gaze sustains the faux neutrality and invisibility of whiteness, defining the focus and orienting the field of vision away from itself.

The white gaze continues to shape visual media globally, including in the realm of HIV prevention marketing. Objectifying bodies of color in HIV prevention is thus only one example within a longer history of visual cultures that situates bodies of color as alluring, exotic, and available for consumption.

When exploring historical violence, sexual racism, and interracial desire, porn studies scholar Linda Williams (2004) invokes philosopher Frantz Fanon's notion of "negrophobia as a form of white sexual anxiety," arguing that contemporary white desire for Black bodies (as well as violence toward them) has roots in slavery and fear of Black male genitalia: "The white gaze sees the organ of black skin and immediately feels fear" (p. 277). According to Fanon (1967), at its core, this fear is a result of a pathological projection on the part of the white man of his own repressed multidimensional sexuality. Others have argued this fear is a natural reaction to a long history of white men raping Black women and fears of revenge; as critic Wesley Morris (2016) puts it, "Sex, for them, was power expressed through rape. And one side effect of that power was paranoia: Wouldn't black revenge include rape? Won't they want to do this to our women?" Williams (2004) expands these arguments to assert that fear, while initially generated by white male masters to keep white women and Black men apart, is the source of contemporary erotic tension situated in interracial desire. By understanding Black–white interracial desire as grounded in a fear, Williams contends that "we begin to recognize the validity of varieties of commodification in contemporary visual culture" (p. 281), especially, as they also argue, "the white man's power remains the pivotal point around which these permutations of power and pleasure turn" (p. 286).

HIV prevention ads—including several already discussed—repeatedly provide evidence of how race is commodified by and through the white gaze. In particular, both the SFAF safer sex ad (Figure 6.1) and Fenway's "Swallow THIS" PrEP ad both feature naked Black bodies, which are presented in ways that "offers them up" for consumption by an imagined white audience. Most notably, this effect is achieved through visual technique of cropping whereby a focus on a specific body part makes up for the whole (Cascalheira & Smith, 2020; Fusco, 2003; Mercer, 1994). In SFAF's advertising, we encounter a headless Black behind, while the white body, also without a head, is literally shielded from our gaze by the Black body. In the Fenway image advertising PrEP, the viewer is invited to swallow "the pill" but positioned in place of a headless Black man's penis so as to instead suggest swallowing his dick. In both ads, the image of a headless Black body evokes the work of prolific 20th-century photographer Robert Mapplethorpe, who, as art historian Kobena Mercer describes, often "decapitated" Black male subjects through cropping to "perpetuate the racist stereotype that, essentially, the black man is nothing more than his penis" (Mercer, 1994). There are clear parallels in

122 REPRESENTATIONS

how cropping is used between the earlier cited HIV prevention ads and some of Mapplethorpe's most notorious works. Such strategic cropping reflects the white gaze and its commitment to "confine [bodies of color] to a narrow repertoire of 'types'" in which one body part (in this case bum and the penis) stand in for a whole (Mercer, 1994, p. 133).

Naturally, the white gaze does not limit itself to representations of Black bodies. Scholar and filmmaker Richard Fung (1991) argues that the visual media continually works toward desexualize and feminize men racialized as Asian. Following Fanon's logic about white men's fear of (and suppressed desire for) big Black penis, Fung (1991) argues that, in opposition, "the Asian man is defined by a striking absence down there" (p. 148). In gay men's sexual vocabularies, this absence translates into stereotypes of and desires for submissive and receptive Asian partner (Chong-suk, 2007). This white racialization of gay Asian men's sexualities manifests in HIV prevention materials in two prominent ways. First, for a long time Asian men have been outright excluded from HIV prevention efforts—including marketing materials—in the "Western" (North American, western European, and Australian) world (Chng et al., 2003; Sen et al., 2017). As with Black men, this exclusion uses race to essentialize HIV risk in ways determined and driven by the white supremacy of traditional institutions of health. Second, when Asian men are included in HIV prevention materials, this inclusion tends to reproduce the racial hierarchy and ethnosexual stereotypes described here.

In white-dominant countries, models of Asian descent are rarely featured in HIV prevention marketing. Sexual stereotypes of Asian men as unsexual alongside a racialized understanding of these populations as "low risk" for HIV offer compelling explanations for this lack of representation, even though data from the United States highlight the need for their inclusion in prevention initiatives (Centers for Disease Control and Prevention, 2019). Australia is one country that has sought to include greater representation of Asian models, including in a 2016 PrEP campaign called "Be in the Moment." In this ad by ACON (formerly the AIDS Council of NSW), two shirtless models embrace; one racialized as white is positioned to look taller than the model racialized as Asian, the resulting effect that he is (metaphorically and literally) looking down. Also, the Asian model's facial expression signals sexual excess that I read as a visual permission for the white male on the left to act on and consume; the expression is more open and sexual than the white model, who by comparison reads as cool and collected. Further the model racialized as Asian has his arms raised and placed behind his neck, a naturally vulnerable pose that signals openness and submission. This visual analysis is, of course, just one reading of which there are probably countless others. Interestingly, when the editorial team approached ACON for permission to reproduce the ad in this collection, they—in contrast to all other organizations—refused. In one of several conversations about this issue, a member of their team explained their decision thus: "We are not interested in opening ourselves up critiques of racism when all we are trying to do is improve representation." Regardless, this piece is publicly accessible online to anyone interested (https://endinghiv.org.au/wp-content/uploads/2016/07/Be-In-The-Moment.jpg).

I have touched on some racialized dimensions of HIV prevention ads, examples of how the white gaze evokes racial difference and stereotype as sources of desire and curiosity within a larger "colonial fantasy." This fantasy relies on stereotypes produced and reproduced by the white Euro-American imagination, which has carried on fetishizing, exploiting, and commodifying nonwhite peoples since the 15th century (Fusco, 1994; Mercer, 1994; Perez, 2015). To this end, it seems racial alterity is always related to the logic of (white) desire; or, put it differently, desire is always already racialized and thus, predicated on racial power dynamics that are implicit in the workings of the white gaze and its processes of gendering, racializing, and sexualizing. To see this aged and enduring fantasy manifest in HIV prevention marketing is, therefore, not surprising. Indeed, it would be more surprising if this were not the case!

Undoubtedly my interpretation of the racialized dynamics here is influenced by my positionality as a white man from south central Europe and a scholar invested in antiracist work, although perhaps this affords a useful perspective on the subtle ways in which the white gaze shapes HIV prevention materials and how they are ultimately read by (white) consumers. From this perceptive, the primary question I consider below is about strategies to *undesire* the white gaze and *undo* sexual racism in the world of HIV prevention—including marketing. In other words, what are some useful strategies to disrupt the white gaze in HIV prevention so as to ensure the meaningful inclusion of Black and other MSM of color?

Prevention as Consumption

Cultural critic Susan Sontag (1990) argued the marketing of HIV prevention and the consumption of condoms serves the economic interests of and

124   REPRESENTATIONS

strengthens the existing commodity capitalism (that great ideology of white supremacy). The logic of biomedical consumption—focused on marketing condoms, treatment, and PrEP—is, therefore, is an expression of and reinforced by interlocking systems of capitalism, whiteness, and racism, which work together to shape the visual vocabularies of HIV prevention ads geared toward MSM. Thus, it is important we ask questions about the actors involved with creating these materials. Who decides a campaign is needed? Who creates HIV prevention ads? Who is in the room when decisions about the visual aspects are being made? Who has the final say on decision-making? Who pays the bills and sponsors these projects? Who signs off on production? Who decides where campaigns are displayed? And across all of these different actors and contexts, I wonder: what are their racial politics and positionalities?

Prevention campaigns are usually a result of a collaboration between state health agencies, private donors, pharmaceutical companies, and advertising corporations (Cooter & Stein, 2010), which in the North American and western European contexts are almost exclusively run by (and for) white people. Stemming from interlocking systems of white supremacy and other privileges (e.g., cisgenderism), since the early 1980s the work of HIV organizations has followed the priorities of white, able-bodied cisgender, gay men, resulting in very specific prevention modes and modalities, which mainly position MSM as desirable consumers. Historian John D'Emilio's (1993) work is crucial for understanding white gay men as consumers, which frames public health as a matter of individual decision-making and consumption, rather than communal intervention. This point, then, highlights a major problem with HIV prevention marketing: it prioritizes individual behaviors over the systems that give rise to HIV disparities, forefronting a neoliberal model predicated upon notions of consumption, personal responsibility, and choice (Geary 2014; Gossett 2014).

Relatedly, scholar Michael Bronski (2015) argues capitalism has been a crucial force in developing and defining "gay male culture" more broadly. Access to same-sex pleasure, for example, has long been a money-making enterprise through businesses like sex theaters, bars, and bathhouses. Without access to truly public spaces, "gay male culture" and "gay male identity" in the West developed in and through these businesses, which—it bears repeating—are primarily concerned with making money. That such businesses became sociocultural spaces and then later spaces for promotion of HIV prevention is important.

For the communities, cultures, movements, spaces, and public health of Western gay life to be forged in the fires of capitalism—systems that derive from and reinforce colonial ideologies of racism and capitalism—is no small point. These venues emerged during the 1970s as spaces where a sense of gay culture was further developed, while in the 1980s they became venues for promoting HIV prevention. During the proliferation of HIV and AIDS, the advertising of safer sex and condoms landed in an already established gay (nightlife) market. When AIDS organizations started eroticizing condoms, they were building on those markets and associated subcultures, creating alliances with gay bars to display prevention materials. Since contemporary gay male cultures are still heavily informed by the residues of the so-called sexual liberation derived from this period (itself a project defined by the precepts of whiteness), prevention marketing continues to center 20th-century white politics of gay men's pleasure and traditional masculinity as pivotal sites of marketing in HIV prevention.

In considering how racism continues to shape HIV prevention marketing, it is necessary to engage with notions of masculinity. Prior to the first wave of the AIDS crisis, masculinity was used as a backdrop for the creation of post-Stonewall gay male identities; parts of gay male community that displayed traditional masculinity as a base of their identities and presentation embraced a "gay clone" aesthetic that drew heavily on heterosexual working-class occupations and appearances that were all rooted firmly in whiteness (Dean, 2002; Levine, 1998; Mercer, 1994). To achieve desired aesthetics, gay clones replicate attributes of traditional white heterosexual masculinity that rely on multiple racial, gender, and sexual exclusions and hierarchies. Having this backdrop in mind, it is no surprise then that HIV prevention established during the first wave of the epidemic replicates gay clone aesthetics established during the earlier decades.

For instance, the poster "Are You Man Enough?" (1985) (see Figure 6.3), created by the West Hollywood CORE program, portrays a black and white illustration of three figures racialized as white in gear associated with leather culture, including a leather hat, harness, armband, belts, and chaps. Based on their suggestive poses, we could imagine that the scene takes place in a sex club or some other gay men's cruising site. By asking the question in large bold black letters about sufficient masculinity, the ad proposes that safer sex is a "manly" endeavor and that the use of condoms does not endanger but actually enhances one's masculinity and, in turn, their sex appeal. However, the ad also suggests another

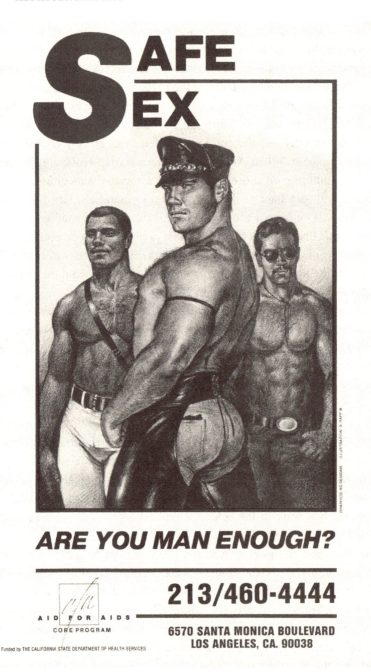

Figure 6.3 "Are You Man Enough?" Aid for AIDS Core Program, West Hollywood (1985).

significant point: some men are not enough and that there is a specific norm when it comes to sufficient masculinity. If such a claim is placed in relation with other prevention ads that include masculinities of different races, it becomes clear that masculinity is always already unmarked and thus white, established as such in relation to other masculinities and racial stereotypes produced by the white gaze, such as overly aggressive Black and Latin men or effeminate Asian men that are either excluded or hypersexualized in clone cultures.

In replicating aesthetics from publications targeted to gay men in the 1970s by employing clone aesthetics, prevention geared toward MSM was thus also fascinated with race as a selling point. According to the sociologist Martin P. Levine (1998), a clone was most often middle-class white man, but men of color and working-class men were often more highly prized for tricks and had a higher currency in clone cultures. Some men of color internalize racial stereotypes to "advertise" themselves in the sexual marketplace (Han, 2021, p. 180), while at the same time they reinforce the power of whiteness and its gaze to sexually consume men of color. I believe such an approach is noted in safer sex ads that centralize interracial desire to market and commodify safer sex.

Resisting the White Gaze, Undoing Sexual Racism

Prevention marketing materials are not the only ways in which HIV and AIDS organizations have struggled to include men of color. Some larger AIDS organizations, including SFAF and the New York City–based Gay Men's Health Crisis (GMHC), have faced criticism over their lack of services for MSM of color, including a lack of outreach to minorities, a lack of recruitment for employees and volunteers of color, and overwhelmingly white-identified leadership structures. White supremacy in HIV activism and service delivery has a long history in the West, with cisgender gay white men consistently directing resources to causes defined by and in support of their politics (Callander et al., 2017). In response to these limitations, many such organizations have explicitly sought to engage communities of color through a range of initiatives. The use of racially diverse explicit sexual imagery has remained a popular strategy, although the tone and tenor of this work has shifted remarkably over time.

128   REPRESENTATIONS

A 1990 poster by SFAF that portrays two nude Black men in an embrace, kissing, while advertising condoms. The text above the image reads "Get Carried Away" and continues below it "With Condoms" (see Figure 6.4). Even more sexually explicit is a poster by the GMHC, "Once, Twice, Thrice: Fierce!" (1991), composed of five photographs depicting two Black men engaging in safer sex using a condom with lubricant (see Figure 6.5). While the men in these campaigns are naked and depicted as explicitly engaged in sexual acts, what is important about these examples is that they also depict moments of intimacy and pleasure. In "Get Carried Away," the men are naked and positioned in an erotic way, but they are embracing in a manner that can be read as tender, while in "Once, Twice, Thrice" although the models are explicitly engaged in sexual acts they are also smiling and embracing in a way that suggests enjoyment, fun, and pleasure. These depictions of intimacy and pleasure stand in sharp contrast with the headless dehumanization of 1984's "YOU CAN HAVE FUN" campaign (see Figure 6.1) and they situate Black men as lovers—including of other Black men—in a way that I read as decentering the white gaze. Thus, through these examples we see it is possible for HIV prevention to be erotized without necessarily manifesting sexual racism.

Of course, such sexualized representation of Black MSM in HIV prevention was not immune to critique, as some perceived these images as harmful for Black men who were already ostracized by the intersectional workings of racism and homophobia (Brier, 2009; Cohen, 1999; Mumford, 2019, p. 187). Working against these partial or nonexistent programs in HIV prevention, in the late 20th century some Black gay men worked to consolidate cultural movements with a mission to reinvent a strong Black gay personhood and reimagine how to relate to one another with respect, care, and affection (Bost, 2019; Cohen 1999; Mumford, 2019). These cultural movements often adopted discourses of "brotherhood." More broadly, the brotherhood approach developed in response to systematic oppression, exploitation, and degradation, and continuous denial of Black men's full access to economic structures of power by white supremacist hierarchies and double-measures (Lemelle, 2010, p. 1; Mumford, 2019, pp. 42, 52–56). In such a climate, Black men turn toward each other to create collectivity based on familial values such as sharing, caring, and respect, as opposed to the hierarchies and competitive spirit that define whiteness. While sexual racism influences how gay men of color relate to one another intimately, writer and revolutionary

UNDESIRING WHITENESS AND UNDOING WHITE GAZE 129

Figure 6.4 "Get Carried Away with Condoms." SFAF (1990).

130 REPRESENTATIONS

Figure 6.5 "Once, Twice, Thrice: Fierce!" GMHC (1991).

Joseph Beam (1986) proclaimed that "Black men loving Black men is the revolutionary action of the 80s" (p. 9), a saying that still mobilizes communities of Black artists and activists today, and the one that has also influenced practices in HIV prevention.

As has been the case with discourses of queer sex and ball cultures, HIV prevention efforts in the United States used vernaculars and discourses of brotherhood to engage men of color (Arnold & Bailey, 2009; Bailey, 2009; Escoffier, 1998). Historian Jennifer Brier (2009) suggests the discourse of brotherhood in HIV prevention "invoke[s] a communal responsibility for AIDS that provided the grounds for men not blaming one another for diseases that they had transmitted, knowingly, unknowingly, or in ignorance of the ultimate consequences" (p. 39). In prevention ads, there have been multiple campaigns that use discourses of brotherly love and depart from explicit sexual imagery to a more vanilla approach that foregrounds familial and traditional values. This effort can be noted in the only two campaigns GMHC made specifically geared toward Black MSM in 1993, as a result of criticism that had to do with lack of services aimed at these populations.

A combination of visuals depicting two Black men in a love clinch combines with discourses of brotherhood in GMHC's safer sex brochure "Brothers Loving Brothers Safely" (see Figure 6.6). Unfortunately, focus group research conducted with men of color in 1993 identified reservations about this campaign. Specifically, participants were concerned with the explicit homoerotic undertones: "It feels it's good for the gay population, but not for the homeboy in Fort Green or Bed Stuy," shared one participant, referring to two Brooklyn neighborhoods commonly populated by people of color (Cohen, 1989). To recuperate poor reception among targeted communities, GMHC published a brochure "Listen Up!" that completely shifts from romantic gestures and envisions "the homeboy" as a targeted audience member. Geared toward "street-smart, inner-city men who are primarily black and [L]atino and homosexually active, ages 18–30," "Listen Up!" embraced hip-hop aesthetics and Black vernaculars to increase resonance with the targeted audiences (see Figure 6.7).

The "Listen Up!" campaign used language like: "So, if you do men, you can fuck, suck, eat ass, whatever. Just do it safely. . . . When fucking, 'doing the nasty,' or 'the wild thang' or whatever you call it, use a condom," "Don't be messing around. Drinking and drugging ain't down," "YO! Be cool. Your mama didn't raise a fool, so protect yourself" (Gay Men's Health Crisis, 1993). Although this brochure departs from sexual imagery that defined much HIV prevention marketing of the time, it still evoked sexualized vocabularies, such as fucking, sucking, eating ass, assuming that sexuality is a major point

132 REPRESENTATIONS

Figure 6.6 A safer sex brochure: "Brothers Loving Brothers Safely." GMHC (1993).

of identity in its targeted audience. However, Latino and Black "homeboys" rarely embrace sexuality as priority, since gayness and whiteness are often synonyms. In addition, while this advertising relies on aesthetics of hip-hop that has been largely consumed both by white audiences and audiences of color, words such as "street-smart" and "inner-city men" read as code-words for Blackness and race overall.

UNDESIRING WHITENESS AND UNDOING WHITE GAZE   133

Figure 6.7 A safer sex brochure: "Listen Up!" GMHC (1993).

As an extension of a tradition that has sought for liberation in promoting affection among Black MSM, there is currently a number of PrEP prevention campaigns that depart from overt sexualizing and instead foreground narratives of romantic and platonic affections. For instance, "Love Your Brotha" (2017) by the Philadelphia Department of Public Health and the marketing agency Better World Advertising, include a close-up image of two men of color, dressed in casual clothing, gazing into the camera. The

134 REPRESENTATIONS

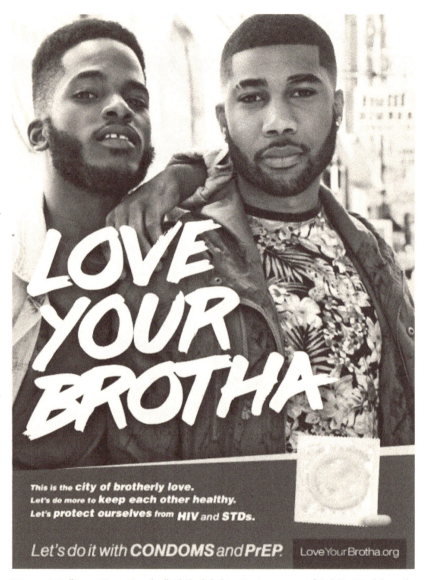

Figure 6.8 "Love Your Brotha." Philadelphia Department of Public Health and Better World Advertising (2017).

text below the photograph urges the spectator to "Love Your Brotha" in "the city of brotherly love" (see Figure 6.8). Unlike marketing boards for HIV marketing in the 1980s and early 1990s, which suffered from predominantly white and male structures (that in turn produced prevention materials with the white gaze as a point of departure), in 2022 the agency Better World Advertising is composed of a diverse group of artists, activists, marketers, communicators, and strategists that out of eight people, included four people of color, including two Black men and a Black woman (Better World Advertising, 2023).

Another variation of the brotherhood discourse is the notion "boo," which is to say a boyfriend and or an admired one. For example, GMHC's campaign "I Love My Boo" (2010) portrays fully dressed Black men from everyday life being affectionate toward one another in a variety of quotidian situations (see Figure 6.9). In a statement accompanying the campaign's release, GHMC highlighted the intentional desexualization: "[r]ather than sexualizing gay relationships, with chiseled bodies and glossy imagery, the beauty of this campaign is that it features intimacy and focuses on what is possible for gay men of color as they boldly and unapologetically express trust, respect and commitment for one another" (Gay Men's Health Crisis, 2010).

Figure 6.9 "I Love My Boo." GMHC (2010).

136   REPRESENTATIONS

Compared with ads from the 1980s and 1990s, more contemporary ads that center discourses of brotherhood may represent a step toward undoing sexual racism in HIV prevention marketing. The brotherhood campaigns that turn away from erotic imagery, strategically mobilize affection as a main site of HIV education and prevention. This visual indexing challenges the demands of the white gaze and recreates the representation of Black men. More importantly it functions as a world-building strategy because it directly foregrounds health, well-being, and holistic care of men of color. In addition, since it has been quite difficult to create an HIV prevention ad that would cover a large variety of MSM groups, including Black men who do not identify as gay or the ones who are turned off by the images of overt sexualization, the brotherhood ads could be observed as a good compromise. However, while one may say these PrEP ads desexualize men of color to reach out to them more successfully, one must also take into consideration that sex is a part of HIV transmission, and to ignore it is to ignore a central part of many people's humanity. Either way, although I have sought to expose and explore how whiteness uses the white gaze to shape HIV prevention, the reality is that avoiding or foregrounding sex in HIV prevention marketing ultimately cannot solve the system-level problem: neoliberally imagined public health, which treats individuals and communities as consumers.

Conclusion: The Antiracist Promise of Desire

This chapter underlines how sexual racism of the white gaze constructs safer sex marketing for MSM in the United States. I have argued that HIV prevention ads geared toward MSM have relied on and reproduced white supremacist notions of gender and sexuality for the pandemic's first 40 years. Put differently, since its beginnings, HIV prevention and management oriented toward MSM has been entirely underwritten by sexual racism and the reproduction of a masculinity defined by whiteness. Moreover, since gay men's cultures have continued to center white masculinity from a much larger historical lineage, its omnipresent focus on images of beefy, well-built men as well as visual practices that commodify and hypersexualize bodies of color in HIV prevention can also tell us something about the nature of (white) gay male culture and their identities overall; they do not exist apart from sexual racism that fuels and makes them a "real" and tangible reality. Or, put differently, if white gay masculinity comes to life by creating hierarchies among masculinities of color, sexual racism mediates these hierarchies and is, therefore, integral to sustaining white supremacy. In this regard, HIV prevention advertising is only one instance that replicates racism as an integral part of longer gay male histories, worldviews, and identities. The question that yet needs to be unpacked is: If the hierarchies of desirability that sexual racism reproduces among different types of masculinities would be diminished, what would happen to white gay masculinity? Since these hierarchies sustain its central and privileged status, would it disappear or, at least, come to a crisis?

Although scholarly reflections can offer intellectual tools for destabilizing the white gaze, operationalizing this in reality is a difficult project. As scholar and artist Coco Fusco (1994) warns us, "psychic investment in [racial stereotypes] does not simply wither away through rationalization" (p. 153). Accordingly, although those of us invested in HIV prevention may understand and consciously work toward undesiring whiteness and undoing sexual racism, we nevertheless still enact racism and, through our labor, reinforce the systems and ideologies from which racism originates. Instead of pure rationalizing then, perhaps desire itself, observed by the scholar Sharon Holland (2012), can lead us toward some answers. As we saw, the work of desire informs large chunks of HIV prevention ads. Regardless of the point of departure, different types of ads, the ones that depict interracial desire or the ones that draw on narratives of brotherhood, are envisioned to foster a psychic investment or response, whether this response be an arousal, affirmation, or solidarity. While desire seems to be a problem, as a major integral part that constitutes a core of gay male identities and it stands as a major mobilizing force in HIV prevention, it cannot be fully dismissed. Desire is messy; it facilitates, enables, and depends on racism, but by that same rationale it can also empower antiracist work, resistance, and consolidation.

Acknowledgments

Beginning its journey as part of a dissertation, this chapter has undergone various transformations and evolved into its current form under the patient guidance of Denton Callander. The author would like to express gratitude to him, as well as other members of the editorial team.

138   REPRESENTATIONS

References

Applebaum, B. (2016). Critical whiteness studies. *Oxford Research Encyclopedias, Education*. Retrieved March 9, 2022, from https://oxfordre.com/education/view/10.1093/acrefore/9780190264093.001.0001/acrefore-9780190264093-e-5

Arnold, E. A., & Bailey, M. M. (2009). Constructing home and family: How the ballroom community supports African American GLBTQ youth in the face of HIV/AIDS. *Journal of Gay and Lesbian Social Services, 21*, 171–188.

Bailey, M. M. (2009). Performance as intravention: Ballroom culture and the politics of HIV/AIDS in Detroit. *Souls, 11*(3), 253–274.

Beam, J. (1986). Caring for each other. *BLACK/OUT: The Magazine of the National Coalition of Black Lesbians and Gays, 1*(1), 9.

Better World Advertising. (n.d.). Who we are. Better World Advertising. Retrieved January 12, 2023, from http://www.socialmarketing.com/who_we_are

Bost, D. (2019). *Evidence of being: The Black gay cultural renaissance and the politics of violence*. University of Chicago Press.

Brier, J. (2009). *Infectious ideas: U.S. political responses to the AIDS crisis*. University of North Carolina Press.

Bronski, M. (2015). *A queer history of the United States*. Beacon.

Callander, D., Holt, M., & Newman, C. (2017). Gay racism. In D. W. Riggs (Ed.), *The psychic life of racism in gay men's communities* (pp. 1–13). Lexington Books.

Cascalheira, C. J., & Smith, B. A. (2020). Hierarchy of desire: Partner preferences and social identities of men who have sex with men on geosocial networks. *Sexuality and Culture, 24*, 630–648.

Centers for Disease Control and Prevention. (2019). *HIV and Asians*. CDCP.

Chng, C. L., Wong, F. Y., Park, R. J., Edberg, M. C. & Lai, D. S. (2003). A model for understanding sexual health among Asian American/Pacific Islander men who have sex with men in the United States. *AIDS Education and Prevention, 15*, 21–38.

Chong-suk, H. (2007). They don't want to cruise your type: Gay men of color and the racial politics of exclusion. *Social Identities, 13*(1), 51–67.

Cohen, C. (1999). *The boundaries of blackness: AIDS and the breakdown of black politics*. University of Chicago Press.

Cohen, M. (1989). *Evaluation of the brochure "Brothers loving brothers safely."* April 25, 1989. Gay Men's Health Crisis records, 1975–1978, 1982–1999 (bulk 1982–1993), New York Public Library, Mss Col 1126, Brochures b. 221 f. 1 Notes on GHMC brochures 1989, 1992–1995.

Cooter, R., & Stein, C. (2010). Visual imagery and epidemics in the twentieth century. In D. Serlin (Ed.), *Imagining illness: Public health and visual culture* (pp. 169–192). University of Minnesota Press.

Crimp, D. (1987). How to have promiscuity in an epidemic. *October, 43*, 237–271.

Dean, T. (2002). Sameness without identity. *Umbr(a): Sameness*, 25–42.

Demens, D. (2014, April 24). The poster that "normalized" gay sex. danieldemens.com. Retrieved April 4, 2020, from http://www.danieldemers.com/The-Poster-That-Normalized-Gay-Sex.php

D'Emilio, J. (1993). Capitalism and gay identity. In H. Abelove, M. A. Barale, & D. M. Halperin (Eds.), *The lesbian and gay studies reader* (pp. 467–476). Routledge.

Dyer, R. (2003). On the matter of whiteness. In C. Fusco (Ed.), *Only skin deep: Changing visions of the American self* (pp. 301–312). International Center of Photography in association with Harry N. Abrams.

Escoffier, J. (1998). The invention of safer sex: Vernacular knowledge, gay politics and HIV prevention. *Berkeley Journal of Sociology, 43*, 1–30.

Fanon, F. (1967). *Black skin, white masks.* Grove.

Fiahlo, A., & Katz, D. (2013). *Safe sex bang.* Center for Sex & Culture Gallery.

Fung, R. (1991). Looking for my penis: The eroticised Asian in gay video porn. In Bad Object–Choices (Ed.), *How do i look? Queer film and video* (pp. 145–168). Bay Press.

Fusco, C. (1994). The other history of intercultural performance. *The Drama Review, 38*(1), 143–167.

Fusco, C. (2003). *Only skin deep: Changing visions of the American self.* Abrams.

Gay Men's Health Crisis. (1993). "Listen up." Gay Men's Health Crisis records, 1975–1978, 1982–1999 (bulk 1982–1993), New York Public Library, Mss Col 1126, b. 220 f. 15 GMHC 1990–1995.

Gay Men's Health Crisis. (2010, September 27). GMHC announces anti-homophobia campaign, "I love my boo," to be in NYC. *The Body.* Retrieved September 30, 2021 from https://www.thebody.com/article/gmhc–announces–anti–homophobia–campaign–i–love–boo–nyc

Geary, A. M (2014). *Antiblack racism and the AIDS epidemic: State intimacies.* Palgrave Macmillan.

Gilman, S. L. (1995). *Picturing health and illness: Images of identity and difference.* Johns Hopkins University Press.

Gossett, C. (2014). We will not rest in peace: AIDS activism, black radicalism, queer and/or trans resistance. In J. Haritaworn, A. Kuntsman, & S. Posocco (Eds), *Queer necropolitics* (pp. 31–50). Routledge.

Han, C. W. (2021). *Racial erotics: Gay men of color, sexual racism, and the politics of desire.* University of Washington Press.

Holland S. P. (2012). *The erotic life of racism.* Duke University Press.

Johnson, E. P. (2003). *Appropriating blackness: Performance and the politics of authenticity.* Duke University Press.

Lemelle, A. J. (2010). *Black masculinity and sexual politics.* Routledge.

Leonard, W., & Mitchell, A. (2000). *The use of sexually explicit materials in HIV/AIDS initiatives targeted at gay men: A guide for educators.* Commonwealth Department of Health and Aged Care, Public Affairs, Parliamentary and Access Branch, Publications Production Unit.

Levine, M. P. (1998). *Gay macho: The life and death of the homosexual clone.* New York University Press.

Mercer, K. (1994). *Welcome to the jungle: New positions in black cultural studies.* Taylor and Francis.

Morris, W. (2016, October 27). Last taboo: Why pop culture just can't deal with Black male sexuality. *New York Times Magazine.* Retrieved November 15, 2022, from https://www.nytimes.com/interactive/2016/10/30/magazine/black–male–sexuality–last–taboo.html

Mumford, K. J. (2019). *Not straight, not white: Black gay men from the march on Washington to the AIDS crisis.* University of North Carolina Press.

Pérez, H. (2015). *A taste for brown bodies: Gay modernity and cosmopolitan desire.* New York University.

Sen, S., et al. (2017). HIV knowledge, risk behavior, stigma, and their impact on HIV testing among Asian American and Pacific Islanders: A review of literature. *Social Work in Public Health, 32*(1), 11–29.

Sontag, S. (1990). *AIDS and its metaphors.* Penguin.

Williams, L. (2004). Skin flicks on the racial border: Pornography, exploitation, and interracial lust. In L. Williams (Ed.), *Porn studies* (pp. 271–308). Duke University Press.

Wilkins, L. C. (2021). Black folk, white gaze: Folklore and Black male precarity. *Journal of Folklore Research, 58*(3), 77–98.

Yancy, G. (2017). *Black bodies, white gazes: The continuing significance of race in America.* Rowman & Littlefield.

7

Amitis Motevalli

Exorcising Orientalism

Anuradha Vikram

Amitis Motevalli is an Iranian-born Los Angeles–based artist, who confronts desire as Othering; embodying and figuring the woman of color as a "problem condition" in a culture that simultaneously lusts for foreign plunder while displaying crippling xenophobia. As an Iranian American, Motevalli occupies a racially ambiguous space as part of a community that has been granted "white" status when it serves the majority, while also racialized in other moments. Legally white yet socially Othered by religious and cultural bias, Motevalli refutes the imperative to assimilate her Iranian American identity into whiteness by deploying disidentifications aligned with what José Esteban Muñoz has described as Vaginal Davis's "terrorist drag," wherein the artists inhabit racialized personas that touch on cross-cultural anxieties and deliberately provoke emotional responses that are often negative (Muñoz, 1999). Motevalli uses multimodal artistic methods, drawing on tropes of sex work, Iranian pop culture, and the history of revolutionary social movements in her reversal of white society's interrogative gaze.

In this text, I will examine works in Motevalli's oeuvre from the perspective foregrounded in this book on sexuality and race, while considering intersecting concerns including gender, class, xenophobia and Islamophobia, and immigration rights. I became aware of her work nearly a decade ago upon moving to Los Angeles to work at 18th Street Arts Center in Santa Monica, where she had participated in a 2011 exhibition that put Iranian American artists alongside artists from Tehran, performing *Baba Karam Lessons* (Figure 7.1). That project, "Postcards from Tehran," was organized with the Aaran Gallery in Tehran and curated by Nazilla Noebashari (2011).

Anuradha Vikram, *Amitis Motevalli* In: *Sexual Racism and Social Justice.* Edited by: Denton Callander, Panteá Farvid, Amir Baradaran, and Thomas A. Vance, Oxford University Press. © Oxford University Press 2024.
DOI: 10.1093/oso/9780197605509.003.0008

Figure 7.1 "Baba Karam Lessons." Amitis Motevalli (2011).

I invited Motevalli to perform at "We the Artists," a celebration of 18th Street Arts Center's 30th anniversary in 2018. We have remained in contact about her work and the intersectional range of concerns that she addresses in her practice.

SWANEA (South and West Asian and North and East African) identity is a complex framework that encompasses people racialized as Black, Brown, and white by Western systems. Politically, this grouping represents a coalition of communities who are impacted by Western Islamophobia in immigration, policing, and hiring/inclusion, whether or not individuals are in fact Muslim. The region includes practitioners of Hinduism, Judaism, Christianity, and Buddhism, although Islam is widespread and predominates in many areas. Within Muslim communities such as the Shi'a majority in contemporary post-Revolution Iran, there are further distinctions, given that the majority of neighboring Arab countries are Sunni-majority as is Pakistan on the South Asian side. Iranians are further distinguished from other SWANEA communities in that they are ethnically distinct from the populations of Arabia, North and East Africa, and South Asia—though each of these different racial groups experiences a version of the same blurring of their ethnic identities within a discourse of white and Black.

Motevalli's work ranges from drawing and painting to interventions in public spaces and in museums. In each, she toys with symbols of race, ethnicity, religiosity, sexual availability, and moral panic. The hijab, an emblem of Muslim women's sexual subjugation for Anglo-Americans, becomes a marker of radical politics in the figure of AK-Ami (2005–2013) (Figure 7.2), which took the form of a series of skills-sharing workshops, street interventions, and performative photo shoots with collaborator Mallika Kubra. AK-Ami wears combat fatigues and sandals, a belt of puka shells, a T-shirt reading "Support Insurgency," and a floral headscarf. She stands defiant atop a pile of construction debris, her hand raised high in a peace sign.

Is the rubble of historical catastrophe on which she stands located in Baghdad, Kabul, or Oakland? In any case, the sexual hysteria wrought by American puritanism has mapped onto the settler colonialist raison d'être, leaving poverty, sexual violence, and ecological destruction in "the wake," as Christina Sharpe describes, "as the conceptual frame of and for living blackness in the diaspora in the still unfolding aftermaths of Atlantic chattel slavery" (Sharpe, 2016). Motevalli was motivated to make this work after witnessing state-sanctioned surveillance of Black and Brown high school students as a teacher in the Los Angeles Unified School

144 REPRESENTATIONS

Figure 7.2 "AK-Ami." Amitis Motevalli (2005–2013).

District from 1999 to 2001 (California Division 3 Second District Court of Appeal, 2004).[1]

In *AK-Ami*, Motevalli dons the hijab—the very garment that white feminists claim SWANEA women must be liberated from, lending social justice credibility to United States military interventions in the region—to embody a radical revolutionary posture in opposition to those interventions and in response to injustices perpetrated on communities of color domestically and abroad. *AK-Ami* is informed by the street activist and community-building principles of the Black Panthers, and by Motevalli's own experiences. Her manifesto reads:

Insurgency in a simple definition is the struggle of a people to defend themselves from dominant oppressors.

Was this picture taken in Baghdad or East LA? In the rubble of Fallujah or Oakland? In the rubbish and destruction of Kabul or New Orleans? Asmara or South Central LA? Port Au Prince or South Side of Chicago? Oaxaca or the Bronx? Housing Projects in France? US?

This is indeed photography of globalized destruction, land being stolen, its people looted and raped. The food, soil and water, toxic and unhealthy. There is a full attempt to erase the cultures that are thriving. This is a neo-colonial urban setting that happens to be El Sereno, California in the US. But here a common struggle is shared with other parts of the earth termed as the "third world." (Motevalli, 2005a)

AK-Ami led workshops and street interventions citing Fanon's maxim, "Decolonization is always a violent phenomenon" (Fanon et al., 2007). Rather than allow herself, a woman of color, to be used by white administrators to enforce a criminalization agenda on Black and Brown students, Motevalli as a teacher for the school district had resisted and aligned with the oppressed. But as a woman of color, and not white, she was already employed in a contingent role that made it easier to silence her. This is increasingly the

---

[1] Motevalli sued Los Angeles Unified School District for wrongful termination on the grounds that her contract at Locke High School in South Central Los Angeles had not been renewed after she twice refused to allow officials to conduct a random weapons search according to District policy, citing the Fourth Amendment protections of her majority Black and Brown students, and instructing the students of their own legal right to refuse the search. The suit was decided in Motevalli's favor by a jury but later dismissed on appeal on the grounds that Motevalli, as a contract employee, had no reasonable expectation of renewal and thus no property interest with which to enforce a claim.

146 REPRESENTATIONS

norm for the education sector, where contingent faculty are more likely to be female-identified and of color while full-time faculty and administrators are overwhelmingly white and largely male, with a disproportionate influence on learning objectives (Whitney & Collins, 2021). AK-Ami's headscarf identifies her visually with "the Other" in a revolutionary posture.

Motevalli's performances of female masculinity are informed by Iranian traditions and the work of feminist artists including Adrian Piper and Eleanor Antin. SWANEA femmes such as Motevalli experience sexual scrutiny according to white standards, examined for deviation from the white aesthetic of beauty (and thus a "good girl") versus nonwhite aesthetic of sexually available and lascivious (and thus a "bad girl," but inherently so, without the liberatory implications that term connotes for white women). Cultural assimilation into whiteness abets a good reputation, a phenomenon that is hypervisible in Motevalli's home city of Los Angeles, where the most visible celebrities and influencers are often white-adjacent (SWANEA examples include Natalie Portman, who is Israeli, and Kim Kardashian, who is Armenian). Meanwhile, Los Angeles is home to enormous Persian, Armenian, and East African diasporic communities who are scarcely represented on the city council or county board of supervisors, and whose concerns are generally ignored by the city's cultural institutions, like those of many immigrants whose contributions are recognized by economic power without commensurate cultural or political visibility.

In Motevalli's work, the threat of latent racialization of "white" women and its counterpart, anxiety about masculine women, are put to provocative use. Her characters resist the rhetoric of male visual pleasure and white feminine purity that has been enacted on the bodies of SWANEA femmes for centuries through conventions such as the art historical form of the Odalisque. In paintings by Gérôme, Sargent, Ingres, Manet, and other 19th-century Euro-American artists, the Odalisque presents a mix of socially acceptable signifiers of white femininity with hypersexualized and Orientalized (Said, 1995) SWANEA characteristics such as yellow-tinged skin, ample hips, and loose hair that contribute to an ornamentalized and objectified reading of their bodies (Cheng, 2019). I will look at how *Stretch Manifesto* (Figure 7.3) adapts the "exotic dancer" uniform of a string bikini and stilettos in surprising ways: stretched across a Hollywood Boulevard intersection or transformed into intricate painted mandalas. *Baba Karam Lessons* (Figure 7.1) diverges from acceptable feminine behavior and presentation with Motevalli adopting the Tehrani "jahel" street tough as a drag archetype to engage audiences in a

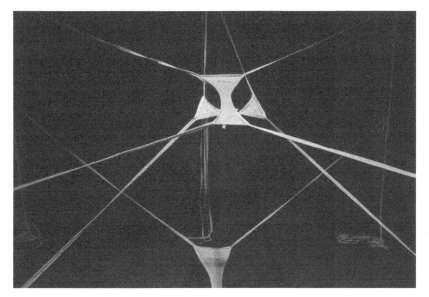

Figure 7.3 "Stretch Manifesto." Amitis Motevalli (2017).

dance-based cultural identity lesson inspired by Adrian Piper's *Funk Lessons*. Another intervention, *The Sand Ninja* (Figures 7.4a–c), is a sexually ambiguous immigrant hustler using sexuality to decolonize nightclubs and galleries. These characters all challenge acceptable social and economic roles for Iranian American women at the intersection of sexuality and whiteness.

Stretch Manifesto: Mahvash, Parivash, and Friends (2017) is a series of drawings and painted works in watercolor on paper, each 52 × 52 inches. Similarly spawned from biographical events, these works refer to Motevalli's experiences as an "exotic dancer" when a college student and recent immigrant in her 20s. In her drawings, Motevalli removes the female body completely so that only the dancer's string bikinis, their acrylic nails, and their stiletto heels appear. The rainbow palette and repeated patterns of these works turn them into mandala-like meditations. Each radiating pattern is named for the women mentioned in a song by Iranian pop singer Jalal Hemati, "Parivash," typical Iranian women's names. The repeating patterns are drawn from mathematical abstractions in Islamic Art. Motevalli explains, "the repetition becomes a metaphor for market and surplus in an industry that commodifies humans but cannot mass manufacture the body through automated means," with the repeated forms signifying the interdependency and endlessness of feminine power (Motevalli, 2017).

148 REPRESENTATIONS

Figure 7.4 "The Sand Ninja., Amitis Motevalli (2005–ongoing).

Figure 7.4 Continued

The very use of the phrase "exotic dancer" when referring to nude dancing, denotes a euphemism that suggests cultural or racial Otherness attached to the performance of sexuality by a body coded feminine. As an Iranian American, Motevalli embodies a classically Caucasian beauty, again both white and not quite, resembling women whose historical standard of beauty was evident before whiteness coalesced into a concept. Though makeup was invented 6,000 years ago by Egyptians, it was trade with Iran that introduced makeup-wearing to Europe, creating hallmarks of femininity that have appeared in the European lexicon for only a few hundred years (Farmanfarmaian, 2000).

Since the onset of the café-concert in late 19th-century France—the precursor to the modern burlesque—anxiety about women's sexual availability, their class, and their proximity to whiteness have been wrapped up in the spectacle of modern leisure. Now that the contemporary strip club and the contemporary dance hall have parted ways, the echo of the café-concert's anxious negotiation of women's labor and their sexual currency remains in the figure of the pole dancer, wrapped up in fantasies of male visual pleasure from the aforementioned French Romantic painters who depicted white

150   REPRESENTATIONS

women in orientalized postures, clothes, and scenarios, as contrast to the ideals of neo-Classicism applied to the female body after the Renaissance.

Motevalli locates her interventions in active spaces where the business of worldly affairs is paramount, creating a dramatic tonal tension between her rituals and the public. If dancing and femininity are at play in *Stretch Manifestos* then dancing and masculinity are put to equally provocative effect in works like *Baba Karam Lessons* (2011/2016/2018) and Motevalli's collaborations with *The Sand Ninja* (2005–ongoing). In these works, the artist performs masculine personas that are distinctly SWANEA-coded, incorporating dark facial hair (mustache, thick eyebrows), exposed and copious body hair (chest, pubic), and a stereotypically lascivious posture when interacting with people in public spaces like the Hammer Museum and the Discostan nightclub. *Baba Karam Lessons'* Amir Khoshgele is a "jahel" or Iranian street tough, and Motevalli's performance of this Iranian cultural convention is in line with a historical performance of what Jack Halberstam has termed "female masculinity" that brings the contours of masculine social conditioning into high relief (Halberstam, 2019). Appropriating the form of Adrian Piper's iconic *Funk Lessons* (1983), in which Piper taught an audience of non-Black people at the University of California, Berkeley, how to hear, appreciate, and dance to funk music, Motevalli extended the engagement she was invited to bring to the museum's interior into the street where the museum typically does not interact with members of the large and active Iranian immigrant community of Westwood. Outside the Hammer Museum's Piper retrospective, Baba Karam interacted with passers-by and patrons of Iranian American establishments as well as with museumgoers.

The Sand Ninja is "a diasporic warrior hailing from Ninjastan who fights against neo-colonialism" but she is also "a professional Gold Digger" whose schtick is an endless financial hustle (Motevalli, 2005b). *Decolonize Your Brow* (2006–2010) saw The Sand Ninja distributing unibrows to decolonize faces while sharing information about privatization of land and its role in promoting homelessness and poverty while criminalizing both. *Ninjastan Takeover* at Discostan was a collaboration with Iranian American fashion designer Hushi (Hushidar Mortezaie) involving a team of SWANEA dancers to bring the queer tradition of House and Ball together with Iranian *Roo hozi*, the tradition of street music and dance that produced the "jahel" or Baba Karam (Motevalli, 2005b). The Sand Ninja's mixture of masculine and feminine attributes recalls Eleanor Antin's *The King of Solana Beach* (1974) performances in the suburbs north of San Diego, in which she dressed in a beard and cloak to perform authority and chivalry in interactions with the public, meanwhile maintaining certain feminine attributes such as her physique, voice, and elements of her demeanor. Sporting a prominent unibrow and a thatch of thick pubic hair (often worn over a unitard), The Sand Ninja performs a sexually aggressive posture while mixing up feminine and masculine visual signals to comical effect. The Sand Ninja provokes anxiety precisely because of the blend of archetypes that Motevalli invokes, calling up the sexual agency and desirability of older women with her lack of body shame and her suggestive movements, as well as triggering the fear and social denial of female sexual aggression.

The Sand Ninja is more than a character, more like a rogue agent of the self. Masculine feminism, racial ambiguity, and sexual license in one package can be too much for audience members whose values are oriented toward white acceptability and masculine dominance. In one such instance, Motevalli shared with me an experience of being heckled by an older white male artist at the Hammer, a peer, and while she appears taken aback if amiable in video, documentation of the performance reports him becoming verbally aggressive after the tape stopped running. This reaction from a colleague reflects a discomfort even on the part of white allies with Motevalli's disidentificatory action, what José Esteban Muñoz describes when writing on Vaginal Davis as being "able to enact a certain misrecognition that let me imagine myself as something other than queer or racialized." Muñoz articulates how the subject assimilated into whiteness finds it seductive, albeit taxing, to live under this delusion and "withstand the identity-eroding effects of normativity" (Muñoz, 1999). Motevalli's work is informed by her teenage friendship with Vaginal Davis,[2] and they share a capacity to consistently provoke strong responses by highlighting unspoken power dynamics within social relations in public that many people would prefer not to see. While this kind of performance may appear on its surface to play to racist stereotypes, Muñoz argues that they are instead "restructured (yet not cleansed) so that they present newly imagined notions of the self and the social" (Muñoz, 1999). Muñoz goes on to state that this behavior interrogates presumptions of racial "passing" as preferable and desirable to produce a cultural politics in contrast to white norms and expectations.

---

[2] Motevalli has been informed by artists including Ron Athey and Vaginal Davis, both of whom she met in the 1990s when they performed at the legendary Club FUCK! in Los Angeles. Performers at the club included notorious "supermasochist" Bob Flanagan, queer photographer Catherine Opie, and trans porn actor Buck Angel. For more information see "Club FUCK! at Basgo's Disco," ONE Archives via https://one.usc.edu/archive-location/club-fuck-basgos-disco

Motevalli is an exuberant performer, but she is not afraid to "harsh" a party vibe. Her third performance for Discostan, a SWANEA-centered nightclub event in Los Angeles, in August 2019 was timed to coincide with the Muslim festival of Muharram commemorating the martyrdom of the prophet Husayn. She modeled her performances on observances of Ashura, the festival that commemorates the tenth day of the Muslim month of Muharram. In *Ruquyya's Reverberation* (Figure 7.5), Motevalli underwent the self-flagellation ritual

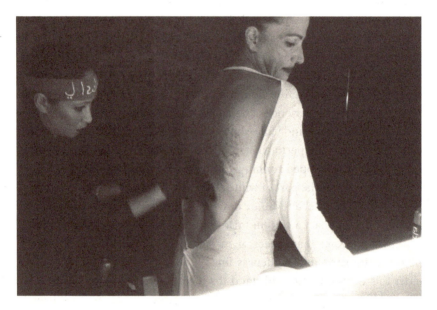

Figure 7.5 "Ruquyya's Reverberation." Amitis Motevalli (2019).

practiced by Shi'a men (and usually not women) with the *zanjeer* or chain flogger, combining religious ritual with BDSM practice in a queering action that reversed the energy flows of the midnight party. Dressed in white, the artist occupied a position within the ritual that is historically forbidden to women and is traditionally performed in private. The severity of her undertaking was out of place in the party setting and provoked controversy even within the largely SWANEA, mixed-gender, and queer-friendly crowd. Some partygoers felt that her relocation of a religious ritual was disrespectful to religion, while others were affronted by the introduction of faith into a space deemed secular and hedonistic.

This work is part of *Golestan Revisited* along with *Masoul*, a performance at Track 16 Gallery in November 2019 for which the artist used her own blood, drawn by a phlebotomist, as ink to paint on a window in a ritual of "self-humiliation as ablution" (Motevalli, 2019). Bathing and shame are interlinked in ritual as in these works, where Motevalli accepts abjection and pain into her own body in an attempt to spare others who are targeted for their distance from patriarchal standards and expectations. Through *Golestan Revisited* Motevalli addressed the history of roses that were imported from west Asia into Europe along with Islamic garden culture during the Crusades, resulting in Anglicization of the names and uses of plants such as *Rosa gallica* ("French rose" in Latin) which was historically cultivated and used in contemporary Iraq, Iran, Afghanistan, Lebanon, and Syria (Figure 7.6). Indeed, both roses and textiles in the West retain the name "Damask" for Damascus, the siege of which resulted in their importation. Motevalli surreptitiously introduced alternative nomenclatures into ornamental gardens around Los Angeles, renaming roses with historic ties to the Middle East with the names of SWANEA femmes killed by neocolonial violence. While many of her performances involve costuming and exaggerated archetypes, the Golestan performances are subdued and mournful. Motevalli performs the Golestan works as acts of memory and resistance to commemorate SWANEA femmes killed by United States imperialism as well as by normalized sexual violence. She locates her critique in the West while also pointing criticism toward SWANEA countries where patriarchy has been fostered and abetted by imperialist aims.

Motevalli is developing a multimedia online database, for which she was awarded a Creative Capital Grant in 2020, containing roses renamed to commemorate women, girls, and femmes who were murdered during occupations of their sovereign territories by Western imperialists or Islamic reactionaries in recent decades. The Golestan project reframes the narratives of "honor killings" and "collateral damage" to foreground the

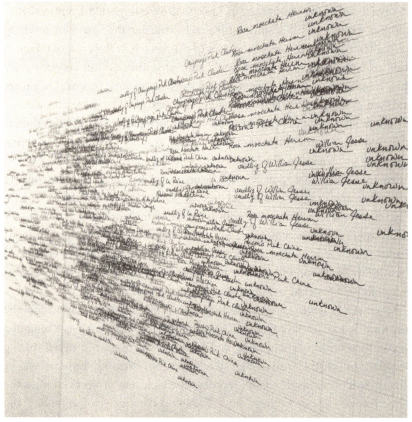

Figure 7.6 "Rosa gallica." Amitis Motevalli (2019).

women, often young, on whose bodies wars of domination and attrition are fought. "Golestan" is a Farsi word meaning "land of the flowers," and refers to the title of a 13th-century poetry collection, *The Gulistan of Sa'adi* (1258 CE). In contemporary Iran, the name Golestan refers to a city, a province, and a palace in Tehran, the latter of which was originally built in the 14th century and makes use of a traditional Islamic walled garden compound design that uses water channels and fountain elements as both irrigation and air conditioning. These innovations were appropriated into European architecture (Pastore, 2017) while the societies that developed them were characterized as barbaric and alien by the church. Women, like roses, were the spoils.

Women, especially young women, specifically young women who have been killed by more powerful men, are not often deemed worthy of public attention (Alter, 2015). As Sa'adi says to his companion, "Thou knowest that the roses of the garden are perishable and the season passes away, and philosophers have said: 'Whatever is not of long duration is not to be cherished'" (Shirzi, 1258). Deviating from this lack of philosophical interest in the figure of the Young-Girl is Tiqqun, the French radical collective who propose that the Young-Girl as a cultural archetype is both radically conformist and immanently radical. For Tiqqun, this contradiction in terms is the condition of present-day digital capitalism, in which affective labor and emotional appeasement become currencies with which to barter one's labor and engage with commodity markets that increasingly operate on speculative grounds. The Young-Girl need not actually be young, nor necessarily a girl:

> What's paradoxical about the masculine Young-Girl is that he's the product of a kind of "alienation by contagion." Though the feminine Young-Girl appears as the incarnation of a certain alienated masculine imagination, the alienation of this incarnation has nothing imaginary about it. She's concretely escaped those whose fantasies she populated in order to stand up against and dominate them. To the extent that the Young-Girl is emancipated, blossoms, and proliferates, she's a dream that turns into a most invasive nightmare. It's the freed slave returning as such to tyrannize the former master. In the end we're watching an ironic epilogue where the "masculine sex" is the victim and object of its own alienated desires. (Tiqqun, 2012)

In that she embodies global capitalism's conflation of youth, sexuality, and commodity fetishism, the Young-Girl is imprisoned by the limitations of her

156 REPRESENTATIONS

role—but in turn, any transgression of those limits represents the potential to overthrow them completely. Motevalli's work toys with this line between constraint and overthrow. Initially, *Golestan Revisited* was conceived as a response to the killing of a 26-year-old French Muslim woman of Moroccan heritage, Hasna Aït Boulahcen. Boulahcen was falsely accused by Parisian police of being a suicide bomber associated with the Bataclan nightclub attack in the press that accompanied her death during the Saint-Denis Raid in November 2015 (Osborne, 2015). Women like Boulahcen are caught between dueling and equally implacable sets of expectations, all prompted by the central role that they play in social reproduction in patriarchal societies, which give them little agency in legal, economic, or political terms but substantial responsibility for home, children, and social welfare.[3] This conflict, according to Tiqqun, gives society cause to understand the Young-Girl as perpetually a martyr, "a stranger to her own desires" who chooses neither debauchery or chastity, merely regulates her needs and wants according to the coherence of the "commodity Super-Ego" (Tiqqun, 2012). In the media narrative, Boulahcen's agency with respect to her faith, her cultural identity, and her sexuality is erased. The Western portrayal of her tragedy positions women of color as victims of their own desires and of the demands of their fathers, brothers, and cousins, who control their mobility and indoctrinate them. Her impossible choice is framed as inevitable in the context of a permanent and intractable war between the medieval East and the commoditized West.

Motevalli used her blood again to handpaint roses and the names of the martyred women and femmes onto the window of venerable performance art venue LACE on Hollywood Boulevard, at midnight, in *An Offering of Honor* (2020), a commemoration of the Shi'a festival of Ashura in the month of August (Figure 7.7). A drummer and vocalist performed a song of mourning for the women as the artist worked through the night, dressed in a green jumpsuit and bandanna to acknowledge her labor as well as the

---

[3] Boulahcen, like many young women whose families emigrated to France from North Africa in the wake of French colonization, has been described as caught between cultures. Friends and neighbors claimed she was sexually forward and highly social, assimilated into white French Young-Girl culture to the degree that she was viewed with some suspicion. Following the attack on the editorial offices of *Charlie Hebdo* magazine on January 15, Boulahcen was said to have changed track, starting to wear hijab and study the Quran. After she was killed when police raided her apartment in search of her cousin Abdelhamid Abaaoud—a suspect in the Bataclan attack—a significant effort was made in the French and British press to portray Boulahcen's shift toward Islamic values as evidence of her involvement in a terrorist conspiracy.

EXORCISING ORIENTALISM 157

Figure 7.7 "An Offering of Honor." Amitis Motevalli (2020).

Iranian Green democracy movement (Daragahi, 2019). The hour-long performance was filmed and was visible from the street through the windows of the closed gallery. Although the culture of Hollywood Boulevard is generally lively until the early hours of morning, COVID-19 had temporarily dampened the flow. This served the somber and meditative tone and magnified the message of mourning for victims of United States aggression overseas at a moment when the failures of racial supremacy and patriarchal leadership were very much on display internationally with respect to the pandemic (Ganguly et al., 2021).

A third Ashura ritual originally planned for August 2021 was stymied by COVID, however Motevalli continued her rituals of mourning that year with *Borrowing Authority from Death* (October 7, 2021) (Figure 7.8), realized at the Leslie-Lohman Museum of Art in lower Manhattan on the anniversary of the United States invasion of Afghanistan following the events of September 11, 2001. In this performance, Motevalli wore a long black dress with her back exposed, and a headdress that she designed with the artist Parisa Parnian and fabricated with consultancy In Favor Of to help her turn her body into a "walking altar" or "alam" memorializing the dead. As with the self-flagellation ritual, Motevalli here used physical pain as a medium and a metaphor, working with the BDSM practitioner Domina Dia Dynasty to pin the "burdens" of the artist's community to her back.

As an aside, Motevalli's use of piercing and the culture that enables it is informed by the Modern Primitives movement popularized by Fakir Musafar, a white American man who studied non-Western body modification and tattooing practices extensively and shared them with Americans

Figure 7.8 "Borrowing Authority from Death." Amitis Motevalli (2021).

in the 1970s and 1980s. Modern Primitives are people of all races who use piercing and tattooing to signify rejection of white European norms and values. Often, they are seekers of transcendental mental states, brought on by experiences of pain or exertion that cause the mind to disassociate from the body. Frequently, they also practice BDSM or nonconventional sexual practices. Modern Primitives have influenced the culture of Burning Man and the aesthetics of alternative rock, two popular outlets for releasing the internalized repression of white culture. The radical queer sensibility of these cultural movements is present throughout Motevalli's oeuvre, particularly in her works that test audience expectations of public and private, or gendered behavior (Vale & Juno, 1989).

Returning to my primary point, Amitis Motevalli's oeuvre is deeply informed by an ethic of social justice that calls the artist to position herself as a target or foil for the social violence of normalization in order to deflect that violence away from others who are more vulnerable to the harm, and less able to withstand the pain. As I have shown in my discussion of *AK-Ami*, her work is rooted in cross-racial solidarity with Black and Brown communities. I addressed Motevalli's skillful use of sexual attraction and repulsion as a disidentificatory strategy in *Stretch Manifestos*, *Baba Karam Lessons*, and *The Sand Ninja*. In considering the Ashura performances that she created for the *Golestan Revisited* project, I explored how her work connects gender segregation within Shi'a Islam and gendered justifications for Western imperialism directed against Muslim countries. That project highlights how not only people but also plants and ideas can be assimilated into whiteness and their historical origins lost.

As an Iranian emigree, Motevalli can openly critique both Western and SWANEA cultural beliefs and practices with less threat of violence than her peers in Iran might experience. As a queer femme with cisgender and beauty privilege, she can both embody and dismantle social expectations around femininity, race, and sexual availability and thereby queer public space. This freedom is also a responsibility that Motevalli feels toward poor communities of color in the United States who are similarly threatened with extreme violence, often by the state. She fulfills that responsibility by extending a simultaneous invitation and challenge to her audiences, occupying a performative space that is half libertine, half killjoy. By activating, confronting, and questioning our desires, Amitis Motevalli's performances and installations lay a foundation for undesiring whiteness.

160   REPRESENTATIONS

References

Alter, C. (2015). Someone is finally starting to count "femicides." *TIME*. Time Publishing. Retrieved February 23, 2023, from https://time.com/3670126/femicides-turkey-women-murders/

California Division 3 Second District Court of Appeal. (2004). Motevalli v. Los Angeles Unified School District. Retrieved February 23, 2024, from https://caselaw.findlaw.com/ca-court-of-appeal/1010302.html

Cheng, A. A. (2019). *Ornamentalism*. Oxford University Press.

Daragahi, B. (2019). *A decade after Iran's green movement, some lessons*. Atlantic Council. Retrieved February 23, 2023, from https://www.atlanticcouncil.org/blogs/iransource/a-decade-after-iran-s-green-movement-some-lessons/

Fanon, F. (2007). *The wretched of the earth*. (R. Philcox, Trans.). Grove Atlantic.

Farmanfarmaian, F. S. (2000). Haft Qalam Arayish: Cosmetics in the Iranian world. *Iranian Studies, 33*(3–4), 285–326.

Ganguly, S., Chin, D., King, E., Mssard da Fonseca, E., Vargas, F., & Greer, S. (2021). World's worst pandemic leaders: 5 presidents and prime ministers who badly mishandled COVID-19. *The Conversation*. Retrieved February 23, 2023 from https://theconversation.com/worlds-worst-pandemic-leaders-5-presidents-and-prime-ministers-who-badly-mishandled-covid-19-159787

Halberstam, J. (2019). *Female masculinity*. Duke University Press.

Motevalli, A. (2005a). *AK-Ami 2005-2013*. Amitis Motevalli. Retrieved February 23, 2023, from http://amitismotevalli.com/#/ak-ami/

Motevalli, A. (2005b). *The sand ninja (2005-present)*. Amitis Motevalli. Retrieved February 23, 2023, from http://amitismotevalli.com/#/the-sand-ninja-1/

Motevalli, A. (2017). *Stretch manifesto: Mahvash, Parivash, and friends*. Amitis Motevalli. Retrieved February 23, 2023, from http://amitismotevalli.com/#/stretch-manifesto/

Motevalli, A. (2019). *Golestan revisited: Performances*. Amitis Motevalli. Retrieved February 23, 2023, from http://amitismotevalli.com/#/golestan-revisited-performances-masoul-and-ruquyyas-reverberation/

Muñoz, J. E. (1999). *Disidentifications: Queers of color and the performance of politics*. University of Minnesota Press.

Noebashari, N. (2011). *Postcards from Tehran: Exhibition at the 18th Street Arts Center*. 18th Street Arts Center. Retrieved February 23, 2023 from https://18thstreet.org/postcards-from-tehran

Osborne, S. (2015). Hasna Ait Boulahcen—Europe's first female suicide bomber—"did not blow herself up." *The Independent*. Retrieved February 23, 2023, from https://www.independent.co.uk/news/world/europe/isis-paris-attacks-hasna-ait-boulahcen-did-not-blow-herself-saint-denis-raid-a6742666.html

Pastore, C. (2017). *Embracing the other: Venetian garden design, early modern travellers, and the Islamic landscape* (Vol. 7). Pennsylvania State University Press.

Said, E. W. (1995). *Orientalism*. Penguin Group Publishing.

Sharpe, C. (2016). *In the wake: On Blackness and being*. Duke University Press.

Shirzi, G. S. (1258). *The Gulistan of Sa'di*. (M. U. Chand, Trans., 2013). Retrieved February 23, 2023, from https://ia800403.us.archive.org/10/items/GulistanSaadiShirziPersianTextEnglishTranslation/Gulistan%20Saadi%20Shirzi%20Persian%20text%20English%20Translation.pdf

Tiqqun. (2012). *Preliminary materials for a theory of the young-girl* (A Reines., Trans.). MIT Press.

Vale, V., & Juno, A. (1989). *Modern primitives: Tattoo, piercing, scarification: An investigation of contemporary adornment and ritual.* V/Search.

Whitney, R., & Collins, J. D. (2021). Advancing racial equity in leadership education: Centering marginalized institutional contexts. *New Directions in Student Leadership, 2021,* 7–13.

Shea Butter and Honey

Ilannah Deshazier

Together we lied, vulnerable, your limbs wound around mine. Our skin glistened in the moonlight, pressed together amidst the Manhattan heat. My dorm room's twin-sized bed left no room for diffidence.

Your green eyes roamed over my dark skin assiduously, analyzing every crevice of my body. I cowered slightly under your gaze, afraid of your scrutiny, reliving the scrutiny of those before you.

Are my eyes too brown? Is my nose too big? Are my lips too full?

You never liked to talk much. My inquisitions about your day rolled off your shoulders carrying little weight. You'd huff out a bit of air, giving me a small smirk before proceeding to lead me to bed. If I were to imagine what you were thinking in that moment, you'd say, "How naïve."

After all, it was 3AM.

A shiver ran through my spine as your left hand carefully found its way to my right thigh, slowly moving upwards. Over the curve of my hips, over my stretch marks, through the valleys and trenches of my torso, up my shoulder, and finally dipping down to my neck, pushing my curls out of your way.

"I've never been with a black girl," you said.

And so he speaks. And your silence was never more welcomed.

I wish you hadn't been another person to say this to me. To say this in my bed. My bed of acceptance and comfort. My bed that engulfs my existence graciously and without delay. You held me in your arms, doting on my greatest success being my black notch in your white headboard. Should I be grateful for that?

POETRY INTERLUDE: SHEA BUTTER AND HONEY   163

Your eyes continued to roam. Slow, beguiled.

Is it lust?

Maybe it's amusement. Is this what you were looking for? The darkness of my flesh to shield yourself from the brightness of my soul?

You twisted your fingers through my curls, breathing into the bottom of your lungs. I didn't speak. I didn't protest.

"Your hair is so soft," you said. "It smells godly." As if you weren't in the presence of one.

"I know."

It's shea butter and honey.

SECTION III
LIVED REALITIES

8

"You Just Got to Own It"

Māori Girls Un/Doing Settler Colonial Sexuality in Aotearoa

Fern Smith and Jade Le Grice

Introduction

Māori girls' contemporary sexualities are shaped through an interface between gender, culture, and settler-colonialism. Settler-colonialism has had devastating effects on Indigenous communities throughout the world—dispossessing Indigenous lands, attempting to erase Indigenous cultures, systems of social control and sovereignty, and instating settler-colonial political and social systems (Avin et al., 2013). In Aotearoa New Zealand, the sexualized racism of Māori girls and women is premised on this wider settler-colonial context, where the land has literally been stripped from underneath our feet. The undermining of Māori women's *rangatiratanga* (leadership) cohered with the removal of land, and disruption to Māori cultural ways of knowing and being that conveyed roles and status of *mana wāhine* (dignity of women) (Dobbs, 2021; Le Grice, 2014; Mikaere, 1994).

While girls' experiences of (hetero)sexuality are permeably shaped by misogyny and sexism (Gavey, 2019), Māori girls' experiences are also interlaced with settler-colonialism (Smith, 1999), racism (Moewaka-Barnes, 2010), and racialized sexism (Le Grice, 2018). Here, the dominance of settler-colonial representations of sexuality, and of Māori sexuality in particular, influence, infiltrate, and elide Māori sexualities informed by Māori cultural ways of knowing and being. While (hetero)sexism, misogyny, Western norms, and Christian values have become imbricated into contemporary Māori girls' experiences, drawing parallels with Pākehā girls, their experiences foreground unique challenges, nuances, and tensions. Often characterized as "at-risk" of unintended young pregnancy, abortion, and sexually transmitted infections (STIs) (Green, 2011), Māori girls' sexualities are often subject to

Fern Smith and Jade Le Grice, *"You Just Got to Own It"* In: *Sexual Racism and Social Justice.* Edited by: Denton Callander, Panteá Farvid, Amir Baradaran, and Thomas A. Vance, Oxford University Press. © Oxford University Press 2024. DOI: 10.1093/oso/9780197605509.003.0009

168 LIVED REALITIES

greater public scrutiny, in ways that restrict their sexual agency. Navigating through these complex sociocultural junctures, some contexts may yield positive sexual possibilities for Māori women and girls, only to become unwritten and undone by dominant settler-colonial narratives about Māori (Le Grice, 2018).

Writing as Māori women, we seek to unravel, and make visible, the influence of settler-colonialism on Māori girls' sexual subjectivities in contemporary sociocultural contexts. Yet, we also seek to delve beyond pathologizing settler-colonial narratives, and center Māori cultural ways of knowing and being to shore up space for Māori girls' *rangatiratanga* and sexual agency—supporting Māori girls to understand themselves, and their sexual subjectivities as significant, full of potential, and knowable beyond the restraints of settler-colonial sociocultural contexts.

The Settler-Colonial Context in Aotearoa: A Brief Note

Integral to the colonialization of Māori by British settlers was the violation of the relationship formalized through Te Tiriti o Waitangi and the Treaty of Waitangi, in 1840. Often referred to as our founding document, Te Tiriti o Waitangi—signed by Māori and British, was written by Māori, with the intention of maintaining Māori *rangatiratanga* (authority) over their people and lands, while allowing the British to rule over their own population. However, the English version, The Treaty of Waitangi, was composed by British settlers with the aim of seizing sovereignty over Māori and their land. Despite discrepancies between these treaties, the signings carved the way for British systems of governance and the marginalization of Māori (Kingi, 2006). After the signings, Māori faced warfare, confiscation and forced sale of lands, and a depleted population (Taonui, 2010). As a corollary, the introduction of missionary schooling, assimilationist policies, and churches entrenched Western ideological structures that were inherently distinct from Māori knowledge and culture (Pihama, 2018).

The undermining of Māori political sovereignty by British settlers extended further to undermining Māori epistemologies and ontologies. While Māori scholars have emphasized ongoing flexibility and fluidity in Māori systems of gender and relational intimacy (Le Grice & Braun, 2017; Pihama et al., 2016; Pihama & McRoberts, 2009), settler-colonialism has exerted impacts on Māori cultural life with Christian religion influencing

Māori sexualities toward rigid and fixed possibilities premised on moralism (Le Grice & Braun, 2018). Settler-colonial depictions of Māori women positioned them as immoral, sexually promiscuous, and readily available to please the sexual appetite of male settlers (Wanhalla, 2011). This is reflected in the ways settlers photographed them in the early 20th century: as sexually inviting through the strategic showing of bare skin, intrinsically violent through the inclusion of traditional and colonial weapons, and as commodified objects through erasing their names and identities (Hudson, 2010).

Māori histories highlight that sexual and gendered diversity were a significant and ordinary aspect of precolonial society (Kerekere, 2017; Te Awekotutu, 1991). Sex and sexuality were spoken about with openness, and visible in precolonial carvings and artwork (Le Grice & Braun, 2018; Pihama & McRoberts, 2009). However, Māori histories have been altered and retold in ways to resemble European cultural mores—including (hetero)sexuality and women's submission to men's authority (Kerekere, 2017; Le Grice, 2018). Christian sexual discourses have influenced some Māori to redefine conversations about sex and sexuality as *tapu*—as too "sacred" to talk about, essentially cloaking these conversations in silence and secrecy (Le Grice & Braun, 2018; Pihama & McRoberts, 2009).

Legacy of Euro-Western Values: Gender and (Hetero)Sexuality

Settler-colonialism created sociocultural contexts that have normalized and naturalized (hetero)sexuality and associated gender binaries, shaping and imbricating these into Māori women and girls' lives (Johnston & Pihama, 1994). In contemporary times, (hetero)sexuality is a pervasive institution (Farvid, 2015; Jackson & Cram, 2003), premised on gender stratification and "social relations between men and women" (Jackson & Scott, 2010, p. 82). Through everyday routine practices, (hetero)sexuality structures normative behavioral expectations for men and women that are reproduced in social interactions (Jackson & Scott, 2010; Pickens & Braun, 2018). It not only assumes (hetero)sexual relationships are natural, but simultaneously assumes gender is restricted to two dichotomous groups— men and women, who have natural and complementary differences (Pickens & Braun, 2018).

170 LIVED REALITIES

Unpacking these gender expectations, discourses shape the organization of (hetero)sexual relationships where men are expected to be always desiring sex, and women are expected to instrumentally use sex to acquire a committed (hetero)sexual relationship with little desire of their own (Farvid, 2015; Foucault, 1982; Gavey, 2019; Hollway, 1989). Together, these discourses scaffold sex around an active masculine subject and a passive feminine subject (Pickens & Braun, 2018). In contemporary sociocultural contexts, these contradictory discourses scaffold a complicated terrain for women and girls to navigate, and experience their sexuality, within. Despite greater social acceptability for women to participate in casual (hetero)sex, the sexual pleasure of men remains centered, while the sexual behaviors of women are subject to scrutiny (Gavey, 2019).

Here, the sexual subjectivities, and sexual decisions of women and girls remain monitored, policed, and controlled through the proliferation of sexual double standards (Farvid et al., 2017). As an example, sexual double standards, underpinned by a sense of male entitlement, are apparent in the context of sending partial or full nude images. Here, boys and men can feel entitled to consume girls' sexualized images, and expect sexual compliance from girls, while simultaneously shaming them for transgressing feminine norms if their nudes become public (Bindesbøl Holm Johansen et al., 2019; Ringrose et al., 2021). Characteristic of a misogynistic system, contemporary sexual double standards evaluate and judge the sexual behaviors and attitudes of women more harshly than men—controlling and restricting the sexual possibilities for women (Gavey, 2019).

For girls in high school, their popularity can be linked to how well they navigate sexual double standards, through appearing as "desirable but not desiring" (Reid et al., 2011, p. 549). Not only are the sexual behaviors of girls monitored, but so are their appearances and attitudes (Farvid et al., 2017). For women and girls of color, they are positioned even further away from a desirable subject position due to their distance from whiteness. Here, "good" and "proper" femininity is synonymous with whiteness and is premised on the abjection of Black women's bodies (Ringrose et al., 2019). Unfortunately, if they deviate too far from femininity, rather than being considered a "victim" sexual double standards and neoliberal logic position them as responsible agents, essentially locating their "bad choices" as personal shortcomings (Bay-Cheng, 2015; Chmielewski et al., 2017). For Indigenous girls, departures from femininity can be met with heighted apathy and social harm (Le Grice, 2018).

Māori Approaches to Gender and Sexuality

Sociocultural meanings of women and girls in *te ao Māori* (the Māori world) highlight their unique *mana* (dignity, prestige) and *tapu* (sacredness, under protection) (Dobbs, 2021). Rangimarie Rose Pere (as cited in Murphy, 2011) describes *mātauranga* (Māori knowledge and wisdom) pertaining to menstruation, whereby Māori women are incredibly tapu while menstruating, conveying a connection to their *whakapapa* (ancestors) and *atua* (Gods). *Te awa atua* (menstrual blood) is considered highly potent with powerful spiritual and protective qualities. Historically, Māori women held the capacity to spiritually shield their *whānau* (extended family), *hapū* (subtribe) and *iwi* (tribal groupings) from danger and instill them *all* with strength and courage (Murphy, 2011).

The unique *mana* and *tapu* of Māori women in *te ao Māori* also extends to leadership, creative, and knowledge-bearing roles (Le Grice, 2014; Simmonds, 2009; Smith, 2015). Historically, Māori women occupied positions of leadership within *hapū* and *iwi* (Webber & O'Connor, 2019), spiritual and military roles (Murphy, 2011) and across political and educational domains (Mikaere, 1994). In contemporary times, Māori women continue to be key forces behind many social movements, as well as land occupation movements that call for the return of stolen *whenua* (Rowe, 2019).

Māori women are the central thread of Māori society and much of our power, strength and wisdom is derived from being keepers of *te whare tangata* (Le Grice, 2014), an embodiment of the womb, literally translated as the house of humanity (Mikaere, 2003). Through divine authority, our unique *tapu* permits access to physical and spiritual worlds (Gabel, 2019). As a corollary, Māori women are revered for our ability to create life and nourish the next generation of a *whakapapa* continuum (descendants of a particular kin group) (Le Grice & Braun, 2017; Smith, 2015). Protecting the sanctity of *te whare tangata* is of paramount importance in Māori society (Norman, 1992; Pihama et al., 2016), distilling unparallel significance onto Māori women (Le Grice, 2014).

These knowledges and histories provide a powerful cultural template for girls and women to understand their own inherent dignity and *tapu*. Understanding girls and women as *tapu*, as "aligned to the moon and earth, and as keepers of te whare tangata" (Moewaka-Barnes, 2010, p. 33), denotes a level of respect and care that is ordinary yet expected in Māori cultural contexts. Importantly, these understandings represent a departure from dominant (hetero)sexuality that limits, confines, and marginalizes. After

172   LIVED REALITIES

drawing out the ways (hetero)sexuality, Christian moralism, and racism structure experiences of harm for Māori girls in sociocultural contexts, this chapter then seeks to consider how Māori cultural ways of knowing and being can structure more expansive and fulfilling sexual possibilities. By supporting Māori girls to stand in their own *mana*, *mātauranga* can provide Māori girls with a sense of safety to negotiate the gendered and racialized harm they experience.

Method

Our project drew from a *kaupapa Māori* research methodology, derived from a theoretical approach that was developed within the praxis of Māori schooling (Smith, 1997) and foundational roots premised within *te ao Māori*, language, culture, and *mātauranga* oriented to Māori relational ways of being (Le Grice, 2014). *Kaupapa Māori* research subverts a Western gaze on us, to instead situate ourselves as experts of our own lives and to research from that basis (Moewaka-Barnes, 2000). Epistemologically, our *mātauranga* and ways of knowing are distinctive, where our esteemed elders are regarded as bearers of wisdom, and validated through their intergenerational experience, and connection to narratives and knowledges of the land (Pihama, 2012; Smith, 2006). Centralizing these diverse knowledges within our research and rendering our communities as experts of knowledge is important to a *kaupapa Māori* approach (Henry & Pene, 2001).

For this project, we interviewed 18 Māori girls and 12 Māori boys via a broad interview schedule that asked about the information they have been given about sex by their family, their experiences with online technology, the way culture informed understandings of their sexual subjectivity, and their personal sexual experiences. (Jade interviewed 15 young people, 2 interviews were completed together, and Fern interviewed 13 young people.) Following the interviews, we delved into their *kōrero* (conversations) seeking to understand: (1) how do Māori girls learn and exercise their bodily autonomy, sexual desire, pleasure, and make sexual decisions? (2) How do misogyny, and (hetero)sexuality shape the way their sexual subjectivities are perceived and/or restricted by others? Simultaneously, we held space to explore how *mātauranga* might also inform counternarratives and possibilities. We recruited these young people from our networks in Te Tai Tokerau, the North of Aotearoa New Zealand. Collaborators were required to identify as Māori, be between the ages of 13 and 24, with close connections to Te Tai Tokerau. Parental consent was given for youth under 16, and the average age was 16. Most collaborators identified as (hetero)sexual, three identified as (bi)sexual, one identified as (pan)sexual, and one expressed they were open-minded and did not want their sexuality to be constrained by categorization.

Our conversations with youth collaborators were guided by a semistructured interview schedule that allowed scope for collaborators to control and steer the direction, generating rich insight into collaborators daily realities, aspirations, struggles, and values (Le Grice & Braun, 2017). Within these interviews, collaborators were given the opportunity to have a support person attend with them (one boy took this up). Interviews were conducted between February 2018 and December 2019, lasted from 45 minutes to 2 hours, were audiorecorded with their consent, and were transcribed verbatim by Fern. Collaborators were given the opportunity to leave at any stage of the interview process, withdraw their audiorecordings or transcripts, and check a written copy of their transcript in case they wanted to edit it. The research obtained ethics approval by the University of Auckland Human Participants Ethics Committee on October 24, 2017, for 3 years (Reference number 020178).

Reflexive thematic analysis (TA)—a form of TA that requires researchers to reflect how they shape the research practice and process (Braun & Clarke, 2012)—was drawn on as a method for identifying, organizing, and analyzing participant interviews by exploring patterns (or themes) shared across collaborators' experiences (Braun & Clarke, 2006). The coding, theme, and analytical processes was led by Fern as part of her master's thesis in psychology, supported and supervised by Jade. Coding followed an iterative process, initially exploring Māori girls' and boys' experiences together, and then branching out to take a focus on girls' experiences for a more fine-grained focus on how gendered and racialized contexts coalesce in shaping Māori girls lives across social and romantic relationships. Through discussions, we chose to craft out two separate but interrelated thematic maps that could attend to the fullness and difference of Māori girls' and boys' experiences and connect to a deeper breadth of codes. While this article attends to the experiences of girls, at times we interweave boys' narratives to highlight the ways Māori girl's sexual subjectives are understood and interpreted by others, providing insight into the racialized and gendered formations Māori girls negotiate. Discussions between the authors about the data were central to the analysis, resulting in a lot of editing and redrafting of potential themes.

174   LIVED REALITIES

In terms of researcher positioning and as scholars committed to reflexivity, both authors are Māori women from Te Tai Tokerau who *whakapapa* (descend) to local *iwi* connected to the youth collaborators. The wider project is led by Jade in collaboration with her *marae* (tribal meeting space) in Te Tai Tokerau, aiming to support Māori youth to live and flourish in their relational lives free of sexual violence. Partaking in *kaupapa Māori* research with the communities we belong to produces unique responsibilities, obligations, and accountabilities. This includes working with our communities from the outset and maintaining and prioritizing our relationships during and after completion of the research. At the time of this research, Fern was 23. As a young Māori woman, my own lived experiences and identities directly informed this research. Throughout this project, I reflected and engaged with my own experiences; to consider the ways my sexual subjectivity was perceived by others, or the way my *mana* was undermined in sociocultural context, bearing some resemblance to collaborators in this study. I relied on this proximity to the research to understand, interpret, and speak about the experiences of other Māori girls in a way that was *tika* (to be true, correct) and *pono* (to be sincere, honest).

Results and Discussion

In what follows, we lay out the entrenched patterns of practice that shaped Māori girls' exploration of their sexuality and experience of sexual relations. The first theme *sexual agency within the restrictive boundaries of femininity* formed the backdrop to their everyday experiences. The second theme, *gendered demand and punishment in/through sexting*, highlights the contradictory, coercive and punitive domain of gendered sexting. The last theme, *Māori girls' resistance: creating flourishing sexual spaces*, highlights the resistance and agency of Māori girls to speak back to settler-colonial influence through their embodiment of Māori ways of knowing and being.

Sexual Agency Within the Restrictive Boundaries of Femininity

While we are amid an ostensibly "pro-sex" (Farvid & Braun, 2014) and even "sexualised" (Gill, 2007) cultural climate, ideals about female sexuality continue to include traditional mores resembling Victorian femininity (Rudman & Phelan, 2008). In some ways, women can still be expected to embody a sexuality that is passive (Pickens & Braun, 2018) yet also receive contradictory pressures to be sexual, sexually literate, available and "up for it" (Barker & Gill, 2012; Gavey, 2019). For Māori girls, these norms become refracted through a settler-colonial gaze, whereby their adherence to these gender norms are monitored through their attributes, qualities, and behaviors. Friends, family, peers and strangers become vigilant informers on their sexuality and any perceived departures from contradictory gendered expectations are made visible to them. In some cases, gender transgressions are reported to adults deemed to be responsible for these Māori girls, requiring strategies to manage these pressures to toe the line of "respectable femininity." Retelling a conversation she was having about sex in non(hetero) sexual and (hetero)sexual relationships, a participant offered the following advice:

> **Mahuika:** Own it [having sex]! If you're going to be ashamed of your actions, why are you doing it [sex] in the first place? That's what I'd say when I was down in [place], I was owning it! Like I'm single, I have no kids, this is how we mingle, this is what [Tinder] the app's for. What's your problem guys? Even when they were trying to talk to mum and being like "oh, can she do that, is she alright to do that?" and she'll be like "well she's got no kids and she's single." And they'll be like "Oh. Oh, yeah." "Well, what do you want her to be doing?" (both laugh) So you just got to own it. Don't be embarrassed about something you're going to do otherwise don't do it in the first place. (Girl; 24; (Bi)sexual)

For this young Māori woman, other people around her queried her sexual curiosity. Having sex outside of a martial (hetero)sexual relationship is deemed as less favorable—potentially leading to judgment from others (Farvid & Braun, 2014). Her desire to be *tika* and *pono* through being transparent and nonapologetic in her use of Tinder (online dating application) was also met with uneasiness by others. Her unflinching boldness in this space was reflective of an active sexuality that has historically been reserved and expected of men (Pickens & Braun, 2018). While women are invited to participate in casual sex, they are also expected to be silent about their experiences. Unlike men, where talking about sex is integral to a successful (hetero)sexual masculine performance (Connell & Messerschmidt, 2005), women are bounded by

176 LIVED REALITIES

subtle pressures to remain quiet about their sexual adventures as it contrasts with appropriate femininity (Farvid et al., 2017). Participating in casual sex for women is wrought with regulations that make it apparent that they are guests in this space (Kalish & Kimmel, 2011). Many Māori girls had to negotiate their sexual agency and bodily autonomy alongside others' judgments, depending on their age. For younger girls who were not engaging in sexual activities, they could be referred as "sluts" and "whores" when their appearance contrasted with femininity.

Māori girls' experiences, negotiations, and enactments of their bodily autonomy and sexual agency, despite misogyny and (hetero)sexuality, closely mirrors international findings (Farvid et al., 2017; Pickens & Braun, 2018; Ringrose et al., 2013). However, settler-colonialism and racism interweave further complications for Māori girls' experiences and understandings of themselves as sexual beings. Settler-colonial instantiations, discourses, and representations of Māori intersect with discourses of women's (hetero) sexualities to subordinate, limit, and restrict Māori girls' sexual subjectivities. Historically, Māori women have been highly eroticized by colonial settlers as primitive and promiscuous (Hudson, 2010; Le Grice, 2018; Te Awekotuku, 1991) with resonances in the contemporary realities of Māori women today, causing some Māori girls to feel anxious and uneasy about exploring their sexuality:

> **Kahurangi:** One of the challenges for *rangatahi* (teenagers) Māori is when some of them [have sex] for their first time and then they get pregnant— they get talked about a lot. "That was her first time and she got pregnant." (Girl; 17; (Hetero)sexual)

This Māori girl, like others in this study, was aware of racism toward Māori in contemporary society. Similar to urban girls of color in the United States (Faulkner, 2003), when asked about the barriers that prevent Māori youth from exploring their sexuality, numerous Māori girls mentioned their fear of getting pregnant. Neoliberal and individualist discourses have constructed early pregnancy as a social problem, leading pregnant Māori women to be perceived as dependent on the state and contributing to heightened poverty, health costs, and welfare spending (Le Grice, 2014; Ware et al., 2017). Here, Māori identity is constructed as a risk factor for early reproduction, contributing to government narratives that seek to control and regulate Māori reproduction and pregnancy (Le Grice, 2014).

Furthermore, through their prisms of meaning, Māori girls and boys articulated an understanding of sex as needing to happen with the right person and within the confines of a committed relationship. However, this ideal was disproportionately imposed on Māori girls and not boys:

> **Ruru:** If you're going out and having sex with all these guys, then you bring that toward yourself. If I met a guy that had lots of women, I'd think he was pretty cool. But if I saw a girl who had lots of sex—I don't know, it's like a streak, you're just getting cooler, but with girls, they just get more sluttier. I feel like girls are more *tapu*. Yeah. I don't know how to explain that. That's pretty hard. (Boy; (Hetero)sexual; 15)

Here, this Māori boy struggles to articulate the sexual double standard that underpins why girls are viewed differently for having numerous sexual partners. To explain this, like other youth in this study, he draws on an understanding of *tapu* that has been altered to align to Christian virtues. Across the dataset, *mātauranga* was often distorted to yield toward a Christian trope, with harmful consequences for Māori girls. These understandings inhibited Māori girls from being able to explore their bodily autonomy and make sexual decisions. While women hold a sacred space as protectors of *te whare tangata*, and are highly *tapu*, within *te ao Māori* (Le Grice, 2014; Pihama et al., 2016), this sanctity has been refracted through a settler-colonial lens that instead functions to shame and inhibit us from making decisions about our bodies. Here, Māori girls are not supported to learn about their sexuality as powerful, diverse and full of possibilities. Instead, these meanings legitimize a landscape where Māori girls are perceived negatively for having autonomous sex, and refract our understandings of *mātauranga* to do so.

Gendered Demand and Punishment in/Through Sexting

One complex and contradictory theme that we identified was related to the sharing of nude or seminude images. Sexting can include digitally sending "sexually suggestive images or nude images" (Lenhart, 2009). "Nude" images may contain full nudity, or partial nudity where specific body parts are highlighted (typically breasts, buttocks, vagina). In our data, sexting was a thorny terrain, fraught with demand for nudes (from boys) but also

178   LIVED REALITIES

social humiliation (for girls) for sharing such images, even under pressure or situations of clear coercion. Similar to overseas studies (Lenhart, 2009; Ringrose et al., 2021), although Māori boys and girls sent full or partial nudes at similar rates the negative consequences for exchanging them were gender-specific. When boys reflected on their experiences, they were more likely to have had their images remain private and generally regarded this experience as positive. In contrast, sending or exchanging full or partial nudes was a complicated and dangerous terrain for Māori girls. As articulated by a Māori boy, the consequences for girls who had their topless images circulated were devastating:

> **Awa:** Well . . . I had an Instagram, and it happened to this girl at my school. She had really big hooters—like really big, and she took—you remember [name]? Her nudes got linked around. It got shared around to different people and it came up on my phone 'cause it was this video thing of "is it a bird, is it a duck, no it's [name]!" and then her nudes would come up. So I quickly exed off [exited out] of that and yeah. (**Jade:** What happened to [name]?) Uh, [name] is just a little hoodrat that lives in town somewhere. And she's had sex so many times that she got expelled from our school. (**Jade:** Was that after the nudes got shared?) Yeah that was way after! She got expelled last year. Next question—oh no I don't feel sorry for her, she used to smoke weed at school and all sorts. (Tane; 13; (Hetero)sexual)

Here, this boy describes physically desirable attributes of the Māori girl whose nudes were shared, such as her breasts. Being recognized as sexually desirable or conventionally attractive has the potential to bring Māori girls a sense of social esteem and/or acceptance. Yet, if this is interpreted in ways that go beyond women's self-management of their images, photos, nudes, it can come at considerable risk. Girls must walk a tightrope between achieving a desirable sexuality that is revered by others and not falling from "prescribed grace" (Lippman & Campbell, 2014). For Māori girls, this fall may be felt more extreme due to racialized undertones that inform others' opinions of them. Terms such as "hoodrat" carry negative connotations and are often weaponized against Māori and people of color (Tyree, 2011). Stereotypes about African American women in early reality television relate to descriptions of a Black woman who was sexually promiscuous, as a "hood rat," who were adventurous, put themselves in dangerous situations, and engaged in sexual behaviors that were deemed morally questionable (Stephans

"YOU JUST GOT TO OWN IT" 179

& Phillips, 2003; Tyree, 2011). For Māori, it conjures up similar images but is also interlaced with being a "hori," a term associated with Māori living in poor economic conditions (Cliffe-Tautari, 2013).

For girls to share an explicit picture of themselves, they then navigate the possibility of being reprimanded as a slut or a whore (Bay-Cheng, 2015; Lippman & Campbell, 2014). In this study, Māori girls who were known to have sent nudes were repeatedly referred to having no morals or integrity. As described by the prior collaborator, this was accomplished by setting up imagery of the type of girl to send nudes: promiscuous, sexually adventurous, risk-taking, involved with drugs, and rebellious, who simply did not care how she was perceived by others. While it is common for European girls to be mocked or bullied after their nudes become "leaked" (Ringrose et al., 2021), Māori girls navigate an added layer of racialized harm. Discursive terms such as "hoodrat" are shored up almost exclusively for Māori, deeming them even less worthy of respect. The "hoodrat" identity, while not solely given to Māori girls when their nudes are leaked may be given and/or reinforced after the occurrence of these events. Layered onto a settler-colonial context where the images of Māori women and girls have been constructed as "overtly sexual" or "promiscuous" (Hudson, 2010), the idea of being considered as sexually desirable by others and to understand oneself as sexually desirable, is a highly precarious subject position for Māori girls. It is one that is subject to apathy, indifference, and abuse, requiring Māori girls to have a thick skin in order to withstand the social punishment meted out.

A pernicious backdrop of misogyny shaped how Māori girls made sense of themselves as sexual beings as well as how others made sense of them. Within the following account, a Māori girl begins to speak to the difficulty of communicating with her school peers on digital platforms, made more complicated by being asked to "send nudes":

Hinetītama: It actually happened to me. I got blackmailed into sending someone nudes, and he showed the whole school. . . . Yeah. It kind of went; "if you don't send me nudes, I'm going to make up this big story about you. And everybody's going to believe me over you," . . . So I've also had someone frame me with weed in my bag at that school, and I got in trouble for that. So I was kind of like "I really don't need something like that to happen so I'll just send you nudes you know?" and thought hey, whatever, I can deal with this. Like I don't really care. But the fact that he showed everyone around the school was like now I care! Now I care. (Girl; 14; (Hetero)sexual)

180   LIVED REALITIES

Māori girls mentioned an array of problematic ways boys tried to coerce them into sending partial or full nudes, including in this instance blackmail and manipulation. Here, teenage girls can negotiate competing pressures to preserve their relationships with boys, yet also keep their reputation intact (Ringrose et al., 2021; Salter, 2016). For this Māori girl, her prior experience of not being believed in a school context strengthened the threat of blackmail. Her experience illuminates the problems of "choice" in contemporary society. The sexual agency and choices of young girls are linked to the wider social and material contexts they are located within (Bay-Cheng & Fava, 2014). Despite understanding the injustice of this situation, her location as a raced and gendered subject constrained the range of responses available to her. Her agency coexists alongside her precarity (Bay-Cheng & Fava, 2014), emphasized by the means of control exerted by a fabricated story. In a social context where women's testimonies are largely ignored (Gavey & Schmidt, 2011), and Māori women have an ongoing history of been silenced and victimized (Le Grice, 2018), *refusing* to send nudes may too have incurred negative consequence as the fabricated story may have been believed by her peers. The confined and restrictive space available to a raced and gendered subject is shored up by a cloth of settler-colonial gender expectations, whereby it is conceivable for a Māori girl to transgress this—teetering on the edge of punishment, derision, social marginalization, and isolation.

Aside from blackmail, collaborators described further strategies to gain sexually explicit photos of girls. In some instances, boys would take bets and challenge their friends to see who could obtain a nude photo of a girl first:

> Whetū: They might be placing a bet or something. I've seen people do that to see who can get who's first (**Fern:** so they will be like "I bet I can get her nudes—") **Whetū:** "before you can yeah." (Boy; 15; (Hetero)sexual)

Here, this boy speaks to an exchange among other boys underpinned by a sense of male entitlement, where persuading girls to send them nudes becomes a game that allows boys to perform their sexual desirability to their friends (Flood, 2008; Hunehäll Berndtsson & Odenbring, 2021; Ringrose et al., 2021). Simultaneously, girls' images and bodies can be interpreted as a form of visual currency (Ringrose et al., 2013). In other studies, boys have employed strategies of flirting and promising not to share explicit photos with their friends to receive nudes (Ringrose et al., 2013). Collecting girls' nudes may construct a space where boys who receive explicit images of girls feel a sense of ownership of not only girls' pictures but also girls themselves (Flynn et al., 2019). This was experienced by a friend of one our collaborators, whose photos were disseminated by an ex-boyfriend in retaliation for ending their relationship and beginning a new one.

Māori Girls' Resistance: Creating Flourishing Sexual Spaces

Despite the sexual injustices evident within Māori girls' experiences, and boys depictions of these, some Māori girls drew on *mātauranga* to guide their sexual journey and create safe, affirming spaces to explore their sexuality. Māori girls who experimented with casual sex mentioned the importance of being *tika* and *pono* with their sexual partners. This included being explicit about consent, sexual intent, and desired outcomes. "Being upfront" (Aroha; Wahine; 21; (Hetero)sexual), as this girl expresses it, allowed them to gain increased feelings of control in their encounters, and mutual satisfaction as both partners knew where they stood. By refusing to be passive about their sexual desire, some Māori girls simultaneously rejected the pressure to feel ashamed about their sexuality—leaning on their mātauranga to navigate risky terrains:

> **Mahuika:** For instance, I was like; "Hey bo, we're just gonna get down and dirty with it cause that's all I want." Cause you know, I feed the cat [participate in cunnilingus] (both laughs). Because I said it out loud, I wasn't giving any of it away to him; it was like mutual understanding of what we're doing. But if I was like "hey, you're so pretty. Do you want to come over and hang out?" you'd kind of feel like a sleazy slut—I dunno. That's how I feel anyway because your intentions weren't pure from the beginning. And if they don't like it then at least they have the first opportunity to be like "nah, you're too crazy bro." (Girl; 24; (Bi)sexual)

This Māori girl was open about her sexual desire, honest about her intentions, and provided space for another to decide whether they wanted to have sex with her. For her, to understand the inherent *tapu* of her own body (Le Grice & Braun, 2018) she needed to be *tika* and *pono*. Positioning herself outside of settler-colonial discourses that may have attempted to redefine her active sexual desires as "slutty" (Farvid et al., 2017) was made possible through understanding herself through this prism of meaning. Not only did she recognize her inherent *tapu*, but she also maintained the inherent dignity of her sexual partner. Going beyond direct translations of *tapu* to sacredness, *tapu* refers to the ways we maintain and sustain the totality of another person, safeguarding their *wairua* (spirituality) and mental and physical well-being (Tate, 2010). By understanding that her sexual desires may not be equivalent to his, and providing space for him to leave, she was denoting significance to the encounter, allowing them to meet "tapu to tapu" (Taane Thomas, as cited in Le Grice, 2014).

For many Māori girls, knowing what they wanted in intimate relationships or during sex allowed them to safeguard their *tapu*. One girl phrased *tapu* as "knowing your worth" (Moana; Girl; 15; (Hetero)sexual): knowing what you want, knowing who you are, and holding onto your values. These understandings scaffolded an expectation that their bodies, decisions, and personhood should be respected in all sexual encounters. Knowing the person with whom they were being sexually intimate was someone who valued them as a person was central to establishing "loving and violence free relationships" (King et al., 2012, p. 94):

> Mārama: Even when we first got together, he was a nice guy. But it was also little things like clarifying this is what I wanted and checking-in afterward. Even though we weren't very involved, it was still being with a person that was respectful. Because obviously if it was someone that was a douche, I wouldn't have spoken to him a second time. (Girl; 23; (Hetero)sexual)

Within some casual sexual encounters, the sexual partners of Māori girls found ways to be affirming and make them feel comfortable. Explicitly seeking consent and prioritizing their well-being ensured these experiences enhanced one another's *mana*. When Māori girls and their sexual partners treat each other as people who had the right to be respected, it not only enhances the experience but leads to positive understandings of themselves and others (Dobbs, 2021). Importantly, it provides a space for Māori girls to explore their sexuality without shame, stigma, or ridicule, and instead, experience sex as fun, exciting, and full of possibilities (Farvid & Braun, 2014).

Reflective of *mātauranga* that values fluid and diverse sexualities (Le Grice & Braun, 2018), resistance to sexual labels swept through the data, with one Māori girl describing her sexuality as "open" due to binarized sexuality terms not resonating with her. Other girls struggled for a while, before settling on a term that most closely aligned with their sexuality. Even those who identified as (hetero)sexual described having same-gender sexual experiences. Girls were socially and politically oriented within their *kōrero* to actively disrupt sexual categorizations. Māori girls' descriptions of their sexuality provided rich insight into how their sexual identity is woven onto an already existent personal identity. Sexuality constitutes one layer of the unique qualities and gifts handed down to them through their *whakapapa* (ancestry) and does not singularly define them. So why are they being defined by it?

> **Tūī:** [I would change] the whole perception around sexuality, if you're bi or gay or if you like boys and girls, or if you like girls and girls, or boys and girls; you shouldn't have to say, but you can just be whatever you want. So if I was like "I like boys" and the next day I was like "I like girls," I shouldn't have the title of "bi"; I should just be whatever I want to be, you know? That's what I wanna change. (Wahine; 15; (Hetero)sexual)

When looking out for the next generations of Māori, many Māori girls imagined and aspired to a future that did not prescribe and define young people through rigid sexual categorizations. Instead, as articulately spoken by this Māori girl they wished for everyone to be understood as people who had the right to be admired and revered in all of their significance and potential. In saying this, given the histories of gay and (bi)sexual peoples, some people may choose to identify with sexual labels as they create space to be queer—allowing them to resist blatant homophobia. Regardless, by challenging (hetero)sexuality and monosexism (Pond & Farvid, 2017), Māori girls opened diverse and fluid identity positions for future Māori youth to step into, and to find a space of belonging.

Conclusions

Settler-colonialism lays out a cloth textured with complicated raced and gendered intersections—layers of identity and influence—providing a complex and contradictory context for Māori girls to negotiate their sexual experiences and relationships and understand themselves as sexual beings. This is evident in the context of sending nudes, where access to the nude images of Māori girls is a cultural metaphor for the gendered and racialized objectification of women's bodies (Hudson, 2010) and men's sense of sexual entitlement to them. Negotiating racialized-sexism, sexual double

184 LIVED REALITIES

standards, settler-colonial discourses, gendered scripts, an cultural knowledge forms are all required for Māori girls to safely explore their sexuality.

However, Māori girls still manage to create spaces of resistance speaking back to settler-colonial influence through their embodiment of Māori ways of knowing and being. By understanding theirs and others' inherent *tapu*, Māori girls hold strong expectations of the way they and others should be treated within a sexual encounter. Being *pono* or "upfront" about their sexual desires, seeking consent and findings ways to treat others with dignity are positioned as fundamental to having positive and healthy sexual experiences. This shows the potential of *mātauranga*, developed by Māori to draw out strategies of agency and overcome contemporary challenges.

It is crucial that we support Māori girls to build on their capacity to respond to challenging contexts, recognize the limitations of settler-colonialism, and support them to exert their *rangatiratanga*. *Mātauranga* sets out more expansive gender and sexual possibilities for exploring sexual desires, curiosities, and pleasures without stigmatization and harm. Currently, dominant sexuality education approaches regard Māori considerations and recommendations as "too difficult" or something to simply "add-on" to the status quo rather than genuinely engaging with and embedding Māori approaches (Le Grice & Braun, 2018). Without adequate representation of *mātauranga* in sexuality education, *mātauranga* becomes vulnerable to misunderstanding as something that is simply grafted onto settler-colonial understandings of gender, which can be weaponized against Māori girls, eroding their dignity and significance. For Māori girls to locate themselves within *mātauranga* first and foremost, they become equipped to understand themselves, and their sexual subjectivities as significant and are reminded of the gendered and sexual fluidity inscribed in their *whakapapa*. The inner strength that becomes possible through being part of a collective, a birthright as Māori girls and woman may provide them with the resolve to step out of gendered and (hetero)sexual systems. Living in the full knowledge they come from *rangatira* (leaders), Māori girls can be supported to fearlessly walk in the footsteps of their ancestors.

References

Barker, M., & Gill, R. (2012). Sexual subjectification and Bitchy Jones's diary. *Psychology & Sexuality*, 3(1), 26–40. https://doi.org/10.1080/19419899.2011.627693

"YOU JUST GOT TO OWN IT"   185

Bay-Cheng, L. Y. (2015). The agency line: A neoliberal metric for appraising young women's sexuality. *Sex Roles*, *73*(7), 279–291. https://doi.org/10.1007/s11199-015-0452-6

Bay-Cheng, L. Y., & Fava, N. M. (2014). What puts "at-risk girls" at risk? Sexual vulnerability and social inequality in the lives of girls in the child welfare system. *Sexuality Research and Social Policy*, *11*(2), 116–125. https://doi.org/10.1007/s13178-013-0142-5

Bindesbøl Holm Johansen, K., Pedersen, B. M., & Tjørnhøj-Thomsen, T. (2019). Visual gossiping: Non-consensual "nude" sharing among young people in Denmark. *Culture, Health and Sexuality*, *21*(9), 1029–1044. https://doi.org/10.1080/13691 058.2018.1534140

Braun, V., & Clarke, V. (2006). Using thematic analysis in psychology. *Qualitative research in psychology*, *3*(2), 77–101. http://dx.doi.org/10.1191/1478088706qp063oa

Braun, V. & Clarke, V. (2012) Thematic analysis. In Cooper, H. (Eds.), *The Handbook of Research Methods in Psychology*. American Psychological Association.

Chmielewski, J. F., Tolman, D. L., & Kincaid, H. (2017). Constructing risk and responsibility: A gender, race, and class analysis of news representations of adolescent sexuality. *Feminist Media Studies*, *17*(3), 412–425. https://doi.org/10.1177/036168432 0917395

Cliffe-Tautari, T. (2013). *Transitory Māori identities: Shape-shifting like Māui; pūrākau of Māori secondary school students experiencing "complex needs"* [Masters dissertation]. University of Auckland.

Connell, R. W., & Messerschmidt, J. W. (2005). Hegemonic masculinity: Rethinking the concept. *Gender and Society*, *19*(6), 829–859. https://doi.org/10.1177/089124320 5278639

Dobbs, T. A. (2021). *Building Taitamariki Māori capacity: Reclaiming and applying Te Ao Māori principles to inform and support their intimate partner relationship well-being* [Doctoral dissertation]. Auckland University of Technology.

Farvid, P. (2015). Heterosexuality. In C. Richards & M. J. Barker (Eds.), *The Palgrave handbook of the psychology of sexuality and gender* (pp. 92–108). Palgrave Macmillan. https://doi.org/10.1080/14680777.2012.724027

Farvid, P., & Braun, V. (2014). The "sassy woman" and the "performing man": Heterosexual casual sex advice and the (re) constitution of gendered subjectivities. *Feminist Media Studies*, *14*(1), 118–134.

Farvid, P., Braun, V., & Rowney, C. (2017). "No girl wants to be called a slut!": Women, heterosexual casual sex and the sexual double standard. *Journal of Gender Studies*, *26*(5), 544–560. https://doi.org/10.1080/09589236.2016.1150818

Faulkner, S. L. (2003). Good girl or flirt girl: Latinas' definitions of sex and sexual relationships. *Hispanic Journal of Behavioral Sciences*, *25*(2), 174–200. https://doi.org/ 10.1177/0739986303025002003

Flood, M. (2008). Men, sex, and homosociality: How bonds between men shape their sexual relations with women. *Men and Masculinities*, *10*(3), 339–359. https://doi.org/ 10.1177/1097184X06287761

Flynn, A., Henry, N., Powell, A., Scott, A., McGlynn, C., Rackley, E., & Gavey, N. (2019). *Shattering lives and myths: Report on image-based sexual abuse*. University of Durham.

Foucault, M. (1982). The subject and power. *Critical Inquiry*, *8*(4), 777–795.

Gabel, K. A. (2019). Raranga, raranga taku takapau: Healing intergenerational trauma through the assertion of mātauranga ūkaipō. In C. Smith, & R. Tiniau (Eds.), *He Rau Murimuri Aroha* (pp. 16–31). Te Atawhai o Te Ao.

Gavey, N. (2019). *Just sex? The cultural scaffolding of rape*. Routledge.

186 LIVED REALITIES

Gavey, N., & Schmidt, J. (2011). "Trauma of rape" discourse: A double-edged template for everyday understandings of the impact of rape? *Violence Against Women, 17*(4), 433–456. https://doi.org/10.1177/1077801211404194

Gill, R. (2007). Postfeminist media culture: Elements of a sensibility. *European Journal of Cultural Studies, 10*(2), 147–166. https://doi.org/10.1177/1367549407075898

Green, J. A. (2011). *A discursive analysis of Maori in sexual and reproductive health policy* [Doctoral dissertation]. University of Waikato.

Henry, E., & Pene, H. (2001). Kaupapa Maori: Locating indigenous ontology, epistemology and methodology in the academy. *Organization, 8*(2), 234–242. https://doi.org/10.1177/1350508401082009

Hollway, W. (1989). *Subjectivity in method and psychology.* Sage.

Hudson, S. P. S. (2010). *Other identities: Portrayals from the past and what remains in the present: An extended essay presented in partial fulfilment of the requirements for the postgraduate degree of Master of Fine Arts at Massey University, Wellington, New Zealand* [Doctoral dissertation]. Massey University.

Hunehäll Berndtsson, K., & Odenbring, Y. (2021). They don't even think about what the girl might think about it: Students' views on sexting, gender inequalities and power relations in school. *Journal of Gender Studies, 30*(1), 91–101. https://doi.org/10.1080/09589236.2020.1825217

Jackson, S. M., & Cram, F. (2003). Disrupting the sexual double standard: Young women's talk about heterosexuality. *British Journal of Social Psychology, 42*(1), 113–127. https://doi.org/10.1348/014466603763276153

Jackson, S., Scott, S., & Books, D. (2010). *Theorizing sexuality.* McGraw-Hill Education.

Johnston, P., & Pihama, L. (1994). What counts as difference and what differences count: Gender, race and the politics of difference. In K. Irwin, I. Ramsden, & R. Kahukiwa (Eds.), *Toi Wāhine: The worlds of Māori women* (pp. 75–86). Penguin Books.

Kalish, R., & Kimmel, M. (2011). Hooking up: Hot hetero sex or the new numb normative? *Australian Feminist Studies, 26*(67), 137–151. https://doi.org/10.1080/08164649.2011.546333

Kerekere, E. (2017). *Part of the whānau: The emergence of takatāpui identity-He whāriki takatāpui* [Doctoral dissertation]. Victoria University of Wellington. http://researcharchive.vuw.ac.nz/handle/10063/6369

King, P., Young-Hauser, A., Li, W., Rua, M., & Nikora, L. W. (2012). Exploring the nature of intimate relationships: A Māori perspective. *Australian Community Psychologist, 24*(1), 86–96.

Kingi, T. K. (2006). *Māori Culture, health and Māori development.* A paper presented at the Te Mata o te Tau Lecture Series, Palmerston North, Te Mata o te Tau Academy for Māori Research and Scholarship, Massey University.

Le Grice, J. (2014). *Māori and reproduction, sexuality education, maternity, and abortion* [Doctoral dissertation]. University of Auckland.

Le Grice, J. (2018). Exotic dancing and relationship violence: Exploring Indigeneity, gender and agency. *Culture, Health and Sexuality, 20*(4), 367–380. https://doi.org/10.1080/13691058.2017.1347962

Le Grice, J., & Braun, V. (2017). Indigenous (Māori) perspectives on abortion in New Zealand. *Feminism and Psychology, 27*(2), 144–162. https://doi.org/10.1177/0959353517701491

Le Grice, J., & Braun, V. (2018). Indigenous (Māori) sexual health psychologies in New Zealand: Delivering culturally congruent sexuality education. *Journal of health psychology, 23*(2), 175–187. https://doi.org/10.1177/1359105317739909

Lenhart, A. (2009). *Teens and sexting: How and why minor teens are sending sexually suggestive nude or nearly nude images via text messaging*. Pew Research Center, Washington, DC. http://www.pewinternet.org/files/old-media//Files/Reports/2009/PIP_Teens_and_Sexting.pdf

Lippman, J. R., & Campbell, S. W. (2014). Damned if you do, damned if you don't . . . if you're a girl: Relational and normative contexts of adolescent sexting in the United States. *Journal of Children and Media, 8*(4), 371–386. https://doi.org/10.1080/17482798.2014.923009

Mikaere, A. (1994). Māori women caught in the contradictions of colonised reality. *Waikato Law Review, 2*, 125–149.

Mikaere, A. (2003). *The balance destroyed: Consequences for Māori women of the colonisation of tikanga Māori*. The International Research Institute for Māori and Indigenous Education.

Moewaka-Barnes, M. (2000). Kaupapa MāoriMāori: Explaining the ordinary. *Pacific Health Dialog, 7*(1), 13–16.

Moewaka-Barnes, H. (2010). *Sexual Coercion, Resilience and Young Maori: A Scoping Review*. SHORE and Whariki Research Centre, Massey University.

Murphy, N. (2011). *Te Awa Atua, Te Awa Tapu, Te Awa Wahine: An examination of stories, ceremonies and practices regarding menstruation in the pre-colonial Māori world* [Doctoral dissertation]. University of Waikato. https://researchcommons.waikato.ac.nz/handle/10289/5532

Norman, W. (1992). He aha te mea nui. *Journal of Te Puawaitanga, 1*(1), 1–9.

Pickens, C., & Braun, V. (2018). Stroppy bitches who just need to learn how to settle? Young single women and norms of femininity and heterosexuality. *Sex Roles, 79*(7–8), 431–448. https://doi.org/10. 1007/s11199-017-0881-5.

Pihama, L. (2012). Kaupapa Māori theory: Transforming theory in Aotearoa. *He Pukenga Korero: A Journal of Māori Studies, Raumati (Summer), 9*(2), 5–14.

Pihama, L. (2018). Colonization and the importation of ideologies of race, gender, and class in Aotearoa. In E. McKinley, & L. T. Smith (Eds.), *Handbook of Indigenous education* (pp. 29–48). Springer Nature. https://doi.org/10.1007/978-981-10-1839-8_56-1

Pihama, L., & McRoberts, H. (2009). *Te Puawaitanga o Te Kākano: A background paper report*. [Unpublished manuscript, Te Puni Kokiri].

Pihama, L., Te Nana, R., Cameron, N., Smith, C., Reid, J., & Southey, K. (2016). Māori cultural definitions of sexual violence. *Sexual Abuse in Australia and New Zealand, 7*(1), 43–51.

Pond, T., & Farvid, P. (2017). "I do like girls, I promise": Young bisexual women's experiences of using Tinder. *Psychology of Sexualities Review, 8*(2), 6–24.

Reid, J. A., Elliott, S., & Webber, G. R. (2011). Casual hookups to formal dates: Refining the boundaries of the sexual double standard. *Gender and Society, 25*(5), 545–568. https://doi.org/10.1177/0891243211418642

Ringrose, J., Harvey, L., Gill, R., & Livingstone, S. (2013). Teen girls, sexual double standards and "sexting": Gendered value in digital image exchange. *Feminist theory, 14*(3), 305–323. https://doi.org/10.1177/1464700113499853

Ringrose, J., Mendes, K., Whitehead, S., & Jenkinson, A. (2021). Resisting rape culture online and at school: The pedagogy of digital defence and feminist activism lessons. In Y. Oldenbring, & T. Johansson (Eds.), *Violence, victimisation and young people* (pp. 129–153). Springer.

Ringrose, J., Tolman, D., Ragonese, M. (2019). Hot right now: Diverse girls navigating technologies of racialized sexy femininity. *Feminism and Psychology, 29*(1): 76–95.

Rowe, D. (2019). *1000 Words: Pania Newton at Ihumataō*. The Spinoff. https://thespinoff. co.nz/atea/28-08-2019/1000-words-pania-newton-at-ihumatao/

Rudman, L. A., & Phelan, J. E. (2008). Backlash effects for disconfirming gender stereotypes in organizations. *Research in organizational behavior, 28*, 61–79. https:// doi.org/10.1016/j.riob.2008.04.003

Salter, M. (2016). Privates in the online public: Sex (ting) and reputation on social media. *New Media and Society, 18*(11), 2723–2739. https://doi.org/10.1177/146144481 5604133

Simmonds, N. (2009). *Mana wahine geographies: Spiritual, spatial and embodied understandings of Papatūānuku* [Doctoral dissertation]. University of Waikato.

Smith, G. H. (1997). *The development of Kaupapa Maori: Theory and praxis* [Doctoral dissertation]. University of Auckland.

Smith, L. (1999). *Decolonizing methodologies: Research and indigenous peoples*. Zed Books.

Smith, L. (2006). Choosing the margins: The role of research in indigenous struggles for social justice. In N. K. Denzin & M. D. Giardina (Eds.), *Qualitative inquiry and the conservative challenge* (pp. 151–174). Left Coast Press.

Smith, R. (2015). *Purposeful conception: Customary traditions and contemporary applications of Te Whare Tangata in the creation of wellbeing*. [Doctoral dissertation]. Massey University. https://mro.massey.ac.nz/handle/10179/6797

Stephens, D. P., & Phillips, L. D. (2003). Freaks, gold diggers, divas, and dykes: The sociohistorical development of adolescent African American women's sexual scripts. *Sexuality and Culture, 7*(1), 3–49.

Taonui, R. (2010). Mana tamariki: Cultural alienation: Māori child homicide and abuse. *AlterNative: An International Journal of Indigenous Peoples, 6*(3), 187–202. https://doi. org/10.1177/117718011000600301

Tate, H. (2010). *Toward some foundations of a systematic Māori Theology* [Doctoral Dissertation]. Melbourne College of Divinity. https://repository.divinity.edu.au

Te Awekotuku, N. (1991). *Mana Wahine Maori: Selected writings on Maori women's art, culture, and politics*. New Women's Press.

Tyree, T. (2011). African American stereotypes in reality television. *Howard Journal of Communications, 22*(4), 394–413. https://doi.org/10.1080/10646175.2011.617217

Wanhalla, A. (2011). Interracial sexual violence in 1860s New Zealand. *New Zealand Journal of History, 45*(1), 71–84.

Ware, F., Breheny, M., & Forster, M. (2017). The politics of government "support" in Aotearoa/New Zealand: Reinforcing and reproducing the poor citizenship of young Māori parents. *Critical Social Policy, 37*(4), 499–519. https://doi.org/10.1177/02610 18316672111

Webber, M., & O'Connor, K. (2019). A fire in the belly of Hineāmaru: Using Whakapapa as a pedagogical tool in education. *Genealogy, 3*(3), 41. https://doi.org/10.3390/genea logy3030041

9

Predators and Perpetrators

Cultures of White Settler Violence in So-Called Australia

Madi Day and Bronwyn Carlson

Introduction

*Content warning: This chapter contains discussion of settler colonial violence and mention of people who have now passed away.

For almost 235 years, white settlers have preyed on and perpetrated violence against Indigenous[1] peoples on this continent—so-called Australia. What began with warships on the shores of Bidjigal and Gweagal Country, and a shot fired, the bullet punching its way through flesh and a shield (see, for example, Daley, 2016), continues with strategic political, social and militant actions against Aboriginal[2] and Torres Strait Islander peoples.[3] White settlers on this continent harass, abuse, and inflict all manner of violence in the service of settler colonialism—a structure designed to eliminate Indigenous peoples for the purpose of land acquisition (Veracini, 2011; Wolfe, 2006). This kind of violence is no longer enacted as frontline combat or state-ordered massacres of Indigenous peoples, although until relatively recently it was (Reynolds, 2013). The war extends beyond the frontier through legislation and other various discursive and institutional methods of state-sanctioned violations against Indigenous people.

Colonial violence is perpetrated at every level of contemporary life for Indigenous peoples including in interpersonal engagements with settlers in the digital world. Aboriginal and Torres Strait Islander people are active

---

[1] We use "Indigenous" in this chapter to describe First peoples of place. This term is in use transnationally to invoke shared precedence and resistance to settler colonialism.
[2] "Aboriginal" is a collective, colonial term for the First People of the mainland continent of so-called Australia and surrounding islands.
[3] "Torres Strait Islander" is a collective, colonial term for the First People of an archipelago between Cape York and Papua New Guinea known to its peoples as Zenadth Kes.

Madi Day and Bronwyn Carlson, *Predators and Perpetrators* In: *Sexual Racism and Social Justice.*
Edited by: Denton Callander, Panteá Farvid, Amir Baradaran, and Thomas A. Vance, Oxford University Press.
© Oxford University Press 2024. DOI: 10.1093/oso/9780197605509.003.0010

190 LIVED REALITIES

and avid users of digital technologies including social media (Carlson, 2020). Like the majority of Australians looking for intimate contact (be it friendship, sex, relationships or love), Aboriginal and Torres Strait Islander people also use dating apps including Tinder, Grindr, and OkCupid (Carlson, 2020; Carlson & Day, 2021). While Indigenous peoples use social media platforms and dating apps for kinship, love, friendship, resistance, activism, community-building, and other life-affirming activities (Carlson & Berglund, 2021; Carlson & Frazer, 2021; Farrell, 2021), these platforms are also weaponized by white users in order to enact harm on Indigenous users of digital technology. White settler behavior online thus connects to a broader, interrelated milieu of white supremacist racism, colonial heteropatriarchy, and systematic harm occurring both off and online (Farrell, 2021). Here, we argue that while there is increasing attention to the impacts of gendered and racialized online abuse toward Aboriginal and Torres Strait Islander people, there is need for greater attention to the behaviors and propensities of the perpetrators and predators—white settlers.

In this chapter, we examine a culture of white settler violence in so-called Australia. We draw attention here to the naming of the continent, which we see as an act of settler colonial violence. In identifying Australia as "so-called" we highlight the fact that people had many names for various parts of the landmass that is now understood as a single nation. We also acknowledge that we have not forgotten our lands and language groups as hundreds of separate entities outside of the concept of a singular homogeneous continent. We offer a big-picture analysis of racial abuse online in a context of gendered, racialized and heterosexualized violence sanctioned by the settler state. To begin, we outline our methodology as an Indigenous futurist approach informed by Indigenous queer studies, Indigenous feminism, and Black studies.

Next, we consider the function of discursive violence in settler colonial projects, and display how settler states operate in a reciprocal system of sanctioned violence with white settler citizens. We discuss how this plays out on social media including dating apps. To do this, we draw on critiques and conversations from Aboriginal and Torres Strait Islander people in news media and public interviews which thoughtfully articulate white settler violence as part of a colonial regime. Alongside this, we engage critically with instances of discursive, institutional, and interpersonal white settler violence throughout to demonstrate the interconnected and systemic nature of behavior that is both predatory and perpetrating on behalf of the settler colonial state. We connect patterns of white settler violence online to larger systems designed to harm Aboriginal and Torres Strait Islander peoples. To conclude, we argue that further research is needed on the patterns of violent behavior exhibited by white settlers, and cultures of settler colonial violence.

For Indigenous Futures, Always

An Indigenous futurist approach can be summarized as: thinking forward as "mob." Mob is an Aboriginal English word that best translates to "community." Aboriginal and Torres Strait Islander notions of community are relationship and place-based as well as cultural and political. They are diverse, intricate, and expansive in ways that are not easily legible to outsiders (Carlson & Frazer, 2021; Dudgeon et. al., 2002; Fredericks, 2013; Peters-Little, 2000; Sullivan, 2020). To be mob is to live and act with great responsibility and obligation to kin (Dudgeon et al., 2002, p. 16). As Aboriginal researchers and authors, we are beholden to ethics and practice that is for and with mob (AIATSIS, 2020). Madi is a Murri transgender PhD candidate and lecturer, and Bronwyn is an Aboriginal woman and professor in Indigenous studies. We work together at Macquarie University on Dharug Country (North Sydney). We approach this chapter as researchers invested in futures where Aboriginal and Torres Strait Islander people are free of oppressive colonial structures and thriving in worlds and societies built up from our own knowledges and values. Part of building these futures is addressing and dismantling the colonial present. To do this work, we draw on growing bodies of literature including Indigenous queer studies (Day, 2021; Farrell, 2021; O'Sullivan, 2021), Indigenous feminism (Duarte & Vigil-Hayes, 2021; Kwaymullina, 2018; Moreton-Robinson, 2015; Tuck & Gaztambide-Fernández, 2013), and Black studies (Benjamin, 2019; Wynter, 2003). Anticolonial and anticarceral praxis is central to this approach, which entails deconstructing complex relations of colonial power including racism, misogyny, homophobia, and transphobia that feed projects of control and harm like the prison industrial complex and domestic and family violence. We treat these not as separate issues but as interwoven "threads in a pattern of the whole" (Day, 2021; Kwaymullina & Kwaymullina, 2010). We cannot envision liberated futures for mob without also addressing the real and violent systems that keep us from one another and ourselves.

This chapter draws on news media and social media in so-called Australia, and data collected as part of Carlson's national research project investigating

192 LIVED REALITIES

Indigenous lives online. The project was funded by an Australian Research Council Discovery Indigenous grant and eventuated in a book (Carlson & Frazer, 2021), which we also draw from throughout. This chapter centers Indigenous women, queer people, and transgender people—groups disproportionately targeted by white settler violence. We use Indigenous scholarship, anecdotal experiences, and representative or ad hoc media data examples to lay out white settler propensities and patterns of behavior for analysis and critique. The chapter works outward from Indigenous knowledges and experiences of settler colonial histories and societies. In this way, we engage in a blend of theoretical argument and empirical analysis, weaving theory with data points to capture the complexities of white settler violence as part of a bigger picture.

A Culture of White Settler Violence

Instances of racial violence toward Aboriginal and Torres Strait Islander peoples are neither historical nor isolated. They are strategic patterns of behavior implemented by white settlers as expressions of coloniality. That is to say, white settler violence is systemic. It is an assertion of colonial power (Moreton-Robinson, 2015; O'Sullivan, 2021). Before delving further into white settler violence online, it is useful to consider the culture of white settler violence and its role in settler colonialism in so-called Australia. It is difficult to appreciate the pervasive nature of white settler violence without acknowledging the specific ways in which white settlers carry out the colonial project on this continent. In so-called Australia, as in many places colonized by the British, white settlers impose themselves, including their culture, religion, and language, violently and by force. This force is not only physical (although it very often is); it is also always discursive, cultural, and systemic.

White settlers impose on the lives and bodies of Aboriginal and Torres Strait Islander people through policies and actions that are widely described as "protectionist." This refers to a historical context beginning in the 19th century where white settler anthropologists produced narratives claiming that Aboriginal peoples were a dying species "capable of casting light on the evolution of human races" (Smith, 1912, p. 374), and thus in need of protection from extinction. This narrative underpins persistent racist discourse that insists that Aboriginal and Torres Strait Islander people are "relics of the past" who are vanishing of our own accord (Behrendt, 2003, p. 62). When

Indigenous people dare to be successful or even visible in the Australian media, white settlers are quick to enforce this narrative. Perhaps the most high-profile example of this involves the Australian Football League (AFL) player Adam Goodes. White settler AFL fans and media commentators successfully harassed Goodes out of his profession with relentless attacks across news and social media, many of which included comparing him to different primates (Carlson, 2019). The former president of Collingwood AFL club, Eddie McGuire, compared Goodes to King Kong; one AFL fan who was field-side called him an ape; another called him "black, monkey looking cunt" (Akbar, 2019). Instances like these demonstrate the ongoing prevalence of narratives based in Social Darwinism, which white settlers weaponize to harm and demean Indigenous peoples.

White settler imaginaries simultaneously lock us into "a romanticised notion of the precolonial past," and vilify us as dysfunctional and inauthentic in an attempt to discredit our existence in the colonial present (Fredericks, 2013, p. 6). In these imaginaries, we must be compliant, disempowered, grateful, and vanishing. If we dare to shatter this illusion by publicly speaking back to discrimination or criticizing the colony itself, white settlers race to remind us how ungrateful and inauthentic we really are. This was the case for actor Miranda Tapsell, who spoke about her experiences of racism in an interview on Channel 9 and said that she did not identify as Australian due to her experiences of marginalization as an Indigenous person in Australian society. An onslaught of social media commentary ensued (see Figure 9.1).

Such commentary speaks directly to histories of racial determinism, biological absorption, and cultural assimilation into white populations—by this logic if Tapsell has white heritage she is "half-caste"[4] thus not "100% Aboriginal" and must assimilate into the Australian population. At the same time, white settlers deem Tapsell Aboriginal enough to call her a "stupid gin" and to criticize her as representative of "Aboriginal groups" who commenters refer to as inept with "effed up" minds (Clarke, 2015). Racist discourse has a significant role in the justification of white settler imposition on Indigenous lives and lands, and social media has enabled faster and further spread of racist narratives and stereotypes popularized by white settlers (Kennedy, 2020). Colonial governments and other settler actors in Indigenous Affairs

---

[4] "Half-caste" is a derogatory term used against Aboriginal and Torres Strait Islander people who have a white parent or white ancestry. In Australia, white settlers primarily use this term to insult Aboriginal people. It is especially offensive due to the history of white settler governments implementing assimilation policies to remove light-skin children from Aboriginal families.

Figure 9.1 Examples of social media comments directed at Miranda Tapsell after she publicly described experiences of racism as an Indigenous person in Australia (2015). Names and photos of those who are not public figures have been redacted.

repurpose this narrative in contemporary expressions of Social Darwinism (Tynan & Bishop, 2019, pp. 223–227) including structures and industries around their desires to "civilize," "discipline," and "protect" the discursively produced, disadvantaged Indigenous subject (Moreton-Robinson, 2009; Tynan & Bishop, 2019). Racist discourse both off and online makes white settler interventions possible. These include but are not limited to systematic attempts at biological absorption and cultural assimilation into white populations, forced removal of children and family from their communities and homelands, controlled movement and finances, and incarceration in both religious and state institutions.

White settler violence directly attacks Aboriginal and Torres Strait Islander lives, bodies, and relationships. Gender, heterosexuality, and race are coconstitutive categories in service of the settler colonial project (O'Sullivan, 2021). European settlers have imposed heterosexualism on Indigenous peoples transnationally as a system of dehumanization, discipline, and coercion designed to naturalize colonial power (Day, 2021; Lugones, 2007).

Christianity and colonial science collaborate on genres that select people on biological and moral grounds as eugenic, and deselect others as degenerate and disposable (Wynter, 2003). Discourses produced by heterosexualism avow sexual and gendered harm toward Indigenous women, and systematic cruelty toward and erasure of Indigenous people who cannot conform to the colonial ideals such as heterosexuality and binary gender formations (Day, 2021; O'Sullivan, 2021; Simpson, 2017). Projects designed to assimilate and harm Indigenous peoples are consistent across Anglo settler colonies (e.g., Canada, Aotearoa/New Zealand). Residential schools and Native Institutes are one strategy shared in common, where white settlers and missionaries removed Indigenous children from their communities, separated them along binary gendered lines, and subjected them to extreme physical and psychological violence in attempts to discipline away their cultural identities, relationship values, and cosmologies (O'Sullivan, 2021; Simpson, 2017). Many children never returned from these institutions, and those that survived live with immense trauma that impacts relationships, cultures, and communities for generations (Atkinson, 2002; Wilson, 2015). To this day, white settlers coerce and harm Indigenous peoples with strategic narratives about Indigenous identity, relationships, and family (Carlson, 2016; Carlson & Kennedy, 2021; Farrell, 2021; Hamley et al., 2021). This is in spite of mounting evidence of societies and cosmologies organized around complex relational kinship systems prior to colonization (Carlson, 2020; Graham, 2008; O'Sullivan, 2021).

The effects of heterosexualism are very much ongoing rather than historical. The *Breaking the Silences* report, which focused on experiences of Aboriginal and Torres Strait Islander LGBTQIA+ people in Western Australia, found that more than 70% of participants had experienced discrimination, 30% reported being followed or harassed, and 12% reported being victims of a crime including assault (Hill et al., 2021, p. 15). More than 50% of participants reported using dating apps, and 40% of participants said they did not divulge that they were Aboriginal on their dating profiles for fear of abuse and discrimination (Hill et al., 2021, p. 16). Across Anglo settler nations including Australia, Canada, and the United States, Indigenous women and queer and transgender people are disproportionately impacted by state-sanctioned violence including sexual assault, gendered and sexual abuse, and murder (2SLGBTQQIA+ Sub-Working Group, 2021; Gregoire, 2021). In so-called Australia, white settlers cultivate a violent colonial culture toward Aboriginal and Torres Islander people that is not only racialized but also gendered and heterosexualist in nature.

196 LIVED REALITIES

License to Hunt and Harm

So-called Australia has a long history of incentivizing white settlers to hunt and harm Aboriginal and Torres Strait Islander people. Colonial officials offered rewards for capture of resistance warriors during the Black Wars and on early frontiers (Reynolds, 2013). After years of relying on endorsed white settler violence, the Crown eventually established policing and prisons to control and displace Aboriginal and Torres Strait Islander populations (Nettelbeck & Ryan, 2018). White settlers continue systemic projects of imprisonment and violence toward Aboriginal and Torres Strait Islander peoples. Aboriginal women are one of the fastest growing populations in Australian prisons and one of the most incarcerated groups of people in the world per capita (McGlade, 2021). At the time of writing, Aboriginal communities in in Geraldton, Western Australia, express their rage and despair at an entirely non-Indigenous jury (McQuire, 2021) that acquitted a police officer of murder after he fatally shot an Aboriginal woman who was surrounded by eight police officers at the time of her death. JC (name withheld) had recently been released from Bandyup prison which is renowned for overcrowding and abuses against Aboriginal women (McGlade, 2021). The police arrived in three cars to a welfare call (McQuire, 2021). The officer who shot JC claimed he acted out of self-defense because she was carrying a bread knife and small pair of pink scissors (McGlade, 2021). CCTV footage of the police surrounding JC revealed that she did not move toward any of the officers. In interviews with Darumbal and South Sea Islander journalist Amy McQuire (2021), and Noongar legal scholar Hannah McGlade (2021), JC's family as well as the wider Aboriginal community have identified the actions of the police officers and justice system as distinctly racialized and colonial.

Not only is the Aboriginal community calling for justice for JC, but they are also highlighting state-sanctioned violence by white settlers both offline and online. Below, are some samples of white settler commentary on the incident shared in below local news media articles on social media (Figures 9.2 and 9.3).

Hannah McGlade documented that similarly to Van Styn, white defense barrister Linda Black joked during the trial that JC was a "ticking time bomb" who "needed to be taken down" (McGlade, 2021, para 7). Both Gregory and McGlade are highlighting a culture of white settler violence. These comments are steeped in racist discourses of Social Darwinism—natural selection,

PREDATORS AND PERPETRATORS   197

Figure 9.2 Comments posted on social media in response to the murder of an Indigenous person by a police officer in the Australian state of Western Australia (2021). Names and photos of those who are not public figures have been redacted.

Figure 9.3 Comments posted by Shane Van Styn, the mayor of the Western Australian town in which the murder of an Indigenous person by a police officer took place, as shared by Bardi woman, Fallon Gregory (2021). Names and photos of those who are not public figures have been redacted.

Meriki (she/her) @Meriiki · Oct 26
It's not a justice system. Stop calling it that. We have legal systems of colonial violence.

#JusticeForJC

Figure 9.4 Comment posted on social media by Gunai and Gunditjmara activist Meriki Onus in response to the murder of an Indigenous person by a police officer in the Australian state of Western Australia (2021).

and protectionist ideologies that claim white settlers need to "fix" and "take down" discursively produced, disadvantaged, and dysfunctional Indigenous subjects (Moreton-Robinson, 2009; Tynan & Bishop, 2019).

Since the Royal Commission into Deaths in Custody 1991, over 475 Aboriginal and Torres Strait Islander people have been killed by police violence, excessive force, and negligence in prisons (Allam et al., 2021). Not one of the perpetrators responsible has been convicted. Unsurprisingly, Indigenous communities across the continent are critical of the acquittal of this police officer. In conversation with Amy McQuire, Mineng Noongar community advocate Megan Krakouer commented, "There is no political will to change the system" (cited in McQuire, 2021, para 13), and "This is what we have to live with every day of the week" (McQuire, 2021, para 14). She concluded, "What we are saying is this decision today has given the police a license to kill" (McQuire, 2021, para 15). This reflects what Gunai and Gunditjmara activist Meriki Onus called "legal systems of colonial violence" (Figure 9.4).

At the time of writing, the hashtag #JusticeforJC is trending on Twitter. Plans for nationwide protests on October 28 are circulating across social media. Aboriginal and Torres Strait Islander people recognize white settler violence is both legal and endemic to settler colonial systems. As Krakouer articulates, the settler state gives white settlers a license to hunt and harm Indigenous peoples. In turn, white settlers both perpetuate and justify state-sanctioned violence both offline and in the digital world.

Predators and Perpetrators Online

The line between predatory white settler behaviors online and offline is indistinct if it exists at all. Despite early dreams of a disembodied racial utopia

(Daniels, 2013), digital spaces are imbued with the same racial prejudices and disparities present in-person. Indeed, many digital technologies are discriminatory and white supremacist by design (Benjamin, 2019). Moreover, access to new technologies, new platforms, and new means of transmission has proliferated cultures and communities based on racism and hate-speech (Klein, 2017). The Internet is yet another tool of predatory white settler behavior enacted on behalf of the settler state. Aboriginal and Torres Strait Islander people are the most targeted group in Australia in terms of online racial abuse (Jakubowicz et al., 2017). The kinds of racial abuse enacted on social media including dating apps against Aboriginal and Torres Strait Islander people are enormous in scope and variety (Carlson, 2019). Below, we focus primarily on interpersonal racial abuse perpetrated by white settlers. However, it is worth noting that cultures of racist humor and anti-Indigenous communities are cultivated in abundance by white settlers using social media in so-called Australia (Carlson & Frazer, 2021, pp. 77–78).

Cultures of violence in the Western Australian police force also extend online. In 2018, an officer commented on a story about Aboriginal people protesting Australia Day.[5] He wrote, "What a pity automatic weapons aren't legal in this State. Oh well, there's always single shot rifles and sharp knives. Your days are numbered." (cited in Carlson & Frazer, 2021, p. 79). This is just one example of how white settler violence occurs not only in communities dedicated to white supremacy, racism, and hate-speech but also as a pattern of everyday predatory actions. It also occurs in interpersonal interactions on dating apps. Like every other interaction in so-called Australia, these are laden with colonial context, and saturated with racial, sexual, and gendered power relations. As Carlson and Frazer aver, just "as Australian culture is founded on notions of racial exclusiveness, settler superiority, and Indigenous inferiority, social media cultures are embedded deeply in the settler project of Indigenous elimination" (2021, pp. 74–75).

Racial discourse about Aboriginal and Torres Strait Islander people is highly gendered and often sexualized. Settler colonialism in so-called Australia relies on the denigration, dehumanization and objectification of Aboriginal and Torres Strait Islander people (Carlson & Day, 2021). One

---

[5] Australia Day is a national holiday celebrated on January 26 annually. It commemorates the landing of First Fleet in 1788.

200 LIVED REALITIES

need only look to comedian and political commentator Trevor Noah's description of Aboriginal women to see the global reach of this discourse:

> "Oh Trevor . . . I've never seen a beautiful Aborigine." But you know what you say? You say, "Yet." Because you haven't seen all of them, right?
> "Plus it's not always about looks, maybe Aborigine women do special things, maybe they'll just like, jump on top of you." (quoted in McGowan, 2018)

Racial stereotypes about Aboriginal and Torres Strait Islander people associate us with excessive and animal-like sexuality in order to justify white settler harm and cruelty including sexual assault and abuse (Day, 2021). White settler violence on dating apps expresses a culmination of desire and disgust for Aboriginal and Torres Strait Islander people (Carlson & Frazer, 2021, p. 101). The result is a barrage of racial hatred entrenched in a history of sexual violence in service of settler colonialism (Sullivan, 2018). In Carlson's study of Aboriginal and Torres Strait Islander people's uses of social media, a transgender Aboriginal woman reported that a white settler on Grindr asked her whether she would like to be treated the way Captain Cook treated her ancestors and referenced rape and mass killings of Aboriginal people (cited in Wilson, 2020). In another interview, a cisgender Aboriginal woman reported being abused by another white settler on Tinder who wrote, "you black cunts are only good for fucking." He also told her he would hunt her down and "fuck you in all your black holes" (Carlson & Frazer, 2021, pp. 108–109). These incidents display white settler propensities to invoke race and histories of colonial violence while being sexually abusive and threatening toward Aboriginal women. Distrust of police and reporting processes obstructs the collection of national statistics about experiences of sexual assault and abuse among Aboriginal and Torres Strait Islander peoples (Deslandes et al., 2022; McCalman et al., 2014).

Estimates from comparative data suggest that Aboriginal and Torres Strait Islander people are among the most targeted by sexual violence, even more so if they are also queer and/or transgender (AIHW, 2020, p. 3). There is very little data available about perpetrators, or incidences that are racially motivated in so-called Australia. Meanwhile, white settlers threaten to shoot, rape, assault, and hunt Aboriginal and Torres Strait Islander people on public Facebook pages (Carlson & Fraser, 2021, p. 79), in comments, and in messages on dating apps. They enact cultures of racial abuse and predatory sexual behavior online and allude to legacies of colonial violence. White settlers stand before juries, looking at themselves reflected, and make jokes about how we need to be "taken down" (McGlade, 2021, para 7). They type that our "days are numbered" (Carlson & Frazer, 2021, p. 79). They are predators and perpetrators of violence sanctioned by the settler colonial state.

Conclusion

White settler violence is endemic to settler colonialism; land that has not been ceded could never be acquired without violating its sovereign owners. Violence is perpetrated at every level of life in so-called Australia and is currently prominent in digital life as well as offline. White settlers use social media to spread white supremacist and colonial discourses that enable and proliferate harm. They are predatory on dating apps, where they invoke legacies of colonial violence to sexually terrorize and abuse Aboriginal and Torres Strait Islander people. White settler violence feeds into broader interconnected systems and structures designed to eliminate Indigenous peoples from their respective lands. Colonial discourse feeds violence disproportionately targeting Indigenous women and queer and transgender peoples. Racism and heterosexualism are coconstitutive of a white settler culture of violence. Digital cultures are embedded in a settler colonial context founded on violence toward Indigenous peoples. White settlers are licensed to hunt and harm Aboriginal and Torres Strait Islander peoples. This kind of violence is state-sanctioned. In turn, white settlers rationalize violence on behalf of the settler state. This pattern of interconnected systems ultimately forms the whole. Yet data about white settler violence including gendered, racially motivated, and sexual violence is sparse. There is need for more inquiry in this space. Indigenous queer and feminist scholars, writers, activists, journalists, and community members offer ongoing critique of white settler violence as state-sanctioned and part of the settler colonial project. We are studying white settlers for what they are: predators and perpetrators endorsed by the settler state.

References

2SLGBTQQIA+ Sub-Working Group. (2021). *MMIWG2SLGBTQQIA+ national action plan: Final report.* Crown-Indigenous Relations and Northern Affairs. https://mmiwg2splus-nationalactionplan.ca/wp-content/uploads/2021/06/2SLGBTQQIA-Report-Final.pdf

Akbar, T. (2019, August 22). The Australian dream: "You black monkey looking c***." *Indigenous X.* https://indigenousx.com.au/the-australian-dream-you-black-monkey-looking-c/

Allam, L., Wahlquist, C., Bannister, J., & Herbert, M. (2021, October 25). Deaths inside: Indigenous Australian deaths in custody 2021. *Guardian.* https://www.theguardian.com/australia-news/ng-interactive/2018/aug/28/deaths-inside-indigenous-australian-deaths-in-custody

Atkinson, J. (2002). *Trauma trails, recreating song lines: The transgenerational effects of trauma in Indigenous Australia.* Spinifex Press.

Australian Institute for Aboriginal and Torres Strait Islander Research (AIATSIS). (2020). *AIATSIS code of ethics for Aboriginal and Torres Strait Islander research.* Australian Institute for Aboriginal and Torres Strait Islander Research. https://aiatsis.gov.au/sites/default/files/2020-10/aiatsis-code-ethics.pdf

Australian Institute of Health and Welfare. (2020). *Sexual assault in Australia. Cat. no. FDV 5.* Australian Institute of Health and Welfare. https://www.aihw.gov.au/getmedia/0375553f-0395-46cc-9574-d54c74fa601a/aihw-fdv-5.pdf.aspx?inline=true

Behrendt, L. (2003). *Achieving social justice: Indigenous rights and Australia's future.* Federation Press.

Benjamin, R. (2019). *Race after technology: Abolitionist tools for the New Jim Code.* Polity Press.

Carlson, B. (2016). *The politics of identity: Who counts as Aboriginal today?* Aboriginal Studies Press.

Carlson, B. (2019). Disrupting the master narrative: Indigenous people and tweeting colonial history. *Griffith Review, 64,* 224–234.

Carlson, B. (2020). Love and hate at the cultural interface: Indigenous Australians and dating apps. *Journal of Sociology, 56*(2), 133–150.

Carlson, B., & Berglund, J. (Eds.). (2021). *Indigenous peoples rise up: The global ascendency of social media activism.* Rutgers University Press.

Carlson, B., & Frazer, R. (2021). *Indigenous digital life: The practice and politics of being Indigenous on social media.* Palgrave Macmillan.

Carlson, B., & Kennedy, T. (2021). Us mob online: The perils of identifying as Indigenous on social media. *Journal of Genealogy 5*(52), 1–13. https://doi.org/10.3390/genealogy5020052

Clarke, A. (2015, October 16). This is what happens when an Indigenous woman talks about being the victim of racism on TV. *Buzzfeed News.* https://www.buzzfeed.com/allanclarke/miranda-tapsell-talks-racism-and-is-abused-for-it

Daniels, J. (2013). Race and racism in internet studies: A review and critique. *New Media and Society, 15*(5), 695–719. https://doi.org/10.1177/1461444812462849

Daley, P. (2016). The Gweagal shield and the fight to change the British Museum's attitude to seized artefacts. *Guardian Australia.* Guardian News Media. Retrieved February 23, 2023, from https://www.theguardian.com/australia-news/2016/sep/25/the-gweagal-shield-and-the-fight-to-change-the-british-museums-attitude-to-seized-artefacts

Day, M. (2021). Remembering Lugones: The critical potential of heterosexualism for studies of so-called Australia. *Genealogy, 5*(3), 71.

DesLandes, A., Longbottom, M., McKinnon, C., & Porter, A. (2022). White feminism and carceral industries: strange bedfellows or partners in crime and criminology? *Decolonization of Criminology and Justice, 4*(2), 5–34.

Doherty, B. (2021, October 23). "It hurts and it's wrong": Family of Aboriginal woman shot dead by WA police officer speak out after acquittal. *Guardian.* https://www.theg uardian.com/australia-news/2021/oct/23/it-hurts-and-its-wrong-family-of-aborigi nal-woman-shot-dead-by-wa-police-officer-speak-out-after-acquittal

Duarte, M. E., & Vigil-Hayes, M. (2021). How we connect: An Indigenous feminist approach to digital methods. In B. Carlson & J. Berglund (Eds.), *Indigenous peoples rise up: The global ascendency of social media activism* (pp. 93–111). Rutgers University Press.

Dudgeon, P., Mallard, J., Oxenham, D., & Fielder, J. (2002). Contemporary Aboriginal perceptions of community. In A. Fisher, C. Sonn, & B. Bishop (Eds.), *Psychological sense of community: Research, applications, and implications* (pp. 247–267). Kluwer Academic/Plenum Publishers.

Farrell, A. (2021). Feeling seen: Aboriginal and Torres Strait Islander LGBTIQ+ peoples, (in)visibility, and social-media assemblages. *Genealogy, 5*(2), 57. https://doi.org/10.3390/genealogy5020057

Farrell, A. (2021). The rise of Black Rainbow: Queering and indigenizing digital media strategies, resistance and change. In B. Carlson & J. Berglund (Eds.), *Indigenous peoples rise up: The global ascendency of social media activism* (pp.140-156). Rutgers University Press.

Fredericks, B. (2013). "We don't leave our identities at the city limits": Aboriginal and Torres Strait Islander people living in urban localities. *Australian Aboriginal Studies, 1*, 4–16.

Graham, M. (2008). Thoughts about the philosophical underpinnings of Aboriginal worldviews. *Australian Humanities Review, 4*(8), 22. http://australianhumanitiesrev iew.org/2008/11/01/some-thoughts-about-the-philosophical-underpinnings-of-abo riginal-worldviews/

Gregoire, P. (2021, March 24). State-sanctioned violence against First Nations women: An interview with Professors Carlson and McGlade. *Sydney Criminal Lawyers.* https://www.sydneycriminallawyers.com.au/blog/state-sanctioned-violence-against-first-nations-women-an-interview-with-professors-carlson-and-mcglade/

Gregory, F. [@FallonGregory]. (2021, October 24). Geraldton, this is your mayor. Context: discussion is referring to the unjust verdict of the police officer responsible for the murder of JC in Geraldton (2019) #JusticeForJC. [Tweet]. Twitter. https://twitter.com/FallonnGregory/status/1452237249568034822

Hamley, L., Groot, S., Le Grice, J., Gillon, A., Greaves, L., Manchi, M., & Clark, T. (2021). "You're the one that was on Uncle's wall!": Identity, Whanaungatanga and connection for Takatāpui (LGBTQ+ Māori). *Genealogy, 5*(2), 54. https://doi.org/10.3390/genea logy5020054

Hill, B., Uink, B., Dodd, J., Bonson, D., Eades, A., & Bennett, S. (2021). *Breaking the silence: Insights into the lived experiences of WA Aboriginal/LGBTIQ+ people, community summary report 2021.* Kurongkurl Katitjin, Edith Cowan University.

204 LIVED REALITIES

Jakubowicz, A., Dunn, K., Mason, G., Paradies, Y., Bliuc, A.-M., Bahfen, N., Oboler, A., Atie, R., & Connelly, K. (2017). *Cyber racism and community resilience: Strategies for combatting online race hate*. Palgrave Macmillan. https://link.springer.com/content/pdf/10.1007/978-3-319-64388-5.pdf

Klein, A. (2017). *Fanaticism, racism, and rage online: Corrupting the digital sphere*. Palgrave Macmillan.

Kwaymullina, A. (2018). Literature, resistance, and First Nations futures: Storytelling from an Australian Indigenous women's standpoint in the twenty-first century and beyond. *Westerly, 63*, 140–152.

Kwaymullina, A., & Kwaymullina, B. (2010). Learning to read the signs: Law in an Indigenous reality. *Journal of Australian Studies, 34*, 195–208.

Lugones, M. (2007). Heterosexualism and the colonial/modern gender system. *Hypatia, 22*(1), 186-219. https://doi.org/10.1111/j.1527-2001.2007.tb01156.x

McCalman, J., Bridge, F., Whiteside, M., Bainbridge, R., Tsey, K., & Jongen, C. (2014). Responding to Indigenous Australian sexual assault: A systematic review of the literature. *SAGE Open*. https://doi.org/10.1177/2158244013518931

McGlade, H. (2021, October 25). Death in Geraldton: how J*** C****(name redacted) became another Indigenous statistic. *Crikey*. https://www.crikey.com.au/2021/10/25/death-in-geraldton-how-joyce-clarke-became-another-indigenous-statistic/

McGowan, M. (2018, July 23). Trevor Noah responds to boycott calls over racist jokes about Aboriginal women. *Guardian*. https://www.theguardian.com/culture/2018/jul/23/trevor-noah-responds-to-boycott-calls-over-racist-joke-about-aboriginal-women

McQuire, A. (2021, October 25). "A license to kill": Family mourn Aboriginal woman JC. *Presence*. https://amymcquire.substack.com/p/a-license-to-kill-family-mourn-aborigi nal?justPublished=true

Moreton-Robinson, A. (2009). Imagining the good Indigenous citizen: Race war and the pathology of patriarchal white sovereignty. *Cultural Studies Review, 15*(2), 61–79. https://doi.org/10.5130/csr.v15i2.2038

Moreton-Robinson, A. (2015). *The white possessive: Property, power and indigenous sovereignty*. University of Minnesota Press.

Nettelbeck, A., & Ryan, L. (2018). Salutary lessons: Native police and the "civilising" role of legalised violence in colonial Australia. *Journal of Imperial and Commonwealth History, 46*(1), 47–68. https://doi.org/10.1080/03086534.2017.1390894

Onus, M. [@Meriiki]. (2021, Oct 26). It's not a justice system. Stop calling it that. We have legal systems of colonial violence. Twitter. https://twitter.com/Meriiki/status/1452 953743918436362

O'Sullivan, S. (2021). The colonial project of gender (and everything else). *Genealogy, 5*(3), 67.

PerthNow. (2021, September 19). *Geraldton mayor Shane Van Styn says the community had been warning for some time about the potential for tragedy in the lead up to Tuesday's tragic police shooting*. Facebook. https://m.facebook.com/perthnow/posts/1015752220 4946192

Peters-Little, F. (2000). *The community game: Aboriginal self-definition at the local level*. Australian Institute of Aboriginal and Torres Strait Islander Studies. https://aiatsis.gov. au/publication/35754

Reynolds, H. (2013). *Forgotten war*. University of New South Wales Press.

Simpson, L. B. (2017). *As we have always done: Indigenous freedom through radical resistance*. University of Minnesota Press.

Smith, W. R. (1913). *Australian conditions and problems from the standpoint of present anthropological knowledge*. Government Printer, No. 2.

Sullivan, C. T. (2018). Indigenous Australian women's colonial sexual intimacies: Positioning indigenous women's agency. *Culture, health & sexuality, 20*(4), 397–410.

Tuck, E., & Gaztambide-Fernández, R. A. (2013). Curriculum, replacement, and settler futurity. *Journal of Curriculum Theorizing, 29*(1), 72–89. https://journal.jctonline.org/index.php/jct/article/viewFile/411/pdf

Tynan, L., & Bishop, M. (2019). Disembodied experts, accountability and refusal: An autoethnography of two (ab)original women. *Australian Journal of Human Rights, 25*(2), 217–231. https://doi.org/10.1080/1323238X.2019.1574202.

Veracini, L. (2011). Introducing: Settler colonial studies. *Settler Colonial Studies, 1*(1), 1–12. https://doi.org/10.1080/2201473X.2011.10648799.

Wolfe, P. (2006). Settler colonialism and the elimination of the native. *Journal of Genocide Research, 8*(4), 387–409. https://doi.org/10.1080/14623 520601056240

Wilson, A. (2015). Our coming in stories: Cree identity, body sovereignty and gender self-determination. *Journal of Global Indigeneity 1*, 4. https://ro.uow.edu.au/cgi/viewcont ent.cgi?article=1011&context=jgi

Wilson, C. (2020, July 3). Indigenous Australians face sexual racism on dating apps: The second he found out about my heritage he was gone. *ABC News*. https://www.abc.net.au/news/science/2020-07-03/indigenous-dating-appracism-tinder-grindr/12406402

Wynter, S. (2003). Unsettling the coloniality of being/power/truth/freedom: Towards the human, after man, its overrepresentation—An argument. *CR: The New Centennial Review, 3*(3), 257–337. https://doi.org/10.1353/ncr.2004.0015

10

Consuming Whiteness/Disciplining Desire

Gene Lim

Introduction

White erotic hegemony profoundly distorts collective sexual life both within Western societies (Green, 2016; Smith et al., 2018) and in non-Western contexts (Ahn, 2018; Pande, 2021). Existing scholarship has extensively interrogated how this erotic hegemony is implicit in the racialization of sexuality, as well as the sexualization of racism. However, the sociological imagination has seldom been exercised to understand how the ingrained desire for whiteness can impact the queer racialized subject. While the contributions of sociological scholarship to current understandings of sexual racism should not be understated, scholars have often failed either to grapple with the nonrational or nonconscious dimensions of racialized erotic desire (Chancer & Andrews, 2014) or to reckon with the racialized desires of the queer, racialized subject (Seitz, 2019a, 2019b). Too often, the distinctions between the visceral dimensions of sexual desire that are fixated on the *flesh*—as opposed to the social desires which tethered to the *body*—have escaped the attention of academic scholarship. Thus, though the project of reforming or disciplining the desire for whiteness has been explored outside the academic sphere (see O'Harris, 2016), these projects are largely omitted from scholarly discourse. What literature exists on this topic paints a pessimistic picture of any attempts to self-regulate one's racialized erotic desire, framing it as either unfruitful or antithetical to romanticized notions of sexual intimacy that position it as uncompelled and instinctual (see Seitz, 2019b).

In this chapter, I attempt to bridge these gaps in current understandings by: (1) exploring the desire for whiteness among queer men of color through the lens of social inquiry, (2) documenting and commentating several personal projects to discipline racialized desire, and finally, (3) considering whether the entrenched desire for whiteness can be meaningfully uprooted through these undertakings. This chapter synthesizes my reflections on my

Gene Lim, *Consuming Whiteness/Disciplining Desire* In: *Sexual Racism and Social Justice*. Edited by: Denton Callander, Panteá Farvid, Amir Baradaran, and Thomas A. Vance, Oxford University Press. © Oxford University Press 2024.
DOI: 10.1093/oso/9780197605509.003.0011

doctoral research project where I investigated experiences of sexual racism and intimate belonging among a sample of 25 queer Asian men (ranging from 22 to 49 years) born in former European or American colonies, and who immigrated to Australia. I derive these insights from a combination of these participants' accounts and life histories, conversations with other queer academics of color as well as my own lived experiences as a queer cisgender man of color.

Retracing Past Ruminations on White Sexual Desire

To say that scholars of sexual racism have obsessively scrutinized and deconstructed the excesses of white sexual desire is an understatement. The resulting body of knowledge offers an excessively ruminative account of the origins, mechanisms, and white intimate parochialism. Broadly, the sexual-racial solipsism of white homosexual men is understood to stem from emotional segregation, the implicit belief that nonwhites lack the same capacity for human emotion as whites (Leung, 2016; Osuji, 2019). Past research has consistently connected these beliefs both to the visceral aversion that whites feel toward their nonwhite counterparts, as well as to their overwhelming preference for white partners (Callander et al., 2017; Han, 2021; Han & Choi, 2018; Shapiro, 2019). This belief is often held even by ostensibly nonracist white persons, who, while holding sanguine attitudes toward the abstract *concept* of interracial intimacy, may be viscerally averse to it within their own intimate lives (Childs, 2005; Shapiro, 2019). These racially homophilous preferences are even theorized to perform a coherent sociological function, as sexuality and heredity have historically been foundational aspects of racism (Carter, 2007; Nagel, 2000), and control over the boundaries and definitions of whiteness are often integral to the maintenance of white supremacy (Nagel, 2000; Theriault, 2018).

In the context of homosexual intimacies, this imperative to maintain white racial purity is instead largely symbolic, accreting into white racial anxieties embedded within the mutable ethnosexual stereotypes commonly affixed to persons of color (Frosh, 2013; Shapiro, 2019). For example, as Shapiro (2019) suggests, the stereotypes of gay men generally as effeminate and promiscuous are projected just onto nonwhite others, predicating popular ethnosexual stereotypes of gay Asian men as feminine and gay Black men as hypersexual. These racial anxieties are further amplified by contact with the

208   LIVED REALITIES

white gay psyche's drive to realign itself to hegemonic (white) masculinities, ostensibly as a means of recovering from its historic abjection (Butler, 1997; Shapiro, 2019). By vehemently disavowing any bonds of recognition across racial boundaries, the white gay psyche is symbolically exorcised of these pejorative connotations through its public denunciations of the "deviant" and somatically inferior racial other—and in doing so, buttresses its tenuous connection to the hegemonic institutions of whiteness and masculinity (Shapiro, 2019).

Other research further indicates that the dehumanizing view of nonwhites as both emotionally and erotically inferior is predominantly propagated via white racial socialization (Riggs, 2013; Shapiro, 2019; Smith, 2017), and is thereafter sustained through either superficial or nonexistent interactions across racial boundaries (Orne, 2017). Likewise, the research provides a sound understanding of the conditions under which interracial intimacy may be deemed acceptable to racist whites. bell hooks (2012) famously dissected the underlying impetuses driving the white desire to sexually consume the racial "other": while long-term, intimate companionship is primarily reserved for other whites, nonwhites offer the possibility of momentary (and, importantly, nonpermanent) exploration and the promise of intense and exciting sexual encounters "spiced up" by the supposedly transgressive nature of interracial intimacy. These dalliances are furthermore conceptualized as an avenue through which the exercise of racial domination can be enacted for erotic gratification (Plummer, 2007; Raj, 2011) or misconstrued within the white racial frame as meaningful challenges to white supremacy (hooks, 1992; Orne, 2017).

Desiring and Consuming Whiteness

Comparatively absent from the literature is a similarly comprehensive and nuanced understanding of the sexual appetite for whiteness held by many queer racialized subjects (see Prestage et al., 2018). To put on a finer point, the sexual appetite for whiteness is *not* an *openness* to intimate encounters or relationships with white persons, nor is it the *willingness* to forge bonds of intimacy and companionship across racial boundaries with white persons. Rather, it is the erotic fixation on bodily, material, and symbolic signifiers of whiteness, which often necessitates the foreclosure of similar bonds with nonwhite persons. The desire for whiteness among persons of color is often simplistically conceptualized as an insidious but ultimately incidental result of racial indoctrination (Chin, 2018; Han, 2015) or is assumed to arise from more pragmatic concerns, such as a desire for upward social mobility (see Kim, 2006; Nemoto, 2008). While scholars can rationally conceive of whiteness as desirable on the basis of its preeminence within quotidian social, cultural, political, and economic systems, the concurrent reification of those bodily signifiers associated with whiteness are largely seen as an unremarkable outgrowth of this fact. Spillers (1987, p. 67) argues, however, that the "flesh" (i.e., material, bodily reality divested of subjecthood) necessarily precedes the "body" (i.e., the amalgamation of symbolic substances that become affixed to the flesh).

While both *body* and *flesh*[1] are essentially regarded as commutative by most scholars, the *flesh* is a "zero degree of social conceptualization that does not escape concealment under the brush of discourse, or the reflexes of iconography" (Spillers, 1987, p. 67). Hence, while the *body* is formed when symbolic meanings are affixed to *flesh*, it is the *flesh* that ultimately tethers and forms the object of those seemingly reflexive erotic responses of arousal and disgust. Citing several autoethnographic accounts of how racialization intrudes on attraction, Shapiro (2019, p. 18) notes that "the visceral quality of racial aversion is further seen in instances where white men move *instantaneously* from attraction to revulsion at the sight of a non-white face." I argue that while the instinctive, recoiling withdrawal that Shapiro (2019) describes may be directed toward the racialized *body*, it ultimately comes to be embedded within the *flesh*. While almond-shaped eyes, snub noses, olive skin, and full lips are all physical traits that undeniably acquire insinuations of erotic undesirability through symbolic association with the racialized *body*, the almost-instantaneous reflexive revulsion these features inspire suggests that negative connotations affixed to these traits eventually acquire a visceral resonance to them that is removed from the more abstract and cerebral qualities of those symbolic narratives attached to the racialized *body*. That a profound distinction between flesh and body exists is further evident in those instances where the desirability of *flesh* can compensate for and even overcome the abjection of the racialized *body*. "You're cute for an Indian guy," "I don't usually fuck Asians, but you're hot"—concessions like these suggest that while the *body* figures preeminently in individual determinations of sexual worth, the

---

[1] Henceforth, reference to Spiller's (1987) concept of the "*body*" and "*flesh*" are denoted in italics.

desires of flesh (excuse the somewhat biblical turn of phrase) can sometimes win out over the erotic liability of inhabiting a racialized body.

The nuances of these distinctions, however, are palpably absent in most discourses about sexual racism. The queer racialized subject is, therefore, seldom constructed as motivated by sexual appetites of the *flesh*, but is instead seen as desiring the white *body* on the premise that substantial benefit can be gleaned through relational proximity to said bodies. Through these framings, the erotic hegemony of whiteness is rendered in two-dimensional simplicity as arising from the desire for socioeconomic status or international mobility among racialized subjects, or an imperative to preserve existing class status among white ones. Alternatively, the racialized subject is more benignly positioned as the collateral victims of an erotic-aesthetic regime that reifies pan-European features as the epitome of erotic desirability and physical beauty. For Seitz (2019b), that existing scholarship on sexuality and race occupies itself predominantly with critiquing and decrying sexual racism inadvertently detracts from considerations of the "complex psychical agency of racialized queer subject [. . . such that] the question or event of queer of colour desire gets sidestepped" (p. 148). This functionally reiterates the misconception that white desire, and the white gaze are all things that "happen" to the passive, racialized subject. More concerningly, it neglects the reality that the desires of the racialized queer subject are often complexly implicated in the disruption and maintenance of white erotic hegemony (see Han & Choi, 2018; Osuji, 2019; Silvestrini, 2020).

This tension was neatly encapsulated in the account of one participant, a Hong-Kongese man who was articulate in his indignation toward the sexually racist white men he often encountered in his intimate life. He furthermore proffered a poignant reflection on how his foundational experiences of racial socialization in British-occupied Hong Kong likely set the stage for his near-exclusive attraction to white men. Subsequently in this interview, the same participant weaponizes the very ethnosexual stereotypes, which he had so insightfully dissected minutes earlier, to denigrate other similarly attracted Asian men. This participant regarded that sheer number of these men statistically minimized the likelihood that he would successfully pair up with his "prince charming," and overtaxed the already-anemic pool of white Australian men who are sexually attracted to Asian men. He lamented that as a naturalized Australian citizen, his affections were absent of the ulterior motives that these opportunistic "visa-chasers" harbored toward their white partners. Oblivious to the irony of his outburst, he rattled off several anecdotes of Asian emigres who "weren't citizens before, and then became a citizen, and they're with a white guy," citing this as evidence that "whatever other Asians were around were taking my potential partners." Examples like these point to an inconvenient fact: much as the white gay psyche can nimbly pivot and reorient itself toward and away from racialized bodies and subjectivities (Shapiro, 2019), so too does the queer racialized subject orient itself toward whiteness (Ahmed, 2006). More specifically, the queer racialized subject may attempt to symbolically hold whiteness by emulating it in both mannerism and affect (Young, 2009), or may attempt to hold it in a more literal sense through its erotic consumption. However, when the queer racialized subject invariably runs afoul of whiteness, it too is able to momentarily pivot away from it as demonstrated by the above participant's deft vacillation between decrying sexual racism and racially vilifying other Asian men.

As such, the erotic desires of queer racialized subjects are demonstrably riddled with complexity and even contradiction. However, white scholars have frequently been unsuccessful in grappling with these nuances—most egregiously, the visceral sexual desire for white bodies and the romantic and social desire for white partners are often conflated with one another. Likewise, lay understandings of racialized desire are also plagued by a lack of sophistication. While the stratification of economic and social capital along racial lines, and the crystallization of racial privilege into tangible material advantage are principles widely accepted as fact (see Fluri et al., 2020), that a similar logic governs collective sexual life appears unfathomable to many laypersons (Bedi, 2015, Smith, 2017). Fundamentally, the *notion* of systemic intimate injustice is at odds with contemporary ideals of intimate attraction, which is commonly idealized as being alien to such concerns (Bedi, 2015). As a result, though sexual racism and intimate discrimination are well-evidenced concepts, they are typically rejected in favor of laissez-faire discourses of racialized desire that construe it as idiosyncratic, untamable, and ultimately harmless (Callander et al., 2017). These discourses are collectively conducive to a distinctly neoliberal conceptualization of erotic desire that implies an individual's sexual desirability to others is a matter that is entirely within their volition (Han & Choi, 2018). Intimate discrimination is consequently framed not as a social or societal issue, but rendered into a trivial concern that ceases to be a hindrance to one's love life once a sufficiently sculpted and muscular physique is cultivated, or once a sufficient (though indeterminate) degree of professional or financial success is attained

(Han & Choi, 2018). That a hypothetical solution to intimate discrimination exists is often brandished as counterpoint against any assertion that arbitrary ethnosexual prejudices unfairly disadvantage persons of color within collective sexual life (see Mattheson, 2013). Yet this ultimately deflects from the fact that certain groups of sexual actors must undertake these arduous projects to even be allowed to participate (from the peripheries, no less) in collective sexual life (see Han & Choi, 2018; Smith, 2017).

For many queer men of color, these debates can feel overly intellectual, purely philosophical, and not particularly meaningful. Their subordinate placement within hierarchical structures of erotic desirability is fundamentally unaltered by whether or not the concept of sexual racism finds widespread acceptance,[2] or if the nuances and contours of intimate discrimination are accurately and precisely described in scholarship. To the queer racialized subject, what matters—from an functional standpoint—is that these structural forces stymie both their romantic and erotic desires from actuation, particularly where white bodies and white partners are the objects of said desires. The conflation of these desires is ultimately unproductive to the goal of undoing the desire for whiteness; by misidentifying these desires as pragmatically instead of viscerally located, the emergent (though misplaced) solution is the economic enfranchisement of racially minoritized groups. Yet, the elevated social standing and socioeconomic status enjoyed by certain racial groups (e.g., Asian Americans) has not been accompanied by an attendant elevation in collective sexual capital (Han, 2021). At the meso-level, past research suggests that concerns of social or economic class are often decoupled from the desire to consume whiteness for Asian men in their partnering decisions. Indeed, many queer men of color may display "hypergamous" tendencies in the sense that they aspire to intimate encounters and partnerships with white sexual actors who categorically hold a greater degree of sexual capital on their race (Lim & Anderson, 2021). Comparatively, both my own findings, and the available evidence suggests that queer men of color are not "hypergamous" in the more conventional sense, and that race often supercedes both social and class status in intimate partner selection (Hammack et al., 2021)—and entirely eclipses either within the context of casual sexual encounters.

---

[2] As authors like Silvestrini (2020) have noted, intimate discrimination can prove remarkable resilient to rectification even when the individual sexual actor harboring these discriminatory attitudes is aware of their biases and attempts to correct them.

For the queer men in my project, the desire for whiteness did not wholly reside in a desire to hold whiteness via proxy, nor was it entirely a product of the entrenched cultural hegemony whites enjoy. Certainly, that some participants conceded to experiencing no small amount of enjoyment from the sexual status implied by their ability to attract white partners—a feat made all the more impressive by the fact of their erotic devaluation—suggests that the palatability of whiteness derives in part from the positive connotation of being recognized as an emotional or sexual equal to one's white counterparts. These concerns, however, are ultimately seen as ancillary to the sexual delight seemingly latent within alabaster skin spangled with tangles of gold and bronze and copper hairs; in striking blue, gray, and green eyes; in angular cheekbones, jawlines, and noses, and in every other outwardly innocuous physical trait that is synonymous with whiteness and white flesh. These bodily traits are not innately erotic (nor, for that matter, are they only found in persons of European ancestry) but are imbued with a powerful insinuation of erotic prowess and desirability through their seemingly incidental, but recurrent associations with erotic pleasure and sensuality.

While these associations are primarily thought to be reinforced through the near-exclusive depictions of white bodies in pornographic media (see Chin, 2018; Salamenca et al., 2018), they appear to increasingly permeate everyday life. From where I write in Australia, a national cult of hard (white) masculinity pervades, and the figure of the Australian tradesman (or "tradie") is concurrently glorified across society as both a national sex symbol and a paragon of "Australian values" (Waling, 2019). The working-class white male, and the somatic signifiers anchoring this abstract notion within the collective national imagination (i.e., "hi-vis" vests stretched over a barrel chest and broad shoulders, muscled legs flecked by light-colored hair, a piercing blue-eyed gaze from beneath a hard hat, et cetera ad nauseum) serve to solidify the erotic symbolism of these bodily traits as "innate" and incidental within the queer male erotic habitus. This eroticization of the white body is, of course, intensified in the gay community, where even Australian sexual health messaging has historically emphasized the virility of the white body (see Bujan, 2023) in stark contrast to concurrent depictions of racial alterity and of bodies of color as "virulent" and as potential biopolitical hazards that demand containment (see Yue, 2008).

For many queer men, irrespective of minoritized ethnicity the sexual consumption of white bodies and white partners is an end unto itself; it facilitates one's ability to enact a truly vast spectrum of erotic fantasies purveyed through popular culture and pornographic media, and transfixed on the physical and visceral dimensions of white bodies. These fantasies are not simply masturbatory aids but provide a narrative context to transform mere mechanical intercourse into a fully fledged erotic encounter. As Žižek (1998, p. 162) points out, "even in the most intense moment of bodily contact with another human being, we cannot simply 'let ourselves go' and immerse ourselves into 'that'—a minimum of narrative support is always needed, even if this narrative is not always announced." As this pertains to the ethnosexual fantasies purveyed by pornography and other erotic media, white men are inherently able to experience these fantasies in a somewhat participatory capacity, finding reciprocal sexual gratification in erotic encounters with *other* white persons. In essence, white queer men are freely able to *access* whiteness for erotic consumption by virtue of the fact that they *hold* whiteness (Leung, 2016). In comparison, queer men of color are often invisible within their own sexual fantasies and desires (Ayres, 1999; Han, 2008), relegated to a kind of pseudovoyeuristic enjoyment that is purged of one's own racialized body. This (literally) disembodied enjoyment of one's intimate fantasies and encounters often stems from the plethora of negative connotations that is affixed to racialized flesh (see Caluya, 2008), which inspires no small measure of sexual disgust.

The amalgam of racist imagery and insinuations of somatic inferiority that accretes around racialized bodies does so via the same mechanisms that enable white bodies to acquire the positive connotations outlined above (Orne, 2017), though the precise narratives and beliefs that confer these connotations are seldom invoked verbatim when one encounters those bodies that are the subject of said beliefs. Evidently, however, racialized bodily traits and features are *somatic intermediaries* that are often suffused with symbolic significance. A particularly interesting example of this was seen in the account of one participant—who self-deprecatingly recounted his purchase of a silicone replica of Brent Corrigan's (a prolific Anglo-American gay porn star) penis at a considerable markup in price over a normal dildo. That the product itself was functionally indistinguishable from most other similarly sized dildos (trust me, I checked) did not appear to detract from the heightened erotic pleasure he describes deriving from its use. This account provides an extreme instance where (a simulacrum of) a bodily, somatic trait—compartmentalized and disembodied though it may be from the broader bodily corpus—retains a considerable degree of erotic symbolism and potency. For this participant, his masturbatory enjoyment is deepened

CONSUMING WHITENESS/DISCIPLINING DESIRE   215

through his symbolic penetration by a popular adult actor whom he will likely never meet and much less bed.

Evidently, the utility of the Brent Corrigan dildo to this participant's masturbatory activities is catalytic, facilitating his immersion in an improbable erotic racialized fantasy. Within these vistas of erotic fantasy, realities that are inconvenient or unconducive (such as, for instance, the fact that not once in 52 films and a 14-year long career has Brent Corrigan costarred opposite an East Asian actor) can easily be set aside, and even the most *unlikely* of fantasies can be believably—if momentarily—indulged. In much the same way, hooks (2012) argues that the white sexual actor often misguidedly imagines the "broadening" of sexual palettes to include nonwhite partners is a symbolic repudiation of white supremacy, a profound betrayal by its very beneficiaries. To hooks (2012), however, these piecemeal attempts at bridging racial difference through one-off erotic encounters are fundamentally self-serving; a "defiant gesture where one denies accountability and historical connection" (p. 369) to the legacies of racial domination underpinning the contemporary desirability of whiteness. Likewise, the racialized queer subject does not participate in these encounters simply for sexual gratification and is not ignorant to the fact that these sexual encounters are often laden with symbolic import. To many of the queer men of color who participated in my research, the successful consumption of whiteness is experienced as an affirmation of one's palatability beneath the white gaze, and was experienced (perhaps somewhat wishfully) as anecdotal evidence of the erosion of white supremacy and white sexual solipsism.

Of note here is how white *flesh* becomes imbued with, and acquires especial erotic substance. This parallels the way that specific physical features become associated with a corresponding ethnosexual subjectivity within the collective erotic imagination. For example, the oversized black penis with black men and black hypermasculinity (Marriott, 1976) or the diminutive Asian penis with Asian men and the purported *lack* of masculinity (Han, 2008). Mirroring the fixation and subsequent objectification of the racial other's flesh within the white erotic habitus, many queer men of color had a likewise-granular understanding of their desires for whiteness. Hence, the desire for whiteness is understood as a harmless proclivity toward specific features like green eyes, or sandy-blond hair—but is quite tellingly a proclivity that is implicitly racially and ethnically specific. That is, these aesthetic preferences are unlikely to be satisfied by, say, an East Asian man wearing green contacts and sporting bottle-dyed blond hair. However, where this *bodily obsession*

216 LIVED REALITIES

differs from the kinds of sexual objectification that transforms both white women and persons of color into sex objects beneath the white male gaze (Kozak et al., 2009; Wood, 2004), lies a disparity of (sexual) capital between white and nonwhite sexual actors. Where whiteness can impel the performance and self-commodification of race by the racialized subject (Green, 2011; hooks, 1992) (for instance, via the eager accentuation and exaggeration of certain racialized characteristics, or the acquiescent performance of specific racial stereotypes), the racialized queer subject who harbors a desire for whiteness is often in no position to make a counterdemand.

This asymmetry is underpinned by the fact that whiteness, as either a cultural characteristic or trait, is highly mutable (Ahmed, 2006). As such, it is not conducive to being "performed" in the same manner that an ethnosexual stereotype, or a stock racial character can be "performed" by the acquiescing, racialized subject to evoke a specific, racialized erotic fantasy. While white sexual actors may *draw attention* to their whiteness to access racial privilege within the erotic marketplace, this is hardly analogous to the nigh-parodical kinds of racialized performance that persons of color may undertake in attempting to capitalize on the racialized fantasies of other sexual actors. Moreover, where persons of color often experience significant pressure to conform to rigid ethnosexual stereotypes to find even a modicum of success within collective sexual life, white sexual actors are able to freely draw on a veritable cornucopia of positive narratives, symbols, meanings and connotations associated with whiteness. This pluripotent mutability, however, is ultimately underscored by a juxtaposing fixity of physical and bodily traits denoting membership to whiteness. This is perhaps, then, why the physical and bodily traits associated with whiteness *alone* are able to transfix queer male desire so utterly (see Han, 2021; Morgana-Sowada & Gamboni, 2021; Ravenhill & de Visser, 2019), whereas the socioeconomic or social signifiers of *whiteness* are oftentimes only capable of captivating desire when accompanied by these bodily traits.[3]

As such, because the *flesh* precedes the *body*, it also enumerates certain parametric limits on what kind of body can become superimposed on this *flesh*. An interesting example of this was related to me by a North Indian participant, whose angular, Indo-European features occasionally caused him to be mistaken as Mediterranean European. Once, while at a circuit party,

---

[3] See, for example, how persons of color are often derided or belittled for "acting white" in both mannerism and speech (Durkee & Gomez, 2021).

where the partygoers were solely illuminated by pink-and-purple strobe-lighting, this participant was approached by another reveler who glibly indicated his sexual interest in him by mentioning his especial fondness for Greek men. Despite this participant's repeated insistence that he was not, in fact, Greek, this man insisted that he could not be mistaken, assuming, I suppose, this participant was being intentionally facetious and obtuse. These were not the only instances of misracialization relayed by my participants. One participant of mixed South and East Asian ancestry, who was frequently misidentified as Hispanic, found that even those other men who were otherwise vehemently opposed to sexual contact with Asians often waived these "preferences" in the hopes of hooking up with him.

Accounts like these demonstrate how the *body* is affixed to the *flesh* and, more importantly, how certain kinds of "bodies" are (mistakenly or otherwise) affixed to certain kinds of "flesh." While these participants experienced sexual racialization as nebulous and error-prone, others like my East Asian participants described interactions where their racial alterity was immediately evident to other sexual actors, being so glaringly apparent as to sometimes cause these other actors to instinctively recoil in seeming disgust from any possibility of sexual contact with these alien others. In comparison, an embarrassment of positive traits and associations can be selected from, and curated to constitute the *body* scaffolded onto white *flesh*. The white *body* is so protean, so malleable that it is seemingly formless and invisible (Frankenberg, 2004) and so nebulously definite that it can, on occasion, be momentarily appropriated by individuals who sit astride delineations of *white* and *nonwhite*. Hence, at least as it pertains to the erotic consumption of race—to "hold" whiteness (and to be able offer it up for consumption), it is not enough to possess a white *body*—given how liminally defined whiteness often is within this context—no, one *has to* possess white *flesh*.

Considering that white *flesh* is considerably more difficult to commandeer than, say, the class signifiers or socioeconomic privilege associated with whiteness as a social category, and because physicality is often the focus of the sexual encounter, white bodily and physical traits accordingly command a higher value within the sexual market. Reflecting on his teenage sexual experiences, one participant spoke about availing himself to the much-older white men who regularly pursued him on hookup apps and dating sites, which was despite realizing he could not muster the same enthusiasm they showed in him. Framing these experiences as a trade-off—his youth for their whiteness—the participant recounted that these men were nevertheless able

218 LIVED REALITIES

to pressure him into sexual acts that he was uncomfortable performing due to a collective awareness of the erotic premium commanded by whiteness and the concurrent "erotic penalty" incurred by racial alterity. hooks (2012) conceptualizes the more superficial forms of interracial sexual contact as "eating the other": the erotic consumption of the racial "other."

hooks suggests that for many whites, interracial sexual encounters are gratifying precisely because they are pregnant with symbolic significance. Here, the white sexual actors' enjoyment of the encounter stemmed from the alien sensuality of racial otherness, and transgressive pleasure derived from the supposed "perversity" of sex contact with the racial other. Similar associations underlie the motivation of the sexual actor of color who partakes in these encounters. For these, the desirability of whiteness is diametrically predicated on favorable connotations appended to it within the erotic imagination, much of which finds a somatic intermediary in the bodily traits associated with whiteness (Green, 2014). Where scholars like hooks (2012) and Seitz (2019a) regard the resultant erotic encounter as essentially constituting a microcosmic reenactment of colonial relations between oppressor and oppressed, this was framed in transactional terms by the queer men of color in my project and some scholars (see Prestage et al., 2019). Given the preferential value commonly ascribed to whiteness, however, this seemingly mutual consumption of racial difference is a demonstrably uneven exchange.

Hark! An Imposter

Often implicated in queer male desires are indelible tensions between adulation and emulation: do I want to be you, or do I want to be with you? This encapsulates a fundamental truth that queer male desire is as much a recognition of the possibility of intimate connection as it is about recognizing the mutability of oneself and the erotic delectation of a potential self as embodied within another man (Landi, 2019). These tensions are not simply poetic musings, and researchers have consistently commented on how gay and bisexual men often evaluate their own sexual worth using the same metrics they apply to prospective partners (Pachankis et al., 2020; Souleymanov et al., 2020). On a broader level, the findings of scholars like Green (2011, 2014) attest to the sublimation of these impulses into a homogenizing impetus wherein those erotic traits ascribed the most value become collective aspirations. The result? Subcultural phenomena like the "gay clone"

CONSUMING WHITENESS/DISCIPLINING DESIRE   219

(Lauritsen, 1993; Levine & Kimmel, 1998), and in a more contemporary context the hypersexual and heteronormative performances pervading dating apps like Grindr (Conner, 2019, p. 7). Given the preeminent desirability of whiteness, it is perhaps unsurprising that attempts to hold or to achieve some approximations of whiteness were common among my participants (see also Ayre, 1999; Caluya, 2008). To Seitz (2019b, p. 55), this specific mode of ethnoerotic emulation is doubtlessly an outgrowth of colonial domination, but is occasionally playful or innocuous harkening to the Lacanian notion of mimicry as "a necessarily ambivalent strategy for colonized and postcolonial subjects" that simultaneously deputizes the subject as intermediaries of the colonial project and also enables these subjects to surreptitiously mock and critique both the colonizer and colonial logic.

Scholars like Fanon (2008) offer invaluable insight into the subjective dimensions of implicit self-identification with and aspirations to whiteness; for persons of color, that whiteness represents the "purest expression of the human race itself" (Dyer, 1997, p. 22) is often misunderstood (particularly within a neoliberal conceptualization of race and racial difference) as a tenable pathway toward a kind of racial embodiment that approximates whiteness (Young, 2009). These fantasies are only later discovered to be misbegotten when other racial actors—particularly white actors—neither abet nor endorse them, or where the insurmountability of one's somatic distance from whiteness is realized. This is particularly true in context of raw physicality of the sexual encounter. As one participant noted, the nonbodily, somatic trappings of whiteness are often easy enough to grasp, and to subsequently co-opt: Ralph Polo Lauren shirts, beige khaki shorts, an Australian drawl, and other shorthand that can be intuited and subsequently deployed to communicate one's "westernized" mindset. In the melee of the sexual encounter, however, where clothes fly off, speech is reduced to passioned moans and grunts, these badges of cultural whiteness are stripped away, leaving only irrefutable somatic dissimilarity—and, within the white racial frame, incommensurability.

Accordingly, the ingrained, erotic appetite for white bodies and whiteness is primarily experienced by queer men of color as problematic because it is unreciprocated and is unreciprocated because whites prize racial mutuality and sameness (Leung, 2016). Couched within that lack of reciprocity, therefore, is an implicit form of denigration because, as Green (2011) asserts, erotic agents predominantly select sexual partners whom they perceive as being of commensurate or greater sexual status. Thus, to be rejected based on

220 LIVED REALITIES

one's ethnicity can be experienced as an assertion of one's racial inferiority. It is a pronouncement that racial identity—and not simply *racial alterity*—is the core of one's apparent undesirability. Consequently, as Marriott (2007) suggests, the internalization of this white gaze inevitably fragments the psyche of color, bifurcating it into two oppositional halves engaged in perpetual conflict. This psychic struggle ultimately threatens to affirm as fact the ever-present suspicion that one's racial identity is indeed the profound and fundamental defect that the white racist other attests it to be:

> To recognize that I resemble the white racist other [. . .] even [if only] in my own desire, would be tantamount to admitting the inadmissible: that I am not myself and that my most proper being is over there, in that reflecting double who enrages (shames, despoils) me. (Marriott, 2017; p. 127)

Marriott's (2007) reflections hint to a crucial point: by internalizing the same kinds of white-biased desires harbored by the white racist other, the racialized subject also internalizes several other beliefs that are concordant with, and which scaffold the view of whites as the only "appropriate" target of intimate desire. As one participant posited, "if I don't find people of my own ethnicity attractive, what does that say about my own self-esteem, what does that say about the way I think of myself?" For Marriott (2007), as for many queer men of color, the preferential or exclusive desire for whiteness is an indefatigable wellspring of racial trauma. Insomuch as these desires simultaneously cement the subordinate position of the queer racialized subject within his own erotic habitus, while demarcating the white other as the solely viable or tenable object of intimate and erotic connection, they functionally guarantee that the queer racialized subject is reiteratively subjected to the kinds of ethnosexual denigration that reliably patterns sexual sociality and sexual interactions between whites and nonwhites.

Marriot's (2007) reflection also reads as an almost-prescient insight into the psychic costs incurred through several decades of intimate antiracism scholarship. Anyone with even passing knowledge of this scholarship is quite likely familiar with urgent exhortations to direct self-scrutiny toward one's racialized desires and to concede one's complicity in oppression. The primary result of these exercises is that we are highly adept at naming, identifying, and decrying sexual racism. I would argue that despite all this work, queer men are no closer to disabusing ourselves of the harmful notion that white sexual actors are the ideal intimate partners or that the bodily features associated with whiteness present the utmost height of erotic and aesthetic desirability. Instead, we develop a panoptic scrutiny toward our own racialized desires that accomplishes little in the way of broadening or democratizing our erotic horizons, instead highlighting our impotence in determining our desires. Anti-sexual-racism scholarship is able to elucidate the threads of sexual racism within collective sexual life, but unable to offer any means of remediation to the (otherwise unspoken) preoccupation with whiteness overshadowing many a sexual life. Inevitably, what arises is a disjunction between the rational self, which is excruciatingly cognizant of the unsightly origins and the unsavory implications of our reflexive predilection for pan-European features and bodies, and our recalcitrant desires, which seem immutably indifferent to any attempt at either discipline or reformation.

Not coincidentally, my participants' comparisons between their inculcated desires for whiteness, and the lingering psychic aftermath of European colonial exploitation were not metaphorical, nor were the reverberations of these legacies an artifact of some distant past. Participants reflected on how the foundations of their sexual palette for whiteness were seeded in their seminal experiences of racial socialization, much of which was subtly inflected by the sociocultural lionization of whiteness and white bodies. This could be seen in the account of one Indian participant, who described being fawned on by relatives and family friends alike during his childhood due to his light skin-tone, and who subsequently developed an uncomfortable awareness of the colorism rampant in many Indian communities once it was pointed out to him. It was evident in the reflections of a Fijian participant whose initial explorations of his sexuality were deflated by the concurrent realization that gay and bisexual men greatly preferred partners of European or mixed-European ancestry, and who routinely found himself labeled "unfuckable" due to his darker skin color. And it was evident in the musings of a Filipino participant who spoke about how Filipinos often mythologized their own family lineages by claiming some far-flung iota of Spanish ancestry—and whose own abortive attempts to "hold" whiteness by closely mimicking the mannerisms and speech of his white Australian peers found disquieting resonance in these mental gymnastics.

In general, these preferential or exclusive desires for whiteness were entrenched on a seemingly visceral level, such that for virtually all participants—cognizant as many were of the complex, racialized power dynamics governing their attractions—merely being aware of these biased desires was insufficient to counteract them. For these men, the habitual, nigh-instinctual erotic response elicited by white bodies and physical traits had to be reined in very deliberately, as they otherwise retained some modicum of influence over one's choice of intimate and romantic partners. As one participant noted of his experiences using dating applications like Tinder and Bumble, unless he was "swiping" through prospective partners in a highly purposive and deliberate manner, he was still liable to automatically "swipe left" on nonwhite faces and users when idly thumbing through potential suitors on these applications. Because platforms like Tinder encourage partner selection on "fast and automatic, but not necessarily completely accurate judgements" (Olivera-La Rosa et al., 2019, p. 3) derived from facial recognition and other social cues, implicit biases often form the entire basis of initial partner selection within these contexts. This apparent immutability of implicit preferences was understandably a source of guilt and frustration for some participants, who viewed their white-biased erotic preferences as an unwitting and thoroughly unwilling form of complicity in the maintenance of white supremacy.

Decolonizing Sexual Desire

The attempts made by queer men of color to captivate the white gaze—whether through projects to tame the body in alignment to culturally dominant body image ideals or by co-opting the cultural signifiers of whiteness—often failed to convincingly bridge the somatic gulf engendered by racial difference and alterity. Consequently, participants sought to resolve psychic conflict through reconfiguring—or as was more commonly stylized, "decolonizing"—their erotic desires. This metaphor of erotic colonization was frequently deployed by my participants to describe the inculcation of self-prejudicial erotic preferences and reflected a consensus the desirability of whiteness was externally imposed and detrimental. As Riggs (2017) notes, the fieldwide aesthetic and erotic devaluation of nonwhite sexualities and subjectivities ultimately benefits white sexual actors by facilitating their access to intimate partners at the expense of nonwhite sexual actors. These participants therefore rightfully surmised that their preferential attraction to white partners were engendered by the same structural forces that constrained their participation in collective erotic life and predicated the ethnosexual discrimination unfailingly encountered within these contexts.

The broadening of decolonial movements and projects to include the intimate sphere is, though relatively novel, by no means unprecedented. Carlson and Frazer (2021) recently discussed this within the context of Indigenous' Australians intentional eschewment of sexual and romantic relationships with white Australians. The subjugation and legislation of Indigenous sexualities have been a long-standing component of many colonial projects. Hence, for Indigenous persons, the rejection of colonial discourses of desire is a means of asserting one's psychosexual sovereignty and constitutes a crucial foundation for securing the collective sovereignty of First Nations peoples. On an individual level, the "decolonization" of one's sexual-racial desires can be a powerful way of asserting one's autonomy in a milieu where dispossession and oppression are nonnegotiable features of everyday existence. As one of Carlson and Frazer's (2021) participants stated, "white people have colonised my land and I'm not gonna let them colonise my body. It's that last part of [the] sovereignty of my body that I want to maintain." These quotes therefore suggest that insofar as the derogation of the Indigenous *body* is an artifact of a broader racial animus prevalent within Australian society, individual Indigenous persons have relatively little control over their *body* (see Brazier, 2018). Crucially, however, these individuals are able to retain a modicum of control over who is allowed access to their *flesh*. Hence, the *flesh* comes to constitute a crucial site for resistance against the erotic privileges that white sexual actors are able to access at the expense of their racialized counterparts (Riggs, 2017).

These projects of rehabilitating one's racialized desires are often acts of resistance and healing (Carlson & Frazier, 2021)—not just indignant fulminations against an unjust sexual status quo—and are carefully mediated challenges to the entrenched and systemic racial privilege enjoyed by white persons within collective sexual life. Similar undertakings were conceptualized by my participants as long-term endeavors meant to dislodge both whiteness and white bodies from their pedestaled positions within their erotic habitus. While these projects were partially conceived as a symbolic repudiation and rejection of white supremacist erotic standards, the goal of these undertakings were primarily restitutive and served to reaffirm to participants that persons of color were desirable and deserving of intimacy. Instead of attempting to convince white men of their sexual desirability (i.e., in the vein of more recent attempts within popular culture to reshape perceptions of the East Asian body as compatible with Eurocentric notions of bodily attractiveness, and to emphasize its somatic similarity to,

224   LIVED REALITIES

the white body, see Ruez, 2017), participants instead overwhelmingly engaged in undertakings to "reprogram" their preferential desires for white partners.

Conscientious (Racial) Consumption

As described, my research involved a series of semistructured life history interviews with a cohort of 25 queer Asian men living in Australia. The transcripts from these interviews resulted in a textual corpus that comprised discussions and painstaking reflection that participants often felt they had few other avenues to process. These discussions often focused on how these participants navigated sexual racism within their intimate lives, and how they attempted to resolve the sexual racism they had internalized over the course of their lives.

Demonstrating a keen awareness of the avenues through which their sexual appetites for whiteness had been inculcated, my participants often embarked on projects to counteract their preferential desires for whiteness. They did so primarily as acts of self-compassion—and as a means of relinquishing both themselves and other queer men of color from constant evaluation against Eurocentric standards of erotic desirability. Crucially, this was also as a means of expanding their erotic and intimate horizons, with many participants attempting to dilate their ethnosexual palettes through mere exposure to bodies and persons of color within an erotic or intimate context. As Orne (2017) outlines, the psychological phenomenon of mere exposure—as it applies to the present psychosexual context—refers to the incremental recognition of racialized subject and subjectivities as intimate equals with whom intimate connection is an acceptable and even desirable proposition, and which ostensibly emerges from sheer, incidental familiarity with said subjects and subjectivities. This operant logic implicitly underpinned a range of discrete and interlinked strategies that participants engage to decolonize their desires, much of which was operationalized as some form of conscientious erotic consumption. These strategies commonly prioritized persons of color as prospective intimate partners and the consumption of pornographic media depicting nonwhite persons and bodies. Importantly, these strategies seldom entirely eschewed either white partners, or the consumption of erotic media involving white persons and bodies.

As relates to the former category, this directive was seen to inform a kind of erotic "affirmative action," wherein participants who experienced little to no attraction to other men of color—particularly in the inceptive stages of these undertakings—nevertheless pursued sexual encounters and relationships with them in the hopes that through the mere exposure effect the kinds of habituated erotic associations that sustained the desire for whiteness could eventually be forged. Expectantly, the resultant encounters and relationships were often marked by sexual indifference and consequently devoid of erotic enjoyment, at least for the participants enacting these strategies. In lieu of this, participants recounted feelings of shame surrounding the realization that they were essentially "using" other men of color as convenient implements to process the racial trauma sustained through one's experiences of race-based sexual discrimination. It did not escape the notice of most participants that these practices were not wholly dissimilar to how some white men are known to "use" racialized bodies as objected to facilitate a greater degree of immersion in their sexual-racial fantasies. This realization seemed to trouble even those participants who overcame this momentary disquiet to reiterate their insistence that these projects were indispensable to their broader efforts to exorcise their white-biased erotic preferences.

At first, I was naively convinced that those participants who vehemently disavowed any erotic interaction with white persons were somewhat oversensitive to these intimate dynamics, and that the benign intentions foregrounding these forms of "sexual solidarity" (as coined by one of these participant) justified this utilitarian—if dispassionate—approach to intimate partner selection. I was given, however, a small glimpse into how it felt to be recruited to such a project when one participant suggested that we head back to his nearby apartment when the interview wrapped up to engage some mutual "antiracist praxis." It did not escape my notice that this suggestion came immediately after this man had taken great pains to explain that sleeping with other Asian men was his challenge to internalized sexual racism (a project, he also revealed, that few others had been willing to join). I politely turned down this offer by citing the need to observe strict ethical boundaries between a researcher and their participants.

Inwardly, I could feel an involuntary grimace creep onto my face, being acutely cognizant of the fact that my desirability is once again reduced to an artifact of my race. Only this time, the kinds of backhandedly complimentary stereotypes about Asian men ("Asian guys have such smooth skin," "Asians are so cute," etc.) that are used as pickup lines by rice queens are

226 LIVED REALITIES

instead replaced by a call-to-action to challenge ethnosexual stereotypes and internalized sexual racism. In either scenario, my desirability is entirely reducible to the fact of my Asian-ness, deriving entirely from this *body* that clings stubbornly to my *flesh*. Irrespective of my attempts to sculpt a physique and an outward appearance (heavily tattooed and somewhat burly) that is deliberately incoherent with the frail, sexually impotent Asian *body* constituted by the white sexual psyche, the other components of my *flesh*—perhaps my facial features or my skin color—remain a somatic intermediary. Or, was it simply that this participant found me desirable precisely because I bore little semblance to this figment of Asian frailty? Was it because my *flesh*, though unmistakably racialized, was far enough removed from this odious stereotype that it would allow him to simultaneously challenge his internalized sexual racism while taking pleasure in the act?

Mulling over these bewildering questions in the days following our interview, I wondered if either the interaction or my gut reaction revealed anything about me. More and more questions rang in my head, over and over: "Should I feel flattered? Should I feel indignant at being racially objectified? Am I failing the movement against intimate racism—did I fail to 'do my bit' by rejecting him out of hand? Would I have accepted this participant's offer if it was made under a different set of circumstances—if ethical considerations were no object? Would my answer be different if he was an attractive white man? Was this person even attracted to me aside from as a way to rehabilitate his racialized desires?"

I found myself wondering if the other Asian men this participant had similarly propositioned were likewise confronted by these uncomfortable thoughts, and if their reticence was truly because they harbored unresolved internal racism. Given the largely incremental nature of any attempted modification of one's ethnosexual desires (see Seitz, 2019b; Silvestrini et al., 2021), the sheer number of similarly stilted attempts at intimate connection presumably necessary to effect any meaningful change to one's ethnosexual preferences ultimately raises the question as to whether such strategies can even be effective where some modicum of visceral, erotic attraction toward bodies and persons of color does not already exist. For some participants, the difficulties they experienced in pursuing these strategies ironically reinforced the belief that the erotic appetite for whiteness was unchangeable and immovable—at least for other persons of color, who shared neither the self-awareness, nor motivation to cooperate with these participants in such endeavors.

For another group of participants, these projects were at least partially motivated by aggrievement at devaluation within collective erotic life. This ethos was discernible in the following participant's example. Having fantasized about an All-Australian boyfriend (replete with dishwater blonde hair and seafoam green eyes) for as long as he could recall, the participant was dismayed to realize that the subordinate position of persons of color within the hierarchy of erotic desirability made it likely that this fantasy would remain just that. In response, he was insistent on *only* dating other men of color, stating, "I find people hot, regardless of race, [but] I make the conscious decision to steer myself away from white guys and to consciously prefer [other] people of colour. If anything, it's almost as if I'm trying to enforce my own sense of justice [. . .] I like to think of it as turning the tables." Resolutions like these superficially parallel the way that many whites are open to momentarily sampling the racial "other," but ultimately decide to cling onto their mainstream positionality by only forming long-term relationships with other whites (hooks, 1992; Shapiro, 2019), particularly since participants like the one above were often open to casual sexual encounters with white men. The view of these intimate practices as constituting a form of "vigilante" intimate justice, however, was often belied by more practical motivations.

For the men who engaged in this form of intimate justice, this outlook often began as a tit-for-tat response to the low erotic esteem they were held in by their white counterparts, but typically grew into a more measured stance which shifted away from plain vindictiveness and toward the viewpoint that long-term intimacy with another man of color was ultimately their only chance at a truly egalitarian relationship. This point was elaborated on by one South Asian participant, who cited his brother's relationship with his white sister-in-law as evidence that while "colorblind" love is not an impossibility, perceived disparities in sexual worth can cast long shadows. These concerns, then, pertained less to the fear of a white partner leveraging their disproportionate sexual capital within said relationship, but often spoke to a sense of incredulity that one's racial alterity—this thing that was the source of so much angst—would be, or that it even could be entirely set aside by a hypothetical white partner. As one participant explained, "it's always the sense that I'm always going to be looked at as the partner who is the one that the white guy settled with. So, it's kind of like, he's settling, and I'm reaching. I'm always going to be the—oh you know, he's an Asian guy, he's so lucky he got a white guy."

The perception that persons of color who formed long-term intimate relationships with white partners were "overreaching" their modest erotic station was a view not only held by white queer men but also internalized by many queer men of color—particularly those who demonstrated an awareness of sexual racism. While many such individuals rationally recognized the possibility of intimate connection occurring across these racial boundaries, they nevertheless tended to view these interracial relationships with derision, and even as a form of hypocrisy on the part of other queer men of color who were likewise cognizant of sexual racism. This was especially true of individuals who were resolved to "decolonize" their desires, and who often view these men with condescension for apparently failing to even attempt likewise. It could be argued the undercurrent of resentment evident within these accounts was tied to a perception that other men of color were not similarly invested in destabilizing the erotic hegemony of whiteness. It could also be argued that it arose from jealousy toward these men for somehow managing to partner with the few white men who were not averse to long-term interracial intimacy. Perhaps both.

Therein lies the chief pitfall of this strategy of erotic affirmative action: reducing a partner to their race not only demeans their personhood but also creates a psychic barrier to intimacy in addition to the deeply rooted ethnosexual biases one is attempting to contravene. By persisting in the prioritization of race as the chief determinant of sexual and romantic selection, these projects do not—and arguably cannot—rectify the visceral desire for whiteness. Instead, these strategies decry and deny these desires in favor of a dispassionate, perfunctory preference for racialized bodies in the hope that the entrenched desire for whiteness—once deprived of any avenue for fulfillment—is eventually displaced onto these racialized bodies for lack of its preferred object. From a more pragmatic standpoint, attempts to rehabilitate one's racialized erotic desires through the exclusive and deliberate consumption of racialized bodies cannot succeed as a solitary endeavor because they definitionally require a critical mass of like-minded others who are similarly willing to (at least temporarily) forswear the consumption of whiteness, and instead subsist entirely on a sexual diet of racialized bodies. As one participant lamented, it was an uphill task trying to get other Asian men to agree to sleep with him when the majority were seemingly uninterested in disciplining their racialized desires through the reiterative reconditioning of their sexual responses.

Finding My Penis: Pornographic Consumption

Perhaps it is much simpler to undertake this "work" in the private domains of one's erotic fantasies and with the help of pornographic paraphernalia. Being that queer men are a demographic group for whom the consumption of erotic media constitutes a particularly prominent component of both seminal and ongoing sexual socialization (Arrington-Sanders et al., 2015), the notion that individual ethnosexual preferences and biases can be sculpted through a regimen of discerning and highly selective consumption is not without merit. After all, scholars have long argued that the seemingly arbitrary preference for white bodies and the concomitant dispreferences for racialized ones held by many sexual actors (see Prestage et al., 2018) are foregrounded by their juxtaposed depictions within most pornographic media (Bishop, 2015; Corneau et al., 2021; Lim et al., 2017). It is therefore unsurprising that many participants' first encounter with the demeaning sexual-racial stereotypes that they would later find immovably affixed to them was through pornographic depictions of racialized bodies. The following participant's reflections exemplified how many participants' formative erotic experiences were deeply intertwined with and underscored by sexual racism. He states:

> I saw male–male sex for the first time, and I think that's also when I started internalising racism, because porn is very much white—exceedingly white. I remember searching for "Asian" themed pornography, sort of just to see people like myself being sexual. But the only available ones were very fetishistic [. . .] They were nearly always presented as being very slim, small, categorised as "twinks," and nearly always bottoms for a white man [. . .] I didn't find them attractive.

The underrepresentation of men of color within pornography was not itself described as having any particularly noticeable impact on the psychosexual development of my participants, whereas previous generations of queer Asian men have cited the absence of Asian *flesh* within pornographic media as a contributing factor to the invisibilization of their own Asian bodies within their erotic fantasies (see Chuang, 1999; Fung, 1991). In contrast, caricaturish depictions of Asian *flesh*—as effeminate, submissive, and as an intermediary through which the racialized *body* is symbolically emasculated—were readily internalized by my participants, even if these representations were infrequently encountered. Within this context,

230   LIVED REALITIES

the imagined deficits of the Asian *body* are viewed as a direct corollary of the phenotypic flaws of Asian *flesh*. That is, because Asian *flesh* is composed of a poorer substance—one that compares unfavorably to the sheer physicality, powerful masculinity, and symbolic gravity[4] seemingly inherent to white *flesh*—its symbolic subordination beneath its white counterpart (e.g., as occurs within erotic hierarchies of desirability) and literal subjugation by the white *body* (e.g., as depicted in pornographic media) is construed as a natural and intuitive consequence of its inferiority. Unsurprising then, that the Asian *flesh* and *body* would be rendered into a feminine parody of the idealized, (white) masculine form, aligning with the aversion toward femininity that is rampant within the gay community (Hoskin, 2019; Mercer, 2017). These depictions, and the cultural narratives couched within subsequently align participants' erotic habitus broadly along the lines of a masculine/feminine dichotomy, wherein the former is viewed as desirable and an inherent quality of whiteness, and the latter undesirable: an irremovable blemish that marks Asian *flesh* (Fung, 1991).

That a connection ostensibly exists between regularly consuming certain kinds of pornography and the resultant inculcation of a concordant ethnosexual preference structure was understood to imply that that one could both: (1) nurture an erotic appetite for bodies of color, and (2) resuscitate self-perceptions of one's own, racialized body by selectively (and consistently) consuming positive depictions of queer racialized subjects. McKee et al. (2008) argue that consuming nonheterosexual pornography is not only instructional for a queer audience but also can be a powerful affirmation of one's sexual desires. In a similar vein, it was reasoned by my participants that consumption of "empowering" depictions of the racialized subject opened vistas of possible erotic embodiment for a group of men who are otherwise accustomed to their limited portrayals as apparatuses of white male desire. These depictions identifiably facilitated a different kind of fantasy—one where racial alterity is not a constraint on sexual self-expression, and where the racial boundaries that structure intimate life are porous and occasionally even nonexistent.

---

[4] Consider, for instance, the heroic implications ascribed to blond or red hair, or the collective romanticization of features common to Caucasian populations, such as pale skin or lighter eye colors. In comparison, the phenotypic diversity inherent within nonwhite populations is seldom the object of similar wonderment or appreciation. Indeed, many "ethnic" features are viewed with derision and are often as a bodily signifiers of inferiority even by "ethnic" persons themselves as indicated by the popularity of so-called ethnic plastic surgery, and the preference for features that can be found in Caucasians.

One participant subsequently found Japanese pornography to be a trove of otherwise-scarce depictions of Asian men as masculine and desirable. Ironically, however, he related that the genitalia of these masculine Asian men were invariably obscured by pixilation in compliance with Japanese censorship laws (Alexander, 2003). Hence, the absent representations of the Asian penis in Western pornography—and the metaphorical castration and feminization of the Asian man (Fung, 1991)—is coincidentally reiterated within these depictions. Moreover, perhaps owing to the ostensible self-alignment of the Japanese racial consciousness to a kind of "cosmopolitan whiteness" (Russell, 2017), the specific configuration of facial features used to denote idealized masculinity within Japanese pornography (i.e., deep-set eyes, a sharp nose, double eyelids) were also virtually indistinguishable from the same within Western pornography (see Mercer, 2017). In general, absent representations of the queer racialized subject within pornographic media, were increasingly replaced by prohibitively narrow interpretations of these subjectivities that emphasized their potential to approximate and approach hegemonically masculine forms of physical embodiment—and through that, the potential to overcome the erotic "deficit" of one's racial alterity. That is, so long as one is a Boomer Banks or Peter Le[5]—hypermasculine, uncannily muscular, and endowed with what one participant termed a "porn dick"—then one would likewise be a leading man, a fully agentic sexual subject who is above all fuckable to one's white counterparts.

Changing the Narrative: Discursive Reframings

Ancillary to these strategies were also discursive reframings of the desirability of whiteness—in essence, attempts to reconfigure the preference for white *flesh* through the destabilization and interrogation of the narrative components of the white *body*. The most common of such strategies involved the deconstruction and reappropriation of established sexual-racial stereotypes to critique the unequal structures of sexual opportunity prevalent within collective erotic life. In past research, one way these forms of "talk" were found to reinforce the undesirability of men of color was through the discursive denigration of their partners. For instance, relationships between Asian men are derided for supposedly mimicking

---

[5] Two prolific adult actors of Asian descent.

232   LIVED REALITIES

female homosexuality (i.e., as it occurs between two *ersatz* women), while men who express interest in Asian men are labeled as "rice queens" who are either too old or undesirable to attract a white partner (Han & Choi, 2018; Jackson, 2000).

Elsewise, these "rice queens" are perceived as race fetishists whose predilections tend toward the pseudofemininity Asian men purportedly hold (Han, 2008), and whose preferences constitute a tacit repudiation of the forms of idealized masculinity that white men inherently possess. In an inversion of these racially pejorative narratives, one participant shared that his group of "gaysian" friends often mutually and light-heartedly teased one another for their choice in white partners, a subtle means of encouraging one another to reflect on their preferential attractions toward white men. This participant recounts playfully admonishing his friends whom he felt tended to suspend their better judgment when seeking out white men for intimate encounters, sharing, "I'll rib them: 'how are you seeing—'or 'how are you talking—'how are you sleeping with this white guy who's clearly so not in your league. You are so much more attractive!" These discourses were evidently underpinned by a begrudging recognition of the fact that satiating the erotic appetite for whiteness often necessitated some compromise on the part of the racialized subject.

This account provided an impression of what a group-level response to individual desires for whiteness might look like. Here, the participant and his friends operate on a mutual understanding of the concessions that persons of color are often required to make in exchange for sexual access to white bodies. These men, however, maintain a jovial yet critical stance, engaging in a form of collective introspection with a kind of levity and playfulness that I seldom encountered in other men of color when discussing sexual racism. At least for the participant, this gradual, sustained, and ultimately well-meaning "ribbing" was a playful way of questioning white erotic hegemony, and undermining its seemingly unassailable ascendancy. For a brief moment, at least among friends, the indelible presence of sexual racism within their intimate lives is reduced into something laughable. Crucially, as well, the desire for whiteness is not pathologized, nor minimized, nor condemned. Instead, it is simply acknowledged, and collective attention drawn to its fundamental absurdity. It is perhaps no coincidence that this participant has one of the most racially diverse sexual resumes among all of the men I spoke to. While both conceding to, and occasionally indulging his appetite for white sexual partners, this individual had also learned to find erotic enjoyment in the kinds of mutual understanding and recognition that were only accessible through intimacy with other persons of color.

Though the disproportionate impact of such a flippant act of resistance may seem surprising, it is well established that deeply entrenched beliefs (implicit or otherwise)—such as those which ascribe preferential value to white persons as intimate partners—are often hideously resistant to direct challenge, as the individual holding these beliefs automatically marshals any number of previously rehearsed (or inculcated) refutations to counter any overt challenge (Kaplan et al., 2016). Conversely, subtle and incremental disruption to these kinds of beliefs often elude these "protective mechanisms" (Ahluwalia, 2000), escaping recognition as a credible threat to these beliefs, which enables them to be substantially altered through sustained, cumulative effort. Hence, it is not unreasonable to think that an individual's implicit belief in the erotic superiority of white persons—and correspondingly, the erotic inferiority of persons of colour—can be destabilized through continual and covert challenges to these beliefs. When accompanied by meaningful, structural change—perhaps of the sort that results in persons of colour being nonprejudicially depicted in both popular and sexual media as fully realized erotic subjects—lasting change to racialized desire can occur.

Incidentally, a change in circumstances that simulated these structural modifications were seemingly experienced by the acquaintance of one participant. This individual had patently refused to entertain the thought of intimacy with Asian men in Australia, but ultimately found a long-term partner in a Singaporean-Chinese man. As recounted, a combination of both casual teasing of the kind described above, as well as his subsequent relocation to Singapore (here East Asian men occupy a hegemonic position within the erotic hierarchy; see Ang et al., 2021), eventually precipitated the "organic" dilation of his racialized desires.[6]

A small number of participants also articulated a more jocular view toward the pedastaled position occupied by whiteness and white bodies within collective sexual life. This was encapsulated in the following participant's droll comment on the experiences of rejection he encountered in his intimate life. He states: "[I get a lot of replies on dating apps going] 'No, I'm not into

---

[6] While a more skeptical interpretation of this development might frame it as the product of necessity and convenience—after all, East Asians are in the numeric majority in Singapore—it should be noted the island hosts a sizable white expatriate population. One large enough that one regularly encounters white expatriates who exclusively date and sleep with *other* white expatriates. Profile descriptions which state 'No Asians!' are also not an uncommon sight on dating apps in Singapore. Take it from a Singaporean citizen.

Asian men,' 'Sorry, no Asians,' or 'Eww, another Asian' or whatever. I'd go 'Uh, it's alright. I'm really not into hairy cavemen. I'm actually into modern, civilized people.'" Discourses like the one above disputed the value commonly ascribed to prominent primary and secondary male sex characteristics such as androgenic hair or excessive muscularity; here, the participant facetiously implies that his preference for "modern and civilized people" is fundamentally incompatible with conventional notions of idealized white masculinity. The ideal homosexual male, he mockingly suggests, is a neanderthal-like creature whose insular stance toward interracial intimacy is explained by the absence of higher-order cognition. This precludes him from being capable of critically examining the racist beliefs that engender his antiquated ethnosexual prejudices. Hence, sexual racists are "uncivilized," and decidedly not "modern": with their ethnosexual prejudices constituting a primitive form of intimate jingoism that betrays a distinct lack of both refinement and culture.

This discursive strategy furthermore harkens to and playfully inverts the kinds of biological essentialism that commonly underpin ethnosexual stereotyping (Han, 2021). For instance, the effeminacy and submissiveness commonly ascribed to the Asian *body* is often viewed as a condition of the inherent physiologic properties of Asian *flesh* (e.g., as weak and sexually monomorphic), ignoring the fact that these phrenological inferences are premised on inaccurate notions about Asian bodies. Applying this logic in a similarly uncharitable manner to white *flesh*, one is able to arrive at a parodically distorted version of the white *body* and the participant is able to demonstrate how the discursive mechanisms that produce erotic disadvantage for racialized persons are almost purposefully designed to disenfranchise the racialized sexual actor. Interestingly, this participant was the sole individual among participants whose entire sexual history was exclusively populated by persons of color. While initially curious about intimacy with white men during his sexual debut, the participant experienced a shocking deluge of racial abuse on both dating apps and the gay "scene" from white actors. To me, it seemed that these discursive reframings were as much a means of critiquing other queer mens' unquestioning acceptance of the narrative components of the white *body* as they were of coping with his deep-seated racial trauma through crass humor. Through the discursive framings discussed above, the desires and erotic preferences of queer racialized subjects are asserted over those of their white counterparts, troubling the notion that the racialized subject ought to occupy a subordinate position within extant hierarchies of desire.

Hence, the ethnosexual discrimination encountered by the queer racialized subject is transformed from a fault of racial alterity—a fundamental and unchangeable "deficiency"—and instead reframed as a fault of the regressive attitudes held by sexual racists toward nonwhites. Notably, these strategies were deployed to modest success, enabling some participants to overcome the distaste they initially harbored toward nonwhite bodies, and broadening previously narrow notions of sexual desirability and worthiness to include both other persons of color as well as themselves. This was in contrast to considerably cruder strategies where participants eschewed intimacy with white persons entirely, or strictly pursued intimacy with nonwhite persons, which were seemingly unsustainable in the long term due to reasons discussed above. Here, I venture that the inability of many participants to successfully enact the latter fundamentally stems from the absence of any paradigmatic change to how one's sexual desires are structured, and thereafter prosecuted. Where whiteness previously transfixes sexual desire, racial alterity is instead nominally elevated in its stead as being desirable, virtuous, and worthy of pursuit. Hence, the reductionist notion that one's skin color is the entire determinant of their sexual worth therefore remains intact, if only momentarily inverted.

Conclusions

Participants sought to unseat their internalized, white-biased erotic preferences through a permutation of projects that broadly attempted to: (1) restrict one's consumption of pornographic media to "empowering" or at the very least, nonderogatory depictions of persons of color and their bodies; (2) eschew the erotic consumption of whiteness all together by refusing intimate interaction with white partners; (3) attempting to limit intimate interactions to only other persons of color, and; (4) discursively reframe the erotic advantage experienced by persons of color.

Insofar as the erotic hegemony of whiteness derives from a multitude of structural inequalities (Green, 2016), it is unsurprising that strategies falling within the first three categories—being as individually focused as they were—saw little success. Considering that sexual socialization is a continual process through which erotic preferences are constantly renegotiated, but which are gradually bought into general alignment with a common structure (Green, 2016), these individualized attempts to alter racialized desire are

236   LIVED REALITIES

situated within (and against) a larger current of ongoing process of socialization that buttresses the erotic hegemony of whiteness. While these desires are readily identifiable, they appear to elude overt rectification (see Silvestrini, 2020); indeed, even by my participants' admissions, such endeavors were only ever partially successful. While many men I spoke to were seemingly able to overcome their sexual indifference (and in some cases, sexual aversion) toward other men of color, virtually none reported any substantial success in subverting their preferential attraction to whiteness.

Of note was the guilt that frequently accompanied these "failures," much of which converged around the implicit belief that ethnosexual preferences were entirely within one's control and that a failure to rectify them was simply owing to insufficient effort or conviction. That "decolonizing" one's desires was almost exclusively framed as a personal project seemed to imply a level of volition over (and thus, personal responsibility for) internalized sexual racism, which did not resonate with neither my nor my participants' experiences. While the consumption of whiteness may be a source of sexual gratification to many queer men of color, I cannot imagine that many are particularly glad for the structural conditions of white supremacy. The current chapter therefore points to the limitations inherent to individualized attempts at re-educating one's erotic desires, at least in the absence of any macrostructural change that first addresses the sociocultural primacy of whiteness. Concurrently, however, it suggests some merit (however modest) to a more nuanced, group-level approach to undermining the erotic hegemony of whiteness, which does not endeavor to legislate desire but instead underscores the farcicality inherent in willingly limiting one's erotic horizons on the basis of skin color.

While white scholars like Orne (2017) have dared to imagine collective erotic life without sexual racism—envisioning it as a utopic terrain consisting of a "queer radical community with people of different races and bodies coming together" (p. 62), and where sexual actors are brought together "across boundaries such as race" (p. 54)—what is perhaps more important in moving toward this vision is to imagine the process by which ethnosexual prejudice can be undone. This question is not exclusively pertinent to the desire for whiteness, and demonstrably retains its relevance even within those contexts where whiteness, occupies position of dominance but not hegemony. Within these contexts, hegemonic ethnosexualities are likewise preferentially sought out for consumption and prized over other racial subjectivities in ways that recognizably translate to the concurrent subordination of said subjects (see Baudinette, 2016; Kang, 2017; Prankumar et al., 2021). The erotic consumption of race in both *body* and *flesh* evidently presents an insurmountable hurdle to realizing this scenario.

It seems clear racial desires cannot be forcibly molded into egalitarian configurations, defying outright attempts at discipline. Perhaps the only way that entrenched intimate prejudice can be meaningfully undermined is through sustained, incremental—and most importantly, subtle—challenges against our inculcated desires for whiteness. As subtlety forms a critical component of such strategies, they are likely impossible to enact within a solitary context, and therefore necessitate a group-level or otherwise collective effort to successfully use. While seemingly onerous, the experiences of my participants suggest that these strategies can often take on a light-hearted, tongue-in-cheek quality and are perhaps even unfeasible otherwise. This makes some intuitive sense: insofar as sexual racism settles into the erotic consciousness in ways that are often insidious and unseen, surely it must be excised through comparably "insidious" means. Admittedly, some might be mortified to imagine undoing the white supremacy of our desires might involve irreverence or frivolity in any measure. But given how (sexual) racism looms constantly over the lives—intimate or otherwise—of persons of color, don't you think we should be allowed to have at least a little fun?

References

Ahluwalia, R. (2000). Examination of psychological processes underlying resistance to persuasion. *Journal of Consumer Research, 27*(2), 217–232.

Ahmed, S. (2006). *Queer phenomenology: orientations, objects, others.* Duke University Press. https://cir.nii.ac.jp/crid/1130282271310909440

Ahn, J. H. (2018). Consuming cosmopolitan white (ness). In J. H. Ahn (Ed.), *Mixed-race politics and neoliberal multiculturalism in South Korean media* (pp. 103–128). Palgrave Macmillan

Alexander, J. R. (2003). Obscenity, pornography and the law in Japan: Reconsidering Oshima's *In the Realm of the Senses. Asian-Pacific Law and Policy Journal, 4*, i.

Ang, M. W., Tan, J. C. K., & Lou, C. (2021). Navigating sexual racism in the sexual field: Compensation for and disavowal of marginality by racial minority Grindr users in Singapore. *Journal of Computer-Mediated Communication, 26*(3), 129–147.

Arrington-Sanders, R., Harper, G. W., Morgan, A., Ogunbajo, A., Trent, M., & Fortenberry, J. D. (2015). The role of sexually explicit material in the sexual development of same-sex-attracted Black adolescent males. *Archives of Sexual Behavior, 44*(3), 597–608.

Ayres, T. (1999). China doll-the experience of being a gay Chinese Australian. *Journal of Homosexuality, 36*(3–4), 87–97.

238   LIVED REALITIES

Baudinette, T. (2016, October). Ethnosexual frontiers in queer Tokyo: The production of racialised desire in Japan. *Japan Forum, 28*(4), 465–485.

Bedi, S. (2015). Sexual racism: Intimacy as a matter of justice. *The Journal of Politics, 77*(4), 998–1011. https://doi.org/10.1086/682749

Bishop, C. J. (2015). "Cocked, locked and ready to fuck?": A synthesis and review of the gay male pornography literature. *Psychology and Sexuality, 6*(1), 5–27.

Bujan, I. (2023). Undesiring whiteness and undoing the white gaze in HIV prevention marketing. In D. Callander, P. Farvid, A. Baradaran, & T. Vance (Eds.), *Sexual Racisim and Social Justice* (pp. 116–140). Oxford University Press.

Butler, J. (1997). *The psychic life of power: Theories in subjection.* Stanford University Press.

Callander, D., Holt, M., & Newman, C. E. (2017). Gay racism. In D. W. Riggs (Ed.), *The psychic life of racism in gay men's communities* (pp. 1–14). Lexington Books.

Caluya, G. (2008). "The rice steamer": Race, desire and affect in Sydney's gay scene. *Australian Geographer, 39*(3), 283–292.

Carlson, B., & Frazer, R. (2021). Desire. In B. Carlson, & R. Frazer (Eds.), *Indigenous digital life* (pp. 95–120). Palgrave Macmillan.

Carter, J. B. (2007). *The heart of whiteness: Normal sexuality and race in America, 1880–1940.* Duke University Press.

Chancer, L., & Andrews, J. (2014). Introduction: The unhappy divorce: From marginalization to revitalization. In L. Chancer, & J. Andrews (Eds.), *The unhappy divorce of sociology and psychoanalysis* (pp. 1–14). Palgrave Macmillan. https://doi.org/10.1057/9781137304582_1.

Childs, E. C. (2005). *Navigating interracial borders: Black-white couples and their social worlds.* Rutgers University Press.

Chin, C. S. (2018). *Yellow fever: Asian representation in western pornography* [Doctoral dissertation]. Chapman University.

Corneau, S., Dominic, B. P., Murray, S. J., Bernatchez, K., & Lecompte, M. (2021). Gay male pornography and the racialisation of desire. *Culture, Health and Sexuality, 23*(5), 579–592.

Conner, C. T. (2019). The gay gayze: Expressions of inequality on Grindr. *Sociological Quarterly, 60*(3), 397–419.

Durkee, M. I., & Gómez, J. M. (2021). Mental health implications of the acting white accusation: The role of cultural betrayal and ethnic-racial identity among Black and Latina/o emerging adults. *American Journal of Orthopsychiatry, 92*(1): 68–78. https://doi.org/10.1037/ort0000589

Dyer, R. (1997). The white man's muscles. In R. Adams, & D. Savran (Eds.), *Masculinity Studies Reader* (pp. 286–314). Blackwell.

Fluri, J. L., Hickcox, A., Frydenlund, S., & Zackary, R. (2020). Accessing racial privilege through property: Geographies of racial capitalism. *Geoforum, 132*, 238–46.

Frankenberg, R. (2004). On unsteady ground: Crafting and engaging in the critical study of whiteness. In M. Bulmer, & J. Solomos (Eds.), *Researching race and racism* (pp. 116–130). Routledge.

Frosh, S. (2013). Psychoanalysis, colonialism, racism. *Journal of Theoretical and Philosophical Psychology, 33*(3), 141.

Fung, R. (1991). Looking for my penis: The eroticized Asian in gay porn video. In Russell Leong (Ed.), *How do I look?* (pp. 145–168). Routledge.

Green, A. I. (2014). The sexual fields framework. In A. I. Green (Ed.), *Sexual fields: Toward a sociology of collective sexual life* (pp. 25–56). University of Chicago Press.

CONSUMING WHITENESS/DISCIPLINING DESIRE   239

Green, A. I. (2016). Sexual capital and social inequality. In C. Meeks, N. Fischer, & S. Seidman (Eds.), *Introducing the new sexuality studies* (pp. 272–281). Taylor & Francis.

Hammack, P. L., Grecco, B., Wilson, B. D. M. & Meyer, I.H. (2022). "White, Tall, Top, Masculine, Muscular": Narratives of Intracommunity stigma in young sexual minority men's experience on mobile apps. *Archives of Sexual Behavior, 51,* 2413–2428. https:// doi.org/10.1007/s10508-021-02144-z

Han, C. S. (2008). A qualitative exploration of the relationship between racism and unsafe sex among Asian Pacific Islander gay men. *Archives of Sexual Behaviour, 37*(5), 827–837.

Han, C. W. (2015). *Geisha of a different kind: Race and sexuality in Gaysian America.* New York University Press.

Han, C. W. (2021). *Racial erotics: Gay men of color, sexual racism, and the politics of desire.* University of Washington Press.

Han, C. S., & Choi, K. H. (2018). Very few people say "No Whites": Gay men of colour and the racial politics of desire. *Sociological Spectrum, 38*(3), 145–161.

hooks, b. (1992). Eating the other: Desire and resistance. In b.hooks, *Black Looks: Race and Representation* (pp. 21–39). Boston: South End Press.

Hoskin, R. A. (2019). Femmephobia: The role of anti-femininity and gender policing in LGBTQ+ people's experiences of discrimination. *Sex Roles,* 81(11–12), 686–703.

Jackson, P. A. (2000). "That's what rice queens study!": White gay desire and representing Asian homosexualities. *Journal of Australian Studies, 24*(65), 181–188.

Kang, D. B. C. (2017). Eastern orientations: Thai middle-class gay desire for "white Asians." *Culture, Theory and Critique, 58*(2), 182–208.

Kaplan, J. T., Gimbel, S. I., & Harris, S. (2016). Neural correlates of maintaining one's political beliefs in the face of counterevidence. *Scientific Reports, 6*(1), 1–11.

Kim, N. Y. (2006). "Patriarchy is so third world": Korean immigrant women and "migrating" white western masculinity. *Social Problems, 53*(4), 519–536.

Kozak, M., Frankenhauser, H., & Roberts, T. A. (2009). Objects of desire: Objectification as a function of male sexual orientation. *Psychology of Men and Masculinity, 10*(3), 225.

Landi, D. (2019). Queer men, affect, and physical education. *Qualitative Research in Sport, Exercise and Health, 11*(2), 168–187.

Lauritsen, J. (1993). Political-economic construction of gay male clone identity. *Journal of Homosexuality, 24*(3–4), 221–232.

Leung, H. (2016). *Being gay and Asian: The journey to finding a voice in New York City,* Doctoral Dissertation, The New School. Available from: https://www.proquest.com/docview/1865658374.

Levine, M. P., & Kimmel, M. (1998). *Gay macho: The life and death of the homosexual clone.* New York University Press.

Lim, M. S., Agius, P. A., Carrotte, E. R., Vella, A. M., & Hellard, M. E. (2017). Young Australians' use of pornography and associations with sexual risk behaviours. *Australian and New Zealand Journal of Public Health, 41*(4), 438–443.

Lim, C. C., & Anderson, R. C. (2023). Effect of sexual racism on partner desirability in gay Asian men. *Journal of Homosexuality, 70*(2), 329–346. https://doi.org/10.1080/00918 369.2021.1948772

Marriott, D. (2007). *Haunted life: Visual culture and Black modernity.* Rutgers University Press.

Matheson, J. (2012, December 14). I'm a sexual racist. Sydney Star Observer. Retrieved from https://doi.org/10.6084/m9.figshare.25050530.v1

240 LIVED REALITIES

McKee, A., Albury, K., & Lumby, C. (2008). *The porn report*. Melbourne University Publishing.

Mercer, J. (2017). Popperbate: Video collage, vernacular creativity, and the scripting of the gay pornographic body. *Porn Studies, 4*(2), 242–256.

Morgan-Sowada, H., & Gamboni, C. (2021). Needing to be "perfect" to be loved: The intersection of body dysmorphic disorder, sexual identity, and gay culture in gay men: A qualitative study. *Sexual and Relationship Therapy,* 1–19. https://doi.org/10.1080/14681 994.2021.1975672

Nagel, J. (2000). Ethnicity and sexuality. *Annual Review of Sociology, 26*(1), 107–133.

Nemoto, K. (2008). Climbing the hierarchy of masculinity: Asian American men's cross-racial competition for intimacy with white women. *Gender Issues, 25*(2), 80–100.

O'Harris, J. (2016, December 19). Decolonizing my desire. *VICE*. Retrieved from https://www.vice.com/en/article/8qgm9g/decolonizing-my-desire.

Olivera-La Rosa, A., Arango-Tobón, O. E., & Ingram, G. P. (2019). Swiping right: Face perception in the age of Tinder. *Heliyon, 5*(12), e02949.

Orne, J. (2017). *Boystown: Sex and community in Chicago*. University of Chicago Press.

Osuji, C. K. (2019). *Boundaries of love: Interracial marriage and the meaning of race*. New York University Press.

Pachankis, J. E., Clark, K. A., Burton, C. L., Hughto, J. M. W., Bränström, R., & Keene, D. E. (2020). Sex, status, competition, and exclusion: Intra-minority stress from within the gay community and gay and bisexual men's mental health. *Journal of Personality and Social Psychology* 119(3), 712–740.

Pande, A. (2021). "Mix or match?": Transnational fertility industry and white desirability. *Medical Anthropology, 40*(4), 335–347.

Pinckney IV, H. P. , Outley C., Brown A., & Theriault D. (2018). Playing while Black. *Leisure Sciences, 40*(7), 675–685. DOI: 10.1080/01490400.2018.1534627

Plummer, M. D. (2007). *Sexual racism in gay communities: Negotiating the ethnosexual marketplace* [Doctoral dissertation]. University of Washington.

Prankumar, S. K., Aggleton, P., & Bryant, J. (2021). Belonging, citizenship and ambivalence among young gay, bisexual and queer Indian Singaporean men. *Asian Studies Review, 45*(1), 155–174.

Prestage, G., Mao, L., Philpot, S., Jin, F., Callander, D., Doyle, M., . . . Bavinton, B. (2018). The role of age and homonegativity in racial or ethnic partner preferences among Australian gay and bisexual men. *Archives of Sexual Behavior, 48*(1), 357–368.

Raj, S. (2011). Grindring bodies: Racial and affective economies of online queer desire. *Critical Race and Whiteness Studies, 7*(2), 1–12.

Ravenhill, J. P., & de Visser, R. O. (2019). "I don't want to be seen as a screaming queen": An interpretative phenomenological analysis of gay men's masculine identities. *Psychology of Men and Masculinities, 20*(3), 324.

Riggs, D. W. (2013). Anti-Asian sentiment amongst a sample of white Australian men on gaydar. *Sex Roles, 68*(11–12), 768–778.

Riggs, D.W. (2017). Introduction: Towards a typology of racisms in gay men's communities. In D. W. Riggs (Ed.), *The psychic life of racism in gay men's communities* (pp. ix–xii). Lexington Books.

Ruez, D. (2017). "I never felt targeted as an Asian . . . until I went to a gay pub": Sexual racism and the aesthetic geographies of the bad encounter. *Environment and Planning A, 49*(4), 893–910.

Russell, J. G. (2017). Replicating the white self and other: Skin colour, racelessness, gynoids, and the construction of whiteness in Japan. *Japanese Studies, 37*(1), 23–48.

Salamanca, P., Janulis, P., Elliott, M., Birkett, M., Mustanski, B., & Phillips, G. (2019). An investigation of racial and ethnic homophily on Grindr among an ongoing cohort study of YMSM. *AIDS and Behavior, 23*(1), 302–311.

Salamanca, P., Janulis, P., Elliott, M., Birkett, M., Mustanski, B., & Phillips II, G. (2019). An investigation of racial and ethnic homophily on grindr among an ongoing cohort study of YMSM. *AIDS and Behavior, 23*, 302–311. https://doi.org/10.1007/s10461-018-2262-7

Seitz, D. K. (2019a). "What do gay Asian men want?": Desiring otherwise in the work of Richard Fung. *Emotion, Space and Society, 31*, 148–154.

Seitz, D. K. (2019b). Looking for Pei Lim's penis: Melancholia, mimicry, pedagogy. *Porn Studies, 6*(1), 48–58.

Shapiro, A. (2019). *Intimate (anti-) racism and white gay men: A psychosocial approach* [Doctoral dissertation]. City University of New York.

Smith, J. G. (2017). Two-face racism in gay online sex. In P. G. Nixon, & I. K. Dusterhoft (Eds.), *Sex in the digital age* (pp. 1–31). Routledge.

Smith, J. G., Morales, M. C., & Han, C. S. (2018). The influence of sexual racism on erotic capital: A systemic racism perspective. In P. Batur, & J. R. Feagin (Eds.), *Handbook of the sociology of racial and ethnic relations* (pp. 389–399). Springer.

Souleymanov, R., Brennan, D. J., George, C., Utama, R., & Ceranto, A. (2020). Experiences of racism, sexual objectification, and alcohol use among gay and bisexual men of colour. *Ethnicity and Health, 25*(4), 525–541.

Spillers, H. J. (1987). Mama's baby, Papa's maybe: An American grammar book. *Diacritics, 17*(2), 65–81.

Silvestrini, M. (2020). "It's not something I can shake": The effect of racial stereotypes, beauty standards, and sexual racism on interracial attraction. *Sexuality and Culture, 24*(1), 305–325.

Waling, A. (2019). *White masculinity in contemporary Australia: The good ol' Aussie bloke.* Routledge.

Wood, M. J. (2004). The gay male gaze: Body image disturbance and gender oppression among gay men. *Journal of Gay and Lesbian Social Services, 17*(2), 43–62.

Young, A. V. (2009). Honorary whiteness. *Asian Ethnicity, 10*(2), 177–185.

Yue, A. (2008). Gay Asian sexual health in Australia: Governing HIV/AIDS, racializing biopolitics and performing conformity. *Sexualities, 11*(1–2), 227–244.

Žižek, Slavoj. 1998. Love thy neighbor? No, thanks! In C. Lane (Ed.), *The psychoanalysis of race* (154–175). Columbia University Press.

11

Sexual Racism as White Privilege

The Psychic and Relational Negotiation of Desire, Power, and Sex

Russell K. Robinson

Introduction

There is a growing cohort of scholars examining how sexual racism is enacted and experienced. While some of this work has considered the dynamics enacted by White people and through systems of Whiteness, rarely has it named and engaged specifically with the concept of White privilege. Because White privilege gives shape to (and derives from) sexual racism, a close examination of its mechanics may help in dismantling the broader systems of power activated through sexual racism. In this chapter, I seek both to center people of color and to focus on how White privilege often functions as an unwritten script in their interactions with White partners. Specifically, I seek to unmask the process of how White privilege unfolds in the relational negotiation of desire, sex, and power within the context of interracial sexualized encounters.

To such ends, this study examined experiences of racial fetishization described in interview data from a racially, sexually, and gender diverse sample of 48 people in the United States. Importantly, this sample was composed entirely of individuals who identified as lesbian, gay, bisexual, transgender, queer, and/or intersex (LGBTQI), a sample that helps broaden previous work beyond a primary focus on cisgender gay men. My analysis yielded three interrelated themes: (1) *White privilege sets the scene* by imposing coconstructed gendered, sexualized, and racialized assumptions on people of color and generally expecting their acquiescence. (2) *White privilege restricts negotiation* because people of color often have difficulty navigating the offensive impositions of White partners and risk losing access to sexual and romantic encounters if negotiations fail. Importantly,

Russell K. Robinson, *Sexual Racism as White Privilege* In: *Sexual Racism and Social Justice*. Edited by: Denton Callander, Panteá Farvid, Amir Baradaran, and Thomas A. Vance, Oxford University Press. © Oxford University Press 2024.
DOI: 10.1093/oso/9780197605509.003.0012

White people do not face this dilemma, and some deploy their privilege to deflect negotiation. (3) *White privilege undermines resistance.* Even though many LGBTQI people of color seek to resist White privilege through vigilance, avoidance, resistance, and education, such strategies appear to be of limited effectiveness and often result in denial or rejection. Further, the modes of resistance themselves demonstrate the dominant influence of White privilege.

Background

Before delving into my analysis in greater detail, it is necessary to establish the conceptual and empirical foundations of this work. Through the chapter, I capitalize "White" specifically to counter the view that Whiteness is the absence of racial identity. As Eve Ewing incisively argues, "When we ignore the specificity and significance of Whiteness—the things that it is, the things that it does—we contribute to its seeming neutrality and thereby grant it power to maintain its invisibility" (Ewing, 2020).

Scholars have separately studied White privilege and sexual racism, and yet White privilege has rarely been used as a framework for understanding the ways in which intimate contact is negotiated between White and non-White sexual partners. Sexual racism can be understood in at least two senses. First, this volume makes evident the foundational role of sexuality in producing White supremacy, and vice versa. For example, fears of interracial commingling have driven White policymakers to maintain segregated schools and neighborhoods (e.g., Hampton, 2006). Beyond structural dimensions, the individual level of sexual and romantic intimacies represents a second layer of sexual racism. Analyzing White privilege creates the possibility of bridging the structural and individual layers. Thus, I contend that not only is White privilege a foundational component of White supremacy but also that it orders how individuals tend to interact in sexual and romantic relationships. It may cultivate sexual situations that benefit White people and create invisible obstacles to people of color's sexual liberty and pleasure.

Critical race theory scholars and critical Whiteness scholars have described the power and simultaneous invisibility (at least to many White people and White-dominated systems) of White privilege (Ewing, 2020; Harris, 1993; McIntosh, 1989). As Barbara Applebaum explains:

244 LIVED REALITIES

> White norms permeate white dominated society, yet these norms appear to be common and value-neutral to the social groups that benefit from them. These norms create the standards by which "difference" is constructed. (Applebaum, 2016)

Moreover, "the set of assumptions, privileges and benefits that accompany the status of being white have become a valuable asset that whites sought to protect. . . . Whites have come to expect and rely upon these benefits, and over time these expectations have been affirmed, legitimated, and protected by law" (Harris, 1993). Whiteness may also be understood as "the veneer of presumed innocence, respectability, and righteousness" that protects White people "like a shield" when they engage in wrongdoing (Ewing, 2020).

The "invisibility" and "innocence" of these practices to White people protects them from meaningful scrutiny in predominantly White spaces (DiAngelo, 2018; Flagg, 1993). People of color, especially African Americans, are more likely than White people to be conscious and critical of racial power dynamics in interracial interactions (Ro et al., 2013; Robinson, 2008). However, asserting the significance of race, including White privilege, may provoke a "fragile" response from a White person who resists seeing their behavior in racial terms or acknowledging the wrongfulness of such power dynamics (Berube, 2001; DiAngelo, 2018). Because such conflicts may disrupt relationships, people of color experience pressure to provide "racial comfort," downplay the significance of race, and enable White people to ignore how they exert their privilege (Carbado & Gulati, 2000). This study seeks to further scholarship on White privilege in the sexual domain by examining sexualized interactions between LGBTQI people of different races in the United States.

Some previous work finds evidence of White privilege in that White cisgender gay men are consistently the most likely to articulate their desires in racially exclusive terms, whereas people of color are more likely to reference race in a self-description or to indicate openness to all races (Callander, Newman, et al., 2012; Phua & Kaufman, 2003). Similarly, research has found that White men of all sexual orientations are the most likely of any racial and gender configuration to receive messages and responses when seeking partners online (Curington et al., 2021; Lin & Lundquist, 2013). Although men and women of various races respond most frequently to White men, the exception is Black gay men, "who appear to privilege other Black gay men." Even when accounting for "age, education, physical attributes, lifestyles, and personal compatibility," a "powerful white male privilege in the online dating market" endures (Curington et al., 2021). The fact that people of color tend to have more limited romantic and sexual options, and White men are widely prized, may create a competitive frenzy within groups such as Asian gay men (Lim & Anderson, 2021). White women also enjoy racial privilege in dating. However, White straight men's and White lesbians' preferences for a same-race partner are somewhat weaker than those of their counterparts (White straight women and White gay men) (Curington et al., 2021).

Despite clear indications of White supremacy, many White gay cisgender men—and some gay men of color—have described their desires as "personal" and "just a preference," a rhetorical move that aims to disconnect their experiences from broader patterns of White supremacy in dating and relationships (Callander et al., 2012, 2016; Smith, 2017). In a 2015 study of attitudes among Australian gay and bisexual cisgender men, Callander et al., found that roughly half of the respondents agreed that "Racism is not really a problem on Internet sex and dating sites." Roughly one-quarter disagreed; and the remainder were neutral. In this sample, White men were more likely than men of color to view sexual racism as harmless (Callander et al., 2015). In this and other research, cisgender gay men have been found to actively resist the very notion of sexual racism (Callander et al., 2023; Smith, 2017), often characterizing such arguments as a threat to hard-won sexual liberties. White privilege can be seen as coursing through such rhetoric, as it imposes one (White) view of sexual liberty and willfully ignores that freedom— sexual or otherwise—is not and has never been universally enjoyed among racialized others.

This brief review of the literature reveals that to-date scholars of sexual racism have predominantly focused on gay, bisexual, and other men who have sex with men (e.g., Callander et al., 2015; Han, 2006; Raj, 2011) and on online contexts (e.g., Prestage et al., 2019; Smith & Amaro, 2021; Wilson et al., 2009). Further, most of this research centers targets of sexual racism, typically gay men of color, and does not fully examine White privilege (e.g., Bhambhani et al., 2019; Hidalgo et al., 2020; Souleymanov et al., 2020). In this chapter, I aim to build on this scholarship by examining how White privilege operates in relational and intimate experiences of sexual racism among a more diverse group of LGBTQI people in the United States. Specifically, the analysis seeks to make visible subtle cultural mechanics that empower White people and oppress people of color in sexual contexts.

Method

Study Design

This chapter draws on data from the LGBT Relationships Study, a qualitative study that began interviewing LGBTQI people in fall 2015 and completed interviews in summer 2019. This study was grounded in intersectionality, which articulates how systems of subordination (e.g., racism, patriarchy, homophobia, biphobia, transphobia) are coconstructed and overlap to produce distinct forms of vulnerability (Crenshaw, 1989). This analytical lens shaped all aspects of the study design, including construction of the research team, interview protocol, sampling method, analysis, and interpretation. For example, we took steps to identify and recruit research investigators and staff identified under the umbrella of LGBTQI but with diversity in terms of gender, race, class, and other characteristics.

The structured interview protocol contained multiple questions concerning the experiences with relationships and discrimination over the participant's entire life span. The interview protocol covered several specific topics including race, gender/gender identity, sexual orientation, family dynamics, sexual behavior, stigma of various forms, and health issues, including HIV, alcohol and substance abuse, and mental health. The design of this study was reviewed and approved by the Institutional Review Board of University of California, Berkeley (protocol number 2014-02-6070).

Recruitment

The study recruited participants from a wide range of venues associated with LGBTQI populations in three major cities in the United States, Chicago, New York City, and San Francisco Bay Area. A list of venues created for a separate project known as the Generations Study was used to identify sites of recruitment (Krueger et al., 2020). A team of LGBTQI-identified research assistants in their 20s and 30s helped to update the database by reviewing online listings and directories, adding newer venues and removing those no longer active.

At identified venues, the research team circulated flyers that directed potential participants to the study website to enroll. The study design deliberately limited the number of participants recruited from each venue to two, being particularly cautious about overreliance on "mainstream" LGBTQI venues (e.g., bars, nightclubs). Other types of recruitment venues included coffee shops, bookstores, barbershops, street fairs, people of color–oriented community groups, and churches. The study also recruited participants through advertisement placed on Facebook and through those distributed via existing professional networks. Finally, participants who sat for interviews referred people in their social networks. Advertisements for the study included a link to a brief online screening questionnaire to assess eligibility. Participants were eligible if they were between ages 18 and 65, identified as one or more identity making up LGBTQI, and had any experience with dating or intimate relationships.

The study design deployed stratified sampling to ensure sufficient subsamples of Black, Latinx, and Asian American participants. Transgender and gender-diverse people were also oversampled because these groups have often been overlooked in dating and relationships research (for more detail, please see Albury et al., 2021). A total of 992 people responded to the eligibility questionnaire. After the research team assessed eligibility and compliance with sampling needs, we invited 120 participants for an interview. The final sample consisted of 99 people who completed an interview, which typically lasted 60–90 minutes and took place in a research office or private location of the participant's choosing. Participants received a $50 prepaid visa card as a token of appreciation.

Sample

People of color (68%) made up the majority of the final sample of 99 participants. Thirty percent of our sample identified as Latinx. Twenty-three percent of participants identified as Black; 13% identified as Asian American; and 31% identified as mixed race (many of whom also identified as Latinx). Thirty-two percent identified as White. Fifty-six percent of participants reported that they were presumed male sex at birth; 41% were presumed female sex at birth; 1% identified as intersex. While the majority of participants were cisgender, nearly one-third were not cisgender, including 10% who identified as transgender, 15% who identified as gender-queer, and 7% who identified their gender as "something else" and wrote in a particular identity or identities.

The analysis described in this chapter focused on White privilege, and thus is limited to the 48 participants who described experiences of

248 LIVED REALITIES

"fetishization" (48.5% of the total sample). While some participants described other experiences of fetishization, the majority were racialized. Here, racial fetishization was defined as experiences in dating relationships that stem from one partner's sexual focus or obsession with racialized aspects of the other partner's identity, a definition sufficiently broad to encompass obsession with both White and people of color identities. This definition, however, is also sufficiently narrow so as to exclude other forms of racism that did not fit the code for fetishization, such as certain racial microaggressions and racial rejections on dating apps (i.e., "No Blacks and Asians").

The racial demographics of this subsample (n = 48) were as follows: 38% Black (n = 18); 23% Asian American (n = 11); 13% White (n = 6); and 10% mixed race (n = 5). Latinx participants, who could identify as any race, were 25% of the subsample (n = 12). The gender demographics were as follows: 54% cisgender men (n = 26), 21% cisgender women (n = 10), 15% transgender men (n = 7), 2% transgender women (n = 1), 4% nonbinary (n = 2), 2% genderqueer (n = 1), 6% some other expression of gender diversity (n = 3), and 2% intersex (n = 1). The sexual orientation demographics were: 48% gay (n = 23), 29% queer (n = 14), 19% bisexual (n = 9), 4% heterosexual (n = 2), 4% lesbian (n = 2), 2% pansexual (n = 1), and 2% "fluid" (n = 1). I note that participants were able to identify as more than one gender, race, and sexual orientation.

Analysis

The research team developed codes and then themes through an inductive approach to thematic analysis recommended by Braun and Clark (2006). Initially, I worked with a graduate student to code all interviews. Several months later, I worked with a different graduate student, and we jointly examined all "fetishization" excerpts and their fuller interviews to understand how Whiteness operated. During weekly meetings, we scrutinized each excerpt to consider the power dynamics in each scenario and discussed at weekly meetings various possible interpretations of the interactions. We looked for explicit and subtle evidence of White privilege, such as leverage in determining the nature of a sexual interaction, as well as evidence of the participants of color resisting these moves. We considered possible connections between a particular interaction and the participant's broader life story and relationship experiences, as context for how they handled the incident. Across the 48 interviews included in this subsample, our analysis yielded 89 excerpts of fetishization, with several participants relating multiple experiences.

Results and Discussion

Participant experiences of racial fetishization helped to illuminate sexual racism as the backdrop for their dating and sexual experiences, a phenomenon visible primarily to LGBTQI people of color. Through my analysis, it was clear White privilege gives structure to the backdrop of sexual racism in three mains ways: (1) White privilege sets the scene, (2) White privilege resists negotiation, and (3) White privilege undermines resistance. These are discussed below in detail and with illustrative data extracts.

White Privilege Sets the Scene

A recurring theme in several interviews was that White privilege enabled White people to set the terms of interracial sexual encounters, determining the distribution of power through subtle or explicit expressions of entitlement. Such entitlement often took the form of assumptions, including perceptions of the sexual orientation or sexual availability of a person of color. For example, James, a Black gay cisgender man from New York described having White women who were strangers aggressively flirt with him in public, even though he was clearly with his White male partner. James recalled being accosted in social spaces: "White women who drink . . .they just, they will invariably start to touch me. . . . It's a thing. It has always been a thing. If I tell them 'stop touching me,' they go . . ., 'How dare you?'" Such responses clearly demonstrate White women's entitlement to experience Black men's bodies (without their consent) and ensuing outrage when Black men do not reciprocate attraction to them.

In this instance, the privileges enacted by these White women not only sexualized this Black man, but also made assumptions about his sexuality while ignoring his relationship with another man. Over time, his White male partner learned to intervene and protect him from unwanted sexual advances from White women, illustrating another way in which White privilege "sets the scene" for interracial sexualized dynamics. In another example

250　LIVED REALITIES

of assumptions, Megan—a Black biracial and bisexual/queer-identified woman in Chicago—reported that White queer women had difficulty recognizing her as queer because she is Black and "really femme." Elaborating on this racialized bi-erasure, Megan stated, "People would never—I always had to prove that I was actually queer. That's still true, I think now that I've had public relationships with men." In examples like these, White people felt privileged to make assumptions about LGBTQI people of color that rendered invisible key dimensions of their sexualities. White heterosexual women's assumption that James was heterosexual subjected him to unwanted sexual advances. By contrast, White queer women who regarded Megan as heterosexual erased her as a potential sexual partner.

Participants' descriptions of racial fetishization repeatedly highlighted how White privilege fostered highly gendered assumptions about their sexualities. It was common for participants to report that White people projected a fetishized sex role onto the subject because of the racial difference in their identities, with the most common role assigned to Black participants that of the "big, Black, buck." Carl, who is Black, cisgender, male, stands about 6'3", is dark-brown-skinned, muscular, and wears dreadlocks, described having White men pursue him because they wanted to experience being with a big Black man. Even though Carl described himself as sexually versatile and far from hypermasculine, White men typically treated him as a top, and at times he acquiesced. "I think the bigger you are," he explained, "the more the idea is that you're going to dominate." Race magnified this effect: "if you're a Black man and you're with someone outside your race, they always tend to, 90 percent of the time, they tend to want you to be the aggressive." He described meeting men that he hoped would be dominant in bed, but when they signaled otherwise in the bedroom he would, "go with the flow." Speaking of one White partner who suddenly discarded him after several months in a relationship, Carl said, "He was attracted to the idea of being a smaller, White guy with this big Black dude. He just wanted to have that moment." By contrast, Black men who were transgender and/or intersex and short said that cisgender gay men (of various races) assumed them to be bottoms and would not permit them to top because they were not cisgender men.

White obsession with Black dominance was not restricted to Black cisgender men. Brittany, a Black transgender woman in her late 30s who described herself as conventionally feminine, noting she was generally perceived by others as cisgender, described "coming out" to her love interest

SEXUAL RACISM AS WHITE PRIVILEGE 251

Nico, an Italian and Colombian cisgender man in his mid-50s. Shortly after she disclosed being trans, Nico asked her to dominate him:

> Well, he sat next to me and he pulled his pants down and he was like, "Hit my butt." I'm like, "Okay." Then, he was like, "Do you like that?" I'm like, "Well, I don't have a feeling toward it." It just became exploratory and then I saw him 12 times. Each time, we took it a step further.

Her Blackness and transgender experience appeared to intersect, in Nico's mind, to undercut Brittany's own sense of self, as well as her sexual desires. When Nico asked Brittany, "Do you like that?," her response was equivocal, but Nico continued to press her deeper into a "Bondage/Discipline, Dominance/Submission, Sadism/Masochism" (BDSM) experience in which she was racialized and gendered as the dominant partner.

Angel, a Latinx nonbinary person in their 30s, said that friends described their gender as "soft masc." Angel, however, had a desire to appear more feminine and complained about being foisted into the role of top. They recounted an exchange with a White man in a San Francisco bathhouse where:

> The man ask[ed] me if I was Mexican. I said yes, and he said he wanted me to fuck him like I was a Mexican, so, which probably meant that he wanted me to be a lot more aggressive and rough.

Angel had sex with the man, but recalled it as uncomfortable because of "performance anxiety." Describing their anxious thoughts, Angel stated, "Okay, you're the top and you're the man, and so you have to be the man in bed. If you're not the man, then this experience is going to be horrible for both of you." Angel's and Brittany's experiences both reflect how gendered norms, racialized sexual ideals, and White privilege allowed their partners to set the scene of their engagement, rather than inquiring into and engaging with their individual identities and desires.

Ramsey, a Black, nonbinary person in the San Francisco Bay Area in their 20s, described similar tension between their race and gender identity while in a committed relationship with Tyler, a White gay cisgender man. Ramsey said that Tyler "always expected, although [he] never said it—he always expected me to be the top in the relationship. . . . He was very adamant on taking pride on being the bottom . . .and particularly bottoming for a Black man." Tyler's prior partners had been Black tops. Ramsey recalls being "very

252   LIVED REALITIES

clear" with Tyler at the beginning of their relationship that he was not a top nor a man, but Tyler projected his own racialized fetishes onto their experience. Ramsey initially acquiesced. However, eventually, due at least in part to multiple racial fissures in the relationship, Ramsey had sex with other partners and ended the relationship with Tyler.

In detailing this theme, I have presented experiences of LGBTQI people with diverse gendered and racial positionalities. Despite this diversity, White privilege and gendered/racialized desires consistently "set the scene" for our participants and was often met with acquiescence or silence. This last point is particularly important, because it suggests not only are LGBTQI people of color in the United States required to exist within a sexualized frame dictated by White privilege, but that they must find ways to navigate a backdrop of sexual racism to maintain their emotional, sexual, and personal well-being.

White Privilege Undermines Negotiation

Building on the first theme, it was clear that participants of various racial backgrounds were navigating and negotiating their own or their partners' White privilege. Some participants of color described scenarios in which White people suggested that racialized fetishes would enhance sexual pleasure . . . for the White partner. As such, participants frequently reported that White people confidently expressed their fetishes to a person of color, casting fetishization as a sexual advance. Jackson, a light-skinned Black cisgender man in Chicago, stated that most White gay cisgender men that he encountered at some point made a racialized reference to his penis (e.g., one stated, "I bet you're Black all over.")

In another example, Megan from Chicago recalled:

> Amber [a White female partner] saying how she always wanted to date a black girl; she had "jungle fever." I hadn't heard it before, but I was like "that's weird, I don't know what to do with that."

The expression "jungle fever" implies that Black people originate from the jungle and evokes a primitive, animalistic, and barbaric state, and has long been examined as a trope in relationships between White and Black partners (e.g., Scott, 1994; Yancey, 2003). Reports like these were common, and the White people involved seemed to intend their racial fetishes to be seen as flirtation. They were generally oblivious that their advances were not taken that way. By contrast, people of color described finding this talk offensive. This represents a phenomenon that I have previously called "perceptual segregation," whereby White people, in general, are socialized to ignore racial dynamics, including their own privilege, while people of color must navigate it in order to survive (hooks, 1992; Robinson, 2008).

Because people of color must continually negotiate their sexuality in the context of White privilege, participants of color were highly cognizant that failure to acquiesce could limit their sexual opportunities. Put another way, they knew that rejecting the racialized scene set by White privilege could mean losing a sexual or romantic opportunity. This potential loss, however, had to be balanced against their sense of self-respect and integrity. Sami, an Asian American transgender man in San Francisco, explained tolerance of fetishization by a White partner, saying, "I think I just was wanting to be in a stable relationship, so I wasn't tryin' to create a lotta issues." This silencing of one's own feelings about racial discrimination to maintain harmony in a relationship was a profound but subtle way that White privilege unfolded—with the perpetrators of the sexual racism often seeming to be unaware that they were behaving in a manner that was racist or offensive to the partner of color.

Kevin, also Asian American, identifies as a gender nonconforming gay man and in his late 20s, recalled the formative experience of hooking up with male sex partners online beginning when he was a teenager. The "vast majority" of profiles that he surveyed in San Francisco either "undesired" or desired Asians for "deplorable reasons." Specifically:

> [t]here were assumptions about how I would treat them, how I would service them, the expectation that I was just more of a receptacle, and my pleasure wasn't really taken into account. . . . I'm just a hole. . . . It doesn't matter if it hurts or if I feel any certain way about it.

Simply being an Asian American man demanded negotiation with White privilege and the assumptions or behavior it encouraged. In Kevin's first sexual encounter organized online, a White man who was topping him yelled the racial slur "chink" right before ejaculating. "It was like he was getting off on [the racial epithet]. That was pretty traumatic." This example demonstrates how the very thing that stimulated Kevin's White partner— the privilege to use a violent racial slur— made Kevin feel used and degraded, a dynamic I have documented previously (Robinson & Frost, 2018).

254   LIVED REALITIES

In this and other encounters, Kevin reported repeatedly being forced to negotiate what he called "ritualized assumptions" about the shape of sex between White men and Asian men. Kevin identified several factors that combined to limit his ability to engage in meaningful negotiations: the context of transactional online sex, with little discussion before the encounter; the submissive role that Kevin was assigned; and the relative lack of men who were open to Asians—but did not describe their desire in racialized terms. Kevin described these White sex partners as bringing an "entitlement" to direct the sex: "they were like, 'You're bottom of the barrel, so what I'm going to do to you, you're gonna like it anyways because you don't really have other choices.'" Kevin found, however, that he experienced more agency over the direction of the encounter when he posted his own advertisement online, as opposed to replying to another man's post. By writing his own ad, Kevin was able to describe his ideal sexual encounter, assert an expectation of safe sex, and try to "weed out" men who desired sexual racism.

During Kevin's long-term relationship with a wealthy White man, he discussed with his partner the sexual racism that he experienced in the San Francisco gay community. Kevin and his partner Bill had an open relationship; they would meet men on a partner-seeking app and often compare their interactions with the same men. Kevin described Bill as a "traditionally attractive" White man who received a "landslide" of messages on the app. The "total transparency" of their relationship agreement meant that Kevin often observed their racially divergent experiences on the app. When Kevin sought comfort from Bill, sometimes Bill was understanding, but sometimes Bill responded by asking skeptical questions:

> "Are you sure this isn't a lens that you have that you have an unrealistic expectation that everyone's gonna be attracted to you? Do you think that maybe these guys, it's not about your race? Sometimes it's just they're not attracted to your body type, or do you think because you've read so much about race, you're projecting a lot of stuff?"

As noted in the introduction, prior research has suggested that gay cisgender men tend to describe their desires as "personal" and "just a preference," and White gay men are particularly likely to regard desire as disconnected from racism (Callander et al., 2012, 2015; Smith, 2017). Bill's rejection of Kevin's assertion of sexual racism echoes this pattern, which he experienced as a form of gaslighting. Although this was "super invalidating," Kevin's reflections on the power dynamic in his relationship with Bill were ambivalent: "I don't think it was all him, and I shouldn't really vilify him to that extent cuz there's only [so] much you can do, too." Kevin's ambivalence was shaped by his sense that other White male partners had been even more dismissive of Kevin's experiences of sexual racism, including the accusation that he was "playing the race card."

Kevin's recollection of his relationship with Bill suggests that one aspect of White privilege is denial that sexual racism exists and the claim that gay men of color "project" the problem onto White men. This refusal to question how racism influences hierarchies of desire in the gay community buttresses White men's dominant position. The emotional intimacy of Kevin and Bill's relationship enabled Kevin to challenge sexual racism—a theme I return to later in this chapter—yet ultimately Bill's defensive reaction may have reinforced Kevin's sense that, as an Asian man, he was "bottom of the barrel." Moreover, one could understand Kevin's ambivalence in sharing the story with me as evidence of the difficulty some people of color encounter in identifying and negotiating sexual racism.

Like Kevin, some Black participants were subjected to racial slurs without consent. During one of Carl's hookups, his White sex partner blurted, "Fuck me, you nigga. Fuck me, you big black nigga." This phrase made Carl "shrivel" and recoil, an "instant turn-off . . . [he] should do a little more homework. That's [something] you should ask somebody before you scream it out while you [are] getting fucked." The White man in this incident was surprised by Carl's reaction and was apologetic. Carl marveled at the paradox of these interracial interactions:

> It's like you [White men] want them [Black men] to dominate you [in bed], you want them to lead you, you want to surrender to them, it's all this stuff that's so opposite of what the other side is [outside of the bedroom], so that's so weird that you would want me to tell you what to do . . . but in the reality, when we walk out the door, your family or the way you think, especially if you're White American, you're thinking, "Oh, they're beneath me."

This example suggests a tension between, on the one hand, certain White men wanting to submit to a Black partner but always enacted through (and working to sustain) White privilege.

Exposure to unwanted race talk during sex was most commonly reported by gay cisgender men, but some cisgender woman reported a similar sexual dilemma. Kelsey, a lesbian in New York City who is half-White and half-Cuban and does not speak Spanish, dated a White woman who was fluent

256   LIVED REALITIES

in several languages, including Spanish. Her partner, Linda, would speak
Spanish during sex. Kelsey objected:

> I'm like, "I don't speak Spanish. I can't do this with you." When you do that,
> even though I tell you that I don't speak Spanish, it tells me that you're not
> really seeing who I am here. You're just having a fantasy that I'm here to
> serve that.

Kelsey reported that Linda continued to speak Spanish while they were
having sex, and that Linda, who had "only dated Hispanic women, would do
what she wanted to do."

Overall, this theme showcases how White privilege undermined meaningful
negotiation by people of color, moving the previously described assumptions
enacted by White partners into a realm of problematic and dehumanizing
actions. Thus, through this theme it become clearer that while White privilege
may "set the scene" for intimate encounters among racially diverse LGBTQI
people, it also works to determine how the actors behave in that scene. And, as
I explore in the third and final theme, there is often a price to be paid should
people of color choose to question or resist the part they are expected to play.

White Privilege Undermines Resistance

By exploring the scene set by White privilege and the required negotiations,
my analysis also identified a theme of resistance enacted by LGBTQI people
of color. Commonly, this resistance manifested as naming, avoiding, challenging, and educating partners in scenes set by White privilege. The
participants of color varied in terms of their awareness of White privilege and
consistency in resisting it, in part because of the sexual dilemma discussed
above: heightened vigilance and attempts to negotiate could mean less sexual
and romantic opportunity.

Some participants described techniques for identifying whether a suitor
had a racial "type," which was viewed as a proxy for racialized fetishes and
sexual racism. Carlos, a Latino gay man in Chicago, explained that:

> [I] try to ignore it as much as possible. There have been times when I've lit-
> erally said to a person, "If you're gonna fetishize me, the least you could do
> is buy me a drink." . . . I will then continue a conversation with them, but
> I take the drink and walk away to friends.

SEXUAL RACISM AS WHITE PRIVILEGE   257

Carlos said that when he first started socializing in Boystown, the main "gayborhood" in Chicago, he did not notice the "huge power dynamic" in the racially segregated city, but over time, he became more aware of it and developed strategies of resistance. "Society does me an injustice, so I will at least get a drink out of it," he said. Similarly, Andre, a Black, bisexual man in Chicago who prefers Black partners, deployed skeptical questions when White men approached him in public. On one occasion, he asked a White suitor "So you like Black men?" After the White man said "yes," Andre followed up with, "You just want a big old Black guy to fuck you?" "Oh, yes," [the White man replied], at which point he said, "Yeah. No." Andre walked away, noting, "He thought I was being—I wasn't being salacious. No. It just is a turnoff to me." Andre leveraged the socialized invisibility of White privilege among those who seek to benefit from it, luring White men into endorsing a racialized fetish and using that confirmation to avoid further interaction.

Further demonstrating resistance through avoidance, Megan—the Black biracial and bisexual woman mentioned above—stopped dating White people altogether and only dated Black men. She described realizing the necessity of this while dating a White man who consistently enacted racial microaggressions. Similarly, Carl refused to have further sexual encounters with the White man who used a racial slur during sex. Carl, however, also described affording non-Black partners some grace, including even those who used a racial epithet. "If [they] say the word 'nigga' [in a nonsexual context], then you sort of let the first one go."

George, an Asian gay cisgender man in his 50s who lives in New York City, described trying to avoid "creepy" White men who seemed "ready to pounce on" Asian men. He was wary of White men who spoke several Asian languages and decorated their apartments to resemble a "Kabuki show." He said that when he was younger he would play along with racial stereotypes, but as he grew older, he became less willing to acquiesce. The result of this internal shift was that he was having less sex. He continued to experience racial microaggressions such as a White man who told him, "Oh, you're good looking for an Asian." When asked, "If somebody said that online or at a bar, would you keep talking to them?" George replied:

Probably not. Unless they were really hot. I probably would walk away. I think there was a time in my life where I was more accommodating, or I was more—I would try to deal with that a little more. I don't know, it's just wearying after a while.

258 LIVED REALITIES

Although this participant had grown tired of tolerating the sexual racism inflicted through White privilege, his caveat "unless they were really hot" alludes to the tension between sexual gratification and resisting racism.

Beyond vigilance and avoidance, some participants described trying to lightly challenge and educate White suitors in ways that might be understood as providing what has previously been called "racial comfort" (Carbado & Gulati, 2000). Jackson, a gay Black cisgender man in Chicago, asserted:

> I'm not exaggerating, 80% of the White men that I have ever spoken to at one point or another either said a Black joke or something about my [penis] size or talked about my race in a way that was condescending.

Jackson's approach was to show restraint when responding to such sexual racism, saying "I try to take those situations and make them into a learning experience rather than an experience of just letting them have it, which I would be well within my right to do."

Brittany, the Black transgender woman whose partner Nico deployed White privilege to enact a fantasy of dominance, used a similar approach to "lightly" challenge and educate Nico. During the interview, she recounted an evening when the two of them were watching a news report about the Black athlete Ray Rice. Rice was suspended by the National Football League after he was caught on video knocking unconscious his then-fiancé, a Black woman. Brittany stated:

> We were in [Nico's] house watching the TV, and he goes, "Yeah, Brittany, why are Black girls so aggressive? She probably hit him first. Look at her. She looks like she probably—they always have the attitude. They're rolling their necks." I was like, "I don't know if that's a fair assumption. I don't do that."

Nico did not seem to notice the irony of him complaining about Black women being "aggressive" when he had urged Brittany to dominate him sexually. Brittany when on to say:

> One of my friends was like, "Why would you let him talk to you about that?" I said, "See? That's a problem. The only way you can affect change is if you allow somebody to tell you what their—what they really think. . . . He has a right to believe whatever he wants." By him seeing a different version

of that, that's gonna affect him going forward because he'll be able to say, "Well, not all girls of colour. I knew one."

Interestingly, Brittany seemed to regard her friend's objection to Nico's comment as the "problem," and Brittany even defended Nico's "right" to espouse a racial/gender stereotype. Brittany's soft challenge to Nico's stereotyping of Black women may have merely established that she is not like "most Black women." It is worth noting that later in the interview, Brittany described great difficulty finding male partners who were willing to date her in public and were not violent or otherwise transphobic. Discerning a pattern in which men aggressively pursued her for sex but refused to be seen with her in public, Brittany began proposing a first date in public. This strategy led to fewer dating and sexual opportunities: "my sexual interaction with people is very—almost non-existent to very rarely."

Brittany's experiences and those from several other participants paint a vivid picture of the emotional labor that people of color may have to perform to try to protect their sense of self and preserve a sexual/romantic opportunity. Indeed, the "light" nature of such resistance affirms the foundational role of White privilege in these dynamics, and the complexities of negotiating them. Thus, even among those who objected to racism, White privilege often dictated the manner of resistance. Participants could decide only to date people of their own race, but doing so ultimately limits their sexual and romantic opportunities.

Conclusions

This study illustrates how White privilege operates to fuel and sustain sexual racism among LGBTQI people in the United States. As I have shown, White privilege sets the scene for sexual and romantic encounters, demands complex negotiations by people of color, and even when they resist, it often exacts a toll. I found that LGBTQI people of color pay for interracial connections in various ways, including but not limited to challenges to their self-respect and mental and emotional well-being. These findings align with much previous scholarship on how people experience and react to sexual racism (Callander, Holt, et al., 2016) and also on the dynamics of White privilege in other contexts (Applebaum, 2016; Ewing, 2020; Harris, 1993). This study suggests that the sexual/romantic realm is an important domain for future

260   LIVED REALITIES

research to further understand how White privilege works and to explore how to dismantle it.

Whereas most sexual racism literature in recent years has focused on cisgender gay and bisexual men as perpetrators and targets of sexual racism, this study supplements that literature by including accounts of cisgender White women (heterosexual and queer) as perpetrators of sexual racism. Furthermore, the targets of sexual racism in this study include cisgender women, transgender men, transgender women, and other gender diverse people. This study highlights the varied gendered and intersectional dynamics implicated in sexual racism and suggests that it is not only a problem among cisgender gay men. Among our diverse sample, these results also help articulate what others have characterised as intersectionality and the mutual coconstruction of race, gender, and sexuality (e.g., Chou, 2012; Crenshaw, 1989; Hill Collins, 2005; Nagel, 2003).

Another valuable insight from this study is that White privilege thrives in and is sustained through silence and assumptions about how a sexual encounter will unfold. As noted, this affirms previous scholarship on White privilege in other populations and in other social spheres (Applebaum, 2016; Ewing, 2020; Harris, 1993), and it suggests that researchers should explore interventions to disrupt such silence and the sexual scripts that White privilege imposes. One intervention may be through teaching sexually active people that racialized fantasies require prior discussion, negotiation, and consent. Sexual and intimate practices that fall under the umbrella term "BDSM" may offer some insight, especially given growing attention to what is known as "race play" (Hernandez, 2004). According to one Black scholar, race play entails Black people "inhabiting, and subsequently taking control of the fetishized stereotypes of Blackness, embodying them in tantalizing performances that are at once both painful and pleasurable" (Smith & Luykx, 2017).

One reason that BDSM may offer a unique challenge to White privilege is because consent to particular sex roles, acts, and language is understood by many as a "cornerstone" of the practice (Pitagora, 2013). Indeed, "consent is considered the main criterion to distinguish BDSM from violence" and is understood as "active collaboration for the pleasure and well-being of everyone involved" (Bauer, 2021; Pitagora, 2013). Such boundaries may facilitate the opportunity for people to explore their sense of self, test their limits, heal from trauma, and more fully inhabit their sexuality (Bauer, 2008; Pitagora, 2013). Some have suggested race play might be able to

SEXUAL RACISM AS WHITE PRIVILEGE   261

support healing in similar ways (e.g., Cruz, 2016; Lindenmann, 2011), including that people of color can find pleasure "by appropriating gendered racial stereotypes to counter standard racist narratives" (Smith & Luykx, 2017). I should note, however, that within many communities, race play is highly controversial. The point here is not to argue for or against race play, but rather to focus on the generative possibilities of the culture of consent suggested by BDSM.

With the explicit introduction of consent, the model of BDSM provides, at least in theory, a stark contrast with the experiences recounted by participants in this study. In looking to BDSM norms as a possible corrective to sexual racism, one must acknowledge potential limitations. According to multiple reports, the BDSM community is predominantly White (Bauer, 2021; Erickson et al., 2022; Robinson, 2018) and it is not immune to the same forces of White privilege I have discussed here. Indeed, the racial "colorblindness" that pervades our societies also appears to stifle frank discussion about race in some BDSM spaces (Bauer, 2008; Norton et al., 2006). Racial stereotypes, the lack of racial diversity, and White people's discomfort engaging race may combine to make it difficult for people of colour to negotiate terms that satisfy their desires while respecting their boundaries (Erickson et al., 2022). Thus, while potentially disruptive and reparative, BDSM does not offer a panacea for the hard work of seeing and working to dismantle sexual practices steeped in White supremacy and White privilege. It does, however, instruct us to ask questions and have conversations about power and consent, including consent to racial fantasies, that some LGBTQI White people in intimate settings appear to sidestep.

Although there are no easy answers, my analysis helps to make visible the powerful presence of White privilege in interracial relationships and the various ways that it dictates and impedes true intimacy. This knowledge might prompt White readers to reflect on how they interact with partners or potential partners who are people of color, while people of color may recognize their own experience of enduring, navigating, and challenging White privilege. Moreover, people of color may borrow some of the strategies of the participants who resisted (e.g., ending a relationship after a partner used a racial slur, letting an offensive suitor buy one a drink and then walking away, baiting a suitor into admitting that his desire is based in racial stereotype and then rejecting him, and writing one's personal profile to minimize exposure to online sexual racism). A heightened consciousness about White privilege's often hidden or subtle dynamics might expand sexual liberty for people of color, create space for frank conversation within LGBTQI communities, and promote healthier, more mutual sexual and romantic relationships.

References

Albury, K., Dietzel, C., Pym, T., Vivienne, S., & Cook, T. (2021). Not your unicorn: Trans dating app users' negotiations of personal safety and sexual health. *Health Sociology Review, 30*(1), 72–86.

Ansley, F. L. (1989). Stirring the ashes: Race, class, and the future of civil rights scholarship. *Cornell Law Review, 74*(6), 993–1077.

Applebaum, B. (2016). Critical whiteness studies. In G. W. Noblit, & J. R. Neikirk (Eds), Oxford research encyclopedia of education (1–23). Oxford University Press.

Bauer, R. (2021). Queering consent: Negotiating critical consent in les-bi-trans-queer BDSM contexts. *Sexualities, 24*, 767–783.

Bauer, R. (2008). Transgressive and transformative gendered sexual practices and White privileges: The case of the dyke/trans BDSM communities. *Women's Studies Quarterly, 36*, 233–253.

Bérubé, A. (2001). How gay stays White and what kind of White it stays. In B. B. Rasmussen, E. Klinenberg, I. J. Nexica, & M. Wray (Eds.), *The making and unmaking of whiteness* (pp. 234–265). Duke University Press.

Bhambhani, Y., Flynn, M. K., Kellum, K. K., & Wilson, K. G. (2019). Examining sexual racism and body dissatisfaction among men of colour who have sex with men: The moderating role of body image inflexibility. *Body Image, 28*, 142–148.

Braun, V., & Clarke, V. (2006). Using thematic analysis in psychology. *Qualitative Research in Psychology, 3*, 101–177. https://doi.org/10.1191/1478088706qp063oa

Callander, D., Ayres, T., & Donovan, T. (2023). A queer history of sexual racism. In D. Callander, P. Farvid, A. Baradaran, T. Vance (Eds.), *(Un)desiring whiteness: (Un)doing sexual racism* (31–50). Oxford University Press.

Callander, D., Holt, M., & Newman, C. E. (2012). Just a preference: Racialised language in the sex-seeking profiles of gay and bisexual men. *Culture, Health and Sexuality, 14*(9/10), 1049–1063. http://www.jstor.org/stable/23524947

Callander, D., Newman, C. E., & Holt, M. (2015). Is sexual racism really racism? Distinguishing attitudes toward sexual racism and generic racism among gay and bisexual men. *Archives of Sexual Behavior, 44*, 1991–2000. https://doi.org/10.1007/s10508-015-0487-3

Callander, D., Holt, M., & Newman, C. E. (2016). "Not everyone's gonna like me": Accounting for race and racism in Australian sex and dating webservices for gay and bisexual men. *Ethnicities, 16*(1), 3–21.

Carbado, D. W., & Gulati, M. (2000). Working identity. *Cornell Law Review,* 85, 1259–1308.

Chou, R. S. (2012). *Asian American sexual politics: The construction of race, gender, and sexuality.* Rowman & Littlefield.

Crenshaw, K. (1989). Demarginalizing the intersection of race and sex: A black feminist critique of antidiscrimination doctrine, feminist theory and antiracist politics. *University of Chicago Legal Forum, 1*(8), 139–167.

Cruz, A. (2016). Playing with the politics of perversion: Policing BDSM, pornography, and black female sexuality. *Souls: A Critical Journal of Black Politics, Culture, and Society, 18*, 379–407.

Curington, C. V., Lundquist, J. H., & Lin, K. (2021). *The dating divide: Race and desire in the era of online romance*. University of California Press.

DiAngelo, R. (2018). *White fragility: Why it's so hard for white people to talk about racism*. Beacon Press.

Erickson, J.M., Slayton, A.M., Petersen, J.G., Hyams, H.M., Howard, L.J., Sharp, S., & Sagarin, B.J. (2022). Challenge at the intersection of race and kink: Racial discrimination, fetishization, and inclusivity within the BDSM community. *Archives of Sexual Behavior, 51*, 1063–1074.

Ewing, E. L. (2020). I'm a Black scholar who studies race: Here's why I capitalize "White." *Zora*. https://zora.medium.com/im-a-black-scholar-who-studies-race-here-s-why-i-capitalize-white-f94883aa2dd3

Flagg, B. (1993). "Was blind, but now i see": White race consciousness and the requirement of discriminatory intent. *Michigan Law Review, 91*, 953–1017.

Hampton, H. (Executive Producer). (2006). *Eyes on the prize* [Film]. PBS Video.

Han, C. (2006). Geisha of a different kind: Gay Asian men and the gendering of sexual identity. *Sexuality and Culture, 10*, 3–28.

Harris, C. I. (1993). Whiteness as property. *Harvard Law Review, 106*, 1707.

Hernandez, D. (2004). Playing with race. *Colorlines*. https://www.colorlines.com/articles/playing-race

Hidalgo, M. A., Layland, E., Kubicek, K., & Kipke, M. (2020). Sexual racism, psychological symptoms, and mindfulness among ethnically/racially diverse young men who have sex with men: A moderation analysis. *Mindfulness, 11*, 452–461.

Hill Collins, P. (2005). *Black sexual politics: African Americans, gender, and the new racism*. Routledge.

hooks, b. (1992). Representing whiteness in the Black imagination. In L. Grossberg, C. Nelson, & P. A. Treichler (Eds), *Cultural studies* (338–346). Routledge.

Krueger, E. A., Lin, A., Kittle, K. R., & Meyer, I. H. (2020). *Generations—a study of the life and health of LGB people in a changing society (Methodology and technical notes, Gallup quantitative survey)*. The Williams Institute. Retrieved from http://www.generations-study.com/s/Generations-Quantitative-Survey-Methods-v20_copy.pdf

Lim, C. C., & Anderson, R. C. (2021): Effect of sexual racism on partner desirability in gay Asian men. *Journal of Homosexuality*. https://doi.org/10.1080/00918369.2021.1948772

Lin, K. H., & Lundquist, J. (2013). Mate selection in cyberspace: The intersection of race, gender, and education. *American Journal of Sociology, 199*, 183–215.

Lindenmann, D. (2011). BDSM as therapy? *Sexualities, 14*, 151–172.

McIntosh, P. (1989). *White privilege: Unpacking the invisible knapsack*. https://psychology.umbc.edu/files/2016/10/White-Privilege_McIntosh-1989.pdf

Nagel, J. (2003). *Race, ethnicity, and sexuality. Intimate intersections, forbidden frontiers*. Oxford University Press.

Norton, M., et al. (2006). Colorblindness and interracial interaction: Playing the political correctness game. *Psychological Science, 17*(11), 949–953.

Pitagora, D. (2013). Consent vs. coercion: BDSM interactions highlight a fine but immutable line. *New School Psychology Bulletin, 10*, 27–36.

Phua, V. C., & Kaufman, G. (2003). The crossroads of race and sexuality. *Journal of Family Issues, 24*, 981–994.

Prestage, G., Mao, L., Philpot, S., Jin, F., Callander, D., Doyle, M., Zablotska, I., Kolstee, J., Keen, P., & Bavinton, B. (2019). The role of age and homonegativity in racial or ethnic partner preferences among Australian gay and bisexual men. *Archives of Sexual Behavior, 48*, 357–368.

Raj, S. (2011). Grindring bodies: Racial and affective economies of online queer desire. *Critical Race and Whiteness Studies, 7*, 55–67.

Ro, A., Ayala, G., Paul, J., & Choi, K. (2013). Dimensions of racism and their impact on partner selection among men who have sex with men of colour: Understanding pathways to sexual risk. *Culture, Health & Sexuality, 15*, 836–850.

Robinson, R. K. (2008). *Perceptual segregation. Columbia Law Review, 108*, 1093

Robinson, R. K., & Frost, D. M. (2018). LGBT equality and sexual racism. *Fordham Law Review, 86*, 2739–2754.

Scott, D. (1994). Jungle fever? Black gay identity politics, white dick, and the utopian bedroom. *Journal of Gay and Lesbian Studies, 1*, 299–321.

Smith, J., & Amaro, G. (2021). "No fats, no femmes, and no Blacks or Asians": The role of body-type, sex position, and race on condom use online. *AIDS and Behavior, 25*, 2166–2176.

Smith, J. G. (2017). "It can't possibly be racism!": The White racial frame and resistance to sexual racism. In D. Riggs (Ed.), *The psychic life of racism in gay men's communities*, 105–122.

Smith, J. G., & Luykx, A. (2017). Race play in BDSM Porn: The eroticization of oppression. *Porn Studies, 4*, 433–446.

Souleymanov, R., Brennan, D. J., George, C., Utama, R., & Ceranton, A. (2020). Experiences of racism, sexual objectification and alcohol use among gay and bisexual men of colour. *Ethnicity and Health, 25*, 525–541.

Wilson, P. A., Valera, P., Ventuneac, A., Balan, I., Rowe, M., & Carballo-Dieguez, A. (2009). Race-based sexual stereotyping and sexual partnering among men who use the Internet to identify other men for bareback sex. *Journal of Sex Research, 46*(5), 399–413. https://doi.org/10.1080/00224490902846479

Yancey, G. (2003). A preliminary examination of differential sexual attitudes among individuals involved in interracial relationships: Testing "Jungle Fever." *Social Science Journal, 40*, 153–157.

The Butcher

Synclaire Warren

She is thought to be a man-made wonder. She is hot succulent dark meat. Juice drips between her thighs to be lapped up by the groins that crave her heat. Her parts are exploited and only admired if they can be devoured. She is a beauty meant to be consumed. Her so-called flaws are covered by dressings. Her fats are salted and her scars are sugared to be chewed down but never swallowed. She is tasted and then spat out so the evidence of her never lies within them. She is made to be a figment, the darkness of shadows. She is an exotic fantasy to them. Their eyes stick to her like honey but nothing sweet is in their stare. She does not delight in this desire nor does she dance in their crazed gaze. She holds fear within her chest as she knows she will never be seen for more than her breasts. She is aware how they would skin her alive only to know that they can. They hate her chuckle, her blackened scoff. Her breath means so little to them unless it is their name she is moaning. She is forced to collect catcalls like compliments. She is to be a catacomb for carnal cravings. She is an offense to whiteness, its culprit. A hate so pure pours out from it. A blame bellowed so loud. She is the echo of envy. I think about her. How her body has said nothing to me that her voice has not already screamed.

SECTION IV
SPOTLIGHTING THE STRUCTURAL

12

Curating Desire

The White Supremacist Grammar of Tagging on Pornhub

Chibundo Egwuatu, Zahra Stardust, Mireille Miller-Young, and Daisy Ducati

> The adult industry largely is run by white men for the consumption of the white male gaze, leaving out the desires of the many Black and Brown people who regularly consume porn for personal pleasure and sexual exploration.
>
> —BIPOC Adult Industry Collective (Rouse, 2020)

"I personally would like to get rid of the "interracial" category entirely," wrote Daisy Ducati in a *Bustle* article in June 2020 (McGowan, 2020). Ducati, a mainstream pornography performer in California, was speaking out against the persistence of racist tagging and marketing practices in the adult industry. In the piece, she recalls an experience where she performed a standard boy/girl scene in Los Angeles with a white male performer. Unbeknownst to Ducati, the scene was titled and marketed in a way that trivialized the #BlackLivesMatter movement, yet she did not find out until it was in stores for sale (McGowan, 2020, n.p.). As Daisy describes:

> I thought everything went well, but when the scene came out on DVD a week or two later, the title was "Black Wives Matter." I had no prior knowledge of that until I saw myself on the box. Later, I found out that no other performers knew. Even the director didn't know—the company that produced it just titled it on their own. Shit like that happens all the time.

Chibundo Egwuatu, Zahra Stardust, Mireille Miller-Young, and Daisy Ducati, *Curating Desire* In: *Sexual Racism and Social Justice*. Edited by: Denton Callander, Panteá Farvid, Amir Baradaran, and Thomas A. Vance, Oxford University Press. © Oxford University Press 2024. DOI: 10.1093/oso/9780197605509.003.0013

270 SPOTLIGHTING THE STRUCTURAL

Daisy's experience is not isolated. Ana Foxxx, another performer, told *Cosmopolitan* the same year, "I'll show up, shoot a scene, and walk away thinking it was a good day. . . . But then the film will come out and it will be labeled 'Black gang bang'" (Lieberman, 2020). In 2021, performer King Noire expressed similar frustration, telling *Mashable*, "At certain points they might just label us as 'Black bitch' or 'big Black negro dick,' or whatever the fuck, so things have been a constant fight, a constant struggle to at least be labelled in ways that the majority of our people are like, 'OK I'm alright with that'" (Thompson, 2021).

These voices join a chorus of performers who are Black, Indigenous, and/or people of color (BIPOC) speaking out about racism in the making and marketing of pornography. In the aftermath of the murders of George Floyd and Breonna Taylor and the viral traction of the Black Lives Matters movement in 2020, a suite of media articles emerged featuring porn performers critiquing not only the eroticization of "cop porn" (Cole, 2020) but also the linguistic systems of tagging that categorize their bodies and identities online (BIPOC Adult Industry Collective, 2020; Dickson, 2020; Klein, 2020; Lieberman, 2020; Perdue, 2021; Rouse, 2020; Snow, 2020; Song, 2020; Thompson, 2021). The BIPOC Adult Industry Collective, who conduct practical, on-the-ground work providing mutual aid, microgrants, and skill-shares for performers, launched a petition to adult media production and distribution companies to end racism and wage discrimination in porn (Rouse, 2020). Some performers, like Daisy, pushed for an entirely reimagined approach, arguing that the interracial tag ought to be prohibited from porn sites that "need to reconsider how they title, tag, and direct [interracial scenes]" (McGowan, 2020, n.p.).

Black porn performers have long criticized the racial stratification of the porn industry. Performers have identified problems in pornographic labor (unequal pay rates in porn production and higher premiums offered to white performers for interracial scenes), problems in representation (privileging of white desire and proliferation of racial stereotypes), and problems in distribution (such as the deployment of racialized terminology in marketing language) (Brooks, 2010; Jones, 2020; Miller-Young, 2014). More recently, these problems are being amplified as streaming sites increasingly rely on automated tagging and machine learning to categorize and sort user-generated content at scale. The coding of racialized tags into algorithms on porn sites has potential both to curate audience desire and impact the visibility (and, in turn, the livelihood) of performers.

In this chapter, we articulate how sexual racism, whiteness, and white supremacy shape the practice of tagging and orient nonwhite bodies in pornography. To do this, we explore how tagging practices on the streaming site Pornhub both presume and manufacture a white gaze by invisibilizing and centering whiteness in their search categories. We are interested in how tagging curates and colonizes desire by producing a "grammaire pornographique" and we argue that recent controversies around tagging stem from a long history of racism in sexuality, which naturally extends to pornography and its distribution, from bookstores to DVD and now tube sites. What is new, however, is that the production of these racialized erotic vocabularies through which viewers understand, make sense of, and consume sexual content are now being magnified by processes of automation that code racism into tech design.

We propose a framework through which to understand this practice—a "white supremacist grammar of tagging"—by which we mean language, syntax, lexicon, semiotics, and logics that are founded on a premise of white superiority. Throughout the chapter we explore how this grammar appears not only in Pornhub's tagging regimes but also in their coding and algorithmic practices, which reinforces a labor context in which nonwhite performers are economically disadvantaged. Beyond exploring and articulating, we view this analysis as part of a larger reparative exercise—a project of social justice centred on "undesiring whiteness, undoing sexual racism," which requires a creative revisioning of tagging regimes, on Pornhub in particular but in sexualities more broadly. This task is the collective and collaborative work to dismantle lexicons through which our bodies, sexualities, identities, and activities have become legible to one another. Such a process involves deconstructing hierarchies that center whiteness while marginalizing people of color, and at the same time advancing alternative erotic lexicons of sexuality, race, ethnicity, identity, and affinity. Further, because white supremacist, capitalist logics of extraction and property define the Pornhub business model, a project of undesiring whiteness is not simply a matter of updating language but one that requires material changes to Internet infrastructure, technology design, and the overall terrain of pornography production and distribution.

Case Study and Approach

If our agenda is to *un*do sexual racism by *un*desiring whiteness, then we contribute to this project by deconstructing how whiteness structures and cultivates desire through an examination of racialized tagging of pornographic content. As our case study, we examine tagging processes on Pornhub, the largest international distributor of pornography. We complement this by comparing and contrasting publicly available data, media statements from Pornhub, and the experiences of BIPOC porn performers as told through media articles following the Black Lives Matter protests. These voices offer insight into the relationships between tagging, visibility, and material impact, and they allow us to contextualize them within broader historical debates. In our analysis, we apply Hortense Spillers's theory of American grammar (Spillers, 1987) to unpack the complexities of tagging. By foregrounding grammar, we analyze how language has emerged historically to constrain and control nonwhite identities, cultures, and meanings. Finally, we consider how BIPOC performers are cultivating and trialing new taxonomies of grammar, identification, and naming with potential to reinscribe new meanings to race, gender, and sexuality.

On pornography, social media, and many other kinds of webservices, tagging serves multiple purposes. Generally, tagging permits people to find content and users based on certain attributes, and it is used to improve search engine optimization, maximize visibility of posts, boost engagement, direct web traffic, increase viewership, and monetize content. Different platforms have different approaches to tagging: tags can be automatically attached to content in a top-down manner, imposed by the platform itself; tags can be attached to content by users, such as via a drop-down menu; and new tags can be created and suggested by users to the platform, who decide whether or not to accept the tag. Tagging practices are increasingly important because they help determine what content is visible and relevant, inform algorithmic outcomes, and ultimately give shape to the experiences of content creators and consumers.

These applications of tagging impose digital experiences that are, implicitly or explicitly, informed by specific grammars and systems of value. In 2019, for example, the video-sharing platform TikTok admitted to suppressing the content of users with disabilities, whom their guidelines identified as being "susceptible to bullying or harassment." TikTok moderators were reportedly ordered to prevent clips from users with disabilities from appearing in the app's video feed when they had reached 6,000–10,000 views, leading to their active exclusion and invisibility as a result of this protectionist and paternalistic narrative (Kelion, 2019). Similarly, for many years the gaming platform Twitch prevented the use of a "transgender" content tag even though many transgender users argued that it limited their ability to connect with each other to form digital communities (Sprayregen, 2021).

Critical race and technology scholars like Ruha Benjamin (2019), Safiya Noble (2018) and Kishonna Gray (2020) have documented how technology design codes oppressive logics into its functions, resulting in racial discrimination, bias, and amplified inequality. Thus, we approach racialized tagging as a function of whiteness. We acknowledge that "whiteness lies at the center of the problem of racism" (Applebaum, 2016, p. 1), and seek to make whiteness visible in order to expose it, displace it and decenter it. A "white gaze" is omnipresent in shaping the erotic imagination in digital media, and yet it is the gaze that is most frequently invisible, unremarkable, and nondescript. As Sara Ahmed writes, "whiteness gains currency by being unnoticed" (2007, p. 149). In sexual commerce, whiteness is constantly present, defining space and permeating erotic possibilities. Whiteness not only exists in the way that sexual laborers are categorized, classified, and assigned value, but also provides a foundation for the business models and industry structures that stratify wages and opportunities and extract and exploit maximum capital from workers. Tags reveal a mechanical ecology of white supremacy in digital worlds that wields algorithms to further annex desire as a site for sustaining whiteness as an ontological ordering mechanism.

Pornhub is an excellent case for the study of tagging in pornography because it illustrates the primary way contemporary digital pornographies are organized through automation as part of tagging, searching, filtering, and recommending systems. Pornhub is also an important case study because their parent company (known at the time of writing as MindGeek, sold in 2023 to Canadian private equity firm Ethical Capital Partners and rebranded as Aylo) controls a significant share of the porn distribution market. Headquartered in Luxembourg, in 2022 MindGeek owned most of the top-ten "tube sites" including Redtube and Youporn and was one of the most high traffic aggregators of sexual videos, citing 130 million visitors per day. Pornhub has engaged in visible corporate social responsibility campaigns, including promoting the site on a billboard in Times Square, making donations to social justice organizations, and publicly supporting #BlackLivesMatter. In 2020, following the murder of George Floyd, the company tweeted, "Pornhub stands in solidarity against racism and social injustice," recommending that followers donate to civil rights organizations like Bail Project, Black Visions, Freedom Fund, Southern Poverty Law Center, and the National Association for the Advancement of Colored People. And

274 SPOTLIGHTING THE STRUCTURAL

yet, Pornhub continues to host videos tagged with racist titles, among other problematic behavior .

While Pornhub has publicly promoted their "advances" in automation (Sawers, 2017), the site faces vehement critiques from independent pornography producers for its market dominance, exploitative business model, piracy practices, verification systems, and tagging regimes. At the time of writing, Pornhub employed a hybrid system that allowed each video to be assigned up to 16 individual tags. Users can tag their own videos as they upload them, selecting from top-down tags provided by the site (which include "ebony" and "interracial"). Performers can also add "Action Tags" to their content at specific parts of the video. Some of the tags available include actions (rimming, scissoring), positions (doggystyle, cowgirl), settings (kitchen, library), objects (dildo, handcuffs), and attributes (petite, trimmed). The tagging process also has an automated component: Pornhub offers "suggested tags" associated with the categories the uploader has chosen. For example, if a performer selects the "anal" category, "ass-fuck" will automatically be tagged. While users can remove suggested tags they don't like, there are limited mechanisms for providing feedback to Pornhub on the tags themselves. In addition, videos can have up to four "pornstar names" that are based on highly searched terms on Pornhub. Porn names can be automatically assigned, and users can upvote or downvote automated name tags. While users can vote to "add a pornstar" and request that a name be added to their database of porn performers, there is no option for users to create their own tags.

As authors, we come together as four individuals with histories as writers, speakers, performers, producers, organizers, and thinkers on sex work, race, and pornography. We have collective experience in pornography performance, sex work activism, media and sexuality studies, and critical race scholarship. Our different disciplines (spanning anthropology, film studies and gender and sexuality studies), geographical positioning (writing from the United States, Germany, and Australia), and professional roles (as both senior and junior academics, students, community advocates, and industry representatives) lend different skillsets, approaches, and knowledges. We present the voices of academics and critics in solidarity with the voices of porn performers who are at the forefront of innovatively and strategically navigating tagging systems, racialized systems of production and capitalist business models. We seek to uplift their voices, compile evidence for their arguments and bring their demands to academic audiences.

From these various standpoints, we make the important step of bringing porn studies scholarship into conversation with Black feminist scholars working in Internet and technology studies. We bring race and sex work to the foreground of Internet studies while bringing a critical algorithm and critical race studies approach to porn studies, centering discussions on structural inequality, racial capitalism, and extraction. The convergence of these fields is necessary and timely, as platforms hosting pornographic material increasingly turn to data-driven models and machine learning systems to enhance their users' search experiences. Just as platform governance scholarship has demonstrated how social media platforms shape media environments, we argue that platforms are not only world-shapers but also "desire curators." Sexual racism, therefore, cannot simply be explained without examining the technological, economic, and infrastructural factors that cultivate and shape the racialization of sexuality and the sexualization of racism. In bringing these fields together, we rely on literature from anthropology and linguistics that threads together how racial and cultural scripts historically move through text, language, and film. We do this to illustrate that sexual racism in pornography or technology is by no means exceptional. Instead, by design it is built into, enacted through, and sustained by multiple systems and mediums.

White Supremacist Grammar of Tagging

The practices of tagging on Pornhub curate and colonize desire by producing a "grammaire pornographique" rooted in white supremacy. Hortense Spillers's *Mama's Baby, Papa's Maybe: An American Grammar Book* (Spillers, 1987) provides a guide for understanding racialized signification work (Smalls, 2020). Spillers's landmark text reflects on the power and weight of naming, unpacking the markers and codes used to describe and control Black women in the United States. Spillers argues that American grammar epistemologically produces Black people's gender as intrinsically other, while constructing a distorted imaginary used to hold African American women captive to the processes of capital:

> The symbolic order that I wish to trace in this writing, calling it an "American grammar," begins at the "beginning," which is really a rupture and a radically different kind of cultural continuation. The massive

demographic shifts, the violent formation of a modern African consciousness, that take place on the sub-Saharan Continent during the initiative
strikes which open the Atlantic slave trade in the fifteenth century of our
Christ, interrupted hundreds of years of black African culture. We write
and think, then, about an outcome of aspects of African-American life in
the United States under the pressure of those events. (Spillers, 1987, p. 22)

Through Spillers's framework for an American grammar, we can see how
the semiotic indexes visual, haptic, legal, labor, future, and even historical
possibilities for racialized subjects. Racialized language is embedded with
symbolic, psychic, and material realities, and pornographic grammar—like
American grammar—must be understood in social, cultural, and historical
context. Raciosemiotics links the phenomenological experience of being an
Other in a white space through an analysis of signs, the body, and the racial meaning-making processes to which they are associated (Smalls, 2020).
Raciosemiotics thinks about the semiotic through a historicoracial schema
(Fanon, 1952) that denaturalizes the white listening subject/interpretant as
the default Human *and* explores the experiences of those who are realized to
be "other than normatively, or optimally, Human" (Smalls, 2020).

Looking at tags from a raciosemiotic perspective permits us to trace the
trajectories of seminal racial tropes throughout varied and transforming
contexts while also subverting moves to exceptionalize racial signification.
In our digital pornographic present, the structuring nature of racialized tags
on porn are methods for the unmarked straight white cisgender man to encounter, experience, and "know" the other. The presumed white consumer is
oriented, from the design of the site and in the language used to navigate the
site, as the intended listening subject for the content hosted on Pornhub. We
see racialized tags on Pornhub as a limiting mechanism, not just indexing
Black women in the (white) digital erotic but also what they cannot be in the
white imagination.

The available tags on Pornhub set up whiteness as the normative bench-
mark against which nonwhite performers are identified, measured, and
marked. On the site, tags related to race, color, and ethnicity are largely reserved for nonwhite performers. Alongside its "Interracial" tag, Pornhub's
descriptors include specific nationalities (such as Brazilian, Indian, Korean,
and Japanese), ethnicities (such as Latina and Arab), race (such as Asian),
and color (such as Ebony). While there are a handful of nationality tags
(for example, Russian, German, and Czech) there are no comparable tags

that specifically reflect the ethnicity, race, or color of white performers. White performers are simply positioned as human beings, while nonwhite performers are sorted, classified, and ranked according to these semiotic tagging regimes. In this way, whiteness "orientates bodies in specific directions, affecting how they 'take up' space" (Ahmed, 2007, p. 150).

Tags on Pornhub index and mark the phenomenology of being as a racialized body. As Spillers writes, names operate as code, laden with historical meaning: "Embedded in a bizarre axiological ground, they demonstrate a sort of telegraphic coding; they are markers so loaded with mythical prepossession that there is no easy way for the agents buried beneath them to come clean" (Spillers, 1987, p. 65). In pornography, the "ebony" tag has become an index for Black feminine content creators, while the "interracial" tag most commonly refers to scenes depicting a white woman performing with a Black man—a fantasy that relies on ideas of Black male sexuality as a threat to an idealized, pure white female sexuality (Williams, 2004). The term "interracial" emerged from the sexual exploitation of slaves and Black people during Reconstruction, when the issue of maintaining color lines depended (as it still does) on sexual control. As performer Isiah Maxwell says in a *Rolling Stone* article, "[interracial] is a smokescreen for what you're really trying to say. . . . It doesn't mean Asian or Latino. It means, 'Are you willing to have sex with a black guy?'" (Dickson, 2020) Pornhub's tagging apparatus thereby produces tags as a means for the white viewer to mediate their experience with the Other.

Race, especially Blackness, has historically been central to the history of pornography in the West, since at least the 19th century and the rise of modern technologies for the mass distribution of photography and film. Black feminist scholars, including Miller-Young (2014), Brooks (2010), Nash (2014), Cruz (2016), Jones (2020), and Horton-Stallings (2015), have explored how colonial fantasies of a mythic Black or African-centered (hyper)sexuality have shaped the production of pornographic media and industries, even where people of color do not appear. Racialized fantasies of a supercharged Black sexuality with the capacity to overcome, defile or transform whiteness, manifests in a multitude of institutional forms and practices. These scholars show that Blackness is central to the creation of whitewashed hierarchies of desirability and hypersexual archetypes, and these Othering logics are further organized via racist schemas of lower pay and fewer job opportunities for nonwhite adult performers, and other problematic material consequences that impact those working in the pornography industry.

278 SPOTLIGHTING THE STRUCTURAL

Tagging, Extraction, and Racial Capitalism

Racialized tagging is essential to the dual white supremacist projects of desiring whiteness and sustaining racial capitalism, as race is wielded as a flavor of, or subgenre of, a supposed normative and unmarked eroticism. As Robinson writes, "world capitalism was developed in a most fundamental way by the particularistic forces of racism and nationalism" (2020, p. 9). In particular, sexual commerce has been built on accumulating capital by extracting value from performers and content creators of color. Tagging as a marketing practice has always involved a certain level of racial exploitation, rooted in commodifying racial difference for the consumption of an imagined white consumer.

Current debates surrounding Pornhub reflect a long history of using racial descriptors to market pornography that predates the Internet. In adult bookstores, video stores, newsletters, and trade magazines, pornographic content has long been organized and sorted according to the presumed tastes of white clientele. In *A Taste for Brown Sugar: Black Women in Pornography*, Miller-Young documents how, during the 1970s, the 8 mm reels available to purchase via mail order would list the title and description of pornographic films in ways that flagged racial signifiers (Miller-Young, 2014). With the emergence of VHS during the 1980s, video store owners would lay out their physical spaces so that customers could navigate content instinctively without having to ask staff for particular titles, while the films themselves employed racialized titles that clearly evoked racial fetishes. This analog means of facilitating consumer searches was reflected in the titling process of films as well as in their box cover art. In the 1980s and 1990s, marketing practices shifted focus to develop an urban Black and Latino male consumer base, gesturing to hip-hop music videos. Across different formats and decades, this language shifted—from "soul sisters" in the 1970s, to "ebony" in the 1980s, to "street hoes" in the 1990s. These categories did not necessarily reflect the racial identities of the performers but rather their cultural constructions by consumers and industry.

In curating their content in the 1980s, video store owners imagined their customer base to be white, suburban, middle-class viewers—those with the income to buy the $100 video tapes—rather than poor whites in the South, or Black and brown urban consumers who tended to be video renters. In fact, some outlets avoided distributing interracial porn in the 1980s in fear of upsetting white audiences (Miller-Young, 2014). As the price of pornography dropped with the advent of DVDs and later online content, porn companies catered to those consumers with purchase power—those who could afford subscription content or premium membership. When "tube" sites emerged in the mid-2000s, they worked to further dispossess marginalized people from their names and images by pirating and remarketing content. In 2006, Pornhub emerged as one of the most aggressive aggregator sites that has defined the "tube era."

MindGeek, formerly Manwin, shifted pornography distribution practices away from subscription sites and "video on demand" by introducing a new industry model that streamed free sexual content and received its income via advertisers. Its model was built on content piracy. Pornhub began as a closed video piracy network where users uploaded videos that infringed copyright. They ripped older VHS material from smaller independent producers as well as large production companies, often buying up production companies and distributors (such as Digital Playground and Brazzers) to secure a monopoly. Pornhub did virtually nothing to enforce the copyright claims of content they were uploading and hosting on their site. They have been criticized by performers for marketing their content using racist, misogynist, transphobic, and fatphobic slurs, as well as stealing queer, feminist, and independent content and rebranding it with their own titles, tags, and loglines that used derogatory or stigmatizing language (Stardust, 2019a).

Now that tube sites provide predominantly free content (although Pornhub does host a premium member section), their customers are not consumers but advertisers. The people who stream and view Pornhub's content merely provide the data that is then sold on to the real customer—corporate advertising companies—to hone their personalized algorithms to market ads more effectively. White designers and white programmers continue to produce white spaces for white people. The experiences, needs, or desires of Black or nonwhite people are rarely a consideration in the design process. In these ways, Pornhub operates as a contemporary example of what Harris calls "whiteness as property," characterized by "the legal legitimation of expectations of power and control that enshrine the status quo as a neutral baseline, while masking the maintenance of white privilege and domination" (Harris, 1993, p. 1715). Increasingly, porn performers and porn scholars are critiquing Pornhub's extractive business models and practices. Maggie MacDonald writes that Pornhub "consolidate[s] media market control in an oligopolistic mode" (2019), while porn performer and director Ovidie exposed many of Pornhub's internal practices of money laundering

280 SPOTLIGHTING THE STRUCTURAL

in her documentary *Pornocracy: The New Sex Multinationals* (2017). It was only recently, due in part to public pressure from independent performers, directors, and studios, that Pornhub began to pitch itself as a platform for which performers, directors, and studios could promote their own work.

Financial motivators continue to perpetuate racial tagging regimes. Without an onslaught of public pressure to change their racialized tagging system, Pornhub continues, business as usual. By comparison, the company rapidly changed its tags when faced with other kinds of public criticism. In 2020, following a highly publicized article by journalist Nicholas Kristof in the *New York Times* about the prevalence of child sexual exploitation material hosted on Pornhub, Visa and Mastercard withdrew their services from the platform, meaning that users could not pay for premium content using those cards. In response, Pornhub made a number of changes to their systems of tagging and verification. They changed the category of "Teen" to "Teen18+" and deleted all content that could not be verified. This was a significant undertaking: according to some reports, this amounted to 80% of Pornhub's total content. This incident demonstrates how quickly Pornhub could act to change their policies and practices where they had the financial or reputational incentive to do so. It was only in response to media outcry and the withdrawal of their payment processors that they belatedly acted to instigate these shifts into their uploading and tagging policies—they managed to implement widespread verification processes within 72 hours of Mastercard and Visa threatening their withdrawal from the site. And yet Pornhub have not changed their practices on using racist tagging systems, suggesting that the concerns of performers and others are not considered sufficient to warrant the effort of designing new ways to tag—or changing to a structure where performers can self-determine their own tags.

Visibility, Searchability, and Undifferentiated Flesh

As we see with Spillers's American grammar, the breaking down of Black people's bodies into parts is not a new process but the continuation of a familiar grammar in the digital. Spillers argues that American grammar turns Black bodies into "undifferentiated flesh" and that sexually assessing Black people's bodies has been part and parcel of white supremacist racial ordering mechanisms from their inception (Spillers, 1987). Not only is it more likely for a content creator's work to have tags that describe them through the white gaze than their actual names, but even when a Black content creator is named, their content is found on the latter pages of a search result for a not necessarily racialized search inquiry (e.g., "blowjob," "stockings," "public") (Jones, 2020; Thompson 2021). In her book, *Camming: Money, Power, and Pleasure in the Sex Work Industry* (2020), Angela Jones found that performers of color were less likely to have their names associated with content on cam sites. Instead they were tagged with racialized descriptors—essentially, they become undifferentiated flesh. King Noire describes this phenomenon directly when he says, "White people are people to a lot of these companies. Black or brown people are fetishes and body parts. . . . When it comes to a lot of Black performers, you won't even see their name in the scene" (Perdue, 2021).

Using "ebony" as an index for Blackness in the white imagination forecloses the possibilities of Black erotic expressions that are not possible under this limiting schema. The possibilities these schemas foreclose for Black content creators includes fair or competitive pay (Goff, 2016), job opportunities (Dickson, 2020), comfortable or even safe working conditions (Lieberman, 2020; Snow, 2020; Song, 2020), retention of their intellectual property (Madison, 2021), to be erotically legible with dark skin, kinky hair, and unambiguously Black features (Lieberman, 2020; McGowan, 2020), and the basic professional standard to be called by their names as a (Perdue, 2021). One of the few means for Black performers to be recognized on a large scale has been through these categories. The "ethnic" category, for example, at the Adult Video News awards, has been a means to recognize nonwhite performers who rarely receive the same attention or visibility as their white counterparts for more general awards such as "performer of the year." Even then, there remain stark differences in how Black men have been able to navigate the awards compared with Black women and trans performers. Black women continue to receive more traction when they talk about race than themselves.

Being nameless creates barriers for nonwhite performers to sustain their own brands, fan-base, clicks, views, traffic and, ultimately, income. This is particularly problematic, as Perdue points out, because Pornhub's own annual awards ceremonies, the Pornhub Awards, are based on internal data about whom daily visitors have searched for and viewed the most. Perdue notes that "[w]hile this positions 'data' as an impartial third party, these metrics are in fact influenced by the structure around them, in which nonwhite performers get more traction by including racial terms than their names" (Perdue, 2021). In this manner, Pornhub's model incentivizes the use of racist descriptors. Racialized tags create feedback loops between the platform and the users. Platforms that stream video content rely on enormous amounts of data from their users, from popularity to user input to viewing patterns in order to recommend content and offer content suggestions to viewers. When platforms make suggestions for what to view next, "it is largely a matter of consumers getting back their own processed data" (Bucher, 2018, p. 2). If performers depend on racialized descriptors to ensure their content is seen, and performers know to search for those descriptors to find the content they enjoy, those terms crystalize and the descriptor becomes the means through which that performer is legible to audiences.

The existence of racialized tags leaves performers in a predicament where many want to challenge rather than cultivate racist desires, but cannot necessarily afford to turn down racist money. As Demi Sutra told *Rolling Stone*, "You never know who really needs the money, because there just aren't so many opportunities for black actresses" (Dickson, 2020). These tags (and their underlying fantasies) are therefore connected to material reality for workers. The interracial tag can be way for Black performers to be visible, legible, and searchable among a proliferation of pornography organized according to white sexual tastes, tropes, and fantasies. Some performers use terms such as "interracial" and "ebony" in their self-marketing, and monetizing this language may be seen by some as compensation or reparations. Dillon Diaz described this dilemma at an adult panel called Flip the Script: "I'm very unsure of what my position is on [search engine optimization] and tags. . . . Some of it is needed to be able to find what one is looking for, but some of it may also be fetishizing and exploitive. Finding where the line is drawn is hard" (Klein, 2020).

Because the searchability and visibility of tags is directly linked to the ability of BIPOC porn performers to earn an income, nonwhite performers are therefore consistently navigating racialized systems in order to survive. Savannah Skye similarly describes in *Cosmopolitan*, "We have to force ourselves into spaces to be accepted. . . . I don't like being tagged as 'ebony' or 'interracial,' but in order to make money, we have to submit ourselves to that" (Lieberman, 2020). To remove these racial markings leaves the question of how to deal with the invisibility of Blackness in an oversaturated market centered on the primacy of white beauty and white sexuality. At the same time, engaging with racialized language—and indeed, race play—can also be a site for BIPOC performers to explore their own desires, sexualities, traumas, and fantasies. Both Jennifer Nash (2014) and Ariane Cruz (2016) write about how such spaces allow for Black women to enact their own critiques, to push against the logic of the system and to politically engage, and that we ought to tune out the white director in order to subtly attend to Black women's performances and agency.

In June 2020, the BIPOC Adult Industry Collective, a performer and sex worker–led collective, issued a Media Statement Regarding Racism in the Adult Entertainment Industry. Notably, the Collective did not support the elimination of terms such as "interracial," "ethnic," and "IR," concerned that this may impact the searchability, visibility, and work opportunities of BIPOC performers. The elimination of terms such as "interracial" and "ethnic," they write, "may do more harm than good" and "will affect product sales, brand management, and the possible deletion of BIPOC from nominations and awards altogether" (2020, n.p.). However, they did support expanding the definition of such terms to include a wider variety of interracial scenes and ethnicities. In addition, they demanded that platforms reject derogatory terms and mockery, and that performers should have autonomy over how they were identified.

Performers are now demanding more control over their own data and processes for seeking their permissions for how that content and data can be used. In an interview on the *Tamron Hall* show, porn performer TS Madison called out the co-optation, extraction, pirating, and theft of Black trans women's intellectual property and the concentrated, privatized, and white ownership of digital infrastructure by media monopolies that contributes to vast inequalities in wealth and power. Madison recalls many women she met who worked in pornography as "being controlled by the man, not taking ownership of their Black skin, not knowing how powerful their Black skin is, not having control over it. And many of those girls have passed on now. And some of them passed on broke and people are still monetising off their intellectual property" (Madison, 2021).

Not Just a glitch: Automation, Coding Whiteness, and the Curation of Desire

Existing sociological discourse on sexual racism focuses largely on its manifestation in individual preferences, intimate exchanges, and personal desires. Indeed, sexual racism permeates and colonizes inner desires and psyches on an individual level. Desire, however, is also infrastructural. Recommended content and search engine results on platforms play a role in *curating* the desire of consumers. Through racialized tagging grammars we see the extension of raciosemiotic circumscription of Black existence, not only through natural language but inscribed in computer code; a racialized digital present where white supremacist racial stratifications and ideologies are imbricated in the very structure of online dwelling and maintained through algorithmic reifications. Recommender systems now rank, sort, filter, and suggest information to users, based on a range of data including user behavior and preferences. Pornhub has a "Recommended For You" section on their homepage as well as their "Recommended Categories" and "Recommended Porn Stars," where they direct users to particular videos, categories, and performers. In this way, the white supremacist grammar of Pornhub is now being amplified via the use of automation and data-driven analytics. Categories of race and color are reproduced by users who are searching for particular content, meaning that performers need to engage with (and label themselves with) these terms in order to effectively reach their audiences. Pornhub reportedly employ over 1,000 tech workers to analyze user consumption data, which is used to sell targeted ads—Gustavo Turner refers to this as Pornhub's "vertically integrated data porn empire" (Turner, 2019).

Because tagging and recommender systems are usually proprietary, it is difficult for researchers or users to fully analyze how they rank, sort, or organize information. Some analysis has been conducted on Pornhub, including a project called "Pornhub—Tracking Exposed," a browser extension that analyzes how Pornhub's personalization algorithms impact user experiences, including the kinds of content they recommend (2021). Indeed, Rama et al. (2022) collected data for 1,600 variations of Pornhub's homepages, in addition to 25,000 videos suggested to 10 accounts with differing self-declared gender identities. They found that "Pornhub's algorithmic suggestions and the structure of the platform concur to reiterate a heteronormative perspective on sexual desire, sexuality, and gender identities" (2022, p. 1). Pornhub itself provides selective research data and analysis about their viewer's consumption practices on their website Pornhub Insights. Their reports include the most searched terms, top searches by country, and trends in popularity of different kinds of content (e.g., breasts, lesbian hentai). However, their use of machine learning and computer vision technology to scan content and recommend and suggest tags at scale on Pornhub is likely to reproduce systems that categorize and type human gender, race, and sexuality using white, heteronormative, and ciscentric logics. Pornhub does not generally provide their disaggregated data sets for researchers or the public, and it is likely that Pornhub's racist tags influence the kinds of data they produce and the kinds of claims they make about human sexuality and desire.

In Pornhub's 2019 *Insight Report*, for example, 8 of the top 25 most popular search terms were nonwhite racial, color, or ethnicity descriptors (Pornhub, 2019). Using data publicly available extracted from Pornhub's landing page, in January 2022 there were 137,928 videos tagged with racialized categories, which increased to 141,986 in July 2022 (Figure 12.1). Demonstrating the enduring popularity of a racialized *grammaire pornographique*, this increase by 2.9% was on par with the overall increase of tagged videos on Pornhub, which rose by 2.8% during the same period. Importantly, this list does not include any reference to a "white" tag, because one is not provided by Pornhub. Further, as former digital media specialist at Pornhub, Noelle Perdue, has previously reflected, terms like "caucasian" or "white" have never appeared on Pornhub's top search lists (Perdue, 2021). As Katrin Tiidenberg and Emily van der Nagel write in *Sex and Social Media*, "Entering the search term 'white' into Pornhub returns videos captioned with references to white stockings or women with the surname "White," as often as this term is used to refer to the race of someone in the video" (2020, p. 70). At the same time, nonwhite performers become boxed into existing categories—for instance,

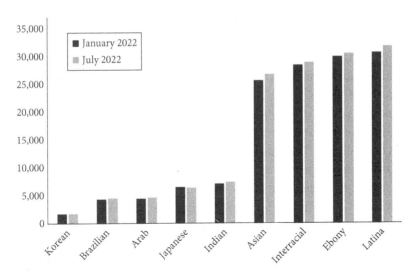

Figure 12.1 Number of videos with racialized "tags" on the website, Pornhub, January–July 2022.

in their examination of the history of Native American characters in pornography, Mackay and Mackay note that "actual Native performers are insistently placed in inaccurate racial categories such as Asian and Latina" (2020). Nonwhite performers have been systemically fetishized and their cultures conflated for the easy consumption by a presumed white porn audience.

In Spillers's discussion of how the transatlantic slave trade and the production of a race (and the following production of that race as chattel), we see the white supremacist move as defining what a racialized body cannot be rather than what it is or even what it *can* be. In her book, *Intersectional Tech*, Kishonna Gray implores us to examine "how technology is mobilized to fulfill the project of white masculine supremacy" (Gray, 2020, p. 4). Because technology is designed by humans, the values of its creators are coded into the hardware. Increasingly, critical race scholars working across technology and Internet studies warn of the potential for automated systems to replicate and reproduce existing inequalities. In *Algorithms of Oppression*, Safiya Umoja Noble reminds us that discriminatory impacts of algorithms are not simply the result of bias or mistake, but rather problems of design: "Algorithmic oppression is not just a glitch in the system but, rather, is fundamental to the operating system of the web" (Noble, 2018, p. 10). As Pornhub accelerates its use of machine learning to automate tagging processes, the white supremacist grammars found in their existing system become coded into the software itself.

Of further concern is not simply Pornhub's data-driven analytics based on the metrics of porn consumers but also their collection of porn performers' biometric data. In order to combat nonconsensual intimate imagery and child sexual abuse material, Pornhub now requires performers to verify their identities before they can post content. The collection of performers' legal names—a project of legibility and knowability—puts them at risk, especially where they are working in environments where porn production may be criminalized. Where performers' legal and work names are connected, they are at risk of stigma and discrimination in other parts of their lives, including in other employment, in accessing goods and services, in child custody matters, in immigration cases, and in accessing justice. Marginalization changes how data interacts with bodies—the collection and analysis of biometric and identity data has disproportionate effects for BIPOC porn performers. And yet these measures are accepted as appropriate from a white normative citizen positionality.

In 2017, Pornhub began using computer vision software to identify porn stars and automate content tagging (Sawers, 2017). They pitched their new approach as a technological fix to their outdated tagging systems, one that would bring efficiency at scale. In an article for *Venture Beat*, Pornhub Vice President Corey Price stated:

> We had an antiquated system for tagging videos that just wasn't cutting it anymore. Now, with the influx of technology, particularly regarding AI and computer vision, we're able to update our system and implement a model that will significantly improve content tagging. (Sawers, 2017)

Pornhub's approach was to feed thousands of videos into the computer vision software alongside official images of porn stars, tag the videos, and ask users to "upvote" or "downvote" the tags. For example, if a video is tagged incorrectly with the wrong name, users could downvote the tag, providing feedback to the site about the accuracy of their software. They created this software by scraping their existing content. Described in an official diagram as "Get pornstar data from 1000s of pornstar images," Pornhub described their aim to help users navigate and find desired content with more accurate results (Figure 12.2). There is indication that Pornhub sought the specific consent of performers to use their content for the purposes of creating this computer vision software.

It is not clear from Pornhub's public statements whether their new AI system also operates to recognize and automatically tag the racial and ethnic backgrounds of performers. However, this is conceivable, given that they announced their plans to scan all videos on their site (5 million at the

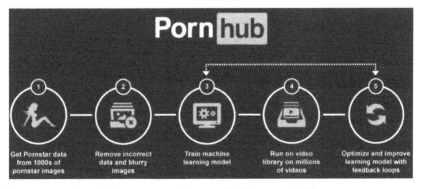

Figure 12.2 Pornhub computer vision model (Sawers, 2017).

time) to recognize outdoor environments, sexual positions, and "physical traits." Such a task brings a series of issues. Aside from the problems with reproducing and reconsolidating a set of problematic racial categories, machine learning systems struggle to accurately identify context and consistently misidentify race, age, and gender. Classifiers are often based on flawed assumptions and unrepresentative training data sets. Facial recognition technology has been shown to have high rates of error and significant racial bias. The Gender Shades study, which analyzed three commercial gender classification systems, found that darker-skinned females were the most misclassified group, with error rates of up to 34.7% compared to 0.8% among lighter-skinned males (Buolamwini & Gebru, 2018). If Pornhub's machine learning model is trained on Pornhub's existing videos and existing tagging system, with its problematic and conflated categories of race, and with feedback on accuracy coming from consumers rather than performers, it is likely to reproduce a white supremacist grammar of tagging at scale.

In *Race After Technology*, Ruha Benjamin demonstrates how automation "has the potential to hide, speed up, and deepen discrimination while appearing neutral and even benevolent . . . by explicitly amplifying racial hierarchies" (2019). Pornhub's "suggested tags"—rather than simply automating navigation tools—have potential to reinforce white supremacist benchmarks and perpetuate the marginalization, stereotyping, and fetishization of nonwhite performers. This is particularly the case where they amplify the content of white performers and derank content by nonwhite performers. Numerous studies have critiqued recommender systems on platforms that boost and amplify content that features white, cisgender, slim, able-bodied women (for example, see van der Nagel, 2103, on Reddit Gone Wild). As André Brock writes, "online identity has long been conflated with whiteness, even as whiteness is itself signified as a universal, raceless, technocultural identity" (Brock, 2020, p. 1). Improving error rates of algorithms for more accurate tagging will not necessarily address the problematic categories of racial identity that underpin them. We ought to understand code, and the relevant algorithms it produces, to be a series of performative utterances that develop the digital as intrinsically racialized. Through a semiotic investigation, we see not only that the racialization of space and those within it is continuous in both the physical and the digital but also that these spaces themselves are facets of a continuous reality. Code is speech, working across both physical and digital planes.

Alternative Grammars of Tagging

What potentials exist for advancing social justice by undesiring whiteness and undoing sexual racism through semiotic means? How might the work of performers and linguists of color provide us with potential paths out of this matrix? Spillers suggests that the project of linguistic undoing is both a deconstructive and creative task: "In order for me to speak a truer word concerning myself, I must strip down through layers of attenuated meanings, made in excess over time, assigned by a particular historical order, and there await whatever marvels of my own inventiveness" (Spillers, 1987, p. 65). The project of undesiring whiteness may entail discohering race as a subgenre—of a normative, that is a white, erotic. Undesiring whiteness requires reimagining an erotic where whiteness is not the listening subject or interpretant, and where Blackness is not performed to be assessed by a more Human audience. Undesiring whiteness requires undoing an intrinsically racialized erotic habitus that is entrenched in the very structures of our sexual, social, and digital worlds.

Various approaches have emerged to address this task. Precisely because accurate tags are necessary for user searchability, Daisy Ducati has argued that porn companies need to "train our fans to use non-racist terminology" (McGowan, 2020). In June 2020, the Adult Video News awards announced they would eliminate the "interracial" and "ethnic" categories from their awards. In a press release, the CEO remarked, "For too long, we've heard the same excuses for these: it's what the market demands. But we choose whether or not to serve that market. As an industry, we can no longer deny that these films amplify racism and discrimination" (South, 2020). There is an obvious role here for white people in industry change. As Evie Muir asks:

> Is it not white people who are the main owners and benefactors of the porn industry? White porn stars who get paid more? White sex workers who dominate discussions on sex worker rights and liberation? It needs to be these communities, both allies and perpetrators of this very specific type of racialised, sexualised harm that are stopping, listening, platforming, advocating, and ultimately changing the sector with the power and racialised privileges they possess. (Thompson, 2021)

Permitting performers to generate their own tags to describe their gender, sexuality, ethnicity, ancestry, or other aspects of their identity, culture, or place of belonging could further work to both manage user expectations and

290 SPOTLIGHTING THE STRUCTURAL

encourage self-determined expression. There are plenty of examples of the ways in which nonwhite content is described, labeled, and marketed in ways that are self-deterministic, respectful, and celebratory. Performer Destinee describes how this language could shift: "I would like to see Black kink and BDSM, Black fetish, Black queer love, Black queer sex, [and] Black trans folks" (Klein, 2020). On independent queer porn sites such as Pink Label Tv, run by Shine Louise Houston, the content is broken down into a range of categories that include "BIPOC Porn: Celebrating People of Colour in Adult Films." Black-owned, independent porn producers such as Jetsetting Jasmine and King Noire, of Royal Fetish Films, are creating their own vocabulary to signal to their audiences. As King Noire says, "We've been working on different ways to label our scenes to get them found for what they actually are, whether it be passion or fetish" (Thompson, 2021). Their content is tagged with an extensive variety of descriptors from "Black love" to "Black Goddess."

As a critical porn-watching/making public, we have to make this erotic lexicon collectively (with the challenges, failures, and successes that involves), with content creators of color at the helm of this change. Feminist pornographies have embarked on such a task over recent decades, attempting to revision, redefine and rework industry practices and lexicons, to varying degrees of success (Stardust, 2019a). While they have certainly intervened in both production and distribution practices, they have also risked reifying and essentializing (rather than undoing) categories of "real sex," "porn for women," and "authenticity" in the process (Stardust, 2019b).

In the award-winning film *Kitchen Talk: Reclaiming our Image*, a group of BIPOC adult performers, including Caritia, Lina Bembe, Bishop Black, and Kali Sudhra, talk openly and honestly about their experiences in the industry and how to heal, reclaim, and move forward together. Independent porn producers in Central and South America are currently engaged in projects to decolonize pornography and rearticulate relationships between sex, self, community, land, and sovereignty. For example, Erica Sarmet's curated Abya Yala collection at the 2020 San Francisco Porn Film Festival decenters and reorients the white gaze in a way that positions whiteness—through its history of colonialism, epistemicide, and genocide—as fundamentally undesirable (Sarmet, 2020). Performers are also using the technology of tagging toward naming their own identities and desires. In 2020, BIPOC performers gathered as part of an event called "Flip the Script," hosted by Kink.com, in which involved panels on representations, inclusivity, industry change, and how consumers should support performers directly by subscribing to their independent content. Sir Jon Julius, founder of Black Porn Matters, suggested that performers ought to tag their videos with self-identified terms and flood social media feeds with those hashtags: "It's not English we're fighting, it's code. Take a lesson from the hackers—if you want to take over a hashtag, overwhelm the feed with your content" (Gillespie, 2020). Listening to these articulations is critical.

But notably, there is a shift away from a politics of inclusion and a push toward performers creating their own platforms, spaces, languages, and companies in order to role-model new industry terminologies and practices. Sex educator Tyomi Morgan claimed, "We are always looking to be included. . . . But the real solution is more POC creating production companies where we can control the narrative . . . placing POC in places of power in companies so they can advocate, being involved in spaces that weren't made for us, and calling out POC to step it up to create more production companies" (Gillespie, 2020). As part of this move toward autonomy, TS Madison has advocated for trans communities learning to code in order to build self-deterministic spaces in which performers can retain ownership of their image and intellectual property (Madison, 2020). Establishing her own production company, Raw Dawg Entertainment/RDE Multimedia group, in 2009, she joins Black content creators such as Lexington Steele (who started Mercenary Motion Pictures in 2003) and Misty Stone (who started Misty Stone Productions in 2013) and a raft of new performers building their own companies. In thinking about how to undesire whiteness in porn, we follow the lead of performers of color as they design and perform the work of recuperating from being called outside their names.

There are practical, short term design steps that platforms can take immediately to intervene and alleviate existing harms: removing racist descriptors from platform categories, allowing performers to self-identify their content, building in consent mechanisms before scraping porn stars' content, or developing more nuanced and less biased search engines and recommender systems. These steps could work toward untangling the systems of legibility that require nonwhite performers to become legible to the white gaze. However, we ought to remember that tech and design fixes alone cannot undo sexual racism. Systems to amplify the content of independent producers are important, but they will not necessarily address the widespread precarity of porn labor or interrupt the dominance of Pornhub's monopoly. Simply reforming tagging practices—whether on social media or porn tube sites—will not necessarily result in the system changes necessary to benefit or empower marginalized users.

The BIPOC Adult Industry Collective reminds us that tagging is merely the tip of the iceberg. On their website, the collective states that they "know that our strength lies not only in the words we stand by but most importantly through the actions of our activities" (2021, n.p.). They are advocating for a broader range of changes that seek to support economic opportunities for BIPOC performers in addition to changing the material structures of industry production and marketing. Among other things, their statement calls to eliminate wage disparities; increase paid BIPOC staff involved in production and distribution; establish an industry-funded career-development pipeline; produce educational resources on marketing language, pay diversity, and intimacy consultants; introduce filters and policies to block racially charged language and abuse; and inform performers of scene titles as part of the booking process and build in a process to opt-out where the title changes.

These demands are significant because they diagnose the problem of tagging very differently. Instead of being a problem that is simply about reforming labels, which invites simple tech fixes, it is a problem of white supremacy at the industry level and the appropriate response involves overhauling the standards and processes of production and the mechanics of distribution altogether. Instead of focusing on the assimilatory goals of inclusion and diversity, platforms ought to be asking themselves how they can actively resist their ownership of nonwhite bodies. Challenging embedded, ingrained sexual racism requires the decentralization of online space, the redistribution of wealth and material resources, the dismantling of media monopolies, an end to white supremacy, and significant shifts toward design justice in technology conceptualization and development.

References

Ahmed, S. (2007). A phenomenology of whiteness. *Feminist Theory, 8*(2), 149–168.

Applebaum, B. (2016). Critical whiteness studies. In G. W. Noblit & J. R. Neikirk (Eds), *Oxford research encyclopedia of education.* Oxford University Press. https://doi.org/10.1093/acrefore/9780190264093.013.5

BIPOC Adult Industry Collective. (2020). *Media statement regarding racism in adult entertainment industry.* BIPOC–AIC | YNOT.

Benjamin, R. (2019). *Race After Technology: Abolitionist Tools for the New Jim Code.* Polity.

Brock, A., Jr. (2020). *Distributed Blackness: African American cybercultures.* New York University Press.

Brooks, S. (2010). *Unequal desires: Race and erotic capital in the stripping industry.* SUNY Press.

Bucher, T. (2018). *If . . . then: Algorithmic power and politics.* Oxford University Press.

Buolamwini, J., & Gebru, T. (2018). Gender shades: Intersectional accuracy disparities in commercial gender classification. *Proceedings of Machine Learning Research, 81*, 1–15.

Chang, E. (2019). *Brotopia: Breaking up the boys club of Silicon Valley.* Penguin Random House.

Cole, S. (2020, July 31). Fuck the Police: Why does cop porn still exist? *Motherboard: Tech by Vice.* (vice.com)

Cruz, A. (2016). *The Colour of Kink: Black Women, BDSM and Pornography.* New York University Press.

Dickson, E. J. (2020). Racism in porn industry under scrutiny amid nationwide protests. *Rolling Stone.* Retrieved October 20, 2021, from https://www.rollingstone.com/cult ure/culture-features/racism-porn-industry-protest-1010853/

Fanon, F. (1952). *Peau Noire, Masques Blancs.* Editions du Seuil.

Goff, K. (2013). Is the porn industry racist? *The Root.* Retrieved October 11, 2021, from https://www.theroot.com/is-the-porn-industry-racist-1790895844#replies

Gray, K. (2020). *Intersectional tech: Black users in digital gaming.* Louisiana State University Press.

Gregory, T. (2021). A decolonial critique of "authentic" pleasure in contemporary Australian heteroporn. *Porn Studies, 9*(2), 1–17.

Harris, C. I. (1993). Whiteness as property. *Harvard Law Review, 106*(8), 1707–1791.

Horton–Stallings, L. (2015). *Funk the erotic: Transaesthetics and black sexual cultures.* University of Illinois Press.

Jones, A. (2020). *Camming: Money, Power and Pleasure in the Sex Work Industry.* New York University Press.

Kelion, L. (2019, December 3). TikTok suppressed disabled users' videos. *BBC News.*

Klein, J. (2020, September 15). Your porn is racist: These Black performers are fighting back. *Input.* https://www.inputmag.com/culture/how-to-fight-rac ism-in-porn-by-using-seo

Lieberman, H. (2020). Black performers make millions for porn sites—while being underpaid, verbally abused, and subjected to racism. *Cosmopolitan.* Retrieved October 9, 2021, from https://www.cosmopolitan.com/sex-love/a34642666/racism-porn-industry/

MacDonald, M. (2019). *Desire for data: PornHub and the platformization of a culture industry* [Doctoral dissertation]. Concordia University.

Mackay, J., & Mackay, P. (2020). NDNGirls and Pocahotties: Native American and First Nations representation in settler colonial pornography and erotica. *Porn Studies, 7*(2), 168–186.

Madison, T. S. (2021, March 17), *Interview on the Tamron Hall show.* https://www.faceb ook.com/watch/?v=1006526216422299

McGowan, E. (2020, June 24). Daisy Ducati thinks the interracial porn tag is racist, period. *Bustle,* n.p.

Miller–Young, M. (2014). *A taste for brown sugar.* Duke University Press.

Moreton–Robinson, A. (2015). *The white possessive: Property, power, and indigenous sovereignty.* University of Minnesota Press.

Nash, J. C. (2014). *The Black body in ecstasy.* Duke University Press.

Noble, S. U. (2018). *Algorithms of Oppression: How Search Engines Reinforce Racism*. New York University Press.

Perdue, N. (2021). How porn's racist metadata hurts adult performers of color. *WIRED*. Retrieved October 20, 2021, from https://www.wired.com/story/porn-racist-metadata-hurts-adult-performers-of-color/

Pornhub Insights. (2019). The 2019 year in review. *Pornhub.com*. December 11. https://www.pornhub.com/insights/2019-year-in-review

Pornhub-Tracking Exposed. (2021). *Pornhub.com*. https://pornhub.tracking.exposed/

Rama, I., Bainotti, L., Gandini, A., Giorgi, G., Semenzin, S., Agosti, C., Corona, G., & Romano, S. (2022). The platformization of gender and sexual identities: An algorithmic analysis of Pornhub. *Porn Studies*, *10*(2): 154–173.

Robinson, C. J. (1983). *Black Marxism: The making of the Black radical tradition*. Zed Books.

Rouse, K. (2020). *Petition by the BIPOC Adult Industry Collective to adult media production companies and distributors to end racism and wage discrimination in porn*. BIPOC-AIC. https://campaigns.organizefor.org/petitions/end-racism-and-wage-discrimination-in-porn?share=169f4ea8-1933-415d-b4dd-5004521ba57a&source=copy_email&utm_source=copy_email

Sarmet, E. (2020). *Abya Yala*. San Francisco Porn Film Festival.

Sawers, P. (2017, October 11). Pornhub taps computer vision to identify porn stars and automate content tagging. *Venture Beat*. https://venturebeat.com/2017/10/11/pornhub-taps-computer-vision-to-identify-porn-stars-and-automate-content-tagging/

Smalls, K. (2020). Race, SIGNS, and the body: Towards a theory of racial semiotics. In H. Samy Alim, Angela Reyes and Paul V. Kroskrity (Eds.), *The Oxford Handbook of Language and Race*. Part 3, Chapter 12. Oxford University Press.

Snow, A. (2013). Interracial sex still taboo for many porn stars. *Daily Beast*. Retrieved October 10, 2021, from https://www.thedailybeast.com/interracial-sex-still-taboo-for-many-porn-stars

Snow, A. (2020). Black porn stars come forward with their racism horror stories. *Daily Beast*. Retrieved October 8, 2021, from https://www.thedailybeast.com/black-porn-stars-come-forward-with-their-racism-horror-stories

Song, S. (2020). Meet the couple fighting porn's race problem. *Paper Mag*. Retrieved October 22, 2021, from https://www.papermag.com/royal-fetish-porn-race-problem-2648632642.html?rebelltitem=12#rebelltitem12

South, M. (2020). Will AVN's elimination of "ethnic" categories hurt performers of color? *Mike South*. June 2, 2020.https://mikesouth.com/avn/will-avns-elimination-of-ethnic-categories-hurt-performers-of-color-57545/

Spillers, H. (1987). Mama's baby, Papa's maybe: An American grammar book, *Diacritics*, *17*(2), 64–81.

Sprayregen, M. (2021, May 28). Twitch adds transgender tag after years of protests from trans community. *Them*.

Srnicek, N. (2019). *Platform capitalism*. Polity Press.

Stardust, Z (2019a). Alternative pornographies, regulatory fantasies, resistance politics. [PhD thesis]. School of Arts and Media, University of New South Wales. https://www.unsworks.unsw.edu.au/permalink/f/5gm2j3/unsworks_59501

Stardust, Z. (2019b). From amateur aesthetics to intelligible orgasms: Pornographic authenticity and precarious labour in the gig economy. *AG About Gender—International Journal of Gender Studies*, *8*(16), 1–29.

Thompson, R. (2021). Porn, and porn sites, bolster racist tropes by design. *Mashable*. Retrieved October 15, 2021, from https://mashable.com/article/porn-racist-tropes

Tierney, A. (2016). Are your porn habits racist? *Vice*. Retrieved October 11, 2021. https://www.vice.com/en/article/kwxm9n/what-canadians-race-specific-porn-searches-say-about-us

Turner, G. (2019, January 1). My stepdad's huge data set. *Logic Mag*. https://logicmag.io/play/my-stepdad's-huge-data-set/

Van der Nagel, E. (2013). Faceless bodies: Negotiating technological and cultural codes on Reddit Gonewild. *Scan: Journal of Media Arts Culture, 10*(2), 1–10.

Williams, L. (2004). Skin flicks on the racial border: Pornography, exploitation and interracial lust. *FGS—Freiburger GeschlechterStudien, 10*(2), 9–10.

13

White Supremacy and the Sex Industry

The Racialized Stratification of Sex Work in Four Distinct Legal Contexts

Panteá Farvid, Sarah Epstein, Leigh Lumpkin, Thyme Canton, and Michelle King

Introduction

Commercial sex is an evolving industry that stratifies people, desire, bodies, income, and access to sex along many lines. In the heterosexual market where straight, cisgender men buy sex from cisgender or transgender[1] women (hereafter referred to as women) there is an invisibilized but deeply rooted racial hierarchy. While race is a social construct, it has real-world material consequences regarding access to power, capital, and safety, based on one's proximity to racial and ethnic whiteness (Salter et al., 2018). Racial stratification affects all sectors of the commercial sex industry, ranging from those that do have sex with clients (e.g., standard to full-service sex workers) to those who do not have sex with clients (e.g., strippers, Dominatrixes, fetish providers, cam models, phone sex operators, and pornographic performers). Standard services for in-person sex work typically involve penetrative sex (vaginal and anal), manual sex, and oral sex (one-way or mutual) and sometimes kissing (Henry & Farvid, 2017). Full-service sex work can also include more intimate social and romantic experiences, referred to as the "girlfriend experience," such as cuddling, kissing, and chatting (Milrod & Monto, 2012). Adjacent to girlfriend experiences, escorts offer social and romantic companions for buyers (e.g., joining a buyer for dinner or a party/event), but not all escorts engage in sex with clients (Barker, 2023). In this

---

[1] For simplicity and brevity, we use transgender as a catchall term for trans* and other gender diverse people, with the understanding that language is limited for the multiplicity of identities that people inhabit and that we cannot capture.

Panteá Farvid, Sarah Epstein, Leigh Lumpkin, Thyme Canton, and Michelle King, *White Supremacy and the Sex Industry* In: *Sexual Racism and Social Justice*. Edited by: Denton Callander, Panteá Farvid, Amir Baradaran, and Thomas A. Vance, Oxford University Press. © Oxford University Press 2024. DOI: 10.1093/oso/9780197605509.003.0014

chapter, we focus specifically on racial stratification of full-service style sex work, including its dictation of whom is sought by clients and why, earnings, the location where one can work, and the extent to which police enforce the criminalization of sex work.

The commercial sex industry, in particular full-service sex work, has historically fueled various sociopolitical moral panics and fierce academic debates (see Farvid, 2017). These include whether sex work challenges or upholds traditional cisgendered, heterosexual power dynamics (Gerassi, 2015); biased public health concerns (Nova, 2016); gender-based violence against women; and the exploitation and subjugation of women within the industry (Farley, 2004). Acute criticism of the industry often comes from an unexpected alliance, namely political conservatives and abolitionists (including some radical) feminists. Traditionally, criticisms of sex work from conservative factions have been most concerned with explicit displays of female sexuality and moral outrage for sex taking place outside of committed heterosexual relationships, while feminist critiques have centered on sex work as an inherently exploitative extension of patriarchal power relations (e.g., Farley, 2009).

Other feminist perspectives vary in their critiques, running the gamut between pro- and anti-sex work stances (Henry & Farvid, 2017). Liberal and pro-sex work feminists hold that sex work provides women individual autonomy and access to economic mobility (Doezema, 2002). Critical feminists see sex work both as replicating oppressive constructs of binary male and female sexuality, traditional heterosexuality, and other oppressive structures (e.g., capitalism), and as offering women access to material wealth in constrained economic contexts (Farvid & Glass, 2014). Marxist feminists typically see all work—including sex work—as exploitative within a capitalist system, particularly if people do not own the modes of operation and/or lack autonomy over their laboring bodies (Beloso, 2012). Further, the intellectual assignment of "agency" afforded to sex workers tends to vary across feminist approaches: radical/abolitionist feminists have been critiqued for positioning sex workers only as victims (e.g., of abuse, neglect, economic hardship, and patriarchy), while liberals feminists uphold limited sentiments of individual empowerment (typically based on the experience of white middle-class and educated sex workers). By contrast, critical and Marxist feminist approaches apply intersectional perspectives, focusing on the various interplay of power and capital. Some critical feminists seek a more nuanced analysis of the broader systems of inequity and power relations

298 SPOTLIGHTING THE STRUCTURAL

that create the gendered, and at times highly exploitative, sex industry, while championing sex workers' rights to safety and autonomy, in constrained social, political, and economic contexts (see Farvid, 2017, for a full discussion).

Racialized stratification in the commercial sex industry refers to the inequities sex workers experience based on their race, ethnicity, and—at times—immigration status (Verdugo, 2008). While some existing research considers racism within the commercial sex industry (e.g., Butler, 2015), further analysis is important for identifying inequities and interrogating legislation and activism, where race or ethnicity might be overlooked. In this chapter, we examine the contours of full-service sex work in four distinct, but culturally adjacent, Anglo-legal contexts: The United States, where buying or selling sex is almost entirely illegal/criminalized; The United Kingdom, where sex work is legal but regulated;[2] Canada, where buyers, but not sellers, are criminalized (often referred to as the "Nordic Model"); and Aotearoa/ New Zealand,[3] where sex work was nationally decriminalized in 2003. We argue that while sex work is profoundly shaped by racism across all geographic and legal contexts, each place has unique historical nuances that affect current-day racial/ethnic relationships and rights. While proximity to "whiteness" or "Blackness" shifts in different geographic locations, what remains constant is the elevation of whatever is most proximate to whiteness and the degradation of whatever is most closely aligned with Blackness.

To achieve this chapter's aims, we first outline the theoretical, historical, and intersectional grounding that provides the entry point to these issues. Second, we give a brief overview of men who buy sex and how "demand" in the sex industry is racialized. Third, we discuss the legal parameters of sex work in each country and how the industry unfolds in particularly racialized ways. We also pay attention to how other oppressive structures, such as colonization, heteronormativity, patriarchy, sexism, and xenophobia are implicated in the racialized matrix of sex work. As argued by others before (e.g., Crenshaw, 1990), these systems of oppression are mutually constitutive and create profound harms, particularly for those who sit at intersections of marginalization. Indeed, our analysis pays attention to how various axes of

---

[2] Sex work is legal in the entire United Kingdom except for in Northern Ireland, where it is illegal to pay for, but not to sell, sex (City of London Police, 2023).

[3] "Aotearoa" is the Indigenous name given to New Zealand by Māori, the Indigenous people of the country (translating to "the land of the long white cloud"). "Aotearoa" is commonly used on its own in the country to refer to the country. When writing for an international audience, it is now common to use both terms—acknowledging that New Zealand already had a name, before the process of colonization began.

identity (e.g., race, gender, class, education, immigration status) intersect to create unique and uneven experiences within the sex industry. Finally, we offer ways forward for sex work scholarship, activism, and policy, concluding any effort that does not seriously center race in its framework is not only limited but ultimately flawed.

Historically Situating Racialized Desire, Sex, Gender, and Sexuality in the Sex Industry

Sex work is touted as a long-standing trade, with the notion of race profoundly affecting its practice both historically and in the contemporary context. Since the creation of race as a supposed biological category that differentiates humans, those in positions of power (e.g., rulers, colonizers, knowledge producers) have mobilized it to stratify humans in unequal ways (e.g., through force, rules, norms, ideals), tying race to sexual stereotypes, sexual worth, desirability (e.g., fetishization, exoticization), and devaluation (Stoler, 1995). Racial classification is a fluid concept that has changed over time based on the political and economic agenda of those with most power. During the "Enlightenment Period," white European male scientists purported that racial categories were biologically and evolutionarily derived, carried by blood, and covaried with distinct morphologic features (Jackson et al., 2005). Race was conceived of as part of the evolutionary process; each race was considered a separate species within a larger "natural" hierarchy (Jackson et al., 2005). Physical characteristics were considered observable expressions of unobservable virtues. Christian western Europeans, marked by stereotypically "white" features (e.g., pale skin, blue eyes, narrow/straight noses, straight/smooth hair) were considered the superior "human" species. Africans, with stereotypically "Black" features (e.g., dark skin, dark-brown eyes, wide noses, curly hair) were considered closer to apes and inferior (Jackson et al., 2005).

Scientific racism dehumanized those deemed not white, justifying colonization; genocide of Indigenous peoples; the transatlantic slave trade (Rattansi, 2020); public health scapegoating (Barr et al., 2021); economic, labor, and sexual exploitation; and, later, restrictive and punitive immigration policies (Ball et al., 2022). Race, ethnicity, sex, gender, sexuality, and class intersect to create subhierarchies within an overarching racial hierarchy of the modern period (Ball et al., 2022). As recently as 1905, for example,

300   SPOTLIGHTING THE STRUCTURAL

British colonizers placed the Irish far below themselves in the racial hierarchy, indicating that whiteness itself is not a monolith, while also revealing the political motivation of such categorization (O'Malley, 2022).

Although the concept of biological race was fully discredited by the 1930s (Hirschman, 2004), it nevertheless remains a powerful sociopolitical tool shaping individual and collective lives. Whiteness continues to be the standard by which feminine physical beauty and sexual desirability is measured. Eurocentric beauty standards—thin, toned, and hairless bodies, straight/smooth, light hair, and light eyes—are idealized (Robinson-Moore, 2008). Sex workers who fulfill Eurocentric ideals have more sexual and economic capital, are given enhanced privilege and opportunity, and are less frequently criminalized (Raguparan, 2019). At the other end of the spectrum, Black bodies are fetishized, hypersexualized, demonized, and projected as deviant, guilty, and "dirty" (Collins, 2004). In between, there is a range of other stereotypes attached to, for example, Asian women (e.g., subservient), Muslim women (e.g., asexual), and Latino women (e.g., fiery)—with their worth and desirability closely aligned with the proximity they hold to whiteness and their distance from Blackness. As we turn to later, these racialized stereotypes give shape to the sex industry, including how, why, and from whom men buy sex.

Racialized Demand: Men, Power, and Privilege

Cisgender men who buy sex are a vital component of the sex industry. Yet, their experiences, engagements, and investments in the industry remain woefully underexamined in contrast to the research, debates, and public representations of women who sell sex. Sex work as it largely unfolds today (no matter the legal context) is an extension of asymmetrical and normative heterosexuality, although the exchange of capital is rendered more crystallized and transparent. Traditional modes of female sexuality bar women from public displays of overt sexuality and disparage direct profiting from sex and sexuality, while more subtle forms of a sexual/money exchange are largely normalized (e.g., heterosexual marriage) (Farvid, 2017). Historically, men were positioned as having an uncontrollable (animalistic) sexual urge that required an outlet (White, 1993). Sex workers who met such a need were seen as lower-class "fallen" women who were morally reprehensible (Gordon, 2002). Hence, a double standard has long been associated with sexuality and sex work. Men could relieve their "primitive desires" (White, 1993, p. 7) by paying for sex (before and during marriage) and still retain a respectable moral character. In contrast, women's sexuality was either "virtuous" or "depraved," depending on their perceived sexual conduct. In a similar vein, the continued prominence of a male sex-drive discourse positions men as in need of sexual release (Gavey, 2019). If release cannot occur through relationships or (unpaid) casual sex, then commercial sex is positioned as a viable option. Despite this "push" for sexual markets, the women who provide such sexual services are likely to be depicted in vulnerable, negative, and disparaging ways (Farvid & Glass, 2014). In addition, in most countries, debates related to prostitution law reform, have largely focused on the rights and well-being of women sex workers space without examining men's engagement and interests in the industry (Barrington, 2008).

Research on buyers is limited in comparison to sellers. Anywhere from 9% to 80% of racially diverse (but majority white) men aged 16–80 (average 35) years report purchasing sexual services, with them differing little in class, education, religiosity, relationship attitudes and relationship status (Farley et al., 2009; Sanders, 2008; Sanders et al., 2020). There are four types of typical buyers: (1) the occasional, purchasing sex once or a few times; (2) the repeat, purchasing various sexual services across their lifetime; (3) the regular, frequenting the same establishment or sex worker habitually; and (4) the sugar daddy, providing a sex-worker long-term financial upkeep (e.g., Sanders, 2008; Sanders et al., 2020). There is also a strong digital element to contemporary sex work in these four countries. Most of it is initiated online; roughly 50% of buyers find sex workers online and choose sex workers based on an expanding "review culture" of establishments and individuals (Sanders et al., 2020). In countries like the United Kingdom, most men purchase sex in an indoor setting (brothels, massage parlors, independent workers), but clients report that they find the least expensive sexual services through street markets. The digital divide positions the working class and more marginalized racial, ethnic, and economic groups to buy and sell on the street (Sanders et al., 2020).

Demand for paid sex is not simply a substitute for the demand for free sex, with motivations for commercial sex defined in three clusters. The first is seeking sexual release, power, and control. These men buy into dominant or hegemonic versions of manhood, purchasing sex in order to "feel like a man again" (Shumka et al., 2017). When in relationships

302 SPOTLIGHTING THE STRUCTURAL

that do not fulfill their sexual needs, these men also report a preference for buying sex over having affairs (Warr & Pyett, 1999). The second is seeking thrills and/or rejecting conventional committed relationships (Reback et al., 2019). These men may seek the thrill of engaging in unconventional, taboo, illicit, or risky sexual practices, and/or variety in sex acts (Monto, 2010), or in types of women (Farley et al., 2017). Some report choosing women based on racial stereotypes or skin color to meet fantasies of the racially or ethnically "different" (Malarek, 2011). Lastly, seeking to fulfill emotional and other intimacy needs (Milrod & Monto, 2012). These men report having difficulty forming conventional sexual and/or romantic relationships—due to their working hours, geographic displacement, anxiety, or disability (Warr & Pyett, 1999). Overall, engaging in the sex industry might also be deemed a leisure activity, but typically as a reported means by wish to fulfill sexual/emotional needs or desires (Sanders, 2008).

Across these buyer categories, particular versions of heterosexual masculinity, sexuality, and sex exist. The first is a traditional model of heterosexual masculinity with male sexuality positioned as biologically sex-driven and "needy" (Hollway, 1989); if men cannot procure sex via conventional means (e.g., a relationship, casual sex) they can purchase sex directly. The second centers on sex as a sybaritic, leisure activity, resting heavily on liberal sexual ideals and the availability, accessibility, and normalization of the sex industry. Here, men tend to prefer sexual variety, can find relationships a burden, and see paid sex as a useful commodity (Malarek, 2011). The last discourse fits within a softer version of manhood depicted as lacking the capacity for social connection or not being able to meet intimacy needs (Sanders, 2008). Although these men would prefer relationships with women who are not sex workers, their only access to sex and intimacy is through direct commerce. In all accounts, men's need for and access to sex is taken for granted, and sex is increasingly constructed as a diverse commodity within late-capitalist and neoliberal economies (Monto, 2010).

Case Studies

We now turn to outline the manner in which the sex industry is racialized in four Anglo countries, where sex work legislation falls on a continuum from complete criminalization to complete decriminalization. Systematic colonization by Britain underpins racialization in three contexts. British colonization of the Americas began in the mid-1500s, taking root permanently in 1607 (Warren, 2016). Britain officially annexed A/NZ in 1840 (NZ History). While the United States gained independence from Britain in 1776, Canada and A/NZ are still commonwealth countries and under the British Empire. All four countries share similar, but not identical, histories of racial/ethnic violence, inequality, and genocide. Of particular importance are the coinciding histories of mass genocide, forced displacement, and dispossession of Indigenous populations, and the trafficking and enslavement of people from Africa, the Caribbean, and their descendants. All but A/NZ engaged in the transatlantic slave trade.

While this history is brief and far from comprehensive, it sets the stage for understanding the prevailing sense of entitlement to nonwhite bodies, and their exoticization, pathologization, and criminalization, within the four contexts we examine. Alongside racial stratification we also address the experiences of devaluation, exploitation, misogyny, and racism sex workers report.

The United States (Near Total Criminalization)

The history of colonization and slavery sets the stage for current racial stratification of sex work in the United States. In Canada and the United States, white male colonizers used the systematic assault of Indigenous women to exert power over Indigenous populations and white women (Smith, 2003). In the United States, white slave owners routinely raped enslaved Black women, regularizing forced reproductive labor in order to increase their profits and ensure replenishment and growth of an enslaved workforce (Roberts, 1997). The United States and Canada presented and treated Black and Indigenous people as "deviant," "savage," "uncivilized," "hypersexual," and "unrapeable" (Roberts, 1997). Black women, particularly in the United States, were cast as hypersexual and as always consenting (Collins, 2004). While Black and Indigenous women were seen as "savage" and "hypersexual," Asian immigration and World War I and II positioned Asian women either submissive or villainous in the white imagination (Matsumoto, 2020). In the United States sex industry, portrayals of women of color still fit these sexualized stereotypes (e.g., the "jezebel," "squaw," "lotus blossom," and "dragon lady") (Egwuatu et al., 2023).

304 SPOTLIGHTING THE STRUCTURAL

Racism and xenophobia also underscored public nuisance, immigration, and public health laws in the United States, where im/migrant women, women of color, and indigenous women are cast as threats to public health, safety, and decorum (Nova, 2016). Various social justice movements—such as the civil rights movement of the 1960s and the more recent Black Lives Matter movement—sought to address the systematic dehumanization of nonwhite people in the United States. Yet, a prevailing racial hierarchy undergirded by profound anti-Blackness remains (Saito, 2020). Such racism is evident when discussing the "agency" of sex workers. White sex workers are typically afforded space for first-narrative accounts, positioning them as truth tellers of their own experience, advocates for the choices they have made in their pursuit of independence. Sex workers of color, however, are rarely given the opportunity to tell their sex work stories and are subject to tropes of "forced coercion," or survival sex (Bernstein, 2007a, 2007b). In a series of interviews with majority white, sex workers from class-privileged backgrounds, Elizabeth Bernstein (2007a) found that due to their social capital, these workers commanded high rates, worked in niche sectors, and had access to distinctive skills acquired through education and childhood wealth. This stratification came into sharp focus when the COVID-19 pandemic deepened a digital divide within sex work, pushing sex work online (or hidden and indoors) for white/privileged sex workers, while street-based sex workers of color were left juggling a much more complex terrain of less technologically-facilitated, street-based sex work (Farley, 2023).

Today, an estimated 1.2 million sex workers operate (illegally[4]) in the United States—though experts believe this to be an underestimate—generating over 14 billion dollars annually (Sawicki et al., 2019). State, rather than federal laws govern sex work in the United States; only Nevada allows full-service sex work, and limits it to licensed brothels in rural areas, with strict policies regarding licensing and regular sexually transmitted infection (STI) testing (Heineman et al., 2012). Due to criminalization and stigma, many sex workers hide their occupation; most research is skewed toward survival sex, trafficking, and forced sex, relying on convenience samples from jails, sexual health clinics, antitrafficking agencies, and substance-use treatment programs (Sawicki et al., 2019). People of color in the United States face greater police violence and targeting than their white counterparts, and this is true for sex workers (ACLU, 2020). Sex work criminalization adds another

[4] Excluding parts of Nevada, where sex work is legal but highly regulated.

layer of vulnerability to street-based sex workers, majority of whom have marginalized identities and compounding vulnerabilities (e.g., unhoused, substance dependence) (Sawicki et al., 2019). While Black people accounted for 14% of the U.S. population in 2023 (Moslimani et al., 2023), Black women constituted 42.2% of federal arrests for sex work and commercialized vice in 2019 (FBI, 2019).

Black sex workers, especially Black transgender sex workers, are at greater risk of police targeting and incarceration (Fernandez, 2016). Police officers rarely offer sex workers safety. For example, reports abound regarding ignored 911 calls, verbal, sexual, or physical harassment, assault, extortion, and exploitation (SNaP Co, 2016; Thukral & Ditmore, 2003). When threatening arrest, police use condoms as evidence of sex work, forcing workers to forgo carrying sexual safety paraphernalia, increasing workers' health risks (Wurth et al., 2013). Police accuse transgender women of color of being sex workers based on stigma and stereotypes linking transgender identity with sexual depravity, hypersexuality, and sexual availability (SNaP Co, 2016). Racialized, undocumented sex workers are targeted at a higher rate than their white or white-passing counterparts, facing threats of deportation and arrest (Fernandez, 2016). Previous arrests and incarceration can impact access to legal work, housing, and custody (Sex Workers and Allies Network, 2020).

In the 1990s sex work shifted from a primarily outdoor (street-based) market to an indoor and cyber market (e.g., massage parlors, escort agencies, online webpages) (Jones, 2015). In 2005, the indoor market constituted up to 85% of all sex work activity in the United States (Urban Justice Centre, 2005). Today, sex work has increasingly moved online, with sex workers advertising services and distributing videos and images through social media platforms and mobile applications (Jones, 2015). Sex workers who lack technological access or skill, or sufficient savings to quit their other jobs, have difficulty transitioning to online markets (Nelson et al., 2020). The public and archival nature of online sex work opens up other forms of harassment, violence, and privacy abuse for sex workers (Jones, 2020). Sex workers whose identities lean toward "Blackness" are disproportionately represented in outdoor markets. These include low-income sex workers of color, sex workers with substance dependencies, Indigenous workers, undocumented workers, and housing- and job-insecure workers. Asian women, who historically reside in the middle of the racial hierarchy between "white" and "Black," and white European im/migrants, are disproportionately represented in the indoor erotic massage market (Engel, 2014).

Racial discrimination, racialized sexuality, and fetishization impacting the legalized sex industry can be extrapolated outward and applied to the illegal industry. Women of color working as erotic dancers experience more violence, greater wage gaps, and less access to lucrative shifts and performance venues than their white counterparts (Brooks, 2010). Buyers at clubs more frequently ask dancers of color for sex acts, paying them less than white dancers (Brooks, 2010). Online, sex workers of color discuss outright racism and discrimination from buyers and technology platforms (e.g., shadow banning—where social media administrators block a sex worker's profile without warning and without their knowledge, limiting their visibility and income) (Locker, 2018). Sex workers of color who fit racialized stereotypes (e.g., "big beautiful Black women") experience racial and ethnic fetishization and are more sought out than women of color who do not fit those stereotypes. For example, in Chapter 12 of this collection, Egwuatu and colleagues showcase how racialized desire appears via "racial tagging" on Pornhub. Sex workers of color—often, Black women—encounter requests for "race play," a sexual practice eroticizing racial and ethnic discrimination (Liang, 2022).

Canada (Buying Sex Is Criminalized, But Selling Sex Is Not)

Above, we have focused on how the sex work discrimination in the United States coincides with criminalization. We will now focus on how Canada's commercial sex industry illuminates the ways in which race, immigration, and indigeneity coincide to stratify desire and fetishization in a British colony. Beginning in 2014, Canada passed end-demand legislation, named the Nordic, Swedish, or equality model, criminalizing buyers and oversight profiteering, but not sellers (i.e., sex worker themselves). Touting it as a feminist framework, Sweden implemented this model in 1999, followed by Norway and Iceland in 2009. Asymmetric criminalization rests on a theoretical stance situating sex work within a larger matrix of violence and exploitation against women (SWARM, 2020). For those who are support the Nordic model in Canada, sex work is seen as stemming from socioeconomic inequality where impoverished individuals (imagined as Indigenous, im/migrant, and women of color) living under white supremacy and heteropatriarchy sell sex to survive (NSWP, 2017). Here the legislation it

WHITE SUPREMACY AND THE SEX INDUSTRY   307

seen as a tool to reduce trafficking and other forms of sexual exploitation, which, due to histories of colonization, disproportionately affect Indigenous women.[5] The advocacy organization Global Network of Sex Work Projects (NSWP) has critiqued the Nordic model, positing that it creates more vulnerability to violence, discrimination, and exploitation for sex workers (NSWP, 2017). NSWP argues that decriminalization (importantly) separates sex work from trafficking, offers workers more choice, promotes sex work as a "legitimate" profession, and is a tool to dismantle colonial domination (NSWP, 2017).

The majority of violence against sex workers in Canada affects Indigenous women and girls, who make up 2%–5% of Canada's population but occupy over 50% of high-risk, street-based, survival sex work (Wilson Narciso, 2020). Street-based workers experience higher amounts of harassment, assault, and STI transmission (including HIV), as street-based work often overlaps with the injectable drug market (Shannon et al., 2007). Indigenous women are 12 times more likely to be murdered or to go missing relative to non-Indigenous women, and these odds increase for Indigenous sex workers (McBride et al., 2020).

As in the United States, those in outdoor sectors in Canada often lie at the intersection of multiple oppressions, including housing insecurity, substance dependence, economic disparities, and other identity-based discriminations. Outdoor sex work is more visible, and police are more likely to target outdoor sex workers (many of whom are Indigenous) under the guise of antitrafficking legislation (McBride et al., 2020). A longitudinal study published in 2020 showed sex workers in Canada with marginalized identities reported increased negative interactions with police after end-demand legislation passed in 2014 (McBride et al., 2020). Racialized sex workers and especially im/migrants face severe health, civil, and human rights inequities, including racial targeting and profiling by police, and bureaucratic barriers to reporting violence. Antitrafficking legislation is built into the Nordic model but is often used to target sex work rather than trafficking. It relies on paternalizing ideologies rooted in colonization. For instance, Christian missionaries and church representatives employed salvation narratives to justify dismantling Indigenous families and communities (Johnson, 2018).

---

[5] A note on language: the Canadian constitution recognizes the legal rights of three distinct groups of people original to North America—Indian/First Nations, Inuit, and Métis—collectively referred to as Aboriginal peoples or Indigenous peoples.

White colonizers imagined themselves as "civilizing" Indigenous people whom they viewed as "savage"—in essence, "saving" Indigenous people from themselves (Johnson, 2018). In the current narrative, trafficked women are envisioned as Indigenous women (and other women of color) in need of saving by the state, unable to govern or care for themselves. Legislation targeting buyers also creates rushed negotiations between outdoor sellers and buyers that are potentially dangerous to sex workers' health and safety, and also reduce sex workers' earnings (Wilson Narciso, 2020).

Canadian immigration policy prohibits temporary residents and im/migrants with open work permits (i.e., permits legally authorizing employment) from engaging in sex work (McBride et al., 2020). However, compared to Indigenous sex workers, im/migrant sex workers are more likely to work in call-in sex work venues (e.g., massage parlors, microbrothels, agencies) than in outdoor and public spaces (e.g., streets and parks) (McBride et al., 2020). Im/migrant sex work in indoor venues is often conflated with trafficking, and more often targeted by police in sting operations and immigration sweeps (McBride et al., 2020). Discrimination, language barriers, privacy concerns, and precarious legal statuses amplify racialized im/migrants fears of authorities. Since 2014, end-demand legislation prompted a slew of antitrafficking raids across Canada, resulting in the arrests, charges, and detention and deportation of im/migrant sex workers (McBride et al., 2020). Im/migrant sex workers report reluctance to call police, fearing criminal charges and police prejudice. Lack of legal protections for sex workers and police stigma against sex workers sets the stage for violence by predatory buyers (McBride et al., 2020).

Indigenous people are underrepresented in Canada's labor market, and Indigenous women are marginalized in the workforce (Block et al., 2020). Anti-Indigenous legislation (e.g., the Indian act passed in 1876 and still enacted with amendments) limited the freedoms of First Nation people living on reservations and those registered as First Nation Status (Borrows, 2008), and has disadvantaged Indigenous people from assimilating into the larger labor market (Hu et al., 2019). Sex work is an alternative to low-paid, care-based labor where, typically, Indigenous women and women of color work under white managers (typically, white women) (Raguparan, 2019). Sex work can offer indigenous women an entry point into upward economic mobility they would be otherwise unable to access. Indigenous and racialized sex workers contend with the same race-based labor hierarchy, receive better renumeration and, as an outgrowth, greater autonomy (Benoit et al., 2018).

However, access to income in indoor venues is racially stratified; Indigenous sex workers who pass as white or leverage racial stereotypes to fulfill buyers' racialized sexual fantasies, report easier market entry and higher pay within third-party sectors (Raguparan, 2019).

Compared to the outdoors, indoor sectors (e.g., agencies, escort services) constitute around 80% of the sex work market in Canada (Raguparan, 2019). Being able to access the indoor industry offers greater protection from legal punishment (Raguparan, 2019). However, indoor venues can also carry management-based risks; workers may lack control over their work conditions and may face exploitation from owners and managers (Benoit & Millar, 2001). Overlapping with managed indoor markets, independent sex workers operate out of their home or privately rented space. Although sole operators self-manage various facets of their work (e.g., scheduling, security, space rental) they do not have to contend with the same management conditions as other indoor workers (Benoit & Millar, 2001). Whether indoor or outdoor, sellers also experience sexual violence (Raphael & Shapiro, 2004).

In one study, Menaka Raguparan (2019) discusses how indoor managers "restrict the inclusion of women who do not meet Eurocentric beauty ideals" (p. 99) (e.g., blond, tall, slim, light-skinned, blue-eyed) and thus perpetuate racial stratification within the industry. Across North America (including the United States), the indoor sex industry is a more "upscale" or "bourgeois" sector that mostly women who are, or pass as, educated, middle- or upper-class (i.e., economically privileged) can access (Bernstein, 2007a). Canadian sex workers of color experienced the Canadian sex industry as "preoccupied with catering to the needs, desires, and fantasies of middle-class and upper-class patrons . . . mostly White heterosexual males seeking the services of White heterosexual sex workers" (Raguparan, 2019, p. 108). Venues seek to entice buyers with high incomes who will not attract law enforcement's attention. As in the United States, (anti-Black) racial stereotypes imagine "desirable" and "respectable" clientele as white.

Sellers report that racialized desire structures buyer demand; white men tend to book white women who fit narrow, idealized, and pornified Eurocentric beauty ideals (Raguparan, 2019). Black men tend to book women of color, but due to the aforementioned racial stereotype, Black men are less prevalent within agencies' customer bases. Black and Indigenous sex workers with lighter skin tones and more "anglicized" features are more likely to get hired (Raguparan, 2019). Women of color "have limited opportunities

310 SPOTLIGHTING THE STRUCTURAL

to work in third party sites, their hourly rates are lower, and they often work unfavourable hours" (Raguparan, 2019, p. 112). East Asian massage parlors run by Asian women often only employ other Asian women. Catering to buyers' racialized desires offers an economic entry point for some Asian women to settle in Canada (Malla et al., 2019). As in other labor markets, Black and South Asian women with dark skin must work harder than their light-skinned counterparts and light-skinned White, East Asian, and Southeast Asian women to make the same amount of money (Raguparan, 2019). Women who appear closer to "Blackness" have to find creative ways to market themselves and remain competitive.

White customers often fetishize women of color, seeking out varieties of women of color for services as a way to expand their sexual repertoire. Sex workers report that unlike mainstream labor markets, the sex industry allows them to have control and agency over racial tropes, where they can leverage and strategically perform racial tropes on their terms (Ehrenreich & Hochschild, 2003). In the Canadian sex industry, a complex matrix of fetishized and racialized desire juxtaposes against racist, Eurocentric beauty standards. Whiteness and Blackness both carry with them fetishized extremes.

United Kingdom (Legal but Regulated)

The United Kingdom legalized exchanging sex for money in 2003 under the Sexual Offences Act, but sex work is heavily regulated through legislation and social norms. Public solicitation, advertising services, managing or owning a brothel, managing sex workers, and "kerb crawling" are illegal (Mac & Smith, 2020). There is a high cost to legal entry; sex workers cannot work in pairs or groups, cannot share a workspace, co-own, or co-rent a workspace, and cannot legally work outdoors (City of London Police, 2023). Working alone prevents sex workers from easily sharing important information and creates safety risks and vulnerabilities. Working with others provides greater safety, which is why restrictions of this kind are so dangerous. In Wales, massage parlors that conduct illegal sex work have cameras and other security features (Hanks, 2021). Tacit police and neighborhood acceptance offer workers networks of surveillance that they can use for safety. Disallowing advertising services pushes sex workers into the shadows, stigmatizing sex work and fostering social attitudes that dehumanize and marginalize sex workers.

The history of sex work in the United Kingdom lives within a sociopolitical history of moral panic. Historical sources commonly referred to sex workers as "morally corrupt" and "vectors of disease" (Fernandes, 2019). We can draw a direct throughline of sex work stigma from the Contagious Disease Act (1864–1886) to the New Labour policies of 2004 and 2006, the latter of which classified sex work as an "antisocial moral aberration" (Hanks, 2021, p. 133). The Contagious Disease Act justified the rigid regulation of women's sexuality, forcing any woman accused of sex work to register with the police department and undergo a forced gynecological examination (Hamilton, 1978). Women with STIs were sentenced to prison or hard labor (Hamilton, 1978). The Street Offences Act (1959) targeted street-based sex and institutionalized a class-based hierarchy within the industry; those who could afford it moved indoors, while low-income workers were relegated to the criminalized street sector (Laite, 2008). While most sex workers currently work indoors, street-based sex work—the street sector—remains the primary workspace for the most marginalized and vulnerable women, who are most visible and most widely targeted by police (Mac & Smith, 2020).

Sex workers of color in the United Kingdom typically experience disproportionate rates of homelessness, substance dependence, police targeting, arrest, imprisonment, financial extortion, sexual violence from the police, and abuse, assault, and harassment from clients, intimate partners, and other community members (Platt et al., 2022). In the early 1990s, police were more tolerant of less visible (or white indoor) working sectors because the customer-base was white, middle, and professional classes; "the public (Black) spaces of streetwalking and car sex were more violent, heavily policed, and stigmatized" (McClintock, 1992, pp. 86–87). Currently, those working in street-based, low-income sectors are primarily younger im/migrants who have comparatively more clients and are paid the least (Platt et al., 2022). Those with marginalized racial and ethnic identities and vulnerable economic groups are still buyers and sellers in the street sector (Lanau & Matolcsi, 2022). These workers face more risks, as well: outdoor sex workers are three times more likely to be killed than indoor sex workers (Preble et al., 2019). Indoor workers in high-income sectors experience greater safety, begin in the industry at an older age, and generate higher income.

312 SPOTLIGHTING THE STRUCTURAL

Street-based workers are often targets of greater physical violence and harassment (Platt et al., 2022).

In the United Kingdom, racialization is also tied to visible markers of citizenship (e.g., accent). U.K.-born residents hold greater power than im/migrants or those perceived as im/migrants; even if they are white. Rhetoric regarding im/migrant groups in the 19th century categorized "other [white] Europeans" as inferior to white British "natives" (Bonnett, 1998). Like scientific racism in the United States, these other European groups were thought to share inherited, negative traits that were a threat to Britain's national identity, health and safety (Bonnett, 1998). Racialized bodies in Victorian England included nonwhite Protestants, who were the sites of derision, mockery, mortality fears, and ultimately national threats. The British cultural imagination paints the idealized British citizen as U.K.-born, with a British accent, white, Protestant. and middle- to upper-class. Those veering too far from the idealized "British" citizen have to legitimize their presence within the United Kingdom. Current-day prejudice extends beyond visible markers of "Blackness," including anyone visibly marked as having non-British nationality (e.g., through skin tone, religious garb, accent). White, im/migrant Eastern European women, for example, occupy a lower social position than white British nationals—and within this context, occupy a lower status within the sex industry. During the 2015 Brexit referendum, the leader of the United Kingdom's right-wing Independence Party, Nigel Farage, painted im/migrants as an epidemiological threat to, and economic drain on, "the Nation" (Hanley, 2022). The xenophobia fueling Brexit similarly shapes the United Kingdom's commercial sex industry, where sex workers perceived as European im/migrants are targets for police and client violence (Hanks, 2021).

As of 2009, im/migrants accounted for roughly 40% of sex workers in the greater United Kingdom, and roughly 80% worked in London (TAMPEP, 2009). Im/migrant women constitute most street-based sex work. They earn less than indoor workers, charge and command lower rates, are younger, and are easier for police to target (Hanks, 2021). Despite the legality of selling sex and legal protections barring deportation of im/migrant sex workers, police often raid and arrest sex workers and threaten them with deportation. Im/migrant sex workers are often targeted based on accent and harassed by clients (Hanks, 2021). Clients who are denied services, refuse to pay, or otherwise antagonize workers use deportation to exploit sex workers (Mac & Smith, 2020). Im/migrant sex workers are barred from accessing state welfare, housing, and healthcare, and deportation fears limit im/migrant sex workers' use of police and other protective government services (Mac & Smith, 2020). New migration policies bar those flagged as sex workers from entering the United Kingdom, further stigmatizing sex work (Hanks, 2021).

Aotearoa/New Zealand (Decriminalized)

Decriminalization is the legal model typically preferred and sought by sex workers (NSWP, 2012). This model generally acknowledges sex work as "real work," addresses legal double standards that criminalize sellers and not buyers, reduces police targeting, and better addresses buyer violence. Through the passing of Prostitution Reform Act (PRA) Aotearoa/New Zealand (A/NZ) decriminalized sex work in 2003 after a long period of activism and campaigning by the New Zealand Prostitutes Collective and a range of politicians and other supporters (Aroney, 2021). While the Nordic model was also considered, A/NZ favored decriminalization, enabling the commercial sex industry to function as any other service industry. Situated within a labor rights and harm reduction perspective, the New Zealand Government offered a very detailed (100-page) guide, *Occupational Health and Safety in the New Zealand Sex Industry* (Scarlet Alliance, 2004). While the government does not morally condone the industry, it does not regulate it either, making it subject to general labor laws like any other work (Armstrong & Abel, 2020). One caveat put in place in order to deter trafficking was that no person coming to A/NZ with intention of being a sex worker may enter the country (there is a threat of deportation if this is discovered), and those on temporary visas cannot engage in sex work (Armstrong & Abel, 2020). Legally, sex workers can deny services to customers and report assault, abuse, or harassment to police, and clients must legally abide by sexual safety measures during a sexual exchange (Armstrong & Abel, 2020).

Twenty years on, New Zealand's legal model has proven mostly effective. While most sex workers (70%–80%) still report entering the industry due to financial hardship (see Abel & Brunton, 2007), sex work is safer than before decriminalization, rates of entry into sex work have not seemingly increased, and harassment cases against brothel managers/owners who have mistreated workers have even been successful in getting convictions (Abel, 2014). No cases of adult cross-border sex trafficking that have been reported, but domestic sex trafficking exists and is hidden, unrecognized,

314 SPOTLIGHTING THE STRUCTURAL

or inadequately addressed by authorities (Farvid, 2018). As an extension of gender-based violence, domestic sex trafficking refers to instances where parents, partners, or other family members force someone (usually a young person) into sexual slavery, while taking all or most of the profits (Thorburn, 2017). At times, but not always, this form of trafficking overlaps with underage sex work, which also exists in A/NZ (Thorburn & de Haan, 2017). Furthermore, the A/NZ sex industry remains highly inequitable—along race/ethnicity, class, and gendered lines. While legal, the work continues to be (socially) stigmatized, and sex workers dehumanized, with moral panics about the "visibility" of the industry (particularly in residential areas) flaring up every so often (Farvid & Glass, 2014). As such, decriminalization is certainly not a silver bullet when it comes to inequities that remain within the industry. It *is*, however, the first step to addressing the racial (and other) inequities—as Schmidt (2017) has aptly noted about the A/NZ situation: "while the PRA may not challenge the gendered nature of the industry, it protects the immediate interests of the women who work within it" (p. 36). Hence, decriminalization is a fundamental baseline for a socially just legal model that would reduce the harms for sex workers. Yet, decriminalization should not take away from continued efforts to address structural inequities *within* the sex industry itself.

As noted above, A/NZ has a colonial past and remains part of the Commonwealth. It is a small and relatively progressive country (with a population of 5 million); it was the first country to legalize same-sex marriage and decriminalize sex work (as previously noted), is relatively queer-friendly, and has pretty robust immigration from multiple countries. The Indigenous population of A/NZ are the Māori people. The first European contact was in 1642, and ensuing wars between Māori and the crown culminated in a "truce" with the signing of *The Treaty of Waitangi* in 1814 (Iorns, 2006). Unlike other colonial contexts, The Treaty of Waitangi clearly indicated that Māori have sovereignty over A/NZ land (Iorns, 2006). While much of this land was illegally taken during the process of colonization, efforts have been made to remedy past wrongs with reparations being made to various *iwi*/tribes (Iorns, 2006). One of the distinct features of A/NZ is its bicultural legal and social system, where Māori culture and knowledge are woven into the governance of the country (Dionisio & Macfarlane, 2021). With this said, while Māori make up about 17% of the population, they are overrepresented in negative demographics (such as incarceration, youth suicide, health issues) (Abel et al., 2007). Prior to the PRA, Māori women were the most affected by police actions against the sex worker population (Abel et al., 2007). A/NZ, and Auckland in particular, is very multicultural. While most of the population is Pākehā (non-Māori New Zealanders of European descent), there is also a large im/migrant population (Bennachie et al., 2021).

When it comes to the decriminalized A/NZ sex industry, racial/ethnic inequities persist alongside the continued effects of colonialism, heteropatriarchy, and transphobia. We address each of these issues in turn, by exploring various contours of the A/NZ sex industry, such as location of work, compensation, underage sex work, and domestic trafficking. In terms of establishment types and the manner in which sex work unfolds in A/NZ, this ranges from street-based sex work (about 10% of sex work in NZ) to indoor sex work (the rest of the industry)—which includes brothels and other managed establishments, massage parlors, and independent work (Abel et al., 2009). After the PRA, significant numbers moved from managed to private sectors enabling sex workers to advertise without having to register with the police (Abel, 2010). In terms of ethnic/racial demographics Māori, Pacific Islanders, and transgender sex workers account for the largest percentage of street-based sex work (Abel et al., 2007), and are paid the least while at the highest risk for violence, robbery, and harassment. The second tier, in terms of safety and earnings includes massage parlors (typically with Asian/southeast Asian sex workers), followed by brothels (typically young and white, but with a peppering of diversity), and finally "independent" workers, who tend to be Pākehā (i.e., white New Zealander), older, and middle-class (Farvid, 2017). Those who earn the most tend to be young and Pākehā or work independently. And, while Māori only make 17% of the population, they make up close to 35% of the sex worker population, with Pākehā at 50%, Pasifika at 5%, and "other" at 15% (Abel et al., 2007). Transgender sex workers, in particular, are typically kept out of any established indoor work, as well as, at times, individuals with substance dependencies. Im/migrant sex workers (who are work illegally), tend to come from southeast Asian countries and are more at risk of harm, violence, fear of deportation, threat of sexual violation via blackmail, inappropriate policing, and health concerns (Bennachie et al., 2021). When it comes to underage and forced sex work, Māori and Pacific Islanders account for the majority (Abel et al., 2007).

Hence, race/ethnicity, indigeneity, and im/migrant status give shape to the A/NZ sex industry. Advocacy work needs to continue addressing the inequities within a decriminalized context. One risk that decriminalization runs is that in its goal to position sex work as a legitimate form of labor, and safer, it can remove critical engagement with the structural inequities of the sex industry. In addition, broader engagements with challenging and/ or dismantling conventional modes of male sexuality, racialized desire, racialized inequities, as well as the economic systems that create, shape and mediate contemporary sex work.

Conclusion

Sexual racism continues to profoundly shape the inequities within sex work. In this chapter, we have outlined the way in which it does so across four Anglo-legal contexts. At its core, there is an invisibilized but deep-rooted racial hierarchy that shapes the industry, manifesting in who is sought by clients, who earns the most, the location that they work, the extent to which they are criminalized or targeted by law enforcement for doing sex work, and the extent to which they are stigmatized and are the victims of violence from clients, the public, and police. Greater attention needs to be paid to how whiteness, cisgenderedness, heterosexuality, wealth, citizenship, and ultimately, humanness, shape the hierarchies of who is desirable and respectable within sex work. For example, cis-heterosexual (white) men's (often unquestioned/unexamined) entitlement to sex (on demand), and their desire for the "exotic," juxtaposed with historic and current constructions of the "pure" white woman, the docile or subservient East Asian woman, the hypersexualized Black woman, and the "deviant" transgender woman— require further direct examination and critique.

Sex work legislation is torn between past and future; deeply rooted in histories of colonial conquest, profound racism, resource extraction, and economic incentive for the few, while envisioning and fighting for labor rights and a better future for sex workers. Whiteness, as historically determining worth, unconsciously and consciously underscores interpersonal desire—which extends to the commercial sex industry in more overt ways. Sex work criminalization, buyer criminalization, and heavy legal regulations push workers into the shadows, maintaining avenues for vulnerability. Decriminalization is not a panacea but begins the process of peeling back centuries of harm and stigmatization that sex work has weathered. Those who have suffered the most have been historically ostracized, devalued, dehumanized, feared, and abused by those in power (e.g., transgender,

Black, Indigenous, im/migrant). Based on our work here, we argue that it is highly likely that, in whatever geographic and/or legal context you find yourself, similar trends would abound—and we urge other to carry out similar analyses that center race in the analysis of stratification.

Whiteness forms the modes of engagement and governance when it comes to sex work. Colonialism and white supremacy will evoke racism through various modes of desirability, respectability, and criminality, even while trying to address inequities. By bringing to the fore the taken-for-granted privilege of, and desire for, whiteness within the sex industry, we advocate for shifting focus onto the intersecting webs of power, social norms, and implicit beliefs that undergird the commercial sex market. Race is a critical factor of economic justice and needs to be at the center of sex worker rights campaigns and decriminalization efforts. All sex workers deserve legal status and protections—it is both hypocritical and dehumanizing to denote sex work should be illegal, due to arbitrary moral values, implicit racism, essentialist beliefs about the gendered "natural order," and in what domains sex should take place. Many forms of "transactional sex" are fully embedded in the most traditional of intimate arrangements—such as traditional heterosexual marriage (where women exchange their domestic, sexual, and childcare labor for financial upkeep—see Farvid, 2017). This parallel was perfectly captured by a fictionalized sex worker in the 2002 Iranian film *Ten* (by Abbas Kiarostami). When asked by the married woman taxi driver "why" she does such work, and after a long exchange, the sex worker illuminatingly notes: "You're the wholesalers. We're the retailers (laughs)." The exchange of money for sex— and hence sex work—is not inherently criminal, even if it is profoundly unequal. Framing it as criminal and/or as an extension of organized crime further disadvantages those who are at the margins and keeps them in a place of vulnerability, precarity, harm, and, at times, desperation.

To address the issues within the commercial sex industry, and in the context of decriminalization, we must ensure that those with the least privilege are protected, and that starts with centering race within decriminalization efforts. Using an intersectional lens is vital for dismantling this hierarchy of desirability and perceived respectability, addressing how racism, sexism, transphobia, xenophobia, and anti–sex work stigma create material realities of profound inequality within the sex industry—ultimately privileging white supremacy and cis-heterosexual men. Strategies for addressing such inequalities at the community, policy, and social level should not only center race and an intersectional approach in campaigns for decriminalization and/

318 SPOTLIGHTING THE STRUCTURAL

or sex worker rights but also make sure that these efforts continue, and a racial analysis remains alive, even in the context where sex work is legal or decriminalized.

References

Abel, G. (2010). *Decriminalisation: A harm minimisation and human rights approach to regulating sex work*. [Doctoral dissertation]. University of Otago. http://hdl.handle.net/10523/3362

Abel, G. M. (2014). A decade of decriminalization: Sex work "down under" but not underground. *Criminology and Criminal Justice, 14*(5), 580–592. https://doi.org/10.1177/1748895814523024.

Abel, G., Fitzgerald, L., & Brunton, C. (2007). *The impact of the Prostitution Reform Act on the health and safety practices of sex workers*. Prostitution Law Review Committee. University of Otago.

Abel, G. M., Fitzgerald, L. J., & Brunton, C. (2009). The impact of decriminalisation on the number of sex workers in New Zealand. *Journal of Social Policy, 38*(3), 515–531. https://doi.org/10.1017/S0047279409003080

ACLU. (2020). *Is sex work decriminalization the answer? What the research tells us.* American Civil Liberties Union. https://www.aclu.org/report/sex-work-decriminalization-answer-what-research-tells-us

Armstrong, L., & Abel, G. (Eds.). (2020). *Sex work and the New Zealand model: Decriminalisation and social change.* Bristol University Press.

Aroney, E. (2021). Changing minds and changing laws: How New Zealand sex workers and their allies shaped decriminalisation in New Zealand. *Sexuality Research and Social Policy, 18*(4), 952–967. https://doi.org/10.1007/s13178-021-00564-z

Ball, E., Steffens, M. C,, & Niedlich, C. (2022). Racism in Europe: Characteristics and intersections with other social categories. *Frontiers in Psychology, 13.* https://doi.org/10.3389/fpsyg.2022.789661

Barker, R. (2023, February 7). A glossary of sex worker terminology. *Vice.* https://www.vice.com/en/article/n7zxy8/a-glossary-of-sex-worker-terminology

Barr, J., McKay, R. A., & Doroshow, D. B. (2021). The dangers of "us versus them": Epidemics then and now. *Journal of General Internal Medicine, 36*(3), 795–796. https://doi.org/10.1007/s11606-020-06368-y

Barrington, J. (2008). *Shapeshifting: Prostitution and the problem of harm: A discourse analysis of media reportage of prostitution law reform in New Zealand in 2003.* [Master's Thesis]. Auckland University of Technology.

Beloso, B. M. (2012). Sex, work, and the feminist erasure of class. *Signs: Journal of Women in Culture and Society, 38*(1), 47–70. https://doi.org/10.1086/665808

Bennachie, C., Pickering, A., Lee, J., Macioti, P. G., Mai, N., Fehrenbacher, A. E., Giametta, C., Hoefinger, H., & Musto, J. (2021). Unfinished decriminalization: The impact of Section 19 of the Prostitution Reform Act 2003 on migrant sex workers' rights and lives in Aotearoa New Zealand. *Social Sciences, 10*(5), Article 5. https://doi.org/10.3390/socsci10050179

WHITE SUPREMACY AND THE SEX INDUSTRY 319

Benoit, C., Jansson, S. M., Smith, M., & Flagg, J. (2018). Prostitution stigma and its effect on the working conditions, personal lives, and health of sex workers. *Journal of Sex Research, 55*(4–5), 457–471. https://doi.org/10.1080/00224499.2017.1393652

Benoit, C., & Millar, A. (2001). *Dispelling myths and understanding realities: Working conditions, health status, and exiting experiences of sex workers.* The Michael Smith Foundation for Health Research.

Bernstein, E. (2007a). Sex work for the middle classes. *Sexualities, 10*(4), 473–488. https://doi.org/10.1177/1363460707080984

Bernstein, E. (2007b). *Temporarily yours: Intimacy, authenticity, and the commerce of sex.* University of Chicago Press.

Block, S., Galabuzi, G. E., & Tranjan, R. (2020). Canada's colour coded income inequality. *Directions (Canadian Race Relations Foundation), 9*, 63–80.

Bonnett, A. (1998). How the British working class became white: The symbolic (re)formation of racialized capitalism. *Journal of Historical Sociology, 11*(3), 316–340. https://doi.org/10.1111/1467-6443.00066

Borrows, J. (2008). *Seven generations, seven teachings: Ending the Indian Act.* National Centre for First Nations Governance. https://fngovernance.org/wp-content/uploads/2020/05/john_borrows.pdf

Brooks, S. (2010). *Unequal desires: Race and erotic capital in the stripping industry.* State University of New York Press.

Butler, C. N. (2015). A critical race feminist perspective on prostitution and sex trafficking in America. *Yale Journal of Law and Feminism, 27*(1), 95–139.

City of London Police. (2023). *Sex worker safety.* City of London Police. https://www.cityoflondon.police.uk/advice/advice-and-information/sw/sex-worker-safety

Collins, P. H. (2004). *Black sexual politics: African Americans, gender, and the new racism.* Routledge.

Crenshaw, K. (1990). Mapping the margins: Intersectionality, identity politics, and violence against women of color. *Stanford Law Review, 43*(6), 1241–1299. https://doi.org/10.2307/1229039

Dionisio, R., & Macfarlane, A.H. (2021). Tikanga rua: Bicultural spatial governance in Aotearoa New Zealand. *New Zealand Geographer, 77*(2), 55–62. https://doi.org/10.1111/nzg.12303

Doezema, J. (2002). Who gets to choose? Coercion, consent, and the UN trafficking protocol. *Gender and Development, 10*(1), 20–27. https://doi.org/10.1080/1355207 0215897

Ehrenreich, B., & Hochschild, A. R. (Eds.). (2003). *Global woman: Nannies, maids, and sex workers in the new economy.* Metropolitan Books.

Engel, P. (2014). What the sex industry looks like in 8 big US cities. *Business Insider.* https://www.businessinsider.com/what-the-sex-industry-looks-like-in-8-us-cities-2014-3

Farley, M. (2004). "Bad for the body, bad for the heart": Prostitution harms women even if legalized or decriminalized. *Violence Against Women, 10*(10), 1087–1125.

Farley, M. (2023). Prostitution, the sex trade, and the COVID-19 pandemic. *Logos Journal.* https://logosjournal.com/2020/prostitution-the-sex-trade-and-the-covid-19-pandemic/

Farley, M., Bindel, J., & Golding, J. M. (2009). *Men who buy sex: Who they buy and what they know.* Eaves.

Farley, M., Golding, J. M., Matthews, E. S., Malamuth, N. M., & Jarrett, L. (2017). Comparing sex buyers with men who do not buy sex: New data on prostitution and trafficking. *Journal of Interpersonal Violence, 32*(23), 3601–3625. https://doi.org/10.1177/0886260515600874

Farvid, P. (2017). The politics of sex work in Aotearoa/New Zealand and the Pacific: Tensions, debates and future directions. *Women's Studies Journal, 31*(2), 27–34.

Farvid, P. (2018, October 4). Sex traffickers are more often intimate partners than international slave traders. *Vice.* https://www.vice.com/en/article/a3p48e/sex-traffickers-are-more-often-intimate-partners-than-international-slave-traders

Farvid, P., & Glass, L. (2014). "It isn't prostitution as you normally think of it. It's survival sex": Media representations of adult and child prostitution in New Zealand. *Women's Studies Journal, 28*(1), 47–67.

FBI. (2019). *Arrests by race and ethnicity, 2019.* Federal Bureau of Investigation. https://ucr.fbi.gov/crime-in-the-u.s/2019/crime-in-the-u.s.-2019/topic-pages/tables/table-43

Fernandes, S. (2019). An uneasy pleasure: Representing the dangers of skin-to-skin contact in eighteenth-century London "The William Bynum prize essay." *Medical History, 63*(4), 494–511. https://doi.org/10.1017/mdh.2019.46

Fernandez, F. L. (2016). *Hands Up: A systematized review of policing sex workers in the U.S.* [Master's Thesis]. Yale University. https://elischolar.library.yale.edu/cgi/viewcontent.cgi?article=1084&context=ysphtdl

Gavey, N. (2019). *Just sex? The cultural scaffolding of rape.* Routledge.

Gerassi, L. (2015). A heated debate: Theoretical perspectives of sexual exploitation and sex work. *Journal of Sociology and Social Welfare, 42*(4), 79–100.

Gordon, L. (2002). *The moral property of women: A history of birth control politics in America.* University of Illinois Press.

Hamilton, M. (1978). Opposition to the Contagious Diseases Acts, 1864–1886. *Albion, 10*(1), 14–27. https://doi.org/10.2307/4048453

Hanks, S. (2021). Increased vulnerabilities: Considering the effects of xeno-racist ordering for Romanian migrant sex workers in the United Kingdom. *International Journal for Crime, Justice and Social Democracy, 10*(1), 130–142. https://doi.org/10.3316/agispt.20210518046859

Hanley, A. (2022). Migration, racism and sexual health in postwar Britain. *History Workshop Journal, 94,* 202–222. https://doi.org/10.1093/hwj/dbac018

Heineman, J., MacFarlane, R. T., & Brents, B. G. (2012). Sex industry and sex workers in Nevada. *Social Health of Nevada: Leading Indicators and Quality of Life in the Silver State, 71,* 1–26.

Henry, M. V., & Farvid, P. (2017). "Always hot, always live": Computer-mediated sex work in the era of "camming." *Women's Studies Journal, 31*(2), 113–127.

Hirschman, C. (2004). The origins and demise of the concept of race. *Population and Development Review, 30*(3), 385–415. https://doi.org/10.1111/j.1728-4457.2004.00021.x

Hollway, W. (1989). *Subjectivity and method in psychology: Gender, meaning and science.* Sage Publications.

Hu, M., Daley, A., & Warman, C. (2019). Literacy, numeracy, technology skill, and labour market outcomes among Indigenous Peoples in Canada. *Canadian Public Policy, 45*(1), 48–73. https://doi.org/10.3138/cpp.2017-068

Iorns, C., (2006). *Reparations for Maori grievances in Aotearoa/New Zealand.* Victoria University of Wellington Legal Research Paper No. 48. http://dx.doi.org/10.2139/ssrn.2175397

WHITE SUPREMACY AND THE SEX INDUSTRY   321

Jackson, J. P., Weidman, N. M., & Rubin, G. (2005). The origins of scientific racism. *Journal of Blacks in Higher Education, 50*(50), 66–79.

Johnson, S. K. (2018). On our knees: Christian ritual in residential schools and the Truth and Reconciliation commission of Canada. *Studies in Religion/Sciences Religieuses, 47*(1), 3–24. https://doi.org/10.1177/0008429817733269

Jones, A. (2015). Sex work in a digital era. *Sociology Compass, 9*(7), 558–570. https://doi.org/10.1111/soc4.12282

Jones, A. (2020). *Camming: Money, power, and pleasure in the sex work industry.* NYU Press. https://doi.org/10.18574/nyu/9781479842964.001.0001

Laite, J. A. (2008). The association for moral and social hygiene: Abolitionism and prostitution law in Britain (1915–1959). *Women's History Review, 17*(2), 207–223. https://doi.org/10.1080/09612020701707209

Lanau, A., & Matolcsi, A. (2022). Prostitution and sex work, who counts? Mapping local data to inform policy and service provision. *Social Policy and Society,* 1–15. https://www.cambridge.org/core/journals/social-policy-and-society/article/abs/prostitution-and-sex-work-who-counts-mapping-local-data-to-inform-policy-and-service-provision/4C1D289B9CFEFAA3AFC48EAB2E896F76

Liang, M. (2022). Playing with power: Kink, race, and desire. *Sexualities, 25*(4), 381–405. https://doi.org/10.1177/1363460720964063

Locker, M. (2018). Why sex workers are ditching Twitter for Switter—And why it matters. *Fast Company.* https://www.fastcompany.com/90178614/why-sex-workers-are-ditching-twitter-for-switter-and-why-it-matters

Mac, J., & Smith, M. (2020). *Revolting prostitutes: The fight for sex workers' rights.* Verso Books.

Malarek, V. (2011). *The Johns: Sex for sale and the men who buy it.* Simon and Schuster

Malla, A., Lam, E., van der Meulen, E., & Peng, H. Y. J. (2019). *Beyond tales of trafficking: A needs assessment of Asian migrant sex workers in Toronto.* Butterfly (Asian and Migrant Sex Workers Support Network). https://www.butterflysw.org/_files/ugd/5bd754_a35d8e085c21475fa97e1ff759d26648.pdf

Matsumoto, K. (2020). Orientalism and the legacy of racialized sexism: Disparate representational images of Asian and Eurasian women in American culture. *Young Scholars in Writing, 17,* 114–126. Retrieved from https://youngscholarsinwriting.org/index.php/ysiw/article/view/305

McBride, B., Shannon, K., Bingham, B., Braschel, M., Strathdee, S., & Goldenberg, S. M. (2020). Underreporting of violence to police among women sex workers in Canada: Amplified inequities for im/migrant and in-call workers prior to and following end-demand legislation. *Health and Human Rights, 22*(2), 257–270.

McClintock, A. (1992). Screwing the system: Sexwork, race, and the law. *Boundary 2, 19*(2), 70–95. https://doi.org/10.2307/303534

Milrod, C., & Monto, M. A. (2012). The hobbyist and the girlfriend experience: Behaviors and preferences of male customers of internet sexual service providers. *Deviant Behavior, 33*(10), 792–810.

Monto, M. A. (2010). Prostitutes' customers' motives and misconceptions. In R. Weitzer (Ed.), *Sex for sale: Prostitution, pornography, and the sex industry* (pp. 233–254). Routledge.

Moslimani, M., Tamir, C., Budiman, A., Noe-Bustamante, L., & Mora, L. (2023). *Facts about the U.S. Black population.* Pew Research Center. https://www.pewresearch.org/social-trends/fact-sheet/facts-about-the-us-black-population/

322 SPOTLIGHTING THE STRUCTURAL

Nelson, A. J., Yu, Y. J., & McBride, B. (2020). Sex work during the COVID-19 pandemic. *Exertions*. https://saw.americananthro.org/pub/sex-work-during-the-covid-19-pandemic/release/1

Nova, C. (2016). Vectors of disease: Sex workers as bodies to be managed. *QED: A Journal in GLBTQ Worldmaking, 3*(3), 196–200. https://doi.org/10.14321/qed.3.3.0196

NSWP. (2012). *Decriminalization*. Global Network of Sex Work Projects. https://www.nswp.org/sites/default/files/sg_to_decriminalisation_prf05.pdf

NSWP (2017). *Smart sex workers' guide: Challenging the introduction of the Nordic model*. Global Network of Sex Workers Projects. https://www.nswp.org/resource/nswp-smart-guides/smart-sex-workers-guide-challenging-the-introduction-the-nordic-model

O'Malley, P. R. (2023). Irish Whiteness and the Nineteenth-Century Construction of Race. *Victorian Literature and Culture, 51*(2), 167–198. doi:10.1017/S1060150322000067

Platt, L., Bowen, R., Grenfell, P., Stuart, R., Sarker, M. D., Hill, K., Walker, J., Javarez, X., Henham, C., Mtetwa, S., Hargreaves, J., Boily, M.-C., Vickerman, P., Hernandez, P., & Elmes, J. (2022). The effect of systemic racism and homophobia on police enforcement and sexual and emotional violence among sex workers in East London: Findings from a cohort study. *Journal of Urban Health, 99*(6), 1127–1140. https://doi.org/10.1007/s11524-022-00673-z

Platt, L., Grenfell, P., Bonell, C., Creighton, S., Wellings, K., Parry, J., & Rhodes, T. (2011). Risk of sexually transmitted infections and violence among indoor-working female sex workers in London: The effect of migration from Eastern Europe. *Sexually Transmitted Infections, 87*(5), 377–384. https://doi.org/10.1136/sti.2011.049544

Preble, K., Magruder, K., & Cimino, A. N. (2019). "It's like being an electrician, you're gonna get shocked": Differences in the perceived risks of indoor and outdoor sex work and its impact on exiting. *Victims and Offenders, 14*(5), 625–646. https://doi.org/10.1080/15564886.2019.1630043

Raguparan, M. (2019). *"So it's not always the sappy story": Women of colour and Indigenous women in the indoor sectors of the Canadian sex industry speak out* [Doctoral Dissertation]. Carleton University. https://curve.carleton.ca/a33b09b7-81cd-4457-9287-ddbe93b10963

Raphael, J., & Shapiro, D. L. (2004). Violence in indoor and outdoor prostitution venues. *Violence Against Women, 10*(2), 126–139. https://doi.org/10.1177/1077801203260529

Rattansi, A. (2020). Imperialism, genocide, and the "science" of race. In A. Rattansi (Ed.), *Racism: A very short introduction*. Oxford University Press. https://doi.org/10.1093/actrade/9780198834793.003.0002

Reback, C. J., Larkins, S., & Clark, K. (2019). Motivations for a casual or occasional sexual encounter with a man and/or transgender woman among heterosexual men: Toward a better understanding of atypical sexual partnering. *Sexuality and Culture, 23*(2), 359–374. https://doi.org/10.1007/s12119-018-9576-5

Roberts, D. (1997). *Killing the Black body: Race, reproduction, and the meaning of liberty*. Penguin Random House.

Robinson-Moore, C. L. (2008). Beauty standards reflect Eurocentric paradigms—so what? Skin color, identity, and Black female beauty. *Journal of Race and Policy, 4*, 66–85.

Saito, N. T. (2020). *Settler colonialism, race, and the law: Why structural racism persists* (Vol. 2). New York University Press.

Salter, P. S., Adams, G., & Perez, M. J. (2018). Racism in the structure of everyday worlds: A cultural-psychological perspective. *Current Directions in Psychological Science, 27*(3), 150–155. https://doi.org/10.1177/0963721417724239

WHITE SUPREMACY AND THE SEX INDUSTRY   323

Sanders, T. (2008). *Paying for pleasure: Men who buy sex.* Willan.

Sanders, T., Brents, B. G., & Wakefield, C. (2020). *Paying for sex in a digital age.* Routledge. https://doi.org/10.4324/9780429454370

Sawicki, D. A., Meffert, B. N., Read, K., & Heinz, A. J. (2019). Culturally competent health care for sex workers: An examination of myths that stigmatize sex work and hinder access to care. *Sexual and Relationship Therapy, 34*(3), 355–371. https://doi.org/10.1080/14681994.2019.1574970

Scarlet Alliance. (2004). *A guide to occupational health and safety in the New Zealand sex industry, Department of Labour—Archives.* New Zealand Department of Labour: Occupational Safety and Health Services. https://www.nzpc.org.nz/pdfs/OHS.Sex-Industry.pdf

Schmidt, J. (2017). The regulation of sex work in Aotearoa/New Zealand: An overview. *Women's Studies Journal, 31*(2), 35–49.

Sex Workers and Allies Network. (2020). *The harmful consequences of sex work criminalization on health and rights.* Yale Global Health Justice Partnership. https://law.yale.edu/sites/default/files/area/center/ghjp/documents/consequences_of_criminalization_v2.pdf

Shannon, K., Bright, V., Allinott, S., Alexson, D., Gibson, K., Tyndall, M. W., & the Maka Project Partnership. (2007). Community-based HIV prevention research among substance-using women in survival sex work: The Maka Project Partnership. *Harm Reduction Journal, 4*(1), 20. https://doi.org/10.1186/1477-7517-4-20

Shumka, L., Strega, S., & Hallgrimsdottir, H. K. (2017). "I wanted to feel like a man again": Hegemonic masculinity in relation to the purchase of street-level sex. *Frontiers in Sociology, 2*(15). https://www.frontiersin.org/articles/10.3389/fsoc.2017.00015

Smith, A. (2003). Not an Indian tradition: The sexual colonization of native peoples. *Hypatia, 18*(2), 70–85. https://doi.org/10.1111/j.1527-2001.2003.tb00802.x

SNaP Co. (2016). *Research report: The most dangerous thing out here is the police.* Solutions Not Punishment Coalition. https://b81b38ed-3626-4dfb-806d-bee93cc1ddcc.filesusr.com/ugd/04cb5a_744a0e7a16ce4935bffd1d53d46193de.pdf

Stoler, A. L. (1995). *Race and the education of desire: Foucault's history of sexuality and the colonial order of things.* Duke University Press.

SWARM. (2020, December 8). *Everything you ever wanted to know about the Swedish model (aka the Nordic model).* Sex workers advocacy and resistance movement. https://www.swarmcollective.org/blog/the-swedish-model

TAMPEP. (2009). *Sex work in Europe: A mapping of the prostitution scene in 25 European countries.* TAMPEP International Foundation. http://tampep.eu/documents/TAMPEP%202009%20European%20Mapping%20Report.pdf.

Thorburn, N. (2017). Practitioner knowledge and responsiveness to victims of sex trafficking in Aotearoa/New Zealand. *Women's Studies Journal, 31*(2), 77–96.

Thorburn, N., & de Haan, I. (2017). Connecting through chaos: Escape behaviour among sex-working adolescents in Aotearoa New Zealand. *Kōtuitui: New Zealand Journal of Social Sciences Online, 12*(1), 32–40. https://doi.org/10.1080/1177083X.2016.1188133

Thukral, J., & Ditmore, M. (2003). *Revolving door, an analysis of street-based prostitution in New York City.* Sex Workers Project at The Urban Justice Center. https://sexworkersproject.org/downloads/RevolvingDoor.pdf

Urban Justice Center (2005). *Behind closed doors: An analysis of indoor sex work in New York City.* Sex Workers Project at The Urban Justice Center. https://sexworkersproject.org/downloads/BehindClosedDoors.pdf

Verdugo, R. R. (2008). Racial stratification, social consciousness, and the education of Mexican Americans in Fabens, Texas: A socio-historical case study. *Spaces for Difference: An Interdisciplinary Journal, 1*(2). https://escholarship.org/uc/item/3bk1q2dq

Warr, D. J., & Pyett, P. M. (1999). Difficult relations: Sex work, love and intimacy. *Sociology of Health and Illness, 21*(3), 290–309. https://doi.org/10.1111/1467-9566.00157

Warren, W. (2016). *New England bound: Slavery and colonization in early America.* W. W. Norton & Company.

White, K. (1993). *The first sexual revolution: The emergence of male heterosexuality in modern america.* New York University Press.

Wilson Narciso, S. (2020). *Decolonizing sex work in Canada: Assessing the impact of government regulation on the wellbeing of Indigenous sex workers.* https://hdl.handle.net/1807/101880

Wurth, M. H., Schleifer, R., McLemore, M., Todrys, K. W., & Amon, J. J. (2013). Condoms as evidence of prostitution in the United States and the criminalization of sex work. *Journal of the International AIDS Society, 16*(1), 18626. https://doi.org/10.7448/IAS.16.1.18626

14

Sexual Racism and Asian American Egg Donation

Reflections on Experiential Ambivalence

Ellen Yom

In the last 40 years, assisted reproductive technologies (ARTs) like intrauterine insemination, in vitro fertilization, intracytoplasmic sperm injection, and surrogacy have advanced significantly (Covington & Burns, 2006; Quiroga, 2007). Egg donation, which began in the 1980s, is a lengthy and invasive process that involves stimulating and retrieving human egg cells from a donor, fertilizing them, and then implanting the embryo in the recipient for reproduction. This practice has grown into a billion-dollar industry in the United States and is projected to expand as rates of infertility increase (GlobeNewswire, 2021). In just the past decade, egg-freezing technologies have also contributed to increasing use of third-party reproduction, which refers to the use of donated eggs, sperm, or embryos to conceive (American Society for Reproductive Medicine, 2023). While egg donation has been a welcome solution for many people who are unable to conceive through other means, the unregulated way in which it is practiced in the United States has created a complex marketplace with mixed sociocultural ramifications.

Gendered discourses were evident in the earliest gamete donation programs, with sperm donation depicted as a "job" and egg donation as a "gift" (Almeling, 2011). Historically, physicians looked to medical students as potential sperm donors who were paid approximately $25 per sample while the first egg donation programs sought women from the community who were paid $500 after thorough assessment to ensure they were donating for altruistic reasons (Almeling, 2011). The first commercial egg agencies opened in the 1990s due to rising demand. As gamete donation became increasingly commercialized, gendered portrayals of egg and sperm continued to organize the donation process. To this day, Almeling (2011) finds that

Ellen Yom, *Sexual Racism and Asian American Egg Donation* In: *Sexual Racism and Social Justice.*
Edited by: Denton Callander, Panteá Farvid, Amir Baradaran, and Thomas A. Vance, Oxford University Press.
© Oxford University Press 2024. DOI: 10.1093/oso/9780197605509.003.0015

during the screening process, sperm and egg donors are assessed based on their health histories, but only egg donors are also judged for their altruistic motivations. Egg donors are encouraged to create "sellable profiles," which typically include attractive pictures with "altruistic" language notably absent from most sperm donor profiles (Almeling, 2009).

Feminist scholars have also illuminated how gamete donation is not only a gendered process but also a racialized one (Deomampo, 2019). The process of matching donors to intended parents reveals complex and problematic views on race and what it means to be "a family." Specifically, fertility clinics and brokers routinely classify and market donors to potential parents based on their racial and ethnic identities (Hudson, 2015). For example, during a tour of a commercial sperm agency, Almeling (2011) discovered that gametes were routinely organized by different colored caps on the vials "with white tops for Caucasian donors, black tops for African American donors, yellow tops for Asian donors, and red tops for donors with 'mixed ancestry'" (p. 49). This racialization of gametes is significant because research shows that intended parents make donor decisions based, at least in part, on assumptions about the heritability of desirable characteristics like intelligence and physical beauty alongside an interest in being able to "pass" the child as their biological offspring (Almeling, 2011; Quiroga, 2007). Thus, oocytes are racialized and commodified based on a fantasy that they contain and can biogenetically transmit socioculturally defined traits (Deomampo, 2019).

Categorizing and marketing oocytes in this way to both recipients and donors reinforce a bioessentialist understanding of race and racial transfer, with gametes seen as carrying physical and nonphysical racialized characteristics (Fogg-Davis, 2001; Hudson, 2015). The practice of matching donors to recipients by resemblance began in the 1940s when physicians started to seek potential sperm donors among their medical students (Almeling, 2009). Racial "matching" where fertility clinics pair donors and intended parents based on phenotypic resemblance has continued to this day and is revealing of a sociocultural preference for the *appearance* of biogenetic relatedness between parents and offspring (Quiroga, 2007). This preference for physical resemblance is a global phenomenon; for example, there is a law in Spain that *requires* clinicians to physically match donors to recipients to the best of their abilities (Almeling, 2009).

Racial matching in ARTs replicates practices in adoption, which used to be the only solution for infertility when this condition was defined as a social problem rather than a medical one (Quiroga, 2007). The absence of physical resemblance has even been purported to be a risk to secure attachment between parents and their children (Homanen, 2018). This adherence to racial matching in ARTs reinforces "the contours of the American kinship model" (Quiroga, 2007, p. 145), which privileges the kinship of "blood" relations rather than social ones. However, Agigian (2004) reminds us, "It is important to remember that 'blood' (race, family name and property, maleness and femaleness) is never just blood" (p. 27). Blood has long existed as a symbol of "natural" biogenetic kinship, and this linkage has proved to have powerful social and political consequences (Agigian, 2004). In the American kinship model, biological offspring of heterosexual couples are understood to be made of equal parts "blood" from both parents, and therefore similar physically and mentally (Quiroga, 2007; Schneider, 1984). Phenotypic matching also imbues the legacy of antimiscegenation thinking in the United States, which sought to maintain "racial purity" in relation to white supremacy (Callander et al., 2024). Any perceived deviation from this "natural" order has often been caste as something other or less than "a family."

Existing studies show that, among all couples using third-party reproduction in the United States, Asian women are most likely, across ethnic groups, to pursue oocyte donation (Shapiro et al., 2016). Since biogenetic kinship continues to be the preferred family structure (Hudson, 2015), there is a high demand and compensation for Asian American egg donors. As a cis-hetero female Asian American PhD student of clinical psychology, in 2019 I started researching the lived experiences of Asian American egg donors. My research was particularly interested in the embodied experience of racialized commodification. This chapter is an initial reflexive exploration of how I came to understand my research through the lens of sexual racism, while also contending with being married to a White man (and having two children of our own). In what follows, I will outline what brought me to this research, my positionality in relation to the work and participants, how I faced my own assumptions and biases regarding racialized egg donation, and what I learned that helped me recognize my own ambivalence regarding sexual racism as lived experience.

Coming to the Research

While my research was focused on the lived experiences of Asian American egg donors, I did not personally struggle with infertility, nor have I ever donated my eggs. My journey to discovering ARTs as a site for excavating the ways in which race, sexuality, and capitalism interact to (re)shape psyches and (re)produce existing oppressive structures happened by chance. Knowing my interest in Asian American women, Lisa Rubin, an academic mentor and advisor at the institution where I was doing my graduate studies, tasked me to analyze six qualitative interviews with Asian American egg donors participating in a larger study of egg donation experiences. I later expanded on this work through subsequent research projects as part of my graduate work, including through further 12 qualitative interviews with Asian American egg donors in the United States.

Across the different interviews, it was immediately clear that the process of egg donation—recruitment, assessment, compensation, racial and other "matching"—relied on well-known stereotypes of Asian American women. Indeed, I discovered that Asian American egg donors were more highly valuable if they also had a record of academic achievement (Yom et al., 2020). While academic achievement is a desirable characteristic for donors of all races, for Asian American women it has a particular meaning for their value as egg donors as derived from the "model minority" stereotype. The "model minority" stereotype developed in the 1960s and depicts a quiet and compliant racial minority who achieves the "American Dream" through hard work (Wong & Halgin, 2006). All the donors with whom I spoke agreed that the closer they were to the model minority stereotype and conventional forms of Western beauty, the more valuable they were within the gamete marketplace as reflected by the higher compensation they enjoyed. What I could not make sense of, however, was the complex descriptions that were provided of feeling both exploited and valued in this context. Despite feeling racially objectified, the majority of donors did not regret having donated their eggs. In fact, one donor expressed that she felt more desirable as an Asian American woman knowing that her reproductive parts, genes, or eggs were highly valued.

Reflexivity and Positioning the Researcher

Reflexivity, a defining feature of critical feminist psychology, is the practice of "disciplined self-reflection" (Wilkinson, 1988, p. 493). It requires the researcher to be aware of their own positionality, interests, and values because the epistemological stance of critical feminist psychology emphasizes multiplicity and the social construction of reality, rejecting positivism and faux

SEXUAL RACISM AND ASIAN AMERICAN EGG DONATION   329

neutrality. As an Asian American woman and doctoral student who also has struggled with the myth of the model minority, I related to the egg donors' experiences. However, my shame around the ways in which I have benefited from and even exploited this stereotype blinded me from relating to the donors' nuanced experience of being simultaneously valued and objectified because of one's race. This blind spot was clear even in the questions I posed during our interviews, including one that specifically asked about experiences of being racially "devalued" in the context of egg donation. This question often generated countervailing descriptions of feelings of value arising from donation. After engaging more critically with the data, I realized the multiplicity of their experiences as not valued *versus* devalued but a complex blend of both. Unbeknownst to me, I had approached my study with an assumption that being racialized, objectified, and commodified through the systems of egg donation was only experienced as harm, while for these participants the realities were more complex and multidimensional.

Once I accepted this potential for greater complexity, I was able to engage with intersecting narratives of value and objectification. As an Asian American woman, I understood the gravitational pull toward being singled out for my race and gender, including by approximating white beauty standards and molding myself to a version of a model minority. Growing up, being fetishized was both alluring and deeply shameful; on the one hand you are singled out as "other" and all the discomfort that entails, but on the other hand you are positioned as unique and desirable. Although I was not expecting it, these dichotomies and their personal implications rushed forward through my research, resulting in a convergence of my personal and professional selves in a way that was entirely new for me.

Pregnant with my daughter, I interviewed some participants during the first year of the COVID-19 pandemic, which saw a rise in anti-Asian hate rhetoric, and public violence against Asian American women in particular. Nowhere was the terror and sadness of this violence more evident than in a series of mass shootings at massage parlors and spas in Atlanta, Georgia, during which a white man murdered eight people including six Asian women: Soon Chung Park, Hyun Jung Grant, Suncha Kim, Yong Yue, Xiaojie Tan, and Daoyou Feng. During this time, I got an email from an old friend who linked this anti-Asian violence to an incident that I had shared with her some time ago:

> I realized I haven't checked in with you this week and feel terrible about it. I can't imagine how hard this all must be for you—and know that I love

330 SPOTLIGHTING THE STRUCTURAL

you, am here for you, and am thinking about you. I keep thinking about that time you told me about when that orthodox Jewish guy stopped you on the street and propositioned you—how awful that must feel, and how disgusting that is.

I was a teenager when the above referenced proposition was made, and while I had forgotten this incident, I was not surprised that it had occurred. Such an event sits among many similar experiences in my life thus far. Every time I am objectified and sexualized in this way, I get flooded with feelings of shame and disgust. I am now in a place in my personhood where I can deflect these feelings rather than internalize them, but I was not always able to do so and, to be honest, this deflection is never fully complete. I imagine my friend had reached out to me because the Atlanta massacre brought attention to the exoticization and hypersexualization of Asian women. However, "the violence in Atlanta was not an aberration. It is a gendered racialization that haunts Asian women across time and space" (Hwang & Parreñas, 2021, p. 568). As noted, this gendered racialization has repeatedly inserted itself into my life, and I came to realize that it has inserted itself into the lives of my research participants as well. Indeed, it seems clear to me now that there is a single structural dimension that unifies the mass murder of Asian women, the sexual objectification I experienced my whole life, and the literal compensation premium for gametes derived from Asian American women: sexual racism.

Sexual Racism and Affective Ambivalence

The participants' recurring experience of being sought out for their race and sex was first called out by one of this collection's editors, Pani Farvid, as possibly linked to *sexual racism*. The interconnectedness of sexism and racism was of particular interest here. "Yellow Fever" and "Rice Queen" are colloquial terms that refer to Asian fetishes that simultaneously sexualize and racialize Asian women and men, respectively. In fact, these racist and sexist stereotypes are reflective of how the institution of whiteness can pierce the individual psyche to transform intimate desires and preferences that then reflexively reinforce white superiority. If sexual racism is understood as a structural force, then it touches everyone's life. Therefore, it is no great leap to see how sexual racism operates in the context of egg donation, another way in which the racialized desire for a type of Asian American woman is enacted based on stereotypes and gendered ideals. Sexual racism is reinforced when comparing the high desirability for Asian egg donors, who can be compensated as much as $100,000 per cycle (Li, 2012), compared to the demand for Asian sperm donors, who are compensated up to $100 per donation (Gilbert, n.d.). This gendered difference resembles existing hierarchies of racialized and gendered desirability where Asian men are persistently seen as inferior in both hetero and queer communities (e.g., Feliciano et al., 2009). The resulting lived experience of this type of racialized and gendered commodification is one where Asian Americans of all genders feel both valued and idealized as well as objectified and exploited for their race and sexuality.

This phenomenon is illustrated in the case of a participant I call "Fran," who was a 24-year-old doctoral student I interviewed in 2021. Fran had donated two times to one intended parent. Fran discovered egg donation when she saw an advertisement in her university newspaper seeking "a highly intelligent Asian American donor." She was vetted using multiple intelligence, personality, and genetic tests before being selected as the donor. The large compensation and assiduous vetting process made Fran feel valued in a new way that she had not experienced before. For the first time, Fran perceived her reproductive capacities as having more value because of her Asian race:

> I didn't realize how much value it (Asian race) held in a reproductive sense, like being an Asian female. Essentially there are people, obviously, who enjoy dating Asian females because of cultural values or they like the aesthetic or whatever. I don't really know, but it's like beyond that. Right? It's the next step beyond the dating game. It's like, who do you want to have a child with? And I think that's what opened my eyes to like, "Wow you have value past just getting dates," or whatever, you know? How you pass just general dating popularity, I guess? People are interested. I mean that's why mail order brides are such a big thing, right? That it's the same sort of feeling.

Fran hits on several gendered and racialized tropes (e.g., so-called mail order brides) before reporting on the complex and ambivalent feeling of being desired explicitly for her perceived race. She was desired, sought out, and valued in this context, a literal marketplace of biological commodities that derive value from systems of sexual racism and, by extension, white

332 SPOTLIGHTING THE STRUCTURAL

supremacy. She equated this with more than just having a "leg up" in the dating game, but as worthy of long-term commitment and care. With regard to dating, you are nothing more than fetishized sexual object that one dates and then can discard, but when donating your eggs you become a special, carefully selected, and ultimately worthy commodity on which one bases a whole human life. It's a powerful distinction, even though both are based on racialized and gendered oppressions inherent in sexual racism.

Fran's experience exemplifies some of the ways in which structural inequality can be hidden or experienced in ambivalent terms (i.e., having both a negative and positive aspect), particularly in the context of capitalist markets. Fran was sought out for her race, but she still had to prove her worth and value through a range of tests. The intended parent's desire for a "genius" Asian donor with 'excellent' genetic and physical histories as measured by standardized tests reinforces a model minority stereotype of Asian American women, not only setting them up as fetishized objects but also selecting Fran as extra desirable and thus worthy of a high rate of compensation. Hence, Fran's experience of sexual racism is imbued with a complex interplay of both negative and positive affective responses, ultimately constrained by the context of commercial egg donation and the range of power dynamics it represents. Yet, even in such a context, she sees her race as of value and a part of herself in a manner that she did not before, while it is very clear that such value comes within, and from, an already gendered and racialized social and commercial system that singles out Asian American women for egg donation.

Recognizing My Ambivalence

The complicated experiences of racial commodification evident within some participants' accounts eventually tapped into my own complex, hidden, and disparate feelings about sexual racism. As a researcher and a person of color, I am not exempt from the power and pull of whiteness. My own positionality and desires are shaped by racist and sexist sociocultural ideologies in ways that I both know and do not know. Living in a gentrified neighborhood of Brooklyn, I am stunned by the numerous young families that look just like mine: Asian mom, white dad, with cute *hapa*[1] children (Crane, 2020). A child

---

[1] A Hawaiian term meaning "half." It originally referred to those who were mixed Hawaiian and haole, "foreigner" or "white person," and can be used to identify being half Asian and white.

of Korean immigrants, I never previously racially matched my neighbors so closely and feel very much at home in my adult community. I finally belong somewhere after feeling so different for so long. I take solace in the way families look here without always realizing that I too, can perpetuate racial and heteronormative homogeneity. Furthermore, I do recognize that the family configurations are raced and gendered, even though it can be uncomfortable to wonder: *why are all the women Asian and all the men White*? As a social scientist I know it is not a coincidence that I am surrounded by other Asian women with White partners; contending with the sexual racism that must be operating here is difficult and emotional work.

What I learned from the egg donors I interviewed was that sexual racism can be validating, exciting, and intoxicating. But ultimately, it is a destructive and pervasive force that reproduces existing oppressive hierarchies through our individual and collective desires; even—or perhaps especially— if packaged up nicely. I initially felt shame recognizing that sexual racism exists in my most intimate relationship and questioned the authenticity of it. *Was my desire for my husband an enactment of internalized White supremacy? Was his desire for me based on an Orientalist fantasy? If this were true, and our desire for each other is shaped by sexual racism, what does this mean for our relationship? And then, our children?* These were difficult questions to face that made me want to resist acknowledging the validity that my sexuality could be racialized. However, my love for him and my children, the love that I, a couple's therapist, see between other interracial couples, affirms for me that this can all be true at once.

Yes, my desire is racialized because sexuality is not separable from race. However, this does not invalidate my love for my husband or my family. While I feel the urge to remain in the realm of "sexual color-blindness" by ignoring the impact of whiteness on my romantic desire (Chen et al., 2024), I also want to resist this easy "cop out" as a temptation. What does undesiring whiteness and sexual racism look like? In an earlier chapter in this volume, Chen et al. discuss the concept of *sexual humility*, which they define as "a commitment to self-reflection and critique of one's sexual preferences and intimate interpersonal actions resulting from historical power imbalances." Perhaps then, undesiring whiteness and undoing sexual racism in my relationship means talking about it and allowing ourselves the freedom to reflect, explore, and lovingly struggle together. It means being with the "both/ and" of exploration and negotiation. And rather than suppressing my discomfort with sexual racism, perhaps it means helping bring it to the surface

334 SPOTLIGHTING THE STRUCTURAL

where it can be unpacked and examined to deflate its unspoken and often hidden power. As mixed-race couples, the egg donation industry, and, as a society, we have some way to go. I have come to realize, however, that as long as I work to keep unveiling both the overt and hidden ways sexual racism operates, I am moving in the right direction.

References

Agigian, A. (2004). *Baby steps: How lesbian alternative insemination is changing the world.* Wesleyan University Press.

Almeling, R. (2009). Gender and the value of bodily goods: commodification in egg and sperm donation. *Law and Contemporary Problems, 72,* 37.

American Society for Reproductive Medicine. (n.d.). *Third-party reproduction.* ASRM. https://www.asrm.org/topics/topics-index/third-party-reproduction/

Almeling, R. (2011). *Sex cells: The medical market for eggs and sperm.* University of California Press.

Callander, D., Farvid, P., Baradaran, A., & Vance, T. (2024). How do you solve a problem like sexual racism?. In D. Callander, P. Farvid, A. Baradaran, & T. Vance (Eds.), Sexual Racism and Social Justice (pp. 1–30). Oxford University Press.

Chen, X., Kelleher, J., Boiardo, A., Ealey, D., Gaztambide, D. (2024). Anti-black skin, white sheets: Challenging sexual color-blindness through a sexual humility framework. In D. Callander, P. Farvid, A. Baradaran, & T. Vance (Eds.), Sexual Racism and Social Justice (pp. 66–83). Oxford University Press.

Covington, S. N., & Burns, L. H. (Eds.). (2006). *Infertility counseling: A comprehensive handbook for clinicians.* Cambridge University Press.

Crane, L. S. (2020). Invisible: A mixt Asian woman's efforts to see and be seen in psychoanalysis. *Studies in Gender and Sexuality, 21*(2), 127–135.

Deomampo, D. (2019). Racialized commodities: Race and value in human egg donation. *Medical Anthropology, 38*(7), 620–633.

Feliciano, C., Robnett, B., & Komaie, G. (2009). Gendered racial exclusion among white Internet daters. *Social Science Research, 38*(1), 39–54.

Fogg-Davis, H. (2001). Navigating race in the market for human gametes. *Hastings Center Report, 31*(5), 13–21.

Gilbert, S. E. (n.d.). How much are you worth. *Princeton Magazine.* Retrieved March 29, 2023, from https://www.princetonmagazine.com/how-much-are-you-worth/

Homanen, R. (2018). Reproducing whiteness and enacting kin in the Nordic context of transnational egg donation: Matching donors with cross-border traveler recipients in Finland. *Social Science and Medicine, 203,* 28–34.

Hudson, N. (2015). Gamete Donation and "Race." In *Encyclopedia of Life Sciences.* John Wiley & Sons. DOI: 10.1002/9780470015902.a0005596.pub2

Hwang, M. C., & Parreñas, R. S. (2021). The gendered racialization of Asian women as villainous temptresses. *Gender and Society, 35*(4), 567–576.

GlobeNewswire. (2021, July 14). Egg donation market revenue to cross USD 5.5 Bn by 2027: Global Market Insights Inc. GlobeNewswire News Room. Retrieved March 29, 2023, from https://www.globenewswire.com/en/news-release/2021/07/14/2262472/

0/en/Egg-Donation-Market-revenue-to-cross-USD-5-5-Bn-by-2027-Global-Market-Insights-Inc.html

Li, S. (2012, May 4). Asian women command premium prices for egg donation in U.S. *Los Angeles Times*. Retrieved March 29, 2023, from https://www.latimes.com/health/la-xpm-2012-may-04-la-fi-egg-donation-20120504-story.html

Quiroga, S. S. (2007). Blood is thicker than water: Policing donor insemination and the reproduction of whiteness. *Hypatia, 22*(2), 143–161.

Schneider, D. M. (1984). *A critique of the study of kinship*. University of Michigan Press.

Shapiro, A., Barad, D. H., Darmon, S., Albertini, D., Gleicher, N., & Kushnir, V. A. (2016). Racial and ethnic disparities in the use of third-party ART in the US. *Fertility and Sterility, 106*(3), e108–e109.

Wilkinson, S. (1988, January). The role of reflexivity in feminist psychology. *Women's Studies International Forum, 11*(5), 493–502.

Wong, F., & Halgin, R. (2006). The "model minority": Bane or blessing for Asian Americans? *Journal of Multicultural Counseling and Development, 34*(1), 38–49.

Yom, E., Rubin, L. R., & de Melo-Martín, I. (2020). *"I've not told my family I've done any of this": Experiences of egg donation among Asian and Asian American egg donors in the U.S.* [Conference session]. Association for Women in Psychology.

15

Decentering Whiteness in South Africa

Using Empathic Dialogue to Engage With Race, Identity, Privilege, and Entitlement

Matthew Rich-Tolsma and Sizwe Mqalo

This chapter is part of an ongoing discussion about how whiteness is centered in South Africa, including how a process of mutual reflexivity—which we call "empathic dialogue"—can help in the undesiring and decentering of whiteness. This idea of dialogue as necessary to the antiracist project calls to mind the work of South African poet, Mongane Wally Serote who in 1972 wrote:

> *White people are white people,*
> *They are burning the world.*
> *Black people are black people,*
> *They are the fuel.*
> *White people are white people,*
> *They must learn to listen.*
> *Black people are black people,*
> *They must learn to talk*

On this foundation, this chapter details an ongoing conversation between us as two South African scholars: Sizwe Mqalo, a black cisgender woman, and Matthew Rich-Tolsma, a white cisgender man. Our conversation was convened to discuss our experiences of race, identity, privilege, and entitlement, including an analysis of gender, sexuality, and desirability. In what follows, we present summary of our discussions, unpack resulting learnings about the processes of racialization, and offer a methodology toward undesiring and decentering whiteness. In order to make sense of our experience, we have drawn on a wide range of literature including critical race theory, African philosophy, and psychoanalysis.

Matthew Rich-Tolsma and Sizwe Mqalo, *Decentering Whiteness in South Africa* In: *Sexual Racism and Social Justice.*
Edited by: Denton Callander, Panteá Farvid, Amir Baradaran, and Thomas A. Vance, Oxford University Press.
© Oxford University Press 2024. DOI: 10.1093/oso/9780197605509.003.0016

The chapter is divided into three parts. The first part engages with our positionality, how we came to meet, and what our dialogue has consisted of thus far. We provide some context for our meeting and initial conversations, paying close attention to the interactions between us, including moments of discomfort, surprise, and transformation. Here we offer and overview of the reflexive process we refer to as "empathetic dialogue," which we believe can have a key role to play in the decentering of whiteness, including as described in a section on "awkward integration." The second part of the chapter provides some examples of the types of themes and sense-making processes in which we were engaged. This part comprises two sections: "White Privilege: An Education" (which deals with identity, gender, class, and race) and "The Racialized Body: Dis/Connection, Desire, Shame, and Entitlement" (which deals with racialized desire, objectification, and prejudice). Lastly, we offer specific narratives interrogated when it came to our experiences. In the conclusion, we summarize the overarching themes from our empathetic dialogue and address potential risks, pitfalls, and limitations of this approach when its actors exist in different positional spaces.

Situating the Authors

We met only a few months before commencing work on this chapter, during an online nonviolence workshop titled Connecting Across Difference which was facilitated by Matthew. We were both interested in, and affected by, violence at the intersections of race, gender, and sexuality in South Africa. While we both were born under the shadow of South Africa's apartheid system and grew up through a period of profound violence and transition, our different positionalities have meant significant differences in our lived interpretations and sense-making. Matthew was born and raised in the Eastern Cape province of South Africa, spending most of his childhood in the coastal city of East London. He has a background in early childhood education and has lived and worked with children and teachers in South Africa, China, and India. More recently, he has worked in higher education researching transformative learning and leadership and worked as an organizational consultant and nonviolent communication trainer. He has lived in Holland with his Dutch partner for the last decade and is presently training as a group psychoanalyst. Sizwe was born in Amakhuzeni village in the Thyume Valley of Eastern Cape, South Africa. She spent her early childhood years in the

338   SPOTLIGHTING THE STRUCTURAL

village, but then later relocated to a boarding school in East London, where she finished her schooling. Sizwe has worked in vocational Christian ministry in South Africa and in Asia. She has also worked as a communication specialist in the corporate setting. At the time of writing this chapter she is completing her master's degree in African philosophy at the University of Fort Hare in South Africa. We put together a proposal and used this as an uncertain foundation from which to launch into a disorientating and, at times, painful conversation.

Situating the Context: Race and South Africa

> Domination is a regime that involves not just control but conviviality, even connivance—as shown by the constant compromises, the small tokens of fealty . . . individuals are constantly being trapped in a net of rituals that reaffirm tyranny, and in that these rituals, however minor, are intimate in nature.
>
> —Mbembe (2001, p. 66)

Black and white South Africans currently live interdependently. Whites make up a very small minority of South Africa's population,[1] yet the ideological centering of whiteness (in the wake of colonialism and apartheid) mean that whites hold disproportionate representation and privilege in almost every part of society (Chatterjee et al., 2020; Maart 2020). The lives of those living in South Africa are profoundly shaped by centuries of violent struggle and the legacy of colonialism. As a result of the process of colonization, all that is good, right, and virtuous is associated with whiteness, while all things deficient, lacking, and corrupt are routinely associated with Blackness (Lebakang, 2011; Mengara, 2001). Therefore, to truly recant and undesire whiteness is not an easy thing to do. This point is reminiscent of the compartmentalization of the lives described by Fanon (1963) in *The Wretched of the Earth*, where the formerly colonized aspires toward the attributes and power of the white colonizer. The changing political landscape in South Africa has

---

[1] Whites make up less than 8% of the national population and have a declining population, while Black South Africans are a fast-growing population and currently make up about 81% of the national population, coloreds—a multiracial ethnic minority in South Africa with diverse ancestry (including Khoisan [first nations], Bantu, European, Austronesian, and [South and East] Asian descent)— are the second-largest demographic, constituting roughly 9% of the overall population (Statistics SA, 2020).

done little to shift the skewed perceptions about Black and white; while we may chant slogans about political freedom, psychological freedom for Black people is still a work in progress. Unlike most nations that went through a political revolution where colonial oppressors were displaced and rejected, South Africa "chose" to forgive and build an integrated "rainbow" nation. However, in the places of intersection where Black and white people meet, this integration has almost always taken place on white people's terms. And so, patterns of racial oppression continue to be replicated.

Steve Biko, a significant leader of the Black consciousness movement in South Africa who was murdered by police in 1977 at the age of 30, anticipated the problematic nature of an unreflective and unaccountable integration when he wrote, "the biggest mistake the black world ever made was to assume that whoever opposed apartheid was an ally" (1979, p. 63). Biko understood that the influence of Western imperialism ran deep and that the assumption of power by whiteness exists even for those that seek to separate themselves from the deliberate subjugation of Black people. Addressing those who saw themselves as allies of "the cause"—the white liberals who called for integration—Biko questioned the terms of this integration, and the power dynamics that would ensue from it. He was adamant:

> If by integration you understand a breakthrough into white society by blacks, an assimilation and acceptance of blacks into an already established set of norms and codes of behaviour set up and maintained by whites, then YES I am against it. . . . If on the other hand, by integration you mean there shall be free participation by all members of a society, catering for the full expression of the self in a freely changing society as determined by the will of the people, then I am with you. (Biko, 1979, p. 24)

Despite Biko's warnings, ours has been an uncritical and ultimately unequal integration where great amounts of energy have been invested in including whites in a "rainbow nation" without challenging their hold on power in spheres outside of political office (Bojabotseha, 2011; World Bank, 2018). In other words, there has been integration but there has been a failure to create a new political subjectivity in white people, and very little demand has been made on white South Africans to adjust their values and do any work of assimilation into or serious interaction with any African framework in society (Gibson, 2008, p. 702).

340 SPOTLIGHTING THE STRUCTURAL

Situating Our Conversation

The process of finding ways to speak to each other about our experience as South Africans was far more challenging than we imagined. We found our experiences and selves inextricably connected and—at the same time—separated by a seemingly impassable rift. Both attracted and repelled, both in motion and in paralysis. We spoke about topics about which we assumed we had shared convictions, such as racism and gender-based violence, and discovered an earnest resonance and companionship. Our vulnerability was amply rewarded, and yet our conversation was laid over a foundation that was ubiquitous and difficult to name. Attending to the patterns of difference pulsing through our gestures seemed inherently conflictual and threatened the polite veneer of harmony we strove so delicately to maintain. For Matthew, the ongoing recognition of whiteness and the complicity this implied in supporting colonial patterns of power relating was painfully difficult to sustain given that he had enjoyed the lifelong privilege of choosing to ignore it at will, in the white liberal milieu in which he had been raised. For us, this called to mind some of hooks's powerful writing from the late 20th century:

> Often [white people's] rage erupts because they believe that all ways of looking that highlight difference subvert the liberal belief in a universal subjectivity (we are all just people) that they think will make racism disappear. They have a deep emotional investment in the myth of sameness even as their actions reflect the primacy of whiteness as a sign informing who they are and how they think. (hooks, 1992, p. 167)

A pattern revealed itself, we were faced with the choice of either colluding with each other—to gloss over difference and affirm an idealized view of ourselves—or to turn toward the discord and work though the discomfort, in seeking transformation. As the American social pragmatist George Herbert Mead reminds us, the way through such a scenario is embracing how we are recognized and reflected in the eyes of others (Mead, 2000, p. 253). This path entails giving primacy to our experience by attending to moments of "breakdown" in our conversations (Alvesson & Kärreman, 2011). These are what the Danish social psychologist Svend Brinkmann calls "stumble data" (2014, p. 723), situations where surprise and doubt problematized our fiercely defended ways of explaining our life-worlds (Martela, 2015, p. 549).

Choosing such a path of reflexive vulnerability was often anxiety provoking, as it required us to continually call into question our prejudices and our taken-for-granted habitual approaches to sense-making, which were invisible until we collided with them in our recognition of the other (Mowles, 2015, p. 61).

It was hard to know where to begin when we first met. Matthew suggested we start by giving each other some sort of autobiographical account, a description of key experience that had shaped the way that we understood the world. It seemed as good a place to start as any. On this first call, Sizwe was located in Hogsback, a magically beautiful village in the Amathole Mountains where Matthew had often gone to play in the late July snowfall as a child. Matthew was seated in his office in the Netherlands. As Matthew began to launch into the story about his life, Sizwe interrupted him. "I'm sorry," she said. "But the most amazing thing has just happened. The mist is rolling in and everything outside my window is completely white. I cannot even see the trees."

Doing Empathic Reflexivity: An Overview of Our Process

What did empathetic dialogue mean for us, and what made it so challenging? Perhaps we were attempting to create a context in which it was possible to fix a gaze that is often experienced as disparaging and distrustful of the other. For Sizwe, this was an act of subversion, an opportunity to turn the encounter with the white gaze on its head; to approach and encounter rather than seek refuge from what she recognized as a historically unsafe relational space. In essence, we sought to use our dialogue as a counterhegemonic tool. The experience of Western hegemony in South Africa has largely depended on false characterizations and categorizations of Black people to justify the legitimacy of white supremacy and dominance (Lebakang, 2011; Ngwena, 2018; Traoré, 2007). These characterizations are dehumanizing for both the Black people who suffer under them and the white people who have historically benefited from wielding them (Freire, 2005; Oelofsen, 2015).

For the white person, a sense of shame, embarrassment, and rage ensues if and when they face up to the fact that their privilege is built on the dehumanization of others (hooks, 1992; Maart, 2014; Milazzo, 2017). For the Black person, a sense of anger arises toward those perpetrating the dehumanization against them, while often a self-disparaging attitude also arises (Freire,

342   SPOTLIGHTING THE STRUCTURAL

2005; Oelofsen, 2015). But, what if healing (at least some of it) could be found in confronting this gaze, and standing directly in its path, mutually? Standing together to understand the lived experiences resulting from these fraught histories, simultaneously working to deconstruct it, at least on an individual level. This is the hope and purpose of our dialogue. That is what we mean by using the purposeful empathy of our dialogue as a counterhegemonic tool.

The idea of "leaning into" the gaze is inspired by the late Argentine-born feminist philosopher Maria Logunes's (2008) paper " *'World'-Travelling, and Loving Perception.*" Logunes asserts that women of color often have to travel between worlds, a traveling that is often born out of necessity and to worlds hostile to them as outsiders. South Africa offers a particularly interesting context in that Black people make up the vast majority of the population of the country, and yet, nearly three decades after the end of apartheid—and nearly a century after colonial independence—whiteness remains firmly centered in the South African experience (Moreira et al., 2020). Because of these power dynamics, it is generally Black people that must travel into white spaces to leverage opportunities for education, employment, and other forms of social advancement. Thus, Black South Africans often must travel into hostile worlds, world traveling that Logunes argues affords an opportunity to create processes toward identification and love.

The legacy of colonialism is a world divided into compartments of Black and white (Fanon, 1963, p. 39). Relationally, we can either have what Logunes terms an "arrogant perception" or we can choose its antithesis: to perceive ourselves and others with "loving eyes" (Logunes, 1987, p. 5). Through arrogant perception, we objectify people and rob them of their agency, while relating through loving eyes can allow the agency of others to flourish. In general, Sizwe's experience of traveling through white worlds is an experience of being the object of arrogant perception. On the other hand, as a Black woman in a world that privileges whiteness, Sizwe identified how as an act of survival she has assimilated aspects of whiteness into her ways of being. She described how she has in parts viewed her culture, and others with shared cultural roots, with an excruciating sense of shame. A sense of wanting to distance herself from these origins and as such, a want to distance herself from her own self. The colonized body is an object being perceived arrogantly, while simultaneously acting as an agent of arrogant perception. Arrogant perception may be understood as a process of reification through which the other is misrecognized and portrayed as a static and dehumanized object (Freire, 2005).

DECENTERING WHITENESS IN SOUTH AFRICA   343

Clearly it is not only those cast as oppressors who perceive others arrogantly. The process of desiring and centering whiteness means that it exists as the bedrock of "normal" humanity (Hitchcock & Flint, 2015). On this foundation, Sizwe could easily come to see Matthew as a caricature, as a man without a story, a mere cypher for oppression. In so doing, she would reduce him to a reified object, "a failure to love," connection, empathy, and joint humanity (Logunes, 1987). Freire points out this requires a degree of humility, namely that:

> dialogue cannot occur between those who want to name the world and those who do not wish this naming—between those who deny others the right to speak their word and those whose right to speak has been denied them. (Freire, 2005, p. 88)

What is needed is an empathic orientation toward self and other, a mutual recognition of difference, but interdependence (Honneth, 2005; Logunes, 1987). Engaging in a dialogical process through which we come to recognize others in this way can be profoundly destabilizing to our sense of identity as it is paradoxically simultaneously affirming and negating. "Remaining open to the meaning of the other person" as Gadamer (1975, p. 221) put it, means that something in our understanding of who we are is dislodged and needs to be open to change. This can be distressing and anxiety-provoking because we hold "deep identity investment in the distorted images we cherish of others" (p. 295) and, indeed, of ourselves.

To better understand this process of "empathic dialogue" we turn to the Russian literary theorist and philosopher Mikhail Bakhtin. Bakhtin pointed out that due to its constitutive nature, dialogue is perennially forming reality rather than revealing something that has already been formed, which gestures toward the transformative potentials of mutual dialogue offering. It is an inexorable process that produces "once-occurrent uniqueness" or "singularity"; it defies classification and logic that cannot be thought of but only experienced (Bakhtin, 1993, p. 13; 1984). We contend that the understanding of dialogue Bakhtin is defining, much like Logunes's *World Travelling*, is a process of mutual recognition. To this end he wrote,

> I achieve self-consciousness, I become myself only by revealing myself to another, through another and with another's help. . . . Cutting myself off, isolating oneself, closing oneself off, those are the basic reasons for loss of self. (Bakhtin, quoted in Todorov, 1984, p. 96)

344 SPOTLIGHTING THE STRUCTURAL

On similar themes, the black feminist poet Audre Lorde put it this way:

> I have come to believe over and over again that what is most important to me must be spoken, made verbal and shared, even at the risk of having it bruised or misunderstood. (Lorde, 2017)

Making Sense of Our Empathic Dialogue

In this section we will explore some of the significant themes constructed through our ongoing dialogue. We will begin by setting the scene with a discussion of identity and mutual recognition as an awkward integration in a postcolonial and postapartheid context. We will then go on to recount some of the narratives that emerged in our conversation. In this section, we explore part of Matthew's account of his education in and through whiteness as well as Sizwe's responses, evoking themes of race, racialization, and privilege. We also draw into Sizwe encountering the racialization of her body, evoking themes of dis/connection, desire, shame, and entitlement.

White Privilege: An Education

Matthew

Almost my entire early childhood (five out of my first six years) was spent in a national state of emergency, which was lifted in 1990 following the release of Nelson Mandela and the unbanning of the African National Congress (ANC). When I think of my early childhood, I am predominantly aware of a pervasive sense of fear. Everywhere there seemed to be security guards who would search you—I recall the smiling Black ladies who rifled through my mother's handbag with white batons when we entered the supermarket—and constant reminders of imminent violence (like the life-size illustrations of common explosive devices that were displayed prominently outside of my first-grade classroom for informational purposes). Every discarded plastic or paper bag was potentially a bomb, and every Black man walking down the road was potentially a source of danger—die swart gevaar. As children we did not understand what this was all about, and—much like most of the white adults who surrounded us—were too isolated to imagine an alternative. I remember, as a 5-year-old, playing with my brother and attempting to fortify our yard with sandbags in order to protect

DECENTERING WHITENESS IN SOUTH AFRICA 345

us from the encroaching ANC. Neither of us had any real idea what the ANC was, but we intuited that it was something very bad, something of almost mythological proportions.

I have a few memories from the early 1990s which I equate with a burgeoning realization around what the reality of privilege meant for me in a profoundly unequal society. Some of my earliest realizations around inequality relate to a gardener called Witness, who came to work for my parents and live in our outbuildings when he became too frail to continue working for my recently widowed aunt. I know now that he must have had another name, one that was a part of his own language; I regret that I never knew it. Witness smelled of sweat and earth and ash, he had worked most of his life in the mines and the acrid heat of the pits had inscribed a story of years on his bitter cocoa skin. He smoked budget tobacco wrapped in newspaper. He ate brown spirit vinegar on his mielie pap. He washed his hands with a brick and drank water from a chipped enamel cup that my mother left outside the back door. I realize now that my parents accommodated him out of pity, but he always seemed a towering figure to me.

"Cowboy," he barked, his voice was just a variation on the rumbling cough that would kill him in the heat of that summer. "Come here. I'll show you how to do this." My brother and I had been scraping the flakes of paint off of the wooden garage door for my father—it had seemed a good strategy to assuage our boredom before we discovered that it involved actual work—and had now returned to a half-completed game of cricket, leaving a pile of tools in the driveway. I approached him cautiously. He ran his fingers over the edges of the cracked paint, then lifted the scraper like a scalpel with exaggerated skill as if to say, "now watch this." We scraped together in silence (punctuated only by his fits of coughing) until the sun was a red band low on the western horizon; him pulling large strips from the immaculate surface of the door while I chipped the wood releasing a pile of little flakes.

He sighed loudly, pocketing the scraper and stepping back to admire the door with hyperbolic interest. He nodded appreciatively while rolling a cigarette with practiced precision. Finally, he spoke. "Look!" he said. "Finished en klaar"! We grinned at each other for a moment, and as I turned to leave, he reached toward me offering a broad yellow palm. I shook his hand and then he held onto my hand for some moments, his grip firm, his palm like sandpaper. Our eyes met. "Do you want to have supper at my house tonight, Witness?" I asked, my hand still enclosed in his. He smiled sadly. "Hauw! Cowboy, Cowboy . . .," he muttered, shaking his head slowly.

Sizwe

When I hear a story like Matthew's I am struck by the beauty of the innocence of all children and how in that moment of realization that there "had to be" separation between Cowboy and Witness must have been the beginning of a rupture of innocence. What I find myself wondering about now is:

1. *Living in this schema where kindness and charity is given to Black people and yet at the same time their "otherness" is very much apparent and sets the limits of intimacy, how has that shaped Matthew's ability to relate to Black people?*
2. *I often witness relationships of charity by white people toward poor Black people. There's a hierarchy of power there, with whites on top dispensing benevolence. I have also often observed that people who lead in these charitable endeavors often lack meaningful and intimate relationships with powerful Black people who do not need their charity. What does Matthew make of such an observation? Has he seen evidence of this in his own life as an adult?*

Matthew

Reflecting on these questions brings me to think about my relationships with Black peers as a child and adolescent.

When I was a child, older Black people seemed very remote to me. Almost all my interactions with them were as servants. They wore blue overalls and arrived from an unknown place crammed into white and yellow Volkswagen minibuses that my parents (and everyone else I knew) called "black taxis." My first year of primary school was the first year in which the boy's college I attended was desegregated.

It is strange to recognize my complete lack of curiosity about the Black boys I met during primary school (the demographic of my cohort changed every year, and by the time I graduated high school, Black students made up about 40% of the class). I did not associate these boys with the gardeners, maids, petrol station attendants, or security guards, who represented Black adults in my experience. They were different: more like me, but not like me. What strikes me now, reflecting on this, is how my recollections of this experience is entirely about the other. My race is not under scrutiny, there was no need to engage with whiteness, because it was the accepted norm.

It wasn't until I reached high school that it occurred to me, that I could inquire into the lives of my Black peers outside of school, or try and visit their homes or share my experience with them. During high school I developed some friendships with Black peers, but they were always mediated by shared activities and the issue of race was never placed on the table. There were always the jokes that were just for white company, and there were always the conversations in rapid sophisticated isiXhosa[2] that left me behind and actively excluded me. When male friends went off to the bush for Ukoluka (the Xhosa initiation ritual into manhood, which includes a period of seclusion in the wilderness, participation in an "initiation school," and ritual circumcision (Meintjes, 1998; Mdedetyana, 2018)) and emerged subtly changed, we never spoke with them about it. I knew better somehow; to talk about this experience, an experience that was completely alien to me, would mean a recognition of our difference, and as a result the unjust gulf of inequality between us. Perhaps we knew deep down that risking closeness meant the recognition of how much harder we expected these "friends," who we ostensibly cared about, to work; and it might mean that we needed to acknowledge the harm that we had perpetrated (and continued to perpetrate) against them and their families.

The older adult Black people I interacted with as a child were almost always cast as people who relied on my parents somehow, people to be helped, propped up. It was not until I entered adulthood that I established relationships with Black mentors to whom I would willingly submit.

In making sense of the above expositions, we draw on James Baldwin's writing on the predicament of whiteness as a position of dislocation, where whites

> who imagine that history flatters them (as it does, indeed, since they wrote it) are impaled or find themselves trapped by self-authored accounts of their histories and become incapable of seeing or changing themselves, or the world. . . . They are dimly, or vividly, aware that the history they have fed themselves is mainly a lie, but they do not know how to release themselves from it, and they suffer enormously from the resulting personal incoherence. (Baldwin, 1985, p. 321)

---

[2] isiXhosa is the language of the amaXhosa people. The second-largest people group in South Africa. It is Sizwe's mother tongue, and the dominant language in the Eastern Cape province where we both grew up.

348   SPOTLIGHTING THE STRUCTURAL

Baldwin eloquently exposes Matthew's dilemma. The position of whites is a precarious one—sprawling on a pin which they themselves have crafted erases difference. Unable to recognize others or themselves, and therefore cut off from the possibility of resonance and impervious to change. Unable to truly encounter the other and relating to them as a petrified object, a receptacle for the projection of intolerable and disavowed attributes of whiteness. As the British psychoanalyst Stephen Frosh puts it:

> The white subject needs the black to define itself; and it desires the black as the repository of those necessary things—above all sexuality—which it has repudiated out of anxiety and self-loathing. (Frosh, 2013, p. 148)

For both of us, our experiences at school provided the first significant encounter with other racial groups and provides, on reflection, a useful opportunity to see the processes of *habitus* and the centering of whiteness playing out. Due to the legacy of apartheid, schools in Black areas tend to be disadvantaged in just about every material way possible. Apart from infrastructural problems, and underfunding, the teachers themselves in these schools, being Black people, for the most part are products of the Bantu education system (the apartheid system of segregated education for Black students, which came into effect with the Bantu Education Act of 1953). The Bantu education system was deliberately designed to keep Black people undereducated in order to keep them in servitude, often performing menial roles. This claim was attested to by Hendrik Verwoerd, a Dutch-born sociologist and apartheid-era prime minister who is often seen as the architect of the apartheid system. Offering an apology for the apartheid approach to education while serving as Native Affairs Minister in 1954, he said:

> There is no place for [the Bantu] in the European community above the level of certain forms of labour. . . . What is the use of teaching the Bantu child mathematics when it cannot use it in practice? That is quite absurd. Education must train people in accordance with their opportunities in life, according to the sphere in which they live. (Speech as Minister of Native Affairs: June 7, 1954)

As restrictions began to loosen during the death throes of apartheid in the 1990s, many Black parents found themselves turning to the recently desegregated "white" state schools (formerly given the bureaucratic moniker

DECENTERING WHITENESS IN SOUTH AFRICA   349

of "Model C Schools") or to more expensive (white-owned) private schools. These schools were run (and generally still are run) by white principals and majority white school boards (referred to as school governing bodies in South Africa), often with an all-white teaching staff save a token isiXhosa or isiZulu teacher. Black children were viewed as being insubordinate and were often punished for speaking their home languages in class. They were also often discouraged from speaking in their native tongue during their leisure times including recess between classes, ostensibly to help them to improve their mastery of English and/or Afrikaans. Soudien (2004) discusses this type of assimilation as characteristic of integration in South African schools, where the dominant group (the white group) proceeds with the assumption that the Black people come with the threat of lowering their standards. Soudien argues that the end product for the Blacks in this system is that "They are expected to give up their own identities and cultures, and, critically, to acknowledge the superiority of the culture, and by implication, the identities of the groups into whose social context they are moving" (Soudien, 2004, p. 95ff.) This is vividly illustrated in Sizwe's experience as a student in all-girls boarding school.

Sizwe

In a place like my boarding school, a girls' school, it was apparent that a successful education process did not just mean mastering the official subjects of my schooling program, but also being properly cultured into the conceptions of what a proper lady ought to be. That is of course a white lady. A creature that, try as hard as I might, I could never be. Externally, that is, physiologically, I was never built to fit the standards of what makes a white woman beautiful, appropriate, or up to par. Socially, I failed dismally, as the requirements of propriety and culture in my culturally white school often stood at odds with the requirements of my own home culture. Thus, the result is that I became shamed for displaying what was labeled the "savage" attributes of Blackness or Africanness and was rewarded for mimicking whiteness, which in the end created in me an odd mix of belonging and not-belonging. This might be understood as something akin to an abjection of Blackness, a sort of sociopedagogical process through which the Black individual becomes a "Native of Nowhere" (Khumalo, 2018).

My Model C school education taught me shame about every behavior that signified Blackness and every part of my physicality that could not be somehow whitewashed. Here I was taught to cover up and developed a strange and awkward body awareness. Here I learned to view myself in terms of lack

350 SPOTLIGHTING THE STRUCTURAL

and deficiency. Now fully adult, I exist within a state of coloniality of being (Tamale, 2020, p. 93) struggling to disentangle myself from internalized forms of coloniality that inform my way of being in the world.

Fanon (1986) discusses the internal relationship a colonized subject has with herself, how she experiences herself as something or someone that is somehow not herself. This colonized subject is a locus of anxiety and self-alienation who lives in tension within herself and her identity. She is at odds with the identities that have been ascribed to her, yet she takes these ascriptions on in the hopes that through her docile compliance she might rise above the oppressiveness of being viewed as a subhuman. However, she over time also comes to assimilate the views of the powerful colonizers and comes to view herself as subhuman and, therefore, she endeavors to distance herself from this identity. She takes on qualities (such as docility and sub-servience) that are celebrated and mimic the colonizer's ways of being in order that she may feel herself to be more human, more acceptable. As Fanon explains in *Black Skins, White Masks*: "The colonised is elevated above his jungle status in proportion to his adoption of the mother country's cultural standards" (1986, p. 16). Fanon describes this dehumanizing reification as a difficulty in relating to the body: a "negating activity," a "third-person con-sciousness" (Fanon, 1986, pp. 110–111). He described this abject process of disembodiment hauntingly when he wrote,

> Below the corporeal schema I had sketched out a historic-racial schema. The elements that I used had been provided for me not by residual sensations and perceptions primarily of a tactile, vestibular, kinaesthetic, and visual character, but by the other . . . the corporeal schema crumbled, its place taken by the racial epidermal schema. (1986, p. 112)

In essence, Fanon draws attention to the fact that for the colonized subject, their own body is always only understood in relation to whiteness. Even in taking on the qualities of the colonizer, the colonized subject is aware that she is deluding herself. She is still a native and because of this immutable fact, there is no amount of conforming to whiteness that will completely de-liver her to full human status on these terms. Thus, she lives with a sense of internal anxiety about her duality, because if she can never be free from her Blackness and native status, which is projected to be the axis of her inferior status, then she in a constant state of indeterminate inauthenticity.

DECENTERING WHITENESS IN SOUTH AFRICA 351

The school environment was not designed for people like Sizwe, or even adjusted to become an environment where she could be made to feel comfortable. Instead, Black girls were the ones to be adjusted and not the institution, and certainly not white teachers or students. It was a place where, as Fanon put it, "the world-view is white because no black voice exists" (1967, p. 152).

The Racialized Body: Desire and Shame

Black embodiment was not only subjugated under colonization and under the apartheid system in South Africa, but it was also fetishized (Copeland, 2010; Ngwenya, 2018). In *Black Skin, White Masks*, Fanon gives an account of the experience of his own objectification and fetishization when he says:

> My body was given back to me sprawled out, distorted, recoloured, clad in mourning in that white winter day. The Negro is an animal, the Negro is mean, the Negro is ugly; look, a nigger, it's cold, the nigger is shivering because he is cold, the little boy is trembling because he is afraid of the nigger. . . . All around me the white man, above the sky tears at its navel, the earth rasps under my feet, and there is a white song, a white song. All this whiteness that burns me. (Fanon, 1967, pp. 113–114)

In this section, we look at the themes of racialized bodies, shame and desire, examining Sizwe's lived world experience of her Black body in white spaces in South Africa.

Sizwe

As a 16-year-old girl, who was still a virgin, and had never been kissed, I noticed a change in how the people in my environment interacted with me as my body began to change. When my body started to develop from a child's body into a curvier, maturing one of a young woman, I began to perceive once more another shift in how I would pass through the world. I noted that somehow, I had become an object of desire for men, both Black and white, but that the desire from white men came across as shameful. Along with the shameful desire that I experienced emanating from white men, I quickly learned that they had the perception that somehow my body was up for sale and they were the entitled buyers. The perception of me I came to realize, was vastly different from that which was afforded to my white counterparts. They were viewed as innocent, pure young girls who needed to be protected, while the coming in of my breasts and hips seemed to somehow signify some form of moral decay, licentiousness, and hypersexuality (Goff et al., 2014; Epstein et al., 2017). I noticed new encounters where I had ceased to just be a girl or even just a person and had somehow become a sexualized object? I soon learned that the Black body is "a site for aggressive racial fantasy, disavowal and fetishisation" (Ngwenya, 2018, p. 85).

I was walking down the street, on a Saturday in the late morning, through the affluent and verdant neighborhood surrounding my boarding school. I was en route to the boys college that was paired with my school to watch my younger brother play in a cricket match. My hair was in pigtails and, since it was summer, I wore a short minidress, which my father had bought for me three years prior for a school dance, paired with slip-on sandals. Over the past three months my body had begun to change quite rapidly. When my father had bought me the dress I now wore, it had been the smallest size in the adult section and I had drowned in it. Now, three years later, I filled it fully.

This was a street in which the double-storey houses were almost all inhabited by upper-middle-class white families. I walked between a row of palm trees and fecund summer gardens filled with hibiscus, frangipani, bougainvillea, alongside manicured lawns watered by tired Black gardeners. A Mercedes Benz pulled up. An upper-middle-class, respectable looking older white man appeared behind the window. He looked like one of my classmates' dads. He offered me a ride and I declined, saying I was okay. He went on to give me a thorough visual appraisal—perusing my body up and down with his eyes. It had almost felt like he was licking me with his eyeballs. He insisted that he was happy to give me a ride, to which I insisted that I was happy to walk. The way he looked at me felt hungry. Eventually, he asked me if I wanted some money. I told him no and feeling rather distressed I began to walk away from the car, fast. I would have two more encounters with middle-aged white men wanting to get me into their car in the short 15-minute walk to my brother's cricket match.

Years later, as an adult interloper in these same bastions of white privilege, while visiting with white friends, I would have encounters where friends' "uncles" would try to offer me money or other material articles of value to "spend time" with me. On one occasion, a white man just off the street pulled up and offered to pay my university fees, if I would come on a ride with him.

Existence in white spaces of privilege and manicured lawns is a discombobulating experience for someone like me. The general perception that *white people have in these places is that Black people are hypersexual and immoral (Lebakang, 2011; Ngwenya, 2018). The advent of HIV/AIDS and the high numbers of single mothers in Black communities is used as supposed proof for this assumption (Caldwell et al., 1989). I have had white (church) friends ask me point blank, why are Black women so immoral?, pointing to the "facts" mentioned above as the justification of their beliefs about us. Yet, the moral decay evident in the behavior of white men who would dehumanize a young girl by fetishizing her and trying to solicit sexual contact from her is invisibilized or ignored, and hidden from other whites as a dirty (and therefore inherently exciting) secret.*

Matthew

When Sizwe shared these account I felt nauseated. Sizwe was describing the neighborhood where I grew up. These men were my neighbors, my parents' friends, my friends' parents. I felt a flush of rage that barely disguised a deep sense of shame and recognition. Had I not always been told in so many ways that Black lives were more dispensable and less valuable than white ones? Had I not come to accept images and stories of Black women's bodies broken, dismembered, and discarded like trash with a click of the tongue and the bare minimum of horror? It seemed so commonplace. White people, myself included, seem to have been raised to believe that they are inherently superior and that others (those who are not white) should somehow be flattered to associate with them (Kendi, 2020). I found this excruciatingly embarrassing to admit, and I would never seek to sexually exploit any women. But when I recognize how ubiquitously the idea that Black women are sexually available is communicated (to both Black and white men), then this scene starts to make a lot of sense, as a racialized hierarchy of desirability and respectability becomes evident.

Kobena Mercer (1999) described how the white normative gaze shapes the experience of Black embodiment through the use of the logic of fetishization. The logic of fetishization at the core is about the repudiation of difference where the white gazer in this instance conjures up a false representation of the Black other, thereby objectifying them in order to create for themselves an imposed reality in the other. Ngwenya (2018) goes on to explain that under the colonial gaze of oppression, the bodies of Black women are taken from them through the process of fetishization and then given back to them "transformed, disassembled and stereotyped by three main forms of markings—the racial, the gendered and the sexual" (2018, p. 93). Ngwenya further argues that under the discourse of coloniality, race, sex and gender are used to fabricate a portrait of Black women as morally degenerate and hypersexual.

In Sizwe's context, it did not matter that she was a young teenager. The fetishization of her skin color and sexual body parts meant that she was excluded from being viewed as her white counterparts were. She was also excluded from being viewed as capable of morality, as the fetishization created a fantasy of her as a morally degenerate object that was open to transacting sexual favors for material gain. She was not a girl to them, instead she was transformed into a thing, an object of desire in a situation that provided an opportunistic chance for exploitation by a white man, the neocolonizer. Through our dialogue we were able to reveal the way in which this exploitative dynamic of fetishization and the dynamics of projection, envy, and abjection which accompany it are structurally woven into the ways that both Blacks and whites are educated to relate to themselves and each other.

Conclusion

> I have come to believe over and over again that what is most important to me must be spoken, made verbal and shared, even at the risk of having it bruised or misunderstood.
>
> —Lorde (1984, p. 40)

We encountered profound structural and intersectional inequality in our conversations. However, the process we engaged in meant that we were more preoccupied by the peculiarities of individual experience than by a general exploration of issues such as systemic racism, sexism, patriarchy, and colonialism—as well as how these structures create racialized bodies, identities, and desires. So, for instance, while we engage some of these issues within our schooling systems and family structures, we do not touch on issues such as land (re)distribution, wealth, and economic power, which are ongoing material drivers and sustainers of the centering of whiteness in South Africa.

Milazzo (2016) offers a scathing critique of the kind of literature that has become popular in philosophy, where white scholars take to centering the white self with its guilt and shame, thereby inadvertently taking up space and drawing attention to itself, seeking to be cared for. This is reminiscent of DiAngelo's (2011) notion of "white fragility." Milazzo argues that the tendency with this type of analysis is that in the end it disregards the salient features of structural racism that are pervasive in our society and serves to sustain the hold that whiteness has on power. She rightly makes the assertion that the mere reflection on individual attitudes of white people and their feelings toward whiteness do not necessarily translate into a material displacing of whiteness and that "the politics of individualised training act as a smokescreen that leaves institutional racism unchallenged (2016, p. 8)." McWhorter (2020) has leveled a similar critique against DiAngelo herself.

Milazzo calls out the tendency of this type of analysis to highlight the difficulties and burden of living under the unwanted white privilege without owning up to the fact of how white people continue not only to benefit but be complicit in maintaining such privilege. She maintains, "theorisations of white privilege in scholarship by white philosophers often similarly tend to silence white people's investment in preserving such privilege." Again, she asserts:

> The portrayal of white people as subjected to rather than co-creators of and agents in the world informs scholarship that advocates white guilt and white shame as well as scholarship that contests notions of white guilt and white shame. (Milazzo, 2016, p. 9)

Throughout our conversation and our inquiry into its form, we have attempted to be perspicaciously reflexive about the tendency to collapse into these patterns. First, instead of this project being about a white person critiquing themselves in a silo of whiteness or a about a Black person seeking to positions themselves in a white world, we have instead a dialogue between two people who are Black and white so as to exchange the experience of themselves as individuals and the experience of the other in the shared milieu. In this dialogue we explore not only how we have been victimized and dehumanized by the centering of whiteness but also how in turn we have at certain points, albeit inspired by different casualties, acted in a manner that is complicit to upholding the status quo.

Second, the issue of decentering whiteness is not and can never be merely a matter of an interpersonal reflection between two parties as if we were able to "reduce whiteness and white racism to a mere misunderstanding among friends" (Mgxitama, 2011). Transformation in a space takes place multidimensionally; it is inherently polyglossic (Bakhtin, 1981). Where we only engage in sentiment, limiting our analyses to feelings and attitudes and never touching the structural "isms" that maintain oppressions in our society, we are being disingenuous. Further, we are obfuscating what really needs to be done in order to foster change. It is hard to imagine how we might be able to make sense of these embodied social dynamics without speaking with each other about them. This means that dialogue remains an integrally important (but insufficient) factor in the process of finding a constructive way forward together.

Our conversation covered a great deal of ground, and yet it seems to only be scratching the surface. In this chapter we have drawn attention to the potential of a vulnerable reflexive encounter with difference for transforming racialized relationships to self and other. Through our conversation we have been able to empathically support each other as we have engaged deeply inculcated defenses, layer by layer revealing hitherto invisible strands of connection and with them the possibility for healing and truth. We argue for the central role that such an empathic dialogue might play decentering whiteness, through paying careful attention through the embodiment disavowal and envy and the "epidermilization of inferiority" (Fanon, 1967, p. 13). Through this process we come to see each other through loving eyes, creating greater resourcefulness in how we are able to inquire into our experience of the sometimes-violent collisions of complex intersectional identities. The paradoxes of difference/sameness and inclusion/exclusion will never go away—there is no utopian harmony to be achieved—but if we can learn to speak to each other, and to truly listen, transformation is inevitable. Let us continue to practice.

References

Baldwin, J. (1985). *The price of the ticket: Collected nonfiction 1948–1985*. St. Martin's Press.

Bakhtin, M. (1981). *The dialogic imagination*. University of Texas Press.

Biko, S. (1979). *Black consciousness in South Africa* (M. W. Arnold, Ed.). Random House.

Bojabotseha, T. P. (2011). Dualism and the social formation of South Africa. *African Journal of Hospitality, Tourism and Leisure, 1*(3): 1–8.

Chatterjee, A., Czajka, A., & Gethin, A. (2018). *Extreme inequalities: The distribution of household wealth in South Africa* (Research Brief 11/20). SA–TIED.

Copeland, M. S. (2010). *Enfleshing freedom: Body, race and being*. Fortress Press.

Elias, N., & Scotson, J. L. (1965). *The established and the outsiders: A sociological enquiry into community problems*. F. Cass.

Epstein, R., Blake, J., & González, T. (June 27, 2017). *Girlhood interrupted: The erasure of Black girls' childhood*. Available at SSRN: https://ssrn.com/abstract=3000695 or http://dx.doi.org/10.2139/ssrn.3000695

Fanon, F. (1963). *The wretched of the earth*. Grove Press.

Fanon, F. (1967). *Black skin, white masks* (C. Markmam, Trans.). Grove Press.

Freire, P. (2005). *Pedagogy of the oppressed*. Continuum.

Frosh, S. (2013). Psychoanalysis, colonialism, racism. *Journal of Theoretical and Philosophical Psychology, 33*(3), 141–154.

Gibson, N. C. (2008). Upright and free: Fanon in South Africa, from Biko to the shackdwellers' movement (Abahlali baseMjondolo). *Social Identities, 14*(6): 683–715.

Goff, P. A., Jackson, M., Di Leone, B. A. L., Culotta, C. M., & DiTomasso, N. A. (2014). The essence of innocence: Consequences of dehumanizing Black children. *Journal of Personality and Social Psychology, 106*(4), 526–545.

Honneth, A. (2005). *The struggle for recognition: The moral grammar of social conflicts* (J. Anderson, Trans.). Polity Press.

hooks, b. (1992). *Black looks: Race and representation*. South End Press.

hooks, b. (2000). *Feminist theory: From margin to center*. South End Press.

Kendi, I. X. (2020). *Be antiracist: A journal for awareness, reflection, and action*. One World.

Kumalo, S. H., & Praeg, L. (2019). Decoloniality and justice a priori. *Journal of Decolonising Disciplines, 1*(1): 1–9.

Lebakeng T. J. (2011). Discourse on colonial epistemicide and contemporary attempts to re-affirm indigenous knowledge systems, with particular reference to South Africa. *Caribbean Journal of Philosophy, 3*(1): 441–455.

Lorde, A. (1984). *Sister outsider: Essays and speeches*. Crossing Press.

Lugones, M. (1987). Playfulness, "world"-travelling, and loving perception. *Hypatia, 2*(2), 3–19.

Lugones, M. (2007). Heterosexualism and the colonial/modern gender system. *Hypatia, 22*(1), 186–209.

Maart, R. (2020). Introduction decoloniality and decolonial education: South Africa and the world. *Alternation Special Edition, 33*(2020) 15–44.

May, V. (2015). *Pursuing intersectionality, unsettling dominant imaginaries*. Routledge.

Mdedetyana, L. S. (2018). *Medical male circumcision and Xhosa masculinities: Tradition and transformation* [Unpublished MA thesis]. University of the Western Cape.

Meintjes, G. (1998). *Manhood at a price: Socio-medical perspectives on Xhosa traditional circumcision*. Rhodes University.

Mercer, K. (1986). *Welcome to the jungle: New positions in black cultural studies*. Routledge.

Mercer, K. (1999). Reading racial fetishism: The photographs of Robert Mapplethorpe. In S. Hall & J. Evans (Eds.), *Visual culture: The reader*. Sage Publishers.

Milazzo, M. (2017). On white ignorance, white shame, and other pitfalls in critical philosophy of race. *Journal of Applied Philosophy, 34*, 557–572.

Mngxitama, A. (2011). End to whiteness a Black issue. *Mail and Guardian*. http://mg.co.za/article/2011-10-24-end-to-whiteness-a-black-issue.

Ngwenya, C. (2018). *What is Africanness? Contesting nativism in race, culture and sexualities*. Pretoria University Law Press.

Serote, W. (1972). *White people are white people*. Renoster Books.

Soudien, C. (2004). "Constituting the class": An analysis of process of "integration" in South African schools. In L. Chisholm (Ed.), *Changing class: Education and social change in post-apartheid South Africa* (pp. 89–114). HSRC Press.

Traoré, R. (2007). Implementing Afrocentricity. *Journal of Pan African Studies, 1*(10): 62–78.

World Bank. (2018). *Overcoming poverty and inequality in South Africa: An assessment of drivers, constraints, and opportunities*. World Bank.

Zizek, S. (1992). *Enjoy your symptom! Jacques Lacan in Hollywood and out*. Routledge.

Index

For the benefit of digital users, indexed terms that span two pages (e.g., 52–53) may, on occasion, appear on only one of those pages.

Note: Tables and figures are indicated by *t* and *f* following the page number

Aboriginal and Torres Strait Islander peoples. *See* white settler violence in Australia
activism. *See also* HIV prevention marketing; "Sexual Racism Sux" campaign
    Cunanan, Andrew and, 103–4
    introduction to, 1–2, 3–4, 17–18, 21–22
    Māori girls' contemporary sexuality study, 170, 175–76, 178–79, 181–83
    Motevalli, Amitis, 145, 150, 159
    queer sexual racism, 31
    sexual color-blindness, 78
    sex work/sex industry and white supremacy, 298–99, 313
    white settler violence in Australia, 189–90, 198*f*, 201
    white sexual desire and, 215
    white supremacy grammar of tagging on Pornhub, 271, 274, 292
ACT UP, 104, 107
Adult Video News, 281, 289
advocacy, 3–4, 11, 16–17, 21–22, 56, 274, 289, 291–92, 304, 315–16, 317
affective ambivalence, 330–32
African National Congress (ANC), 344–45
Ahmed, Sarah, 4–5, 11–12, 99–100
AIDS activism, 125, 126*f*, 131. *See also* HIV prevention marketing
Algorithms of Oppression (Noble), 286
American Tropics: Articulating Filipino America (Punzalan Isaac), 100
Amnesty International, 52
Angels in America (Kushner), 107
Another Country (Baldwin), 31
anti-Blackness, 2, 79, 304
antimiscegenation, 7–8, 72, 326–27

antiracism/anti-sexual racism efforts, 1, 21–22, 41–43. *See also* "Sexual Racism Sux" campaign
Aotearoa settler colonialism. *See* Māori girls' contemporary sexuality study
apartheid, 92–93, 337–39, 342, 348–49, 351
Applebaum, Barbara, 4, 243–44
Asian American assisted reproductive technologies
    affective ambivalence and sexual racism, 330–32
    introduction to, 325–27
    racial commodification, 332–34
    racial matching, 326–27
    reflexivity and positioning of researcher, 328–30
    research on, 327–28
    white supremacy and, 326–27, 333
The Assassination of Gianni Versace (2018), 99–100, 108
assimilation, 11, 99–103, 104, 141, 146, 151, 168, 193–95, 292, 308–9, 339, 342, 348–50
assisted reproductive technologies (ARTs). *See* Asian American assisted reproductive technologies
attraction, psychology of, 73–74
Ayres, Tony, 103

Baba Karam Lessons (Motevalli), 141–43, 142*f*, 146–47, 150–51, 159
Bacareza Balance, 109
Bakhtin, Mikhail, 343, 344–54
Balance, Christine Bacareza, 99–100
Baldwin, James, 1–2, 31–32, 347–48
ball culture, 131

360 INDEX

Bantu Education Act (1935), 348
Bedi, Sonu, 2–3
Bellis, Alice, 90–92
Benjamin, Ruha, 288
Bernstein, Elizabeth, 304
Biko, Steve, 339
biogenetic kinship, 326–27
BIPOC Adult Industry Collective, 269, 270, 283, 292
Black consciousness movement, 339
Black gay personhood. *See* queer sexual racism
Black Is Beautiful movement, 92–93, 94
Black Lives Matters movement, 270
Black Panthers, 145
Black Porn Matters, 290–91
Black porn performers. *See* white supremacy grammar of tagging on Pornhub
Black Skins, White Masks (Fanon), 350–51
Bondage/Discipline, Dominance/ Submission, Sadism/Masochism (BDSM), 152–53, 158–59, 251, 260– 61, 289–90
Borrowing Authority from Death (Motevalli), 158f, 158
Bourdieu, Pierre, 39–40
Breaking the Silences report, 195
Brent Corrigan dildo, 215
Brier, Jennifer, 131
Brinkmann, Svend, 340–41
British colonization, 302–3
Bronski, Michael, 124
Burk, Ronnie, 103–9
The Butcher (Warren), 265
Butts, June Dobbs, 1–2

Camming: Money, Power, and Pleasure in the Sex Work Industry (Jones), 280–81
camp-recognition, 100–1
Canadian sex work/sex industry, 306–10
capitalism
 grammaire pornographique, 19, 270– 71, 275–77, 285–86
 individualism and, 46–47
 introduction to, 2, 6
 racial capitalism, 278–80
casual sex, 175–76, 181, 182, 212, 227, 300–1, 302

China Dolls (1998), 33f, 33–39, 103
Chong-suk Han, 102
Christian, Michelle, 6
civil individualism, 44
Clarkson, Wensley, 102
Clifton, Lucille, 87–88
Cohn, Roy, 107
colonialism. *See also* white settler violence in Australia
 introduction to, 2, 6, 7–9
 settler-colonialism and Māori girls' study, 18–19, 167–72, 176, 183–84
 sexualization of, 7
 in South Africa, 338–39, 340, 342, 344, 349–50, 353–54
commercial sex industry. *See* sex work/sex industry
condom promotion campaigns, 119, 123– 24, 134f
Connor, Alice, 89
conscientious racial consumption, 224–28
Contagious Disease Act (UK), 311
COVID-19 pandemic, 156–58, 304, 329
Crenshaw, Kimberlé, 108
criminalization of sex work/sex industry, 296–97, 303–10
Criss, Darren, 99–100, 104–7
Cruz, Ariane, 282–83
cultural humility, 76
Cunanan, Andrew
 identification and, 99–103
 introduction to, 98–99
 racialization and, 99–111
 radicalization and, 103–11, 105f, 106f
 white desirability, 98, 99–103, 109–11

Death at Every Stop (Clarkson), 102
decriminalization of sex work/sex industry, 313–16
Demens, Daniel, 116
D'Emilio, John, 124
desexualization, 135
Deshazier, Ilannah, 17–18, 162–63
Desiring Arabs (Massad), 8–9
DiAngelo, Robin, 43–44, 46–47
Diaz, Dillon, 282
digital tagging. *See* white supremacy grammar of tagging on Pornhub

doing sexual racism, 32. *See also* undoing sexual racism
Ducati, Daisy, 269–70, 289
Dyer, Richard, 120

Eddo-Lodge, Reni, 61
egalitarianism, 43–44, 227, 237
egg-donation practices, 19
Eng, David, 68
enlightenment, 7, 299
Enlightenment Period, 299
erotic consumption, 210–11, 213–14, 217–18, 224–28, 235, 236–37
erotic fantasies, 213–15, 216, 229–30
erotic hegemony of whiteness, 206, 210, 228, 232–33, 235–36
erotic penalty, 217–18
erotized HIV prevention, 18
ethnosexual discrimination, 222, 235
ethnosexual stereotypes, 122, 207–8, 210–11, 216, 225
eugenics, 7–8, 194–95
Euro-Western sexuality values, 169–70
exotic dancer, 146–49

Fanon, Frantz, 1–2, 120–21
Farvid, Pani, 330–31
female masculinity, 146, 150
femininity, 170, 174–77
feminism
    critical feminist psychology, 328–29
    Indigenous feminism, 190, 191
    Marxist feminists, 297–98
    pornographic media studies, 277
    reflexivity and, 328–30
    sex work/sex industry, 297–98
fetishization online, 14–15
films, queer sexual racism, 33f, 33–39, 34f
Fire Island (2022), 46
Floyd, George, 270
forced sterilization, 7–8
Foxx, Ana, 270
Frantz Fanon Lab for Intersectional Psychology, 67
freedom, 5, 7, 8–9, 10, 43–44, 58, 70–71, 159, 245, 308–9, 333–34, 338–39
Freud, Sigmund, 75
Frosh, Stephen, 348

Fung, Richard, 122
Funk Lessons (Piper), 150

gamete donation. *See* Asian American assisted reproductive technologies
Gay Asian Male (GAM) pages, 52, 53, 55
gay clone, 125, 218–19
Gaydar website, 52, 55–56, 57–58, 62–63
Gay International, 9
gay male culture, 124–25, 136–37
Gay Men's Health Crisis (GMHC), 127–35
gay politics, 44–46
gay rights, 9, 44–45
gay rights movement, 9
gender-blindness, 72
gender diversity, 17, 242–43, 247, 248, 260
gender nonconforming persons, 253–55
Gender Shades study, 287–88
genocide, 7, 290–91, 299–300, 302–3
Giovanni's Room (Baldwin), 31–32
globalization, 2, 6
Global Network of Sex Work Projects (NSWP), 306–7
Goldstein, Richard, 31
Golestan Revisited (Motevalli), 153–56, 159
Goodes, Adam, 192–93
grammaire pornographique, 19, 270–71, 275–77, 285–86
Grindr, 62–63, 189–90, 200, 218–19

Hagedorn, Jessica, 99–100, 109
Han, Shinhee, 68
Herton, Charles, 1–2
heterosexualism, 194–95, 201
History of the Family, 12
HIV prevention marketing
    condom promotion campaigns, 119, 123–24, 134f
    as consumption, 123–27
    interracial desire in, 120–21, 127, 137
    introduction to, 116–19, 117f, 118f
    men who have sex with men, 116, 126f, 127–37, 129f, 130f, 132f, 133f, 134f, 135f
    pre-exposure prophylaxis, 117–19, 121–24, 133–35, 134f, 136
    undoing sexual racism, 126f, 127–36, 137
    white gaze in, 119–23, 127–36
    white supremacy and, 119, 122, 123–24, 127, 136–37

362 INDEX

Holland, Sharon, 137
Holloway, Wendy, 72
homosexuality, 9, 31–32, 107, 131, 207–8, 231–32, 233–34
hooks, bell, 5
hypergamous tendencies, 212
hypersexualization/hypersexuality, 15, 305, 325–26, 351–52

identity, 67, 99–103, 143, 145
imperialism, 2, 6, 7–9, 11, 153–55, 159, 339
Indigenous persons, 190, 191, 306–10
individualism, 10, 13–14, 38, 39–41, 43–47
individualization, 10, 40–41, 43–45
insurgency, 143, 145
International Centre for Counter-Terrorism, 112
interpsychic realms, 68
interracial desire, 120–21, 127, 137
interracial relationships, 7–8, 12–13, 207–8, 228, 233–34, 252–56
intersectionality, 35, 37, 41, 44–47, 67
intrapsychic realms, 3–4, 68
Islamophobia, 141–43

Jerome of Stridon, 90
Jezebel (Warren), 84
Johnson, E. Patrick, 120
Johnson, James Weldon, 1–2
Jones, Angela, 280–81

Khoshgele, Amir, 150
Kitchen Talk: Reclaiming our Image (film), 290–91
Krakouer, Megan, 198
Kristof, Nicholas, 280
Kubra, Mallika, 143
Kundnani, Arun, 10
Kushner, Tony, 107
Kyung-Hee Choi, 102

Lacan, Jacques, 75
LGBTQI+ people. *See also* HIV prevention marketing; queer sexual racism; White LGBTQI privilege
gay male culture, 124–25, 136–37
Indigenous people, 17

men who have sex with men, 116, 126*f*, 127–37, 129*f*, 130*f*, 132*f*, 133*f*, 134*f*, 135*f*
rice queens, 225, 231–32, 330–31
in Western Australia, 195, 200–1
Linafelt, Tod, 89
Lipovetsky, Gilles, 39–40
Logunes, Maria, 342
Lorde, Audre, 87–89, 93–96, 344, 354

MacDonald, Maggie, 279–80
Madison, TS, 283, 291
Mama's Baby, Papa's Maybe: An American Grammar Book (Spillers), 275–76
mana wāhine (dignity of women), 167
Mansfield, Tim, 54
Māori girls' contemporary sexuality study
approaches to, 171–72
Euro-Western sexuality values, 169–70
introduction to, 167–72
mana wāhine (dignity of women), 167
mātauranga Māori (Māori knowledge and wisdom), 171–73, 177, 180–81, 182–84
methodology of, 172–74
rangatiratanga (leadership), 167, 168, 184
results and discussion, 174–83
settler-colonialism and, 18–19, 167–72, 176, 183–84
sexting and, 177–81
sexual agency and, 174–77
Māori sex workers, 314–15
Mapplethorpe, Robert, 121–22
marginalization on Pornhub, 271, 278–79, 286, 288, 291–92
Marxist feminists, 297–98
Massad, Josef, 8–9
mātauranga Māori (Māori knowledge and wisdom), 171–73, 177, 180–81, 182–84
Maxwell, Isiah, 277
McGlade, Hannah, 196–98
McQuire, Amy, 196, 198
Meeks, Chet, 44
men who have sex with men (MSM), 116, 126*f*, 127–37, 129*f*, 130*f*, 132*f*, 133*f*, 134*f*, 135*f*
Mercer, Kobena, 121–22, 353–54
mere exposure effect, 224–25
Miglin, Lee, 108–9
MindGeek, 279

INDEX 363

misogyny, 39, 103–4, 112, 167–68, 170, 172–73, 176, 179, 191, 279, 303
Modern Primitives movement, 158–59
Moore, Stephen D., 93–94
Morgan, Tyomi, 291
Morris, Wesley, 120–21
Moses, Julia, 12
Most Wanted (Hagedorn), 99–100
Motevalli, Amitis, 141–59, 142*f*, 144*f*
Muir, Evie, 289
Muñoz, José Esteban, 141, 151
Murphy, Ryan, 98–99, 107, 109

Nash, Jennifer, 282–83
Natividad, Beverly Romero, 101–2
negrophobia, 120–21
neoliberalism/neoliberal sexualities, 2, 10–11, 39–40, 43–44, 46–47
The New Black Sociologists (Randolph), 32
New Zealand sex work/sex industry, 313–16
Noble, Safiya Umoja, 286
No Chocolate No Rice (2018), 33–39, 34*f*
nonbinary persons, 248, 251–52
Noongar, Mineng, 198

An Offering of Honor (Motevalli), 156–58, 157*f*
OkCupid, 189–90
online sexual racism, 13–15
Orth, Maureen, 102, 109–10
otherness/othering, 68, 94, 141, 149, 218, 277, 346

Pardes, Ilana, 93–94
Peau Noire, Masques Blancs (Fanon), 1–2
Piper, Adrian, 150
Poetry Is Not a Luxury (Lorde), 87–88, 92–93
population health, 119
Pornhub Awards, 281–82
Pornhub's tagging regimes. *See* white supremacy grammar of tagging on Pornhub
Pornocracy: The New Sex Multinationals (MacDonald), 279–80
pornography, 19, 229–31, 270–71, 275–77, 285–86. *See also* white supremacy grammar of tagging on Pornhub

pre-exposure prophylaxis (PrEP), 117–19, 121–24, 133–35, 134*f*, 136
Price, Corey, 287
Prostitution Reform Act (PRA) Aotearoa New Zealand (A/NZ), 313–16
psychology of attraction, 73–74
Punzalan Isaac, Allan, 99–100, 101

queer sexual racism. *See also* LGBTQI+; "Sexual Racism Sux" campaign
anti-sexual racism and, 41–43
in film, 33*f*, 33–39, 34*f*
future of, 45–47
gay politics, 44–46
gay rights, 9, 44–45
homosexuality, 9, 31–32, 107, 131, 207–8, 231–32, 233–34
individualism and, 10, 13–14, 38, 39–41, 43–47
intersectionality in, 35, 37, 41, 44–47
introduction to, 31–32, 33*f*
personal preferences and, 39–41
white sexual desire, 213–20, 222–24, 228–31, 234–37

Race After Technology (Benjamin), 288
racial alterity, 120, 123, 213, 217–18, 219–20, 227, 230–31, 235
racial capitalism, 278–80
racial commodification, 332–34
racial discrimination, 68, 253, 273, 306
racial dissociation, 69
racial fetishization, 102, 111, 242–43, 247–48, 249, 250, 252–53, 278
racial hierarchy, 2–3, 122, 296–97, 299–300, 304, 305, 316
racialization
of gay Asian men, 122
of sexuality, 2, 3, 8–9, 31–32, 43, 119, 206, 275 (*see also* sexual racism)
of sex workers, 299–300
of white desirability, 99–111
racialized desire, 13–14, 117–18, 206–7, 211–12, 220–21, 223–24, 226, 228, 233, 235, 252, 299–300, 306, 309–10, 315–16, 330–31, 337
racialized women, 87–96

364 INDEX

Racial Melancholia and Dissociation (Eng, Han), 68
racial oppression, 3–4, 338–39
racial purity, 7–8, 207–8, 326–27
racial rejection, 14, 247–48
racial socialization, 208, 210–11, 221
Raguparan, Menaka, 309
Randolph, Antonia, 32
rangatiratanga (leadership), 167, 168, 184
reflexive thematic analysis (TA), 173
reflexivity
  Asian American assisted reproductive technologies, 328–30
  empathic reflexivity, 341–44
  feminism and, 328–30
  self-reflexivity, 17, 19–20
  sexual color-blindness, 77
rice queens, 225, 231–32, 330–31
Ricoeur, Paul, 91–92
Riggs, Marlon, 46
Rosa gallica (Motevalli), 145f, 153
Royal Commission into Deaths in Custody, 198

same-gender attraction, 8–9, 182–83
The Sand Ninja (Motevalli), 146–47, 148f, 150–51, 159
San Francisco AIDS Foundation (SFAF), 116, 128
San Francisco Chronicle, 116
Sarmet, Erica, 290–91
scientific racism, 299–300, 312
Sedgwick, Eve, 100–1
Seidman, Steven, 44
self-love, 94–96
self-reflexivity, 17, 19–20
settler-colonialism in Aotearoa. *See* Māori girls' contemporary sexuality study
settler-colonialism in Australia. *See* white settler violence in Australia
Sex and Racism in America (Herton), 1–2
sexting, 177–81
sexual agency of Māori girls, 174–77
sexual color-blindness
  as benign preference, 70–71, 70t, 71t
  cultural humility and, 76
  ideologies of, 68–70
  individual discomfort over, 78–79

  individual experiences of, 77–78
  intersectional identities, 67
  introduction to, 66–67
  psychoanalytic thinking and, 74–75
  psychology of attraction, 73–74
  reflexive engagement with, 77
  sexual desire and, 71–72
  sexual humility and, 76–77
  sexual imagination and, 79
  undoing whiteness, 79–80
sexual desire
  interracial desire, 120–21, 127, 137
  politics of, 87–96
  racialized desire, 13–14, 117–18, 206–7, 211–12, 220–21, 223–24, 226, 228, 233, 235, 252, 299–300, 306, 309–10, 315–16, 330–31, 337
  sexual color-blindness and, 71–72
  white supremacist grammar of tagging on Pornhub, 283–88, 285f, 287f
sexual humility, 17–18, 76–77, 333–34
sexual imagination, 79
sexualization of colonialism, 7
sexualization of racism, 2, 3, 18, 19, 31–32, 60, 119, 136, 206, 275
sexual liberation, 10–11, 21–22, 38, 125, 243, 245, 261–62
sexually transmitted infections (STIs), 167–68, 304–5, 307, 311
sexual objectification, 215–16, 330
sexual racism
  attempts to undo, 20–22
  defined, 2–4
  interracial relationships, 7–8, 12–13
  introduction to, 1–2
  lived realities of, 11–16
  online, 13–15
  undesiring whiteness, 16–20
  as violence, 15–16
"Sexual Racism Sux" campaign. *See also* antiracism/anti-sexual racism efforts
  approach to, 61–63
  consistency of racism, 59–60
  criticism of, 61
  impact of, 56–59
  lessons from, 59–63
  origins of, 51–54
  overview of, 55–56

INDEX 365

sexual solidarity, 225
sex work/sex industry and white supremacy
  Canadian, 306–10
  case studies, 302–3
  criminalization of, 296–97, 303–10
  decriminalization model, 313–16
  inequities within, 316–18
  introduction to, 8, 296–99
  racialization of, 111
  racialization of sexuality, 299–300
  racialized demand by buyers, 300–2
  United Kingdom, 310–13
  United States, 303–6
Shea Butter and Honey (Deshazier), 162–63
Skye, Savannah, 282–83
Smith, Tom Rob, 107
Social Darwinism, 193–94, 196–98
social justice, 3–4, 14–15, 20–21, 145, 159,
  273–74, 304
social realms, 3–4, 68
societal anxiety, 1
somatic intermediaries, 214–15, 218, 225
Song of Songs in Hebrew Bible, 87–96
Sontag, Susan, 123–24
Spillers, Hortense, 275–76, 280–81, 286
Stember, Charles, 1–2
sterilization, forced, 7–8
Street Offences Act (1959) (UK), 311
*Stretch Manifesto: Mahvash, Parivash, and
  Friends* (Motevalli), 146–47, 147f,
  150, 159
Sutra, Demi, 282
SWANEA (South and West Asian and
  North and East African) identity, 143,
  145, 146–47, 150, 153
Swindell, Todd, 104
Sydney Star Observer, 56

Tapsell, Miranda, 193–94, 194f
*A Taste for Brown Sugar: Black
  Women in Pornography* (Miller-
  Young), 278–80
Taylor, Breonna, 270
Thompson, John B., 91–92
Tinder, 175–76, 189–90, 200, 221–22
Tizon, Alex, 111–12
transgender persons. *See* LGBTQI+ people
transparency, 4, 175–76, 254, 300–1

The Treaty of Waitangi (1814), 314–15
Trump, Donald, 107

undesiring whiteness, 16–22
undoing sexual racism, 4, 14–15, 16–20,
  21–22, 32, 38–39, 42–44, 46–47, 127–
  36, 137, 271, 289, 333–34
undoing whiteness, 79–80
United Kingdom sex work/sex
  industry, 310–13
Uses of the Erotic (Lorde), 87, 88–89
US sex work/sex industry, 303–6

Versace, Gianni, 98
Verwoerd, Hendrik, 348
Vulgar Favors (Orth), 102

Wabyanga, Robert Kuloba, 92–93
Warren, Synclaire, 17–18, 84, 265
Webster, Jamieson, 75
Western Educated Industrialized Rich
  Developed (WEIRD) countries, 73–74
Western imperialism, 159, 339
white desirability, 98, 99–103, 109–11
white fragility, 78, 354–55
white gaze, 119–23, 127–36, 210, 215,
  219–20, 222, 270–71, 273, 290–92,
  341, 353–54
white LGBTQI privilege study
  analysis, 248–49
  background on, 243–45
  design of, 246
  insights from, 259–62
  introduction to, 242–43
  methodology of, 246–49
  negotiation of whiteness, 252–56
  recruitment of participants, 246–47
  recurring theme, 249–52
  results and discussion, 249–59
  sample of participants, 247–48
  undermining resistance, 256–59
whiteness
  defined, 4
  femininity and, 170
  introduction to, 4–9
  as property, 69, 279–80
  undesiring whiteness, 16–22
  undoing whiteness, 79–80

366 INDEX

whiteness in South Africa discussion
   apartheid and, 92–93, 337–39, 342,
      348–49, 351
   authors of, 337–38
   context of, 338–39
   conversation on, 340–41
   empathic dialogue, 343, 344–54
   empathic reflexivity, 341–44
   introduction to, 336–37
   racialized body, 351–54
   white privilege and, 344–51
white privilege in South Africa
   discussion, 344–51
white replacement conspiracy
   theory, 15–16
white settler violence in Australia
   culture of, 192–95, 194f
   heterosexualism and, 194–95, 201
   hunting and harming in, 196–98,
      197f, 198f
   Indigenous futurist approach, 191–92
   introduction to, 189–91
   online predators and perpetrators,
      198–201
white sexual desire
   appetite for whiteness, 208–18
   approximations of whiteness, 218–35
   conscientious racial
      consumption, 224–28
   decolonizing of, 222–24
   discursive reframings of, 231–35
   erotic consumption, 210–11, 213–14,
      217–18, 224–28, 235, 236–37
   erotic fantasies, 213–15, 216, 229–30
   erotic hegemony of whiteness, 206, 210,
      228, 232–33, 235–36
   interracial intimacy and, 207–8,
      228, 233–34
   introduction to, 206–7
   mere exposure effect, 224–25
   past ruminations on, 207–8

pornographic consumption, 229–31
queer men and, 213–20, 222–24, 228–
   31, 234–37
somatic intermediaries, 214–15,
   218, 225
white gaze and, 219–20, 222
white supremacy and, 207–8, 215, 221–
   24, 236–37
white supremacy. *See also* sex work/sex
   industry and white supremacy
Baldwin, James and, 31–32
grammaire pornographique, 19, 270–
   71, 275–77, 285–86
HIV prevention marketing and, 119,
   122, 123–24, 127, 136–37
introduction to, 2, 4–6
sexual color-blindness and, 75
undesiring whiteness, 16–22
white sexual desire and, 207–8, 215,
   221–24, 236–37
white supremacy grammar of tagging on
   Pornhub
   alternative grammars of, 289–92
   case study, 271–75
   in content creation, 280–83
   grammaire pornographique and, 283–
      88, 285f, 287f
   introduction to, 19, 269–71
   overview of, 275–77
   racial capitalism and, 278–80
   sexual desire and, 283–88, 285f
Williams, Linda, 120–21
Woesthoff, Julia, 12
The Wretched of the Earth
   (Fanon), 338–39

xenophobia, 141–43, 298–99, 304,
   312, 317

Young-Girl archetype, 155–56
Yuen, Nancy Wany, 15